EMILY CARR

Also by Maria Tippett

From Desolation to Splendour
Changing Perceptions of the British Columbia Landscape
(with Douglas Cole)

Phillips in Print
The Selected Writings of Walter J. Phillips on Canadian Nature and Art
(Editor, with Douglas Cole)

Art at the Service of War
Canada, Art, and the Great War

Breaking the Cycle, and Other Stories from a Gulf Island

Lest We Forget
Canadian Paintings of the First and Second World Wars

Making Culture
English-Canadian Institutions and the Arts Before the Massey Commission

By a Lady
Celebrating Three Centuries of Art by Canadian Women

Between Two Cultures
A Photographer Among the Inuit, 1958–1968
(with photographs by Charles Gimpel)

Becoming Myself
A Memoir

Stormy Weather
F. H. Varley, a Biography

Bill Reid
The Making of an Indian

MARIA TIPPETT

EMILY CARR

A BIOGRAPHY

ANANSI

First published in hardcover in 1979 by Oxford University Press
Published in paperback in 1982 by Penguin Books Canada
Published in 1994 by Stoddart Publishing Co.

This edition published in 2006 by
House of Anansi Press Inc.
110 Spadina Avenue, Suite 801
Toronto, ON, M5V 2K4
Tel. 416-363-4343
Fax 416-363-1017
www.anansi.ca

Distributed in Canada by
HarperCollins Canada Ltd.
1995 Markham Road
Scarborough, ON, M1B 5M8
Toll free tel. 1-800-387-0117

Distributed in the United States by
Publishers Group West
1700 Fourth Street
Berkeley, CA 94710
Toll free tel. 1-800-788-3123

House of Anansi Press is committed to protecting our natural environment.
As part of our efforts, this book is printed on Rolland Enviro paper: it contains
100% post-consumer recycled fibres, is acid-free, and is processed chlorine-free.

10 09 08 07 06   1 2 3 4 5

Library and Archives Canada Cataloguing in Publication Data

Tippett, Maria, 1944–
Emily Carr : a biography / Maria Tippett.

Includes bibliographical references and index.
ISBN-13: 978-0-88784-756-1
ISBN-10: 0-88784-756-0

1. Carr, Emily, 1871–1945. 2. Painters — Canada — Biography. I. Title.

ND249.C3T56 2006   759.11   C2006-902805-2

Library of Congress Control Number: 2006927555

Cover design: Paul Hodgson
Cover art: detail from *Untitled* (totem pole), 1928, Emily Carr.
Collection of Max J. Miller & Eva Mendel Miller, and Family.
Reproduced by kind permission of Ms. Eva Mendel Miller.
Author photograph: David Thomas

**Canada Council   Conseil des Arts
for the Arts   du Canada**

ONTARIO ARTS COUNCIL
CONSEIL DES ARTS DE L'ONTARIO

*We acknowledge for their financial support of our publishing program
the Canada Council for the Arts, the Ontario Arts Council, and the Government of Canada
through the Book Publishing Industry Development Program (BPIDP).*

Printed and bound in Canada

Contents

Colour Plates

Abbreviations

AGGV Art Gallery of Greater Victoria

BCPM British Columbia Provincial Museum

CBC Canadian Broadcasting Corporation

CHS California Historical Society, San Francisco

HH Hart House, University of Toronto

MMFA Montreal Museum of Fine Arts

NGC National Gallery of Canada

PABC Provincial Archives of British Columbia

PAC Public Archives of Canada, Ottawa

VAG Vancouver Art Gallery

VCA Victoria City Archives

VPL Vancouver Public Library

Preface to the 1994 Edition

Authors rarely have an opportunity to revise the books they write—let alone comment upon the work that has emerged as a result of their publication. Most books are put aside by the author even before the flurry of interviews and reviews announce their appearance. This is generally because the writer has already embarked upon another topic. Though I was well into my study of Canadian art and the First World War before the first edition of this biography went to press, I have been continually prompted to return to Emily Carr. There have been invitations to lecture at home as well as in Europe, South America, New Zealand, the United States, Great Britain, and Japan and to provide essays for exhibition catalogues. While I have enjoyed introducing Carr's work to people, especially outside of Canada, I have never had a chance to reassess my own writing. Now, more than fifteen years after the original publication of *Emily Carr: A Biography*, this new edition gives me an opportunity to do so.

I have corrected the typographical and factual errors that such careful readers of the book as Professor Peter Smith, formerly of the University of Victoria, noted in their reviews. On the other hand, I have decided not to make other alterations. I have retained Emily Carr's own usage of First Nations' names. I do, however, wish to point out that many of these names have changed. For example, the Skeena River settlement of Kitwancool is now called Gitanyow. The First Nations' members of that settlement belong to the Gitanyow Band and to the Gitksan Nation. It should also be noted that the Emily Carr papers that I consulted at the National Archives of Canada— then known as the Public Archives of Canada—have since been deposited in the Provincial Archives of British Columbia. The trunk of unpublished material in the basement of J.A. Parnall to which I was denied access has been deposited in the same archive.

During the course of re-reading my biography, I have pondered over its most controversial aspect, namely, the suggestion that an incident that occurred between Emily and her father, Richard Carr, made Emily turn from her family to the woods, animals, and First Nations' peoples of coastal British Columbia. I have, however, chosen to leave the passage dealing with it substantially intact. I have further reconsidered my discussion of Emily's illness in the East Anglia Sanatorium in England. Again I found little to change. Though I must stress that the 1901 diagnosis of her illness as 'hysteria' must be seen as encompassing everything from neurasthenia, hypochondriasis, and depression, to ambulatory schizophrenia and conversion reaction.

Were I to write a biography of Emily Carr today I would not alter any of my conclusions. Yet I would write that book with the knowledge I have gained through my later studies of the art and culture of Canada. *Making Culture: English–Canadian Institutions and the Arts before the Massey Commission* (1990) has made me more aware of the extent to which artistic reputations are made as much by the patronage or neglect of public and private cultural organizations and institutions as by the quality of the work produced by the artist. While temperament is undoubtedly a large factor in determining an artist's public success—Emily regretted that she went only halfway to meet it—the support of professional and amateur institutions—in Carr's case the Group of Seven, the Victoria Memorial Museum, the National Gallery of Canada, the Ontario Society of Artists, and Oxford University Press—play an equally important role in establishing reputations. *By a Lady: Celebrating Three Centuries of Art by Canadian Women* (1992) taught me that Carr had many female peers whose experience of working in a profession dominated by men was no less difficult than her own. It also confirmed that her visual construct of the forest emerged in the work of her contemporaries: Ina D.D. Uhthoff, Yvonne McKague, and Paraskeva Clark, among others. During the course of researching *Between Two Cultures: A Photographer among the Inuit*, I became more aware of how many non-Native photographers have misrepresented the Inuit and thereby done them an injustice. How far might painters have done this too?

These insights would no doubt have helped set the agenda for a new biography complementing but not superseding what is here.

This new edition has not only prompted me to reassess my own work, it has made me consider its relationship to the studies that have subsequently appeared. This has been an ambiguous experience. It was gratifying to find that in *The Art of Emily Carr*, published a week after my biography, Doris Shadbolt had incorporated all of the substantial revisions I had made for the re-issue, in 1975, of her exhibition catalogue *Emily Carr: A Centennial Exhibition Celebrating the One Hundredth Anniversary of Her Birth* (1971). Ruth Gowers' *Emily Carr* (1987), Paula Blanchard's *The Life of Emily Carr* (1987), and Ruth Stevens Appelhof's exhibition catalogue *The Expressionist Landscape: North American Modernist Painting 1920–1947* (1987) wove biographical details from my work into their own discussion; sometimes with acknowledgement.

Before my book was published, no author had written about Carr's life in detail. During the three decades following her death, there was a flurry of articles and memoirs by Emily's 'listening ladies', Flora Hamilton Burns and Ruth Humphrey, by her painter-friend Edythe Hembroff-Schleicher, and by the young girl whom she wanted to adopt, Carol Pearson. These women were eager to perpetuate the myths of rejection, poverty, and neglect that Carr had already charted in her autobiographical writings. When I set out to challenge some of these myths through a series of articles, Carr's 'keepers of the flame' emerged to extinguish what I had written. Ruth Humphrey wrote 'A Reply' to my first article, '"A Paste Solitaire in a Steel-Claw Setting": Emily Carr and Her Public', which had appeared in *BC Studies* in the winter of 1973–1974. Four years later Edythe Hembroff-Schleicher came out with *Emily Carr: The Untold Story*. This was certainly a polemical work. Indeed, one critic characterized its tone as sometimes being 'unjustifiably plaintive and self-righteous'.

After my biography appeared in 1979, Edythe Hembroff-Schleicher passed her torch to an American writer, Paula Blanchard. In 1987 Blanchard challenged me by recycling some of Hembroff-Schleicher's material. Blanchard—to give but one example—questioned my statement that Carr had been diagnosed with the complaint of 'hysteria' and that, as Emily herself put it, she had 'cracked up in England'. Indeed Blanchard went on to make the sinister innuendo that no such document with the diagnosis of hysteria existed and that it would have been highly irregular for a patient's complaint to have been recorded at all. Had Blanchard made any effort to approach me about the matter I could have enlightened her, for this document had been one of my most exciting discoveries during the course of my research.

I had written to the Sanatorium only to be told that their records had been destroyed. Wanting nevertheless to visit the institution where Carr had been incarcerated for fifteen unhappy months, I travelled to England. There, in May of 1975, I asked yet again: 'Are you certain that there are no old records or case histories somewhere on the premises?' One of the secretaries paused, thought for a moment, then asked me to follow her to a root cellar adjacent to the main building. Flashlight in hand, I made my way into the damp underground storeroom. Lying in a corner on the earth floor were a stack of old ledgers. I quickly located the volume that covered the years 1903 and 1904. In it were the names of men and women who had been diagnosed with complaints such as bronchitis, neurasthenia, syphilitic arthritis, dyspepsia, appendicitis, and hysteria. Running a finger down the column of names on page twenty-four, I found the following entry: Miss Carr, 44 Carr St. Victoria, Brit. Columbia, Came: 12.1.03; Went: 17.3.04; Complaint: Hysteria.

Shortly before her death Carr imagined that the next generation would 'scoff' at her honours and consider her 'trash'. During the next four decades the keepers of the flame prevented this from happening. Indeed, Carr's work became an inspiration for other cultural producers. Jack Shadbolt celebrated Carr's forest at his island retreat on Hornby Island in a series of powerful drawings. Pat Martin Bates, John Koerner, and Gordon Smith, among other artists, produced evocative prints, oil and acrylic paintings that paid homage to Carr's subject matter. Dorothy Livesay and Susan Musgrave wrote poems, 'The Three Emily Carrs' and 'Skookumchuk', respectively. In 1975 Anna Wyman choreographed the ballet *Klee Wyck: A Ballet for Emily* and Toronto film-maker Nancy Ryley produced a two-part documentary film, *Growing Pains* and *Little Old Lady on the Edge of Nowhere*. In 1990 Jovette Marchessault produced 'Le Voyage Magnifique d'Emily Carr' at Montreal's Théâtre d'Aujourd'hui. Long before this the composer Jean Coulthard had paid musical tribute to Carr with the chamber music composition *The Pines of Emily Carr* (1969). And a year later Harry Freedman followed with the orchestral work *Klee Wyck*.

From the early 1990s Emily Carr's legacy became controversial. The most contentious issue among Carr's critics has been her relationship to the First Nations peoples of British Columbia. Some commentators question her sincerity towards and knowledge of the province's indigenous peoples. Others fault Carr for including no Native Indians in her paintings but choosing instead to appropriate their artefacts for her subject matter. And still others have wondered why Carr was so ignorant of the legislative oppression under which her First Nations friends lived.

A careful reading of this book will show that most of these assertions serve contemporary political agendae rather than enlighten our understanding of Carr. While Carr might have idealized or romanticized Native Indians in her prose and paintings, there is no doubt that she was genuinely sympathetic towards them. Nor should her efforts to understand First Nations cultures be dismissed. She consulted an impressive amount of the material that was available to her at the time. Moreover she took great pains to make this material, along with the artwork produced as a result of her travels among Native communities, known to a largely unsympathetic Euro-Canadian public. She gave public lectures, she wrote newspaper articles, and she held public exhibitions of paintings that included portraits of First Nations peoples. Initially Carr recorded the totem poles and the community houses 'for history'. Yet her critics often forget that she eventually abandoned her attempt to paint 'all the totem poles & villages . . . before they are a thing of the past'. Indeed, by 1929 she came to the conclusion that 'while working on the Indian stuff . . . I was copying the Indian idiom instead of expressing my own findings.'

Carr's achievements as a painter of landscape have not escaped the pundits either. She has been depreciated for making no innovative contribution to art. This charge represents the worst sort of whiggish art history. It is true that Carr worked within styles—most notably Northern European Expressionism—that had already been established. Yet this does not detract from her monumental achievement: enhancing our perception of British Columbia's coastal landscape. Other critics have labelled Carr a regional artist. This prompts one to ask: Do British art historians call John Constable a regional artist because his work is confined to a small corner of rural Suffolk in East Anglia? This centrist view of cultural history, however, is peculiarly Canadian. If a work of art is created outside of southern Ontario, the artist must be 'regional'. This line of thinking has worked against Carr in two ways: it has made some westerners claim a unique privilege to write about her; it has prompted some non-westerners to dismiss her as an insignificant regionalist.

Such judgements relating to Carr's work have arisen partly because the oeuvre has not yet been given the searching critical attention it deserves. The existence of two very large—but very uneven—bodies of her work is partly to blame. It is not surprising that some of the paintings housed in the Vancouver Art Gallery and in the Provincial Archives of British Columbia are inferior. No prolific artist paints only masterpieces. Moreover, neither of these collections was carefully selected; they were bequeathed in a lump. What is surprising is that so much of her inferior work is shown. Her best work came during a very short period towards the end of her life. Carr has not lacked attention; she has lacked discriminating attention.

Carr must be considered on her own terms. This means situating her work and her life in the historical context, which will involve sorting out the causes and the conditions that enabled Emily to express herself in paint and in words. Precisely what I have tried to recapture in this biography.

The causes that brought Emily's work to fruition grew out of her inner spiritual tensions. Her challenge was to give those tensions expression through her art. This entailed finding an appropriate style and subject matter. She began by developing her visual language through a dual perception of the landscape. She naturally perceived it through the eyes of the British settler, but she also *wanted* to see it through the eyes of the First Nations people. Her quest was continued by studying theosophy and other esoteric religions, and by fusing Christianity with some of these ideas.

Carr's yearning to express her spirituality through her art can be sensed when she first painted the forest in Tregenna Wood in St Ives. Yet it was only after she encountered the paintings of Lawren Harris that she saw how she might do this in her own work. Her development of a visual language appropriate to the expression of her spirituality began in France, continued through contact with the Group of Seven, then Mark Tobey, Georgia O'Keeffe, Lawrence Atkinson, and Mary Cecil Allen. The conditions necessary for fulfilling these aspirations came with the restructuring of her life to fit the primacy of her art in three ways: by subordinating landlady chores to it; through achieving isolation and propinquity to nature in the forest by the purchase of a caravan; and as a result of discovering the oil-on-paper medium for sketching. Sadly these conditions only fell into place a few years before Emily died.

The spiritual quest that Emily was embarked upon for much of her life might seem strange to people living in the last decade of the twentieth century. But, as this biography shows, it is the key to understanding Carr's art and her life.

MARIA TIPPETT
Bowen Island, October 1994

Preface

It would be difficult to live in British Columbia for any length of time without being confronted with the name of Emily Carr and one or all of her several personae: the lonely, struggling artist; the undaunted traveller; the endearing memoirist; the doughty eccentric. My acquaintance with Emily began when I was a child in her own Victoria and viewed her paintings of Indian totem poles in the corridors of the Parliament Buildings on my Saturday-morning visits to the Provincial Museum; this experience became for me at once an early introduction to painting and to the art of the Northwest Coast Indians. When I grew older and embarked on my studies in Canadian and European cultural history, Emily's several reputations, and the legends about her—some of her own making—attracted and challenged me to discover the real person behind them.

Five years of research and writing have produced this book. If I may anticipate the life that unfolds, it is that of a highly complex woman: a person of strong character, not always agreeable, who was the victim of anxieties and guilts; who had a highly perceptive and penetrating mind while being unintellectual, intuitive, and spiritually inclined; whose remarkable creativity and output as an artist and writer existed in spite of a prodigious expenditure of energy on non-painting and non-writing activities. The period Emily Carr lived in—1871 to 1945—was not one that encouraged a woman of independent spirit to have a life of her own. Yet in conservative Victoria, and against numerous obstacles, that is what Emily had. It was an eventful life—emotionally, creatively, and socially—and to the everlasting gratitude of a biographer, she wrote about it generously and vividly. An unbroken thread running through her adult years was her persistent examination of her relationship to the Indians, to the forest, and to God. In working this out in her painting, she did not pioneer a new artistic movement: her style was a late adaptation of Expressionism. She was an innovator of perception, not of style; and as a result, her reputation remained in Canada. But her efforts were rewarded in a crowning achievement: she saw the landscape and the Indians in a new way, and through her art she enabled others to do so too.

Emily Carr's perception of our forest landscape has implanted itself in the imagination of British Columbians. Indeed, all Canadians who have seen her work will have had their impressions of the B.C. forest and the natives who inhabited it influenced by her vision. This is just one of her achievements. Another is her literary accomplishment: her books are firmly entrenched in the body of Canadian literature. Finally there is the life itself—so rich in human strengths and failings, triumphs and adversities—which filled me with admiration and wonder as I reconstructed it. I hope my readers will have a similar response.

Acknowledgements

In my research for this book I have examined hundreds of Emily Carr's paintings in a dozen cities and towns, and followed her travels from Victoria to San Francisco and the west coast of Vancouver Island; to London, St Ives, Bushey, and the East Anglia Sanatorium in England; to Paris, Crécy-en-Brie, and Concarneau in France; to the Queen Charlotte Islands, and the districts of the Nass and Skeena Rivers in northern British Columbia; and to Toronto, Montreal, and Ottawa. Throughout this endeavour many people have been most helpful and I would like to express my gratitude for their assistance. Foremost among them is my husband, Douglas Cole, who has lived not only with me for the past five years but with Emily Carr.

Helen Gray and Judy and John Kendle made cogent comments upon early versions of my text. I wish to thank them and Martha Dzioba of the Oxford University Press, and my editor, William Toye, who skilfully worked on the typescript and proofs. Deserving of special mention for their generous assistance are Charles C. Hill of the National Gallery of Canada; Harry Milford of the San Francisco Institute of Art; Dr Eric McCormick, Auckland, New Zealand; Dr Patricia Roy of the University of Victoria; Frances Gundry, manuscripts archivist, Provincial Archives of British Columbia; and Dr Regina Seelig, Munich. Tod Greenaway provided photographic assistance for which I am grateful. Several lectures at Simon Fraser University elicited helpful comments from my students, and the Canada Council generously provided research grants. Unfortunately I was denied access to some important material, but I am grateful to those relatives, friends, and admirers of Emily Carr who assisted by sharing their manuscripts, paintings, and recollections with me.

Public institutions that were particularly helpful were the National Gallery of Canada; the Vancouver Art Gallery; the Art Gallery of Ontario; the Art Gallery of Greater Victoria; the Montreal Museum of

Fine Arts; the Glenbow-Alberta Institute; the Public Archives of Canada; the Museum of Man; the Vancouver Public Library; the Vancouver City Archives; the Public Archives of British Columbia; the Simon Fraser University Library; the University of British Columbia Library; the McMichael Canadian Collection; the California Historical Society Library; the Dominion Gallery, Montreal; the San Francisco Art Institute; the Seattle Art Museum; the Jane Walker Hospital, Nayland, Suffolk; the Towner Art Gallery, Brighton; the Architectural Association, London; and the Alexander Turnbull Library, Wellington. To all of them I am most grateful.

M.T.

Bibliographical Note

I have made generous use of the Emily Carr Papers in the Public Archives of Canada, which include an unpublished autobiography, the complete journals, manuscripts of published and unpublished stories and autobiographical writings, and correspondence between Emily Carr and Ira Dilworth. With the exception of numerous quotations from the unpublished autobiography—which was handwritten in three unpaginated scribblers—all quotations and other references are annotated at the back of this book. To avoid peppering quotations from Emily's journals and letters with *sic* after eccentricities of spelling—which, like the quality of her writing, varied with Emily's moods—I have transcribed her words as she wrote them. My references to *Klee Wyck, The Book of Small, The House of All Sorts, Growing Pains: The Autobiography of Emily Carr,* and *Hundreds and Thousands*—originally published in 1941, 1942, 1944, 1946, and 1966 respectively—are to later paperback editions published by Clarke, Irwin & Company Limited.

NOTE: An asterisk preceding a painting title indicates a black-and-white illustration; a dagger indicates a colour reproduction. All measurements are given in inches.

1
Childhood
1871-1891

In the early morning of the fifth of July 1863 the sidewheel steamer *The Brother Jonathan* entered the spacious harbour of Esquimalt near the southeastern tip of Vancouver Island. The vessel docked alongside the wharf, where a collection of wooden warehouse buildings straddled the rocky shore. Most of the passengers had already disembarked the day before at Portland and were now travelling to the mines at Boise, Idaho, so that hardly more than forty people emerged at Esquimalt. One of them, Richard Carr, had left his gold-prospecting days behind him, having made a modest fortune in California. The stout full-bearded man was here as a settler with his small, spare wife, Emily, and two young daughters, Edith and Clara. The family boarded a stagecoach and prepared to be driven three miles through the coniferous forest to their destination—Victoria.

Fort Victoria was established in 1843 by James Douglas, Chief Factor of the Hudson's Bay Company. Two years later the appearance of the Royal Navy reinforced Britain's claim to the ownership of Vancouver Island that was being disputed by the U.S.A. With the Oregon Boundary Treaty of 1846 the Island became British, and in 1849 it was leased to the Company on condition that it would start and develop a colony there. In the mid-1850s, when the Royal Navy established a depot at Esquimalt harbour, the Fort became less dominated by the fur trade and increasingly concerned with farming and lumbering. But a more pronounced change overtook the small community after 1857 when gold was discovered on the bars of the Fraser and Thompson Rivers and thousands of miners from the south passed through the settlement to buy provisions before crossing the Strait of Georgia to the adjacent mainland. In the process of catering to their needs and whims, gambling saloons and dance halls, warehouses and banks, churches and shanties were constructed almost overnight. The British outpost was suddenly transformed into the town of Victoria. A second discovery of gold, this

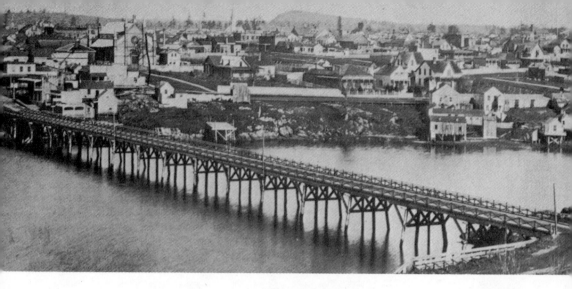

time at Williams Creek in the Cariboo in 1862, brought the town out of the lull that had followed the 1858 boom. Once again miners disembarked by the hundreds at Esquimalt harbour and rode or walked to Victoria before setting off to the mainland for the long trek to the fields.

When Richard Carr and his family arrived in 1863, Victoria had all the characteristics of a boom-and-bust town. Unpainted hovels clung to the gently sloping shores of the narrow inner harbour, or squatted next to newly built brick buildings on the principal streets, Government and Wharf. Across the harbour, massive slant-roofed community houses on the Songhees Indian Reserve housed upwards of 2,000 Coast Salish natives, rivalling the town's white population of 3,000. At the south end of the harbour, opposite a tidal mud flat straddled by an 800-foot bridge, stood an assortment of pagoda-like buildings that had been the headquarters of the legislative assembly and the colonial governor since 1859. Still further south, behind the government buildings, was the city's first residential suburb, James Bay. Here such personages as Douglas, his son-in-law Dr John Helmcken, and the Reverend Edward Cridge, rector of the Church of England, had built fashionable villas on generous parcels of land.

Richard Carr was not displeased with what he saw on his first day in Victoria. He admired the many fine brick and stone buildings and the wooden sidewalks; he found the streets in generally good condition; and he counted a total of seven churches and three daily newspapers. Nor did he fail to note that Victoria was 'beautifully located'.[1] The coniferous forest that covered most of the island remained on the fringes of the settled areas around the city. Groves of Garry oak, expansive meadows, and undulating hills predominated. Across the Juan de Fuca Strait, which separated the island from the territory of Washington to the south, loomed the perpetually snow-covered mountains of the Olympic range.

It was more than the pleasing diversity of vegetation and the similarity of Victoria's gentle climate to that of Cornwall that had brought Richard Carr out of retirement in Barnstaple, Devon. With its gold-rush prosperity, its free port, its plentiful supply of cheap building materials, and its British flag, Victoria offered him the advantages of both New World life and British institutions.

Carr's beginnings were certainly more humble than one might have imagined in observing the well-dressed man entering St George's Hotel with his wife and daughters. He was the youngest of seven children, the son of Thomas Carr, a tradesman who had moved his family from Beckley, Oxfordshire, to Craford, Kent—where Richard was born in 1818—then on to Tenby, Wales, and back again to Beckley. Richard received little more than elementary schooling, but by the age of eighteen he had made a pleasure trip to Paris, Berlin, Warsaw, and Dresden. Not satisfied that he had seen enough, he took passage, probably as a deckhand, on the *Sir Edward Hamilton*, which sailed the following year (1837) to America. Now came twelve years of itinerant jobs: harvesting in Upper Canada, ice and net fishing on Lake Michigan, working as a deckhand on ships touching at Gulf and Caribbean ports, and finally— with camera, plates, and developing equipment—traversing the Yucatan Peninsula on horseback as a daguerreotype photographer. These activities were interspersed with trips back to England—always as a deckhand—and visits to his brothers: Samuel in Toronto and Thomas in Black Water Creek, Alabama. Very much the curious, romantic nineteenth-century adventurer and notetaker, Richard Carr was intent on experiencing all he could. He visited a Quaker settlement in Albany, attended a Methodist gathering at Saratoga, observed the expulsion of the Cherokee Indians from their territories in the West, and witnessed saloon brawls in New Orleans while maintaining a certain British superiority to all his encounters. In his travels throughout North America he did not find one American whom he felt could be called a gentleman. Unlike his brothers, he refused to regard any of the cities where he lingered as more than temporary residences.

Carr's life changed when news of gold discoveries in California reached him in Central America. Arriving in San Francisco in January 1849, he found that he could ask double his usual price for daguerreotype photographs. But he worked as a photographer for only a few days after his arrival. By late January he was in the gold fields, where he remained until November. After accumulating $3,000 in less than a year of prospecting, he invested his money in establishing general stores in Alviso, Gilroy, San José, and Mountain View. His success as a merchant was such that by 1854 he was worth about $25,000. Leaving his Bay area stores in the hands of his assistant, Jacob Shumway, he took a six-month holiday. The purpose of the leave was to accompany Miss Emily Saunders to England, where they were to be married.

Carr had hitherto travelled alone. He had attempted in his wanderings to keep in touch with female acquaintances by correspondence, but this had led to nothing. In San Francisco, however, at the age of thirty-two, he met Emily Saunders while she was living with a Mrs Quantack. How or when or why this girl, eighteen years his junior, came to that city is unknown. Her mother, Mary Saunders, was a single woman.[2] Richard and Emily Carr chose to tell their children little of their courtship or early lives. The close proximity of Emily Saunders' place of birth at Freeland, Oxfordshire, to Beckley—a distance of less than ten miles—led the Carr children to assume that their parents had met in England rather than in California.

After their marriage at Eynsham Parish Church in Oxfordshire, the couple returned to California, took up residence in Alviso, and began their family of nine children: Edith was born in 1856 and Clara in 1857. It had never been Richard Carr's intention to settle permanently in the United States. In 1861, when he had added another $5,000 to his fortune, he decided—against the advice of his American friends—to return to England. He retained some land but sold his stores and became the first man to transport California wheat and flour to England. For this he chartered three ships, one of which, *The Great Republic*, took him and his family. On arrival in England, he sold the grain for a small profit and invested the money in British railway stock and a home in Barnstaple, Devon.

His friends' prediction that he would find life in England disappointing was soon realized. Though he spent his time pleasantly enough working in the small garden of his Devonshire home, tutoring the girls in reading and writing, and travelling occasionally to London, he was not happy. It rained too much, the garden was not large enough to occupy his free time, and Barnstaple, with its mainly professional middle class, was unfriendly: he was uncomfortable among the class his prosperity allowed him to join. 'I used to think there was nothing like England and the English,' he wrote shortly after arriving in Barnstaple, 'but now I find they are not exactly what I thought they were.'[3] With no demanding work, he felt useless and idle; his plan to live the quiet life of an English gentleman was a failure. Adding to this unhappiness were the deaths of two infant sons: William in 1861 and John in 1862.

Barely two years after returning to England, Carr decided that in California or some other newly settled land, preferably under the British flag, his children would have a much brighter prospect before them and he would be able to live more comfortably on his investments and find more activity for his leisure time. Thus in July 1863 he packed a few trunks and sailed with his family for Victoria via San Francisco.

Carr had little opportunity to be bored during his first years in Victoria. A month after arriving, he was occupied with establishing a wholesale firm and commission agency in the town's warehouse district along Wharf Street, and planning a home on a parcel of land he had purchased in James Bay. Within a year his business was flourishing and he had moved into a handsome Italianate villa designed for him by the Victoria architects Wright and Saunders. The house was on part of Beckley Farm, formerly Hudson's Bay Company property, and bordered on uncultivated Beacon Hill Park, only a short distance from the cliffs overlooking Juan de Fuca Strait. The new street was named after Carr.

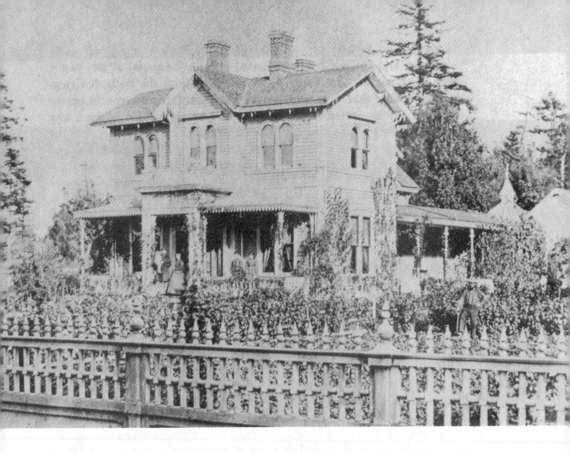

(It lost the name Carr Street shortly after the turn of the century, when it was joined to Government Street.) The cleared land surrounding the house was cultivated in front with formal gardens of hawthorn bushes and banks of primroses and behind with vegetable beds and orchards of apple, plum, and cherry. There were two paddocks for cows, a barn, and a yard for swine. An acre was left in forest. The family were able to enjoy relative self-sufficiency on their eight acres, eating well—Richard Carr did not consider a roast under ten pounds worth serving—but not extravagantly. As one relative recalled, 'It was Bread and Butter OR Bread and Jam, but only on Sundays could it be Bread and Butter and Jam.'[4]

Richard Carr made several business trips to San Francisco, where he still had investments in land. Mrs Carr journeyed south for her health in 1879, but she never accompanied her husband. She was fully occupied supervising Bong, the Chinese cook, and Mary, the native Indian washerwoman, as well as teaching Edith and Clara the rudiments of housekeeping. She made friends with her immediate neighbours, Mrs Bisset and Mrs Cridge, but was not gregarious. An invalid during the last ten years of her life, she was remembered by her children as a sickly, quiet woman who laughed little. But she may have possessed a more forceful personality than her children realized. A family acquaintance recalled that she 'was really the mainstay of the household, although her in-

The Carr house, with Richard and Emily Carr and three of their daughters; Mr Carr is holding Emily, and Edith and Clara are standing on the right. Probably taken in 1874. PABC.

fluence was skilfully exerted so that the father was the nominal head.'⁵

Richard and Emily Carr participated little in the social affairs of the city. Their names were never on the guest lists of the balls of the Victoria elite and they were never 'At Home' for afternoon tea or weekend tennis, as many of their neighbours were. Nor is there any evidence that they frequented the productions of Victoria's amateur theatrical or philharmonic societies or even watched the horse racing and cricket at Beacon Hill Park. They did attend the church of the Establishment, Christ Church, but were neither seat holders nor participants in the congregation's social affairs. This reluctance to mingle caused many of their contemporaries to regard Carr as 'a stay-at-home-man' and his wife as a woman who 'never went out'.⁶ But they did not lack friends. The merchants R.H. Austin and J.B. Robinson, old acquaintances from San Francisco who had greeted them on their arrival in Victoria, were occasionally entertained in the pleasant but plain sitting room, with its heavy mahogany-and-horsehair furniture. And although the tightly knit upper echelon of Victoria's small society generally considered self-made businessmen as having more money than culture, Carr's place of residence in fashionable James Bay enabled him to count some of the élite among his friends and neighbours. The social life of the town held no attraction, however. Carr's interests were in making a success of his business and in creating a comfortable home for his family.

Shortly after arriving in Victoria in 1863, Carr had a disagreement with Colonel R.C. Moody, the land-speculating commander of the Royal Engineers, over the boundary of four acres he had purchased from him. He sued Moody for $600—the estimated value of the property in dispute. At the conclusion of a trial that dragged on for months, Carr lost the case and was left with court expenses. Further trouble concerning land occurred that same year, when he sold one acre at the northeast corner of his property to William Lush, on condition that no public house would be erected on the lot. One was. Carr retaliated by building a large and hideous wooden fence between the two properties. Coinciding with these difficulties was the death of yet another son, Thomas; this time there had been some hope for the baby's survival, as he lived for six months.

Richard Carr & Company prospered in its first two years. But when the gold rush subsided in 1865 and Victoria lost its free-port status, Carr found himself with a warehouse full of goods for which there was no market. Many merchants were forced to close their doors. Carr struggled on for two years, then amalgamated with W.J. Welcker. In 1870, when the economy had recovered from its post-gold-rush slump, the partnership was dissolved. Yet the unstable market had taken its toll on Carr's finances. He was made painfully aware of this when he visited his former business associates in California and found them to be considerably more prosperous than himself. At fifty-two he was not old, but he suffered from attacks of gout so severe that he was frequently confined to bed. Moreover, he was witnessing the deaths of many of his old

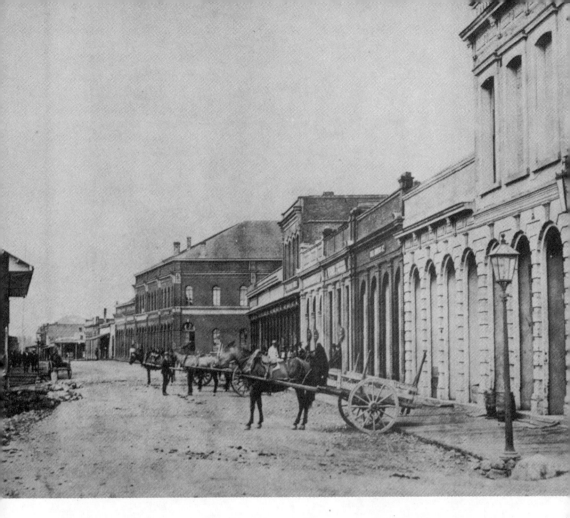

friends. This made him reflect upon his life. 'We know not what an hour may bring forth,' he wrote, 'may we be found prepared is my fervant [sic] prayer.'[7]

From 1868 Carr became increasingly religious. Every morning he conducted family prayers at seven forty-five. Sundays were entirely given over to religious observances. In the morning he led the family to the First Presbyterian Church; in the afternoon he took the children to Mrs Cridge's for Sunday School; in the evening, after attending service at Christ Church, he conducted Bible readings and hymn singing in the family sitting room. The children were baptized by the Presbyterian minister, the Reverend Thomas Sommerville, in 1870, shortly before he departed for Scotland.

More children were born to Mrs Carr. Elizabeth arrived in 1867, Alice in 1869, Emily in 1871, and the longed-for son, Richard, in 1875. Family life was considerably different for them than it had been for Edith and Clara. Soon after her son's birth, Mrs Carr was more often in bed than out of it. Increasing invalidism greatly reduced her contacts with her children, apart from frail young Dick. Though their father appeared to

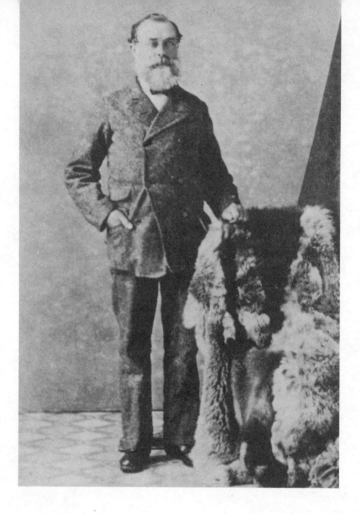

Richard Carr,
about 1876.
PABC.

dominate the family—from the table at mealtimes, conducting daily prayers and Bible readings, leading the children to and from church—he was not the day-to-day disciplinarian of the younger children. That role fell to Edith as the eldest. This trim, rather plain, strongly self-willed young woman, who was nineteen when Dick was born, supervised the children's Saturday-evening baths, their deportment, and religious studies with the utmost efficiency. She also saw to the needs of her ailing mother. (The more attractive Clara was preoccupied with courting Major John Nicholles of the Royal Engineers, whom she married in 1882.) Though Edith's experience with children and her quick sense of humour might have made her a good wife and mother, or allowed her to follow a profession, she laid aside any plans she might have had for her future and devoted herself entirely to the family.

Of the three young girls in Edith's care, slim Lizzie, with straight brown hair drawn tightly off her bird-like face, dreamed of becoming a missionary and learned hundreds of religious texts by heart. Alice, who was small and had masses of auburn hair, spent more time caring for her dolls than learning Sunday-School verses. Midway between Lizzie and

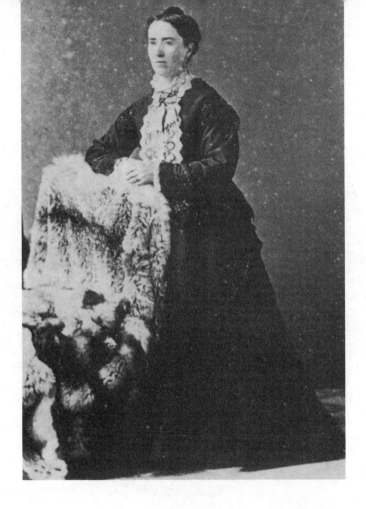

Mrs Richard Carr, about 1876. PABC.

Emily, she was a constant target for their affection, though she would not let either sister monopolize her fully. Emily—who, as the youngest girl, became accustomed to receiving more than her share of the family's attention—was frequently vexed at not having Alice completely to herself.

Chubby, grey-eyed Emily remained the favourite of the family, especially of her father—even after the arrival of Dick, who spent more time with his mother, because of his frail health, than with his sisters. Emily accompanied Richard Carr to and from his store, helped him in the garden, held his hand on the way to church, and slept under his arm during the long Presbyterian sermons. Neither clever at school like Alice, nor adept at memorizing religious texts like Lizzie, she depended greatly on the attention of the family around her. In the case of Edith, this was not always easy to come by. Edith loved her brother and sisters dearly but rarely showed that she did and Emily minded this. She also resented the privileged authority of a sister who, in her mind, should have been an equal. At an early age she came to associate authority and rule with Edith and love and attention with her father.

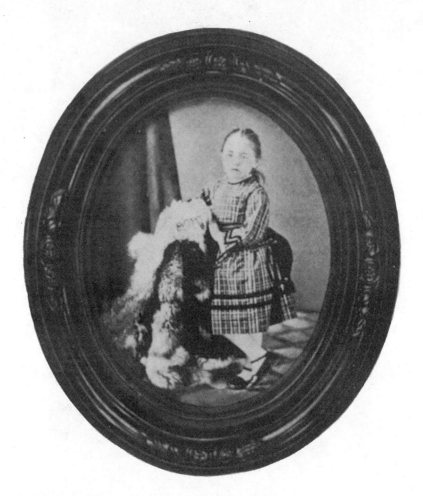

Emily, aged 5.
VPL.

Beyond the realm of family, Emily's childhood world was immense. Beacon Hill Park, to the east of the Carr property, was full of woods and wild flowers, hooting owls, and murky ponds with croaking frogs. Above the park was Beacon Hill itself, covered in spring with carpets of purple camas and clusters of yellow broom whose pods crackled in the warmer months and spread the shrub over the hill and down to the ocean. At the water's edge, below the Dallas Road cliffs and along the log-strewn pebbly beach, were the encampments of itinerant Indians. Emily spent many summer days sitting in the long grass on Beacon Hill, dipping into the icy waters below the cliffs, and gazing into tidal pools along the rocky shore.

The town—lying behind the beach, the cliffs, the hill, the park, the Carr property, and over the James Bay bridge—was a less-favoured haunt. Yet when Emily went there, she found much to see. The streets were alive with two-wheeled dog-carts, four-passenger chaises, Mr Winters' rentable picnic carriage, saddle horses, and, competing with all of these, herds of cattle being driven from the docks through the centre of town to Goodacre's slaughterhouse. Emily also observed the chain gang

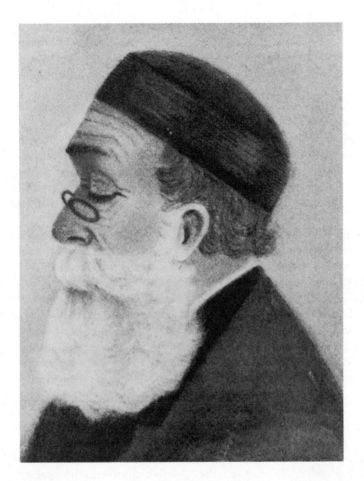

dressed in moleskin trousers, checkered shirts, and blue cloth caps marching under escort from the city jail, across the mud flats and up to Marvin's Hill to work on the rock pile. Among Victoria's 'queer people' who interested her were eccentric old gentlemen who drove about the town in buggies, and Elizabeth Pickering, who roamed the streets intoxicated.[9]

Emily's childhood was not merely spent discovering the peculiarities and beauties of the city and the park. One friend remembered her as a 'rather dumpy and dowdy old-fashioned' girl who was not interested in children's games, preferring to climb fences or trees to watch the birds.[8] She not only watched but longed to handle, and have in her keeping, every wild creature she encountered. Ducks and chickens from the barnyard and a young crow stolen from a nest were only a few of the animals she tamed. It was during this time that she also became interested in art. While attending Mrs Fraser's private school for children, Emily took drawing lessons from Miss Emily Woods once a week. When she later moved on to the Central Public School, where art was not part of the curriculum, her father found lessons for her elsewhere. Along with

Alice and Lizzie, Emily joined the class of Miss Eva Withrow, who had trained as an artist in San Francisco.[10] While Lizzie and Alice painted flowers, Emily learned to draw heads on a grid. A pencil sketch of her father in profile shows that by about the age of nine she could produce a reasonable, though stiff, likeness. Alice, with her watercolour drawings of wild flowers, also showed talent. Perhaps it was their interest in painting that strengthened the two girls' friendship during their later childhood. They exchanged girlhood secrets in their double-dormered bedroom overlooking the park. Wearing their older sisters' dresses, they played 'ladies' in one of the two hay fields until Richard Carr ordered them to exchange fields with the cows. And in the children's garden, assisted by religious Lizzie, they held mock funerals for their deceased pets.

Emily gained many friends among James Bay's elderly residents. Mrs Mitchell frequently entertained her with stories and news from England, and once a week Mrs Cridge read Dickens to the girls while they munched on her drop cakes. Breaking the pattern of everyday life were special events celebrated by the whole family. On the Queen's birthday the children donned their scratchy muslin summer frocks for the first time and, joining friends, rowed up the harbour to the Gorge, where they watched ten oar-cutters, whalers, gigs, and forty-foot Indian canoes race up the inlet. At Christmas the merchants along Government Street tied fir trees to every lamp post and decorated their shop windows with cotton wool, red-lettered greetings, striped peppermint-candy walking sticks, and colourfully illustrated storybooks. In Mr Saunders' grocery-store window a mechanical Santa Claus ground real coffee. In the Carr home the fragrance of pine and cedar boughs permeated the house all season and mingled on Christmas day with the aroma of the boiling plum pudding. Most thrilling to the Carr children was the present-laden Christmas tree around which they joined hands and sang carols. If there was a rare snowfall, sleighbells could be heard in the distance.

Victoria in the late seventies encompassed both frontier and Old-World elements. Though newcomers were still homesteading on the outskirts of town, there were many residents, now comfortably established, who could recall the hardships of life in Fort Victoria. Their drawing rooms were decorated with faded engravings of young Queen Victoria, women sang old English songs to assuage their homesickness, and the next ship from around the Horn was always awaited eagerly for news of home. Richard Carr's Englishness was expressed in his reminiscences of his youth in Kent and Wales, and through his manners, prim garden, imported newspapers, and clothes smelling of Wright's coaltar soap and camphor. But it was he who gave Emily her first taste of the frontier when he entertained her with lively descriptions of impenetrable forests and remote Indian villages after returning from a voyage around Vancouver Island in 1879.

As her father's favourite, Emily came to know him well. Their daily walks together began on the gravel path in front of the house, proceeded

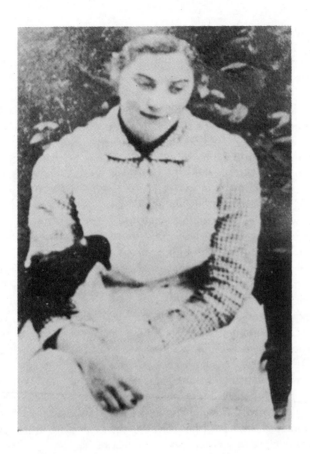

Emily, aged 16, with her pet crow. PABC.

up Carr Street to Toronto Street, then along Princess Avenue and down Marvin's Hill to the James Bay bridge. They not only allowed Emily and her father to share their love of nature, particularly birds, but they provided a respite from the rigid family rituals of Bible-reading, prayers, and church-going. The walks were companionable interludes between school and home, work and family life.

This 'fond and devoted relationship' with her father came to an end when Emily reached early puberty,[11] and something occurred that ever after made her think of Richard Carr as 'a cross gouty sexy old man who hurt and disgusted' her.[12]

> I couldn't forgive Father I just couldn't for spoiling all the loveliness of life with that bestial brutalness of explanation filling me with horror instead of gently explaining the glorious beauty of reproduction the holiness and joy of it.[13]

The emotion that pervades Emily's vague references to the incident—written in old age—suggests that it was something more than an unfeeling and clumsy explanation of the facts of life to an over-sensitive adolescent; more even than the shock of hearing this topic discussed by her father, to whom she was devoted. Her expression of revulsion makes one wonder whether it was caused by a misguided attempt to illustrate the explanation by some action. The 'brutal telling', as Emily was later to call it, remained a secret horror that she was to share with no one until a few years before her death.[14] According to her recollections of the aftermath, Richard Carr suddenly seemed hypocritical and salacious. 'Nobody knew the sinking agonies of terror I had suffered when I had been alone with father, because before I'd been his favourite trotting after him like a dog.'[15] Her love for him turned to hate.

Emily now questioned her father's morals and challenged the sincerity of his religious devotion and his rationale for upholding Edith's overbearing rules. According to her, Carr responded with cruelty. Mrs Carr was merely perplexed by her daughter's insubordination and called her 'black crow' and 'puzzle child'.[16] Alice and Lizzie also remained ignorant of her experience. As they were older, more clever at school, more adept at their religious studies—though no more devout—Emily felt inferior to them, especially now that she was without the favoured attention of her father. The childhood world around which she would later weave some of her stories had come to an end.

The experience had a lasting effect on her sexuality, her maturation, her social development, and her family relations. Already feeling different from her sisters, Emily allowed the 'brutal telling' to widen the gulf that existed between herself and her family. The incident came to provide a justification for being different and resulted in an ambivalent mixture of superiority and guilt. She felt superior because, in discovering fault in her father, she held herself above his standards, to which the entire family adhered. She could not refrain from criticizing, questioning, and finding hypocrisy in virtually every aspect of her family's life.[17] On the other hand she was burdened with a sense of guilt at dishonouring her father, disappointing her delicate mother, and rebelling against family discipline. She scribbled vows—'I really will be good tempered when I go home'—in the margins of her school books, yet she remained querulous and critical. She saw herself as 'the family's sinner', its 'black sheep'.[18]

Mrs Carr died after a lingering illness—probably tuberculosis—in 1886. Emily and Dick now spent their summers with the family of Alexander Green, a Victoria banker who had known Richard Carr in San Francisco. Green had three sons and three daughters and a cottage at Shoal Bay. Though only a few miles from the Carr house, Shoal Bay was far enough away to remove Emily completely from the household for five summers. These were oases in an otherwise unhappy period of Emily's adolescence.

Following his wife's death, Richard Carr began making preparations for his own end. He sold all but a little over an acre of the James Bay property and arranged for it to be left to Edith on condition that she maintain the house and garden as it would be upon his death. In the spring of 1888 he sold the warehouse business to R.P. Rithet. With less garden to occupy his time, and with increasing periods of depression and pain from attacks of gout, he retired more and more to his study to read

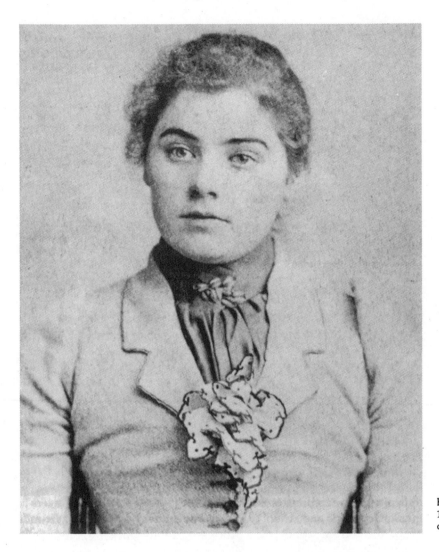

Emily, about
1888. Private
collection.

the papers or just to sit and stare out at the garden. A few months after
selling his firm, in the fall of 1888, he died. (The cause of death was given
as 'lung hemorrhage'.) The newspaper obituaries praised the high reputation he had gained for honourable business dealing, and Senator
Macdonald and Alex Monroe, the Hudson's Bay Company factor, were
among the distinguished citizens who carried his coffin to the family plot
in the Ross Bay Cemetery. Carr left his family an estate of $50,000.
Along with the official guardianship of the children, this was put in the
hands of his old friend, James H. Lawson, a red-bearded former employee of the Hudson's Bay Company.

Almost seventeen when her father died, Emily was now without
parental guidance, the more so as Carr, leaving behind letters of advice
to his survivors, pointedly omitted her. Edith now received the full brunt

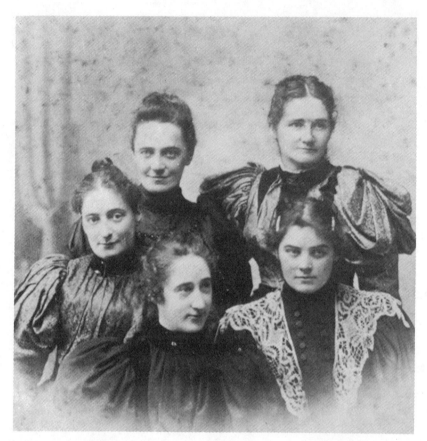

The five Carr
sisters, about
1888, with Emily
in the lower
right, and
(clockwise)
Alice, Lizzie,
Edith, Clara.
PABC.

of Emily's hostility to authority and they frequently quarrelled. For
Lizzie and Alice, the years following their father's death were not so
difficult. More accepting of Edith's rule, they were studying for careers in
missionary work and school teaching. For Emily, however, the three-mile
walk to and from school was a drudgery and the work itself, especially
arithmetic, was difficult and joyless. Nevertheless Emily had graduated
from the Central Public School in the spring of 1888, eleventh in a class
of thirteen. And in the autumn, only shortly before her father's death,
she had entered Victoria High School. She quit the following year.

2
San Francisco and Ucluelet

1891-1899

In 1886 the French painter C.A. de L'Aubinière and his English artist-wife Georgina came to Victoria. The couple put on exhibitions, gave lessons, attempted to establish an art gallery, and generally dominated the small art scene during their year in the city. Emily later scoffed at them as having 'painted a few faraway mountains floating in something hazy that was not Canadian air', then slamming down the lids of their paint boxes and returning to the Old World.[1] Yet she was probably among their students. After they left, she and two girlhood acquaintances, Sophie Pemberton and Theresa Wylde, attended art classes given by the Misses Berry and Jorand in the turret of the old Roccabella mansion on Victoria Crescent, which had been converted into a fashionable boarding house. They sketched together in the park and along the Dallas Road cliffs below Beacon Hill. In 1890, when Sophie Pemberton left Victoria to study in England, and Theresa Wylde was making arrangements to go there too, Emily began thinking about her own artistic career. Not particularly happy at home, and unsuccessful at school, she saw art study as an opportunity to cultivate the only activity in which she excelled.

Emily would have preferred to follow her sketching partners to London, sailing past the Golden Gate, around the Horn, and on to Liverpool, but San Francisco had a good art school and was closer to Victoria. Moreover, there was a strong connection between the Carrs and that city. Her father had made his fortune in central California; business interests and the warmer climate had drawn her parents and elder sisters to the 'Golden City' in the 1860s and 1870s; and the family's rare out-of-town visitors had come from the Bay area. With the intention of going there to study, she approached her guardian, James Lawson, with the idea of obtaining funds from the family estate. She told him that her desire to learn more about art was very real and convinced him that it could lead to a profession. Lawson arranged for a monthly allowance to cover her tuition, room, and board. With the assistance of her former teacher, Eva Withrow, Emily submitted entrance drawings to the California School of Design. She was accepted and left Victoria in the late summer of 1891. One of the Carrs' closest friends, Mrs Hayes, had been appointed Emily's guardian and was waiting on the pier in San Francisco Bay when the ship bearing Emily made its way through the morning fog.[2]

Emily's desire to begin her art studies in London caused her to view San Francisco as relatively new and unsophisticated. Yet that city, although remote from the large centres of the Midwest and East, was already a cultivated metropolis. Fortunes from gold and land, silver and the railroad, had long supported the fine arts. As early as the 1870s San Francisco had been ranked by some second only to New York as a centre for the arts in North America.

The California School of Design reflected the city's cultural reputation. It had been offering first-class instruction since its inception in 1874. The majority of the school's teachers, though largely American-born, had studied in Paris at the Académie Julian or the Ecole des Beaux-Arts. Some had been inspired by the intuitive approach of James McNeill Whistler, others by the flat decorative motifs of Puvis de Chavannes. However diverse their styles, they offered their students sound instruction in the tradition of the best art schools of Europe. A student began in the antique class—drawing in charcoal from a collection of plaster-cast shoulders, arms, feet, and replicas of classical sculpture; then continued to the life class—drawing from an undraped model; then advanced to the still-life class and finally to the landscape class. Unlike most other institutions, the California School of Design allowed women to draw from the nude. They were thus given a unique opportunity to advance beyond still-life and landscape painting.

The school was located above a 'veritable World's Bazaar of edibles'— the famous Pine Street Market.[3] Stairs led up from the street into a long, wide room that was partitioned off by sliding curtains. An enormous skylight and a row of large windows facing the street made it bright and sunny. At one end flies circled lazily around a pile of decaying fruit set out for the still-life class. At the other end replicas of the Venus de Milo, the Apollo, the Discus Thrower, and other works of classical statuary peered down from their pedestals.

Clad in a black sateen frock that almost touched the hem of her long skirt, Emily entered Arthur F. Mathews' antique class. It was a good place to start. Though brusque in manner and known for his caustic remarks to students and fellow colleagues, the dark, mustachioed Mathews was the most revered teacher in the school. His fine reputation at the Paris Salon, his Bohemian life style, and his flirtation with the French Impressionists and Symbolists made students seek him out.[4] But Emily did not continue with him. After completing his antique class, prudery kept her from working in the life class. Vowing never to draw from the nude, she not only missed a privilege given to few female art

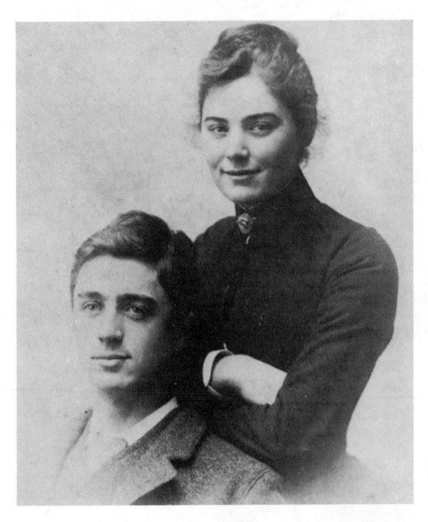

Emily and Dick,
about 1891.
Private collec-
tion.

students at the time, but deprived herself of studying further under the
best artist and teacher in the school. Instead she joined, probably in her
second year, Amédée Joullin's still-life class, exchanging charcoal for oil
paints and classical replicas for fruit and flowers. At the beginning of her
third year she began classes in perspective and landscape painting under
Raymond Yelland, who was replaced by Lorenzo Latimer.

For Emily the first two years of study were dull. The repeated copying
of a plaster cast or an arrangement of apples and flowers, in the hope of
achieving a better likeness with yet another rendering, was sheer
drudgery. So too was working more or less without instruction, as her
teachers appeared only twice a week to give crits. During her third year,
however, she escaped the classroom routine by joining, every Wednesday, thirty or forty men and women at the ferry terminal and
travelling with them to cow pastures, chicken farms, and vacant lots

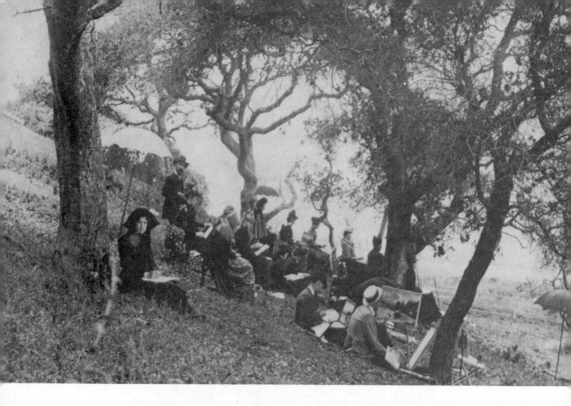

(ABOVE) Raymond Yelland's outdoor sketch class, 1893. CHS.

(BELOW) Detail of above, showing Emily.

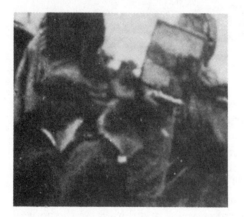

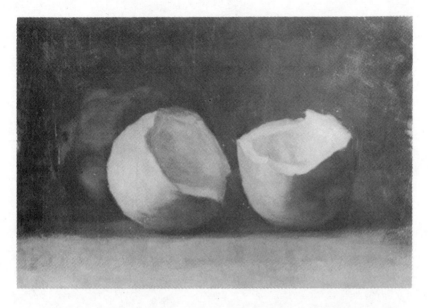

Melons, 1892.
Oil on canvas,
13 3/4 x 19 7/8.
Newcombe Col-
lection, PABC.

surrounding the city. Painting out-of-doors was an exhilarating experience. It demanded a different approach, for the landscape was more
elusive than the well-defined contours and objects she had been copying
in the classroom. Unlike apples and statuary, it could be felt.

While never distinguishing herself in any of her classes, Emily was
encouraged when Joullin told her that her colour sense was good and that
she had the makings of an artist. However, no gold medals or honourable mentions came her way at the end-of-term student exhibitions.
*Melons, one of two unsigned oil paintings attributed to her period in
San Francisco, is the work of an unremarkable student that shows the
influence of Mathews in its loose brush strokes.

A nostalgia for the classrooms above the oyster bars, the rows of
vegetable and fruit stalls manned by screeching vendors, never left
Emily. Though the school was dirty and drab, though the air was soured
by the murk and smells of the marketplace below, it always remained for
her 'a lovely, lowly, humble, starting place'.[5] Whether lunching around
the old stove, viewing parades from the roof, or exploring the props in
the attic, she was never alone. Among her new friends were the rhyme-
making cartoonist Jimmy Swinterton, the crippled Miss Beaner, the
lonely Nellie McCormick, the homesick English 'Stevie', and the insecure
Ishbel Dane. They were her junior by four or five years, and for the first
time in her life Emily was able to play a dominant role. Being older, she
found that they came to her for advice, which she gave gladly. She
became a much-needed companion for Nellie McCormick, who 'had few
friends'; allowed 'Stevie' to take comfort in her own Englishness; and

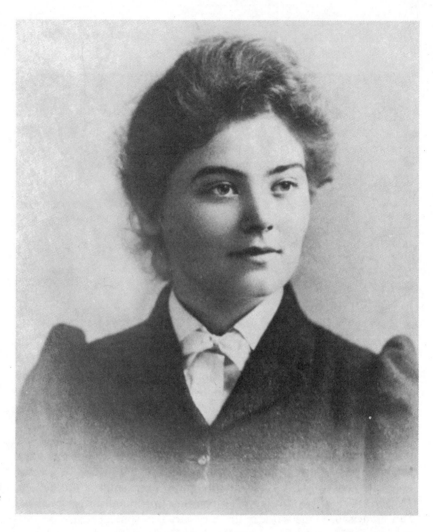

Emily, about
1892. Private
possession.

conscled the taunted 'Beaner' with the gift of a kitten.[6] Yet she herself
needed mothering. Though almost twenty when she arrived in California, emotionally she was little more than a young adolescent—which
is perhaps why she acquired the nickname 'Dummy'. She still thought of
herself as a child, and experienced a sense of family security as she shared
the warnings and advice in the parental letters of her much-younger
friend Adda. Emily rarely enjoyed relationships in which she was neither
mothering nor being mothered. An exception was her friendship with
Nellie McCormick, one of the most accomplished students in the school,
whom Emily still recalled warmly when she was ageing and sick.

Contrived partly as a release from family pressures, Emily's period of
study in San Francisco was more than a respite; it became a way of life. It
gave her, as a student-artist, a niche and the promise of a profession. It
also allowed her to enter an environment in which she found she had the

capacity to please others, to make friends, and to gain attention for her work without fear of hostile criticism or sheer indifference. Emily's two-and-a-half years in San Francisco were dominated not by the study of art but by the free give-and-take among the students, a sense of belonging, and a spirit of unconventionality. This is not to suggest that instruction was taken lightly. She worked hard, spending weekends and often holidays alone above the market finishing what she had failed to complete during the previous week, or copying yet another cast or still-life arrangement. However, this industriousness, verging on overwork, was not coupled with the desire to seek art beyond the classroom. She was unaware of the Vickery Gallery and the Bohemian Club, where the most prominent artists exhibited, for she later complained that the city had 'no galleries, no picture exhibitions'.[7] Nor did she probe her instructors about the location of local galleries or the availability of art books that would have told of the latest European movements. In the presence of her instructors she was childishly shy; they were authorities to be listened to, not queried. As for their work, displayed alongside that of the students at the end-of-session exhibitions, Amédée Joullin's paintings of Pueblo Indian life probably encouraged her depiction of the canoes and houses on the Songhees Indian Reserve that she painted after she returned to Victoria in 1893. And the low-key and dreamy mood of Lorenzo Latimer's landscape paintings can be seen reflected in Emily's subdued watercolour views of Burnside and other points around Victoria. However, with few examples of her pre-1898 work available for study, any discussion of her progress while in San Francisco, and the influence of her instruction there on her later work, must remain speculative.

Apparently Mrs Hayes did not oversee her ward with the scrutiny Edith Carr had requested. Taking full advantage of this lack of restraint, Emily did many things she would not have dared to do at home. From the Hayes' Lyndhurst Hotel on Geary Street where she lived, she innocently discovered the more exotic areas of the city, including Grant Street's redlight district and the squalid slums of Telegraph Hill. She taught herself to sew, took guitar lessons (even joining a banjo, mandolin, and guitar club), and went to church when and where she pleased. Unfortunately this freedom to pick and choose, to come and go, to like and dislike, was short-lived. In the spring that ended her first year of study, she was joined by Edith, Lizzie, and Alice. With Dick boarding at Ridley College in Ontario, Alice and Lizzie not yet embarked on their teaching and missionary careers, and the house rented to Messrs Waddington and Lawson, her three sisters were free to leave Victoria.

For Emily the disadvantages of their visit were many. The McAllister Street apartment into which she now moved with her sisters put her no longer within walking distance of the school. The family excursions and picnics, in which she was now required to participate, curtailed her outside activities and friendships. Living once again with her sisters, she was relegated to a position of inferiority; the confidence she had gained

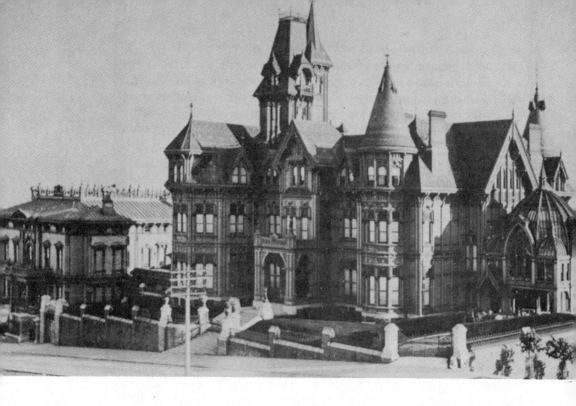

among her new friends at school began to wane. Her sisters took very
little interest in her art, and she resented this. Feeling discouraged,
particularly by Edith, she became lax about attending class. Her laziness
persisted until her sisters returned to Victoria—a year later.

Their sojourn had likely been prolonged by the sudden arrival in
California of young Dick. Never robust, he was found to have tuberculosis, and that illness brought him from Ontario to southern California's warmer climate early in 1893.[8] The sisters remained in San Francisco until early spring, travelling regularly to visit him in a Santa
Barbara sanatorium. After they had resettled in the Carr home in Victoria, Emily visited her brother only once. It was an unsettled period for
her. She moved from the McAllister Street apartment to the cottage of a
destitute artist-mother in Oakland; when she found that commuting
from the suburb was time-consuming, she moved again—this time to a
boarding house not far from the school. Not only did she change her
residence twice, but the school relocated too.

In May 1893 Edward F. Searles presented the former Gothic Revival
mansion of California millionaire Mark Hopkins to the San Francisco
Art Association. The awesome, grey-towered building, surrounded by
huge stone walls reaching a height of forty feet, was luxurious compared
with the ill-ventilated rat-infested Pine Street school. Yet Emily never felt
comfortable in these palatial surroundings, where the students did not
have the freedom to splash and experiment, to sharpen charcoal or to
toss eraser bread-crusts on the floor. The change of location affected
more than the students' relaxed behaviour. Now under the auspices of

the University of California, the school became the Mark Hopkins Institute of Art and established a three-year program leading to a University Certificate of Proficiency in the Graphic Arts. Study from life—the nude drawing that Emily had avoided—was mandatory under the new curriculum. Without it her chances of receiving a certificate were not good. In any event she left before she had completed her third year.

Emily recalled that James Lawson summoned her home because she had 'played at Art' long enough.[9] Certainly the family finances were in a poor state. Though generous and kind, James Lawson was 'no investor', and had not managed the family investments to the best advantage.[10] The economic panic of 1893 was probably a further and very severe blow. The expense of maintaining Emily, on top of the high sanatorium costs for Dick, might have been reason enough to summon her back to Victoria.

She ended her first period of study outside the country in December 1893.

Emily arrived in Victoria a week before Christmas. The family home was smelling of pine and cedar boughs and Edith, Lizzie, and Alice were busy preparing for the Christmas bazaar at the Reformed Episcopal Church, which their mother had attended. Though glad to be home during the festive season, Emily did not likely share her sisters' enthusiasm for the bazaar, which featured an elephant from India. Nor is it likely that she participated in their other interests: the YWCA, the Protestant Orphanage, and the Council of Women. Quite apart from the fact that she wanted to embark on an art-teaching career, she would have been even more under their direction if she had involved herself in their concerns for women and abandoned children. As it was, their attitude towards her had changed little. Though Emily was now a woman of twenty-two and had been living on her own for over a year, her sisters continued to be both over-protective and critical. Exclamations of 'Milly, how can you!' and 'Milly you ought to be ashamed of yourself!' followed her around the house and garden.[11] She responded to this nagging by questioning their authority and mocking their values. As before, her insubordination was directed particularly against Edith. Difficulties escalated when Edith gave Emily a longed-for dog, then had it destroyed after it bit a provoking tease. Emily did not have a forgiving nature.

Though still treated like a child by her sisters, Emily had returned from San Francisco a grown woman. She possessed a generous figure but was not stout. She wore her dark brown hair pulled back into a bun, yet allowed some curly wisps of hair to frame her face, which was dominated by large grey eyes that had a slightly oriental slant; above them were beautifully arched brows. Her beauty so moved a young man with whom she was already infatuated that during a lull in a spring tennis party he took her in his arms and kissed her, an action that convinced Emily she now 'belonged' to him.[12] She fell in love 'with a thoroughness that was terrible',[13] but made the discovery that the kiss had meant 'nothing more to him than a part of all the young loveliness at spring'. The man was clearly 'just a flirt', but she recalled the incident as one that left her 'deeply mortified'.[14]

In an attempt to escape the constant bickering with her sisters, Emily devised a plan to move out of the house. While she was living alone in California she maintained a correspondence with Alice that strengthened their close friendship, or so Emily felt.[15] Now she hoped they could move together from the family home and establish their own residence. She went so far as to find a rentable cottage on the east side of Beacon Hill Park, only a short walk from the Carr house but distant enough to ensure privacy. The cottage stood at the end of Moss Street, amidst a 'tangle of Broom bushes & wild roses';[16] it had a room facing north that would serve as a studio-classroom and a fireplace in every room that would keep them warm when the cool wind blew in from the ocean. However, the proposition was not to Alice's liking. Having won her teaching degree, she wished to pursue her own career rather than keep house for her younger, often difficult, sister. She refused to move, so Emily remained at home.

Emily held her first art classes in the dining room on the east side of the house, which was also used for the social activities of the Reformed Episcopal Church and the YWCA. Predictably the chattering children and the painting mess left by each group interfered with her sisters' prayer gatherings and study groups. There was trouble after every class. Emily decided that in order to keep peace in the family, she would have to convert the barn's hayloft into a classroom-studio.

The 'old loft, smelling of hay and apples, new sawed wood, Monday washings and earthy garden tools', was the 'dearest' studio Emily ever had.[17] She taught boys' and girls' classes of five or six children each. The boys especially felt at ease with their pretty dark-haired teacher, who wore a red apron and acted little older than themselves. They took liberties, like eating their rubbing-out bread, or tormenting Emily until, pretending exasperation, she would drop through a trap door into the cow's manger, run around the barn, and come up the stairs to frighten them all back to work. These were 'dear funny days'.[18] During the winter the students drew from Emily's collection of plaster casts. In the spring and summer they sat in the long grass amid the camas and broom on Beacon Hill and painted the stunted oaks and flowers and the distant snowy mountains. Emily liked the work and enjoyed the children. Moreover, she was able to continue her own drawing and painting. In October 1894 she contributed work to the annual Victoria Fall Fair at the Willows Park fairground.

Victoria did not have an art museum or an art society in 1894, though there was enough enthusiasm among the city's artists to form one. Sketchers could almost always be seen on the grassy slopes, the beaches and rocky cliffs that skirted the sea, or among the arbutus groves on the higher ground. From Beacon Hill, painters could render Mount Baker rising above Rockland Heights, then turn to capture the Olympic range

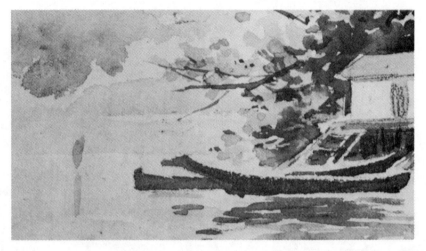

Indian Canoes in Harbour, after 1893. Small watercolour in a sketchbook, 1 7/8 x 3 3/8. Private collection.

floating in a mist across the Strait. The only place where Victoria's largely amateur artists could exhibit their work—apart from Joseph Sommers' furniture and art-supply store, which occasionally displayed paintings—was in one of the wooden buildings at the annual agricultural fair. Their placid watercolours, minutely detailed pen-and-ink sketches, and sombre oil paintings shared exhibition space with bottles of preserved fruit, crocheted antimacassars, and hand-painted china.

Emily's training in San Francisco had prepared her well to exhibit alongside the best of Victoria's British-schooled artists, Thomas Bamford and Edward Shrapnel. The low-keyed tones of her watercolours were in harmony with their own preference for subtle colouring, and she shared with them an eagerness to depict a scene so accurately that the viewer might be carried to the very spot where the painting had been executed. She also shared their love of picturesque subjects, such as ships silhouetted against a pale red sunset and harbour scenes of Victoria, with the inevitable Indian paddling across the bay. She contributed to the Fall Fair a group of pen-and-ink drawings (now lost), which won first prize over Victoria's established artists. 'A nicer bit of work it would be hard to find,' wrote the *British Colonist.*[19] (Edith also captured a first prize for her delicate flower paintings on bone china.)

At this time Emily had had only a distant experience of the primeval forest. On one visit to the heavily wooded area of Millstream, some miles from Victoria, she and her sisters remained timidly at the edge of the brook, as 'we could not have squeezed into the woods had we tried because they were so thick.'[20] She had watched pioneering families in outlying areas of the city struggle to fell trees and uproot stumps. She had heard her father tell how he had been overwhelmed by the terrific density of the growth he had observed during his voyage around Vancouver Island. But however disquieting her associations with the forest had been, she set out to discover it for herself in the summer of 1895, when she took a break from teaching. With two other women—her

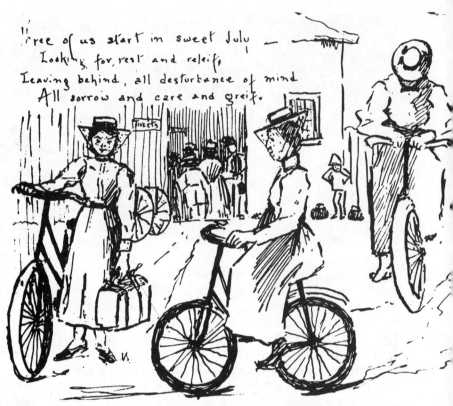

"Three of us start in sweet July —
Looking for rest and releif,
Leaving behind, all desturbance of mind
All sorrow and care and greif.

A page from
Emily's sketch-
book of her
Lake Cowichan
bicycle trip,
1895. Emily is
on the left. Pen
and ink. Private
collection.

girlhood friend Edna Green and 'Mac' (probably Nellie McCormick, who
visited her one summer after her return from San Francisco)—she took
the train from Victoria north to Duncan.[21] From there they cycled almost
ten miles, along a bumpy coach road that cut through the dense forest, to
an inn on the Cowichan River. Emily's impressions of the wilderness on
this excursion may have been coloured by her childhood reading of
Pilgrim's Progress. For the three young ladies, as for the pilgrim in John
Bunyan's allegory, the passage through the woods was a fearful experience. The trees past which they cycled were 'tall' and 'sombre'; the
forest was 'dark' and 'lonesome', its silence 'gruesome'.[22] The possibility
of encountering a bear, a cougar, a snake, or of finding a fallen tree
across their narrow path, was frightening: it was a journey of endurance
rather than of pleasure. When Emily opened her sketchbook after
reaching the Cowichan Inn, it was not the awesome forest she drew but a
view of the river from the window of her second-floor room, and her
friends pushing their bicycles up rocky hills, taking tumbles, and sucking
lemons for refreshment. She had little interest in recapturing the
desolate, frightening wilderness.

More appealing to Emily as subjects for her sketches and watercolours
were the native peoples of British Columbia, particularly the Coast
Salish in and around Victoria, and the Nootka on the west coast of the

Island. Her fascination with Indians probably began in childhood. During the 1870s Victoria had almost as many Indians as whites. The Songhees Reserve was on the west side of Victoria harbour and connected to the city by two bridges. Indians could be seen in Victoria at all times. Some worked in domestic service for white families. Others, usually women clad in brightly coloured print dresses, wandered from door to door selling game and berries. Many were itinerants, visiting Victoria in the autumn to purchase supplies or in the summer to sign on with the whaling and sealing ships, or pausing briefly on their way to or from the hop fields in Washington or the fish canneries on the Fraser River. From the cliffs along Dallas Road, Emily had looked down at their glowing beach fires and canoes when they camped on the pebbly shore. From Victoria harbour she had seen the more permanent dwellings—great flat-roofed houses—of the Songhees. She had watched the family's native washerwoman, 'Wash Mary', bend over the foaming tubs; at Mrs Fraser's school she had shyly observed the half-Indian pupil, Lizzie Mason; and at her father's store she had often encountered natives buying their winter provisions or waiting on the steps for a handout, which Richard Carr was known to give frequently. The Songhees Reserve was 'a glory place of adventure'—but only in her imagination, for entry there was forbidden to children.[23] (And few white men, let alone young ladies, would dream of visiting it.) During early adolescence Emily even wished she had been born an Indian.[24]

Something beyond mere curiosity prompted Emily to identify with Indians. She must have been strongly attracted by their freedom from the restrictions and conventions she suffered under. Furthermore, her father's tales of his experiences among the native peoples of North and Central America, and his kind treatment of local Indians, had made a deep impression on her. Though Victoria's earliest settlers had been greatly dependent on the Indians, and many men—including the governor, Sir James Douglas—took Indian women as their wives, by the 1870s Victorians had adopted a somewhat hostile attitude towards native people. Most now regarded them as drunks, gamblers, and idlers, 'a nuisance and a trouble to the authorities'.[25] They were highly displeased every autumn when upwards of 3,000 gathered on the Songhees Reserve and the noise from their celebrations drifted across to the city.

There is much among Emily's late autobiographical writings that tells of her childhood interest in Indians, though her drawings give no evidence of this until after her return from San Francisco. The group of 1890s watercolours of Victoria harbour include several distant views of the Songhees Reserve. More important is a little cedar-bound book in which she recorded verses related to the Indian. Given to Alice in 1895, it contains in Emily's handwriting a portion of Alexander Pope's *Essay on Man* celebrating the Indian's 'untutored mind', his 'contentment', his lack of greed, his inherent goodness, and his superiority to the avaricious, over-civilized, discontented, sinful European.[26] The native's relationship to God through his intimacy with nature gave him a 'natural religion'.

His freedom from the concepts of sin and atonement, from civilized conventions, appealed to the guilt- and convention-ridden 'black sheep' of the Carr family and offered a beguiling contrast to the discipline imposed by Emily's over-protective sisters and to the suffocating narrowness of Bishop Cridge's sermons at the Reformed Episcopal Church. Three years later, when Emily made her first excursion to an Indian village, she retained the idealized view of the natives she had received from Pope.

The *Willipa* made year-round runs from Victoria up the west coast of Vancouver Island. One summer evening in 1898 it departed from the Canadian Pacific wharf at 8 p.m. with only one passenger on board, twenty-six-year-old Miss Emily Carr. When, early next morning, the steamer turned into the most north-westerly port of Barclay Sound and entered Ucluelet Bay, there came into view several isolated clusters of buildings straddling the rocky promontory between the dense forest and the Pacific. Perched near the government dock was the small white settlement that boasted two stores and a shingle mill. A mile and a half from the dock, nestled in the thick woods, was the former residence of the government Indian agent, now occupied by the Reverend Melvyn Swartout and his missionary assistant.[27] Together these buildings comprised the area known as Ucluelet. Another mile along the shore was the Indian Reserve, where approximately 200 members of the Ucluelet band of the Nootka nation lived. There, in the villages of Etedsu and Quaimta, Emily found big barn-like structures whose supporting beams required the combined strength of 200 men to lift, and one-room dwellings that a gust of wind might cause to collapse. Standing between them was a rough cedar building surrounded by stumps and bushes. Though lacking a belfry, a portico, and even paint, it served as both church and school for the two villages and was occupied by Presbyterian missionaries. This building was Emily's destination. It was here that her sister Lizzie was learning to be a missionary under the supervision of the missionary-teacher Miss E. May Armstrong.[28]

Emily had not arrived in Ucluelet at an ideal time. Since early spring the Indians had been plagued by an epidemic of German measles and whooping cough that, along with tuberculosis, would be fatal to some of them before the end of the summer. It was an unhappy village for other reasons. The gradual depletion of seals had reached a point where many sealing schooners found it unprofitable to continue their annual hunting excursions to the Bering Sea. Economically dependent on these expeditions for their livelihood, the Indians were now forced to seek employment elsewhere. Perhaps symptomatic of these difficulties was a renewed outbreak of drinking and gambling that summer. Several Indians were engaged in the sale of whisky; others had recently learned to make home-brewed beer.

Living conditions on the reserve were unpleasant. Smells from rotting fish and sewage pervaded houses and people alike. Adding to the stench

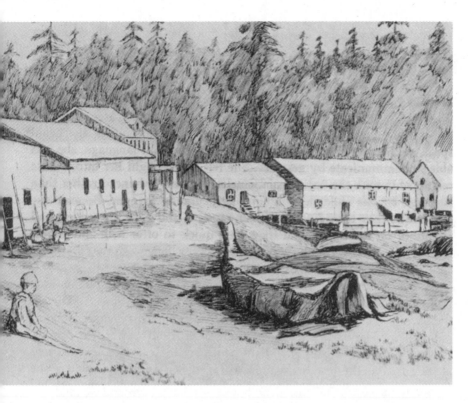

were packs of grey-haired shaggy dogs with tubercular skin and leprous
eyes. During the day they roamed the reserve and snapped at passing
strangers; after dark they shattered the night with their barking and
howling. Part of this depressing scene, and confronted daily with problems caused by whisky and gambling, idolatry and illiteracy, filth and
illness, were Lizzie Carr and E. May Armstrong. In her earnest attempts
to bring the Indian to a knowledge of 'the Resurrection and the Life',
Miss Armstrong struggled through three sermons in Chinook jargon
every Sunday.[29] Despite her coloured charts illustrating the life of Christ,
and her unswerving patience, not one native in the two villages had yet
been baptized.

When Emily recorded her trip to Ucluelet thirty years later she recalled
little of the filth, the epidemics, the economic difficulties, the gambling
and drinking. Because she kept no diary, as she had done on her 1895
excursion to the Cowichan Inn, there is no way of knowing how she
adapted Pope's eighteenth-century conception of the Noble Savage to the
Nootka. However, writing about the visit to Ucluelet in later years, she
expressed total sympathy with the Indians. She blamed their degraded
condition on corrupting European influences that destroyed their natural
order. Before the arrival of the white man, the Indians' closeness to
nature was noble; after, their condition changed to one of humiliation
and subservience. She saw the missionary as the central figure in this

decline. Although she respected Miss Armstrong's fearlessness of the woods and envied her ability in Chinook, the sight of adult Indians squeezed into tiny schoolhouse desks on Sunday attempting to understand the missionary's coloured charts struck her, at least in retrospect, as pathetic.

Emily was quick to make friends with the natives. They called her 'Klee Wyck' (the one who tends to laugh), because they discovered that she was 'not stuck up' and 'knew how to laugh'.[30] Though she could speak neither the Chinook jargon nor Aht, she was able to communicate by gestures. She felt this brought her into a close relationship with the natives of Ucluelet that was enhanced rather than hindered by her childish, laughing, gesticulating manner. She presumed that because she was white, they considered her their superior and gave her respect and attention; on the other hand they were quick to offer help and advice when she seemed to need it, warning her about dangers in the forest and telling her many things of which the white man was ignorant.[31]

Emily's associations with the Indians at Ucluelet brought about a significant expansion of her repertoire of picturesque subjects. The Indian women allowed Emily to sketch them while they wove mats of bullrushes, cedar bark, and rags. The children posed for her after school. She made pencil sketches of Indians bent over their work and of canoes abandoned on the beach. In more detailed pen-and-ink drawings she captured several views of the two villages and from these painted watercolours of the Indians, their houses, and the surrounding landscape. However, the pencil sketches are uncertain, the watercolours muddy, and the pen-and-ink drawings stiff. Nothing raises them above the pictures by other artists who portrayed the Indian as an exotic and picturesque subject. Emily later claimed that she was overwhelmed by the 'one continual shove of growing' in Ucluelet, and had 'no idea of how to tackle it'.[32] The forest appears in these drawings as one great impenetrable mass—a backdrop for the subjects that interested her more: the Indians and their villages.

At the summer's end she boarded the *Willipa* with a portfolio of drawings and watercolours. The excitement of having successfully completed her Ucluelet sojourn was forgotten, however, when she became acquainted with the young man who was the ship's purser.

Four years Emily's junior, William 'Mayo' Paddon—so named after his county of birth—was the son of the Reverend Canon William Francis Locke Paddon, who had brought his family to Victoria from Ireland in 1890. After he and Emily met on the *Willipa*, Mayo became a frequent guest in the Carr home. Emily began to attend his church, St Saviour's Anglican, instead of the family's Reformed Episcopal, and its conversaziones and Bible-study groups. She and Mayo took long walks in Beacon Hill Park and along the Dallas Road cliffs. Mayo was drawn to 'Emmie' because he found her to be deeply religious,[33] and she recalled being attracted to him because of the ease with which she could share her deepest concerns, particularly the burden of guilt she still felt towards

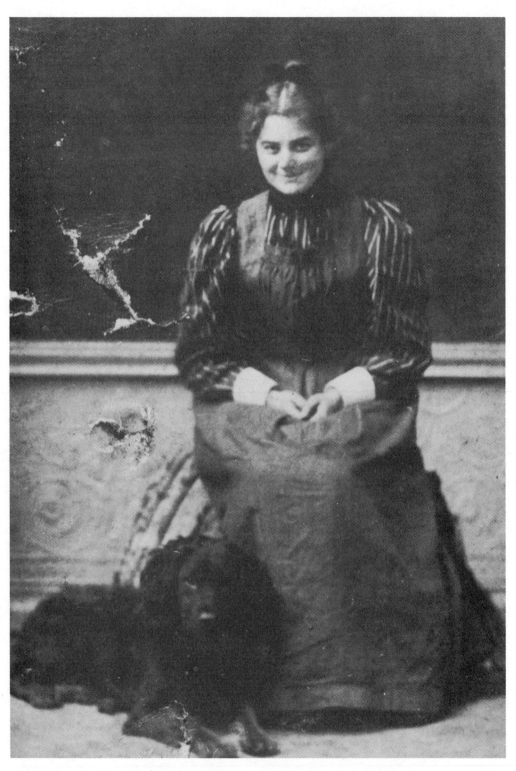

'Emily 1898'. Emily wrote on the back, referring to the tear: 'Excuse monkey / Woo's chewing'. Private collection.

her mother. She confessed to him her regret at being the family's 'black sheep', and her sadness at her mother's disappointment in her 'bad child'. Paddon responded with sympathetic concern, telling her that 'if you *were the bad one*, you may be *shure* [*sic*] your mother loved you just a *little* more than the others.' Such assurances were comforting; they almost made her 'quaver into love for him'.[34]

Mayo Paddon's attentions did not keep Emily from leaving the country once more. She had been easily persuaded by her teachers in San Francisco that the Mark Hopkins was merely a stepping-stone to more serious study in Europe. Also, she had heard that her friend Sophie Pemberton—who had won distinction at the South Kensington School of Art and made her début at the Royal Academy—had entered the Académie Julian in Paris. Having saved money from her teaching for further training, Emily chose to go to England. She left Victoria in August 1899. Alice accompanied her to Vancouver on the boat, then saw her off on the CPR.

3
England
1899-1904

Emily arrived in England in the torrid late summer of 1899. 'The bricks oozed heat, and the air—well there wasn't any.'[1] But she was happy to have the Atlantic voyage behind her: seasickness had forced her to spend the entire ten days shut up in her cabin. As she travelled from Southampton to London, an 'entirely different, pretty, small' world opened before her through the train windows.[2] It was one she had heard much about since childhood. Her parents, like almost every adult she knew in Victoria, were English-born. After the 'brutal telling', Emily had rejected her father's Englishness as 'hard & aggressive', but she continued to build her ideals on the 'homey and lovely' English values of her mother. 'The Church of England, the courtesy of England, the names of England' evoked pleasant images with which she longed to be associated. As she passed through the Kent Downs and acres of verdant English countryside, she was not disappointed. But her destination was grimy, chimney-potted London.

Emily settled in Miss Amelia Green's paying guest-house, an undistinguished row house in West Kensington. From there, on the nineteenth of September, she set out for her chosen art school. She walked across the grass court in Dean's Yard behind Westminster Abbey and entered narrow, two-block-long Tufton Street. Towering above the humble houses on the right was the grim red-brick edifice of the Royal Architectural Museum. Emily entered; passed through a clutter of 'old broken nosed saints & martyrs', mouldings, encaustic tiles, mural paintings, roof ornaments, and stained glass; then climbed the stairs to the second-floor premises of the Westminster School of Art. There she found the school's elderly white-bearded curator, Francis Ford, and paid him six pounds and sixpence to cover her entrance and tuition fees for the first three months of study.

Emily thought the Westminster School was England's best. But her choice exemplified how out of touch colonial Victoria was with the

London art scene. In the 1880s, under the directorship of Frederick Brown, Westminster had become the leading school in London devoted to the study of drawing and painting from life. It had provided instruction in drawing and illustration—which Brown had based on the study of Greek and Roman statuary—to Aubrey Beardsley and Dame Ethel Walker, among others. But in 1893 Brown, followed by his assistant Henry Tonks, left to join the Slade School of Art. By the time Emily enrolled, the institution that had been one of the most enlightened art schools in London had declined to mediocrity. The reputation Brown had established for it, causing its name to reach such an obscure corner of the British Empire as Victoria, was now obsolete. Emily was five years too late. While offering sound instruction in illustration and portraiture, the Westminster School was 'not very exciting', according to the distinguished artist, Duncan Grant, who attended from 1902 to 1905.[3] Only occasionally, he remembered, was a reproduction of a Degas or a Whistler passed around the classroom.[4] With few exceptions the students were oblivious of the French Impressionists, who frequently exhibited in London's West End galleries. They perpetuated the classical and historical painting that kept England in the backwater of European art. Emily may have thought she was attending a leading art school, but it was merely an academy that sustained those conservative ideals she had seen and practised in Victoria and San Francisco.

The three classes in which she enrolled were held on six days and two evenings, making forty hours a week. The ladies' costume model class, the evening class of drawing in black and white (for commercial illustration), and the segregated ladies' life class were simply a continuation of her studies in San Francisco.[5] Though she had vowed never to draw from the nude, Emily forgot her shyness when the model, proud of her shapely figure, mounted the platform. Raising her arm to the easel, Emily allowed the charcoal to follow the soft curves of the illuminated flesh and discovered that nakedness was not shameful but beautiful.

Instruction was no better than what she had received in San Francisco. Mouat Loudan, her teacher in the life class, was a portrait painter of little distinction in the Gainsborough manner; of the other teachers, like James Black, there is even less to be said. Still, there were significant differences between the two schools. At Westminster the classes were segregated, the students were more sophisticated and more serious. Emily was often to look back on the California School of Design as having been more fun. There she had been somewhat older than the other students and had enjoyed a manipulative-protective relationship with those she liked. Here she was among students who were not only her own age but were earnest, cultivated, and mature. She had taken her work seriously in California but had amused herself as well; here there seemed to be only the 'uninspiring Westminster grind'. Moreover, in San Francisco she had recognized herself as British—feeling, if anything, superior to her American friends. At the Westminster School she was a colonial, a status that had a taint of inferiority. Furthermore she lacked sophistication,

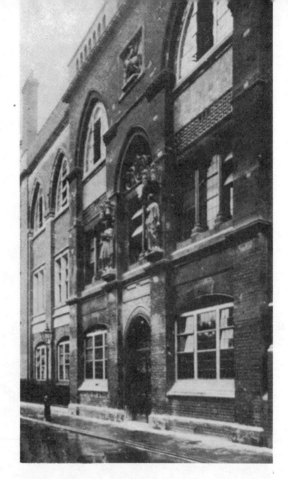

Westminster School of Art
and the Royal Archi-
tectural Museum, 1904.
Courtesy the British
Library, London.

wore dowdy clothes, and according to her later recollections was
thought 'stupid' by her fellow classmates because she did not, unlike
most of them, smoke.[6] (She would shortly pick up the habit.) Emily soon
realized that Victoria's brand of Englishness was not that of the upper- or
middle-class people she encountered at the school. Feeling awkward and
inadequate, she took an almost perverse pride in her differentness, raising what she felt were her and her country's virtues of honesty, forth-
rightness, and naturalness to the point of exaggeration. She did not attempt to be more British, as she did in California, but more Canadian.

Though feeling a misfit, she was quick to make friends during her first
months in England. Alice Watts, a fellow student and the daughter of a
vicar in Cambridgeshire, was particularly supportive and helpful. During Emily's first year, 'Wattie' persuaded her to move from Miss Green's
guest-house to her residence in the Martin Stainford Apartments in
Vincent Square, a respectable neighbourhood of hospitals and churches
that surrounded the playing field of the Westminster Boys' School. The
two women had separate bedrooms but shared a sitting-dining room.
During meals, or walking to and from school, they discussed the virtues
of their respective countries. Wattie praised the traditions and oldness of

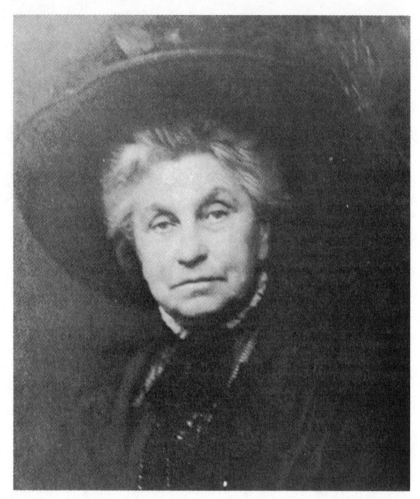

Mrs Redden, about 1900. Courtesy the Emily Carr Arts Centre, Victoria, B.C., and Mrs John A. Farmer.

England, while Emily boasted of Canada's bigness and natural resources. Other friends were Mrs Marion Redden, a Canadian-born widow from Milton, Ont., and her lawyer son, Frederick, to whom Emily had been given an introduction by a young man in Victoria. The sixty-two-year-old Mrs Redden—whom Emily later remembered as having grey hair, a large mouth, wrinkles, and being always dressed in black except for 'some bit of white fuss at the throat'—was a warm, hospitable woman who became her best friend in England. Emily quickly grew to feel comfortable with her, and with her son, whose forehead was already 'hurrying towards the top of his head', though he was not much older than Emily.[7] Their residence in 57 Abingdon Court became Emily's 'Home House', as the Reddens had hoped it would.[8] Every Sunday, her one free day from the school, it was her habit to go there for tea, hot buttered muffins, and cake. The Reddens, their friend Mrs Mortimer, her son Edward, and Samuel Blake (the younger son of Edward Blake,

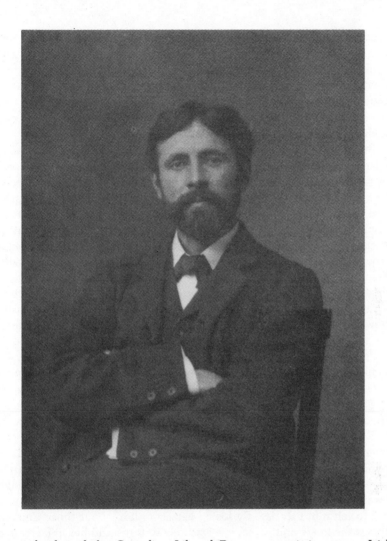

Sammy Blake, early 1900s. Private collection.

former leader of the Canadian Liberal Party, now sitting as an Irish Nationalist in the House of Commons), had one thing in common: they had all formerly lived in Canada.[9] The three young men—all bachelors, all somewhat older than Emily, and all Canadian-born—were lawyers now practising in London. As well as Sunday tea, Emily often joined the three men and two widows for an afternoon visit to the National Portrait Gallery or the Royal Academy or for Evensong at Westminster Abbey. One Saturday they rented canoes and paddled on the Thames from Staines to Windsor. On this excursion, recalled by Emily as 'one of my loveliest memories of England', she shared a canoe with Sammy Blake, the only one of the three men she felt treated her like a mature woman, and was sensitive and charming besides. According to one friend, Blake was a 'blend of poet and athlete', with a 'face of rare spiritual beauty'.[10] To Emily he was not, like his two friends, 'ultra-English'. 'Canada still peeped out of Sammy', and she could not remember him ever wearing a silk hat and frock coat, as his two companions did. Nor could she recall him 'lowering some superior English quality' down on Canada. When he spoke of his native country, it was with fondness. She responded to his treatment of her as a 'sane adult', his appealing nature, and his loyalty to Canada with strong affection. She was always glad when he came to tea on Sundays and definitely favoured him above the other men, especially Eddie, whom Mrs Mortimer hoped she might marry.

Blake's warm regard for Canada was important to Emily, who had few friends who understood her homesickness for the 'West and the woods'. 'Mrs Redden used to schold & be angry with me,' she recalled, because 'she loved London so & thought anyone should be so proud and happy to live there.' The two women frequently clashed, causing Emily to 'fly home in a furious tempest', vowing never to return to her unsympathetic friends.[11] But the following Sunday she would be back in Abingdon Court. Emily seldom discussed her art studies during these visits. Frederick and his mother were 'very fond historically of Art' and Frederick had 'huge volumes of excellent photos of great pictures, arranged according to Century'. Knowing little about the old masters, however, Emily was intimidated by Frederick's knowledge of historical dates and schools. The Reddens went frequently to Paris, where two cousins were undergoing the trials of studio painting. Hearing of this, Emily, who was growing bored with Westminster's conservatism, became envious and felt more inadequate than ever during Sunday tea.

The only subject Emily could discuss with confidence with her new friends were her experiences among the British Columbia Indians. She told comic stories, like the tale of the old Indian who threw a tombstone overboard at the spot in the sea where his brother had drowned, and reminisced about her visit to Ucluelet. Her friends responded warmly, especially the young men, whose boyhood memories of Canada were awakened. They called her by her Nootka name, Klee Wyck, and urged her to tell more stories. By losing herself in talk about those Canadian things she knew and loved, she was able to transcend her unfashionable clothing, her awkwardness, and her colonialness, which Mrs Redden and Mrs Mortimer would have had her change.

Another person who became an attentive listener to her Canadian stories was the placid, wealthy Mildred Crompton-Roberts, a fellow student.[12] 'Crummie', whom Emily initially took to be just a society girl, lived with her mother in Belgrave Square. Though occasionally embarrassed by their insistence that she retell her stories to their friends, Emily did, and became the hit of one of the best houses in a fashionable district of London. Taking comfort in her identification with British Columbia, and enjoying the popularity it aroused, she felt quite at ease there in her starched muslin among their swishy silks; the environment Emily would have formerly dismissed as hypocritical became acceptable and familiar. Perhaps it was no accident that a proudly colonial woman found herself more comfortable in upper-class Belgravia than in middle-class Westminster.

With forty hours of class a week, and Sundays reserved for the Reddens, Emily had little time for outside activities. Some sightseeing was done with Mrs Mortimer, though tourist attractions were a bore. 'The British Museum rolled on me' and Westminster Abbey was 'made a little cheap by sightseers who whispered and creaked.'[13] Exploring London alone atop a horse-drawn omnibus, she went to the slums in Whitechapel, poked into the quaint corners of Paternoster Row, and walked in St James's Park. Courtesy calls were made to family acquaintances, and though she never recorded visits to any relatives, her nephew remembered her contacting their cousins, the Gamages, of Gamages Sporting Goods. Mr Gamage was too busy to see her when she inquired at his office, though he later suggested, in a typewritten postcard, a date when they might meet. Emily replied that 'no gentleman would send a lady a Post Card, much less a typewritten one; that she was only making a duty call which she considered no longer necessary.'[14] She paid a business call on the publisher Frederick Warne in an attempt to interest him in printing a collection of Ucluelet sketches.[15] Her studies in black-and-white illustration at Westminster, as well as the great amount of time she devoted to working up sketches and rhyming verse while in England, suggest that she considered a career as a cartoonist or a book illustrator. However, Warne was not interested in her work and she packed the Ucluelet sketches back in her trunk.

Emily may have taken a brief respite from school by visiting friends in Scotland during her first Christmas abroad,[16] but it was not until the spring break that she was able to relax and enjoy that 'homey and lovely' character she had expected to find in England. The Easter holiday of 1900 was passed in the village of Goudhurst in Kent. Emily travelled there by rail in the company of an unnamed fellow student from Victoria (perhaps Theresa Wylde, who was still in London). A popular retreat for London artists, the medieval hill-top village was a charming place, with long-gabled bow-windowed houses and a view extending to the south coast. The Firth and Bedgebury Woods, the hop gardens and orchards, all epitomized the kind of picturesque setting that attracted so many late-nineteenth-century landscape artists. In its springtime glory, the village offered a happy contrast to London's drabness and dirt. And the undulating landscape, with a view to the distant sea, recalled something of Victoria. But here the English character was neither forced nor affected, as in British Columbia's capital city. The historical associations and the quaintness were honestly indigenous and plentiful. 'Thrushes, blackbirds, every kind of song bird' welcomed Emily as she 'pressed hurriedly into the wood, getting drenched by the dripping greenery.' Here was the England she had expected to find. She was so happy she 'could have died right there.'[17]

Emily returned to London at the end of the Easter vacation. In late May the school closed for three months and she travelled, probably for the second time, to the farm of her friends in Scotland. Her hosts, whom she never mentioned by name, were kind and generous. She 'loved them

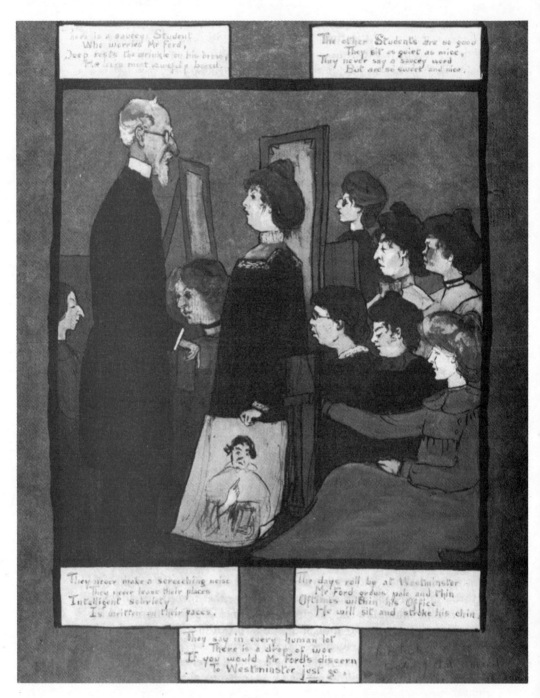

A confrontation with Mr Ford, 1899-1900. One of Emily's satirical sketches of life in the Westminster School of Art. Tempera and pen and ink on brown paper. PAC (C-98905).

all and they'd have done anything' for her. There was plenty of scones and porridge, lengthy country walks, and days filled with socializing when she 'had to be "shewn" to all their friends'. In early September she returned to London. Waiting for her on the Euston Station platform was Mayo Paddon.

Paddon had taken a three-month leave from his position as purser on the *Willipa*, explaining to his family that he wanted to visit the Exposition Universelle in Paris. Though he did go to Paris, the real intent of his trip was to visit 'Emmie', and to persuade her to return with him to Canada so that they might share their lives. Paddon was taking a chance, for Emily had already refused a written proposal. With her refusal she had made this scarcely consoling statement: 'One hour of Eternity, will make us utterly forget a lifetime's desolation.'[18] Attempting to dissuade him further, she had told him that there was 'another'—a reference either to the man to whom she had once 'belonged' or to Sammy Blake, with whom she was infatuated. Yet Paddon did not give up his suit. Putting his trust in God, he wrote in his Bible shortly after his arrival in London: 'I beseech thee, that he that asketh, believing, should receive.'[19]

Initially there was some reason to hope that his desire might be fulfilled. Emily had refused his written marriage proposal by mail but had nonetheless arranged to meet him on her return from Scotland. Standing on the Euston Station platform, he was 'like a bit of British Columbia . . . big, strong, handsome'. She was delighted. He was the first visitor from Victoria she had seen in a whole year. She took pleasure in showing him Kew Gardens, the sights of London, and introducing him to her friends. On Tuesday, the eleventh of September, they took the Central Line northeast to the 5,000-acre forest at Epping. Giving themselves up to 'England's sweetness happily', they hired a horse-drawn cart and rode through the woods until they found a place to picnic. Emily enjoyed herself thoroughly. Paddon preserved the memory of that day by pinning a sprig of heather, given to him by Emily, into his Bible, where it remains. There were few 'perfect' days like that one in Epping Forest.[20] And there was probably none that recreated their earlier friendship. Their activities in London were secular. Paddon was a visitor, Emily his friendly guide. The religious milieu that had brought them together and nurtured their friendship in Victoria had eroded. All that remained were Paddon's insistent marriage proposals—on an average of five times a week.

Paddon had arrived at a busy time. It was the beginning of the school term and Emily was preoccupied. She and Wattie decided to find new rooms; materials and supplies had to be purchased before the term commenced. Paddon was a hindrance to these activities. When she first saw him in London, Emily had to refrain from seeming too glad, but by mid-September he had become a nuisance. He remained in London until the late autumn. His stay was probably prolonged by Mrs Redden's involvement in their relationship. She urged Paddon to have patience. At the same time she tried to persuade Emily to accept his proposal. Emily simply wished the widow would tell Paddon 'how horrid, how perverse' she really was.[21] By early November, Paddon was still hopeful that God would bring them together. 'Hear me,' he prayed, *Thou canst if Thou Wilst.*' But by December he was scribbling fewer prayers in the margins of his Bible. The way seemed 'very dark ahead now'.[22] Shortly thereafter he left England and returned to Victoria.

Paddon suffered greatly. Back on board the *Willipa* he was 'wretchedly ill—backed by a broken heart'.[23] He attempted to console himself by visiting Emily's sisters, by praying in church, and by walking in Beacon Hill Park. Everything he did, however, evoked her memory: communions reminded him of 'those I spent with her . . . when she and I knelt together Sunday by Sunday at the Lord's table.'[24] Walking in the park brought him to the bench where they had last sat. At the end of January he was still 'wretched and lonely'. Desperate, he wrote to her asking if she would 'let things be as they were before . . . . Why should my love kill our friendship?'[25] Emily's short reply was not encouraging. On the eighteenth of March he 'wrote to Emmie in answer to the last

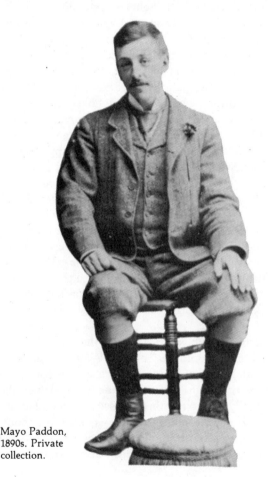

Mayo Paddon,
1890s. Private
collection.

which ends it I suppose.'[26] A few weeks later, having received no further correspondence from Emily, he walked to Rat Bay. There he 'read and burnt *all* her letters'.[27] The pursuit was over. He began taking walks in Beacon Hill Park with another woman, but was unable 'to give her the blessed knowledge of the Saviour' that he and Emily had shared.[28] He continued to visit Alice Carr until the very day before she herself departed for England. Though he did not attempt to write to Emily again, he kept the memory of her alive by frequently writing of her in his diary. 'God bless and keep her,' he wrote after burning her letters, 'and give her to me if it be His will.'[29]

The break-up was upsetting for Emily too. 'It does not hurt the killed,' she wrote many years later, 'it hurts the killer.'[30] The guilt she bore in refusing Paddon's love was immense. She had not only refused a proposal of marriage, but had denied a relationship that seemed sanctioned by God. With Emily's deeply religious sensitivities, this denial seemed to be a negative reflection of her own relationship with God. Years later she wrote that Paddon's love was 'killing me, sapping the life from me'.[31] But was Emily capable of accepting the love Paddon offered? The kind of love she had known previously was undemanding: the love of her mother; the silent infatuation with the man who had kissed her at the spring tennis party, and with Sammy Blake.[32] Even her relationship with Paddon in Victoria—which had never gone beyond holding his hand at the communion table—had existed with the knowledge that she was leaving for study in England. But faced with something so overwhelming and real as the love that brought Mayo Paddon 5,000 miles to England, she recoiled. Years later she wrote regretfully that it had been 'a bad, dreadful thing to do'; that love was 'too beautiful . . . a thing to murder'.[33] Yet the kind of love that had once caused her heart to flutter when she rubbed her cheek against a man's rough tweed sleeve had been mere infatuation. As she later reflected, sleeves were sleeves, cheeks were cheeks, and hearts were blood pumps.[34] Mild infatuations and idealistic loves were fine, but a long-term adult relationship that demanded a normal sexual response was frightening to her. Most likely sexually inhibited, Emily was unable to bridge the gap between playful flirtations and sexual fulfillment. As well as being attractive, she was coquettish, a trait that had brought her, soon after arriving in England, advances from an Irish doctor she had met on her transatlantic crossing, as well as from Mr Hayes, a Liverpool engineer and the brother-in-law of her San Francisco guardian. Emily's relationship with Sammy Blake, remembered so affectionately years later and described to a friend as her only love, was probably a romantic fabrication to mask her lack of matrimonial interest.[35] Unsure of herself and realizing that a permanent liaison with Paddon, or any other suitor, would end in disaster, she focused her attention on her art.

By the time Emily had written her last letter to Paddon, she had almost completed the two-year course of study at the Westminster School of Art. Despite the complications of his visit, the second year had been easier. The first had been interrupted by illness—she had a toe amputated (an incident to which she refers only vaguely in her autobiography, but that must have been frightening and painful)—and by the news of her brother's death in Santa Barbara. Also, she had taken far too many hours of class a week. In her second year she was more prudent. She enrolled in fewer classes, took more time to explore London, and assisted Mrs Redden with voluntary work among the poor for St John's Church. Emily's 'district visiting' in Westminster's slums did not last long, however. 'To pay a kindly little visit in the name of their parish church, [to] take an interest in them & find out if they had any special needs', was the most dreadful thing she ever recalled doing. Her charitable feelings, aroused by Canon Wilberforce's plea for volunteers, quickly evaporated when she encountered 'the smells and dirt, the horrible cockney language', and the 'dreadful creatures', most of whom were uninterested in whatever assistance Emily might give. Her enthusiasm may also have diminished after an incident, recalled years later, that took place in Westminster Abbey. Emily was sitting between Mrs Redden and a black-suited, white-collared cleric. Suddenly she noticed the man's fat white hand moving between the chairs beside her. It slowly found its way to her lap, where it remained to caress her thigh. Mrs Redden continued to worship calmly and Emily, afraid of drawing attention to the cleric's hand, sat motionless. Blood rushed to her cheeks and feelings of resentment against the clergy rose within her. Soon after, she resigned her district visiting, loathing the poor *and* the clergy of London.

During the middle of her second year, Emily changed her residence when Wattie went back to Cambridgeshire. She moved to Mrs Dodds' 'Home for Governesses and Ladies'—at 4 Bulstrode Road, just off Oxford Street—which housed some fifty girls of various ages and nationalities. They lived five to a room, in which a flimsy red curtain that encircled each bed and washstand offered a little privacy; they also had the use of a large sitting room on the main floor. It was 'not luxury and ease', Emily wrote, 'but living in a squeeze'.[36] Yet it proved satisfactory and remained her London base until she departed for Canada.

Though she seemed comfortably established in London by her second year, Emily was becoming increasingly bored with her studies. She regretted not having gone to Paris or Rome to work with the more progressive teachers there. Visits to Paris by Frederick and Mrs Redden and fellow students had excited her interest. The prospect of studying where she believed the modern schools flourished offered an alternative to her not-always-happy life in London. Yet she was unable to move to Paris or Rome because she had neither the finances nor the necessary knowledge of French or Italian. Despite her boredom, Emily showed no initiative outside the classroom to compensate for the Westminster School's dull conservatism. Had she been interested in discovering the avant-garde in London, it would not have been difficult. There was a Bohemian clique at the school that might have drawn her into their crowd. They met at the Café Royal, where such artists as Augustus John and Max Beerbohm gathered to exchange ideas. Granted, there were few galleries where the work of the more progressive members of the New English Art Club could be viewed; and even less evidence of modernism was to be found in such English art journals as the *International Studio* and the *Magazine of Art*. But Emily was in a city where she later claimed one could 'see and hear everything that is worth seeing and hearing'.[37] Yet at the time she was not sufficiently inquisitive, or even interested, to seek out what little modern art there was in London. She decided to escape the city's smells and the tediousness of working indoors by enrolling in a landscape-painting course in the country. In June 1901 she left for Boxford, Berkshire.

It was probably under the aegis of the Westminster Sketch Club that Emily and several other students from the school gathered in Boxford. For two years Emily had been working exclusively from the human figure: sketching the nude in charcoal, the costume model in pen and ink, or modelling it in clay. The new course gave Emily her first opportunity to paint *en plein air* in England. The thatched roofs and weathered tiles of the quaint cottages, the clumps of fir on Hoar Hill, the rolling Berkshire Downs surrounding the village provided a variety of 'ready-made compositions, needing only to be copied'.[38] Emily found the landscape 'well ordered & tidy'—so different from 'the lush pushing exuberance of the Western soil'. 'Everything was faded', the 'colour did not throb so violently' as around Victoria or at Ucluelet.[39] Though she later condemned painting from the English landscape as indolent seeing, during that spring in Boxford she thrived on the misty atmosphere and the picturesqueness of the village and its surroundings. After this experience she never again returned to the stuffy rooms of a London art school but sought instruction in the country.

Shortly after the Westminster School had closed for the summer, Emily welcomed another visitor from home: her closest sister, Alice, who had come to spend the vacation with her. Once again Emily was an enthusiastic guide. But she did not let her sister's visit interfere with her work. As soon as the landscape course began in Boxford, she left Alice in London, returning only on weekends. When it ended in early August, she did not go back to the city but travelled with Alice to Devonshire and Cornwall.

The West Country was a perfectly natural district for the Carr women to visit. It was in Barnstaple, Devonshire, that their parents and two eldest sisters had lived in the 1860s. And it was their parents' description of this part of England that had coloured Alice's and Emily's early impressions of the country. From Devonshire they travelled further south to the Cornish fishing village of St Ives, where Emily would remain for the next eight months. Alice spent the last weeks of her three-month English sojourn as a paying guest in 'Draycot', in one of Mrs Treleaven's hillside cottages overlooking the sickle-shaped beach.[40]

By the time Emily arrived at St Ives in 1901, it was already a well-established art colony. J.M.W. Turner had been the first to appreciate its constant grey light, its rapidly changing sky, and the dramatic craggy cliffs that formed an almost perfect arc around St Ives Bay. After the railroad was opened in 1877, Whistler, Sickert, and a host of other painters were lured to the village by the relatively cheap living, and the mild climate. Many remained. They converted derelict fishing lofts in nearby Downalong and Portmoer into studios and found residences in the finer, newer houses on the hill above the harbour. Their presence attracted students eager for instruction and the opportunity to paint out-of-doors all year round. They lodged with the fishing families in their old stone houses facing the harbour. Emily found a place with Mr and Mrs Curnow, a friendly couple whose stable-cum-bulking-house-cum-antique shop stood adjacent to the vicarage of St Ives Parish Church and backed onto the sea. She enrolled in the class of Julius Olsson and Algernon Talmage, which was held in a converted fish loft at Portmoer Bay. Her fellow students were not pretentious, like those at the Westminster School. She made two close friends—Hilda Ferron, from Ireland, and a much-younger English boy, Noel—and several acquaintances among the younger male students, including the Australian, Will Ashton. There were no stuffy classrooms, nor was there the drudgery of working solely from a model. The variety of subjects was endless. Emily painted the land and sea from the beach or cliffs and sketched the fisherfolk at work along the quay. When it was too windy to paint outdoors, she worked from a model hired by Olsson and Talmage. In the evenings and on weekends she would fill a small sketchbook with portrait studies of village children, whom she and Hilda Ferron paid to pose. When there were no children eager to earn a penny, the two women sat for one another. And when neither Hilda nor children were available to draw, and the light was too poor to work along the quay, Emily would strum her guitar and write doggerel.

That winter she composed everything from an apostrophe to the west wind to a twenty-one-stanza poem about her wax Dutch dolls, the 'Gollywogs'.[41] While some of her verses were written and illustrated to mock others, she herself was often the victim of her ridicule:

> These are the students
> who laughed at her gear
> But now they have left
> Doth she wish they were here
> To jeer at the cloak
> To tell her the time
> That swings from her belt
> On a stout piece of twine
> That kicks o'er the shoes
> That in the wet she doth use
> Which like the mit
> Has no special fit
> That put on the cap
> That got wet through the gap

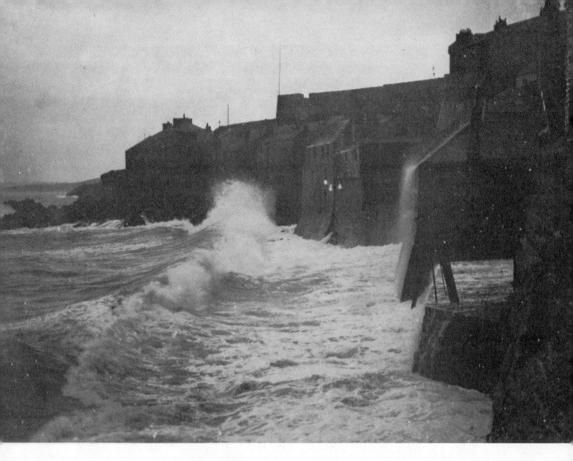

In the side of the gamp
For a rainy tramp
That covered the cape
Of an antique shape
That covered the cloak
With the seams all broke
That covered the coat
Of a date remote
That covered the gown
With a hole burnt brown
That was worn by an
   Olsson Student[42]

The sea wall, St Ives, at the turn of the century. Emily lived in one of these houses. Courtesy A. Lanyon.

Emily's doggerel reveals that her friendship with the younger students did not assuage her immense loneliness—or prevent her health from declining. It was already 'going down hill' when she arrived in the fishing village and it did not improve during her stay there. She was often confined to bed with 'dreadful nervous bilious headaches', which were partly brought on by Olsson's insistence that his students work in the 'strong dazzle of the shore'. A distinguished seascape painter who would win the Gold Medal at the Paris Salon in 1903, Olsson was eager to have his students work on the beach in order to capture the sea in virtually every kind of weather. When he found Emily sketching 'in the narrow

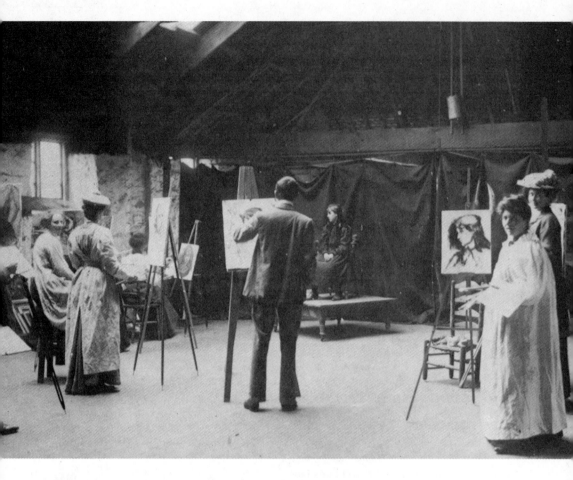

Sketching class in St Ives, 1901-2. Emily, wearing her tam, is third from the left. Courtesy A. Lanyon.

little streets where the wind tore through but the glare was less obvious', Olsson forced her to return to the beach; Emily hated him for making her work in 'that horrible glare', and thereafter they 'remained antagonistic always'.[43] It is not surprising that when Mrs Olsson invited the best students for tea, Emily was not included.

During the Christmas break, with Olsson on vacation in his native Sweden, Emily found a work-place where she was not troubled by the wind and the glare. High on the hill above St Ives she discovered the dark and restful Tregenna Wood. It was here, among the 'haunting, ivy-draped, solemn' trees, that her love for painting the forest originated.[44] Tregenna Wood inspired her to want 'to learn to express the indescribable depths & the glories of the greenery' and to see 'the coming & going of crowded foliage that still had breath space between every leaf.' Olsson's partner, Algernon Talmage, a man her age and a landscape painter who had a 'deep and reverent' love of nature, did not insist that Emily remain on the shore.[45] A patient teacher, he would climb the steep hill above the village to Tregenna Wood and criticize her work there. The gesture was never forgotten; nor was his advice. When her forest

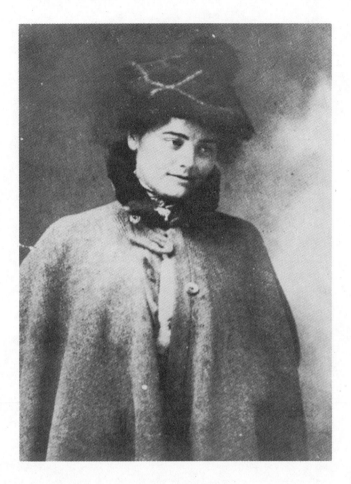

Emily in Corn-
wall, 1901-2.
PABC.

paintings became too dark, he reminded her that there was also 'sunshine
in the shadows'.

By choosing to paint in Tregenna Wood, Emily made something of a
breakthrough: few artists had ever considered setting up their easel in a
forest. Yet Tregenna was not entirely outside the realm of the picturesque. Emily found the trees—leafless, and draped in ivy—'haunting'.[46] The wood possessed a romantic atmosphere her British Columbia
forest lacked. It was not remote but bordered on a farm and overlooked
the fishing village. A ravine cutting through it lent diversity to the
landscape. Sunlight penetrated to the forest floor, and the scarcity of
tangled underbrush made walking through it easy. Instead of the
awesome silence that pervaded the forest at home, songbirds could be
heard. And there were no bears or cougars to make it terrifying. At
Ucluelet the forest had seemed unfathomable, overwhelming, unpaintable. But with the aid of picturesque conventions, Emily found she
was able to paint Tregenna. She would later find these conventions unsuitable for portraying the western-Canadian landscape, but it was here
that she began her conquest of the British Columbia forest.

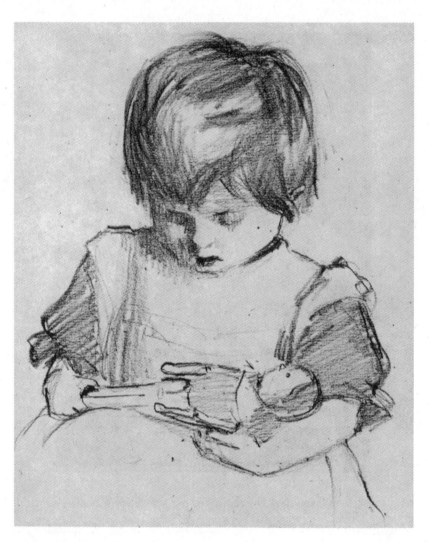

Little Girl with Doll, 1901-2. From Emily's St Ives sketchbook. PAC (C-96824).

When Olsson returned from Sweden, he cursed Emily's 'dark dismal woods'. She returned to the glare of the beach and ocean but remained in St Ives only a few months longer. In early March she travelled with one of the younger male students on a little steamer to the coastal villages of St Erth and 'The Rat Hole' (Mousehole). She then went—probably on Talmage's advice—to the art colony in Bushey, Hertfordshire, where Talmage himself had studied.

Emily never returned to St Ives. She had had eight months of severe nervous headaches, of gaining weight, and much loneliness. Yet the memory of 'keen air, quaint poor people with a tang of melancholy pervading their stone cottages', and 'the sea pounding' incessantly never left her. Nor did she forget that her Cornish sojourn had seen the beginning of her love for the forest, which 'deepened and strengthened' during the rest of her life.

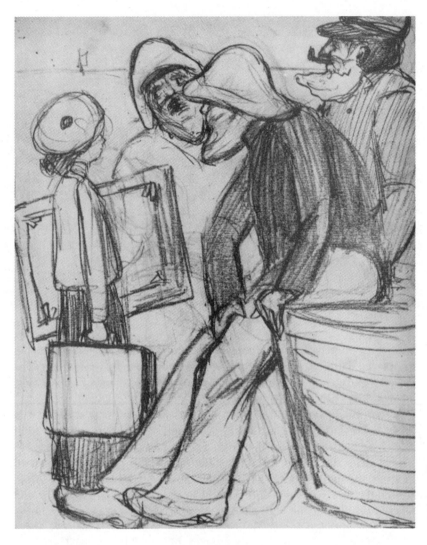

'The old men tell her [Hilda Ferron] how the fish *will* not be caught as they could wish', 1901-2. From Emily's St Ives sketchbook. PAC (C-96875).

The landscape around Bushey, a mere fourteen miles from London's Charing Cross station, offered an immense contrast to the stark, craggy, barrenness of Cornwall. When Emily arrived at Bushey in mid-March 1902, 'everything was yellow-green and pearly with young spring.'[47] The woods were full of birds and the park-like fields were covered with bluebells. In 1883 Herbert von Herkomer, a talented Bavarian artist-craftsman, had established the Herkomer School in Bushey, and with his progressive ideas had attracted artists and craftsmen from all over England. He was particularly well known for giving female students the same chance as male students.[48] In St Ives, and probably in London, Emily had experienced some discrimination. Olsson had favoured his male students and the Reddens had not taken Emily's art study seriously. Women were rarely considered professional artists; most were looked upon as mere hobbyists. Though Herkomer was impartial where wo-

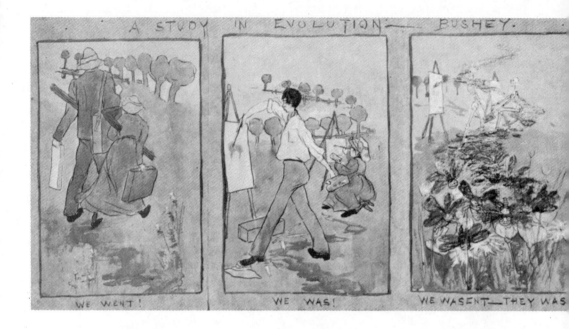

'A Study in Evolution—Bushey', 1902. 'Milford' and Emily sketching. Watercolour and pen and ink on brown paper. PAC (C-98918).

men were concerned, he did have a bias against older students, whom he considered dabblers. He therefore refused to accept any student over the age of twenty-eight. Though Emily wished to study with Herkommer, she was one year too old.

Several of Herkommer's former students had remained in Bushey to work and teach, encouraged by Herkommer, who had generously built studios and workshops for their use. The buildings stood in two rows in a level field 200 yards from his Lululand estate, behind a screen of chestnut and maple trees. The Meadows Studios were most un-Victorian in architecture. High and lofty, with large windows facing north and covered on the outside with corrugated iron, they were functionally designed for frame-making, film, crafts, and painting. In Studio Nine, Emily found John Whiteley, who was not, like his former teacher, reticent about taking older students. Emily enrolled in his class.

Though a landscape painter himself, Whiteley was offering a course in painting from the clothed model, both indoors and out. On the first day of instruction he drew diagrams dividing the head into sections, which his students, including Emily, copied into their notebooks, then attempted to apply to the model. During the course of these lessons Whiteley was 'very shy' and used 'as few words as possible for teaching, and none otherwise.' Though this was a class in portraiture, Emily devoted most of her time to painting the surrounding woods and Whiteley did not discourage her. In fact he followed her to the woods and gave her lessons there. His instruction, like Talmage's, was remembered. Emily learned not to 'paint flat walls' but to 'remember the going & coming among the trees.' In the woods surrounding the Meadows Studios, her 'first notice of tree movement was born.'

While her interest in the forest quickened under the guidance of John Whiteley, her mental and physical condition deteriorated. Always reluctant to write of her health in England, Emily recorded little of her illness during her Bushey sojourn. Perhaps already disappointed at being too old for Herkomer's school, she found her first days in Whiteley's class, where 'nobody told you anything and giggled when you fell through ignorance', an additional emotional strain. Her condition became more acute when she was unable to surmount the initial unease of being a new student. The nervous strain that had brought on her headaches in Cornwall, and the overeating that prompted her to describe herself now as 'just verging on fat', began to increase.[49] The students at St Ives had laughed at her apparel; in Bushey they were 'cold, stand-offish'.[50] Some, she felt, 'despised me for a colonial'. Three girls in the studio were particularly disagreeable, and Emily went out of her way to put them in their place. To spite them she made friends with the male students, sketching with them in the fields and woods and socializing with them after class. This aroused the jealousy of the girls, who were too reserved to make the boys' acquaintance without an introduction. Seeking to befriend Emily because of the boys, they asked her to tea. She recalled that 'this set the devil in me on end' and 'I behaved as badly as I could.' 'Acting the fool,' she 'ate loud', wiped her mouth on her sleeve, 'made faces, used bad grammar, sniffed, gulped, behaved abominably.' Choosing the youngest, most vulnerable girl, she enticed her to follow her in a 'pretty dance' through the hawthorn hedges 'till she bled like a stuck pig.' She also forced the unfortunate girl to smoke cigarettes, 'which she hated'. Thus Emily crudely struck out at 'Mack', the eldest of the trio, who 'did not think me up to her standard'.

Emily mocked not only those who seemed condescending to her, but also those of whom she herself was critical. One Saturday morning, towards the end of the term, she found upon entering the studio a fat baby-faced girl in her early twenties, who was dressed in a lace-trimmed pinafore. Not only was she 'crimped & curled like a baby show infant', but sitting next to her was a chaperone! The sight was too much. Emily spent most of the following day composing and illustrating some verse based on the *reductio ad absurdum* of the whole class bringing chaperones to the studio. She did not exclude Whiteley from her farce:

> And so the room got very full
>   the air was like to choke
> The Master sighed and said Ah me!
>   This is indeed no joke
> But for the sake of decency
>   Tis very plain to me
> That I my gentle wife
>   Must bring
> And she our children three

These lines brought 'peal after peal of chuckles' from the usually shy and retiring Whiteley. They also aroused the envy of 'Mack' when Whiteley gave Emily one of his paintings in exchange for her doggerel.

Her antics were no doubt a manifestation of a growing inner turmoil that was not relieved by the agreeable aspects of her stay in Bushey. Emily was in a lovely English village, enjoying an easy-going relationship with the younger male students, and progressing in her work under the sympathetic John Whiteley. But she was still not happy. Something more than the English disdain for colonials, or her democratic aversion to upper-class conceit, caused her to 'crack up'.[51]

The events of the next seven or eight months—from the time she left Bushey until illness overcame her and she was admitted to the East Anglia Sanatorium—were variously recorded by Emily. In one version she wrote that she was visiting her friends on a farm in Scotland when she contracted bronchitis and influenza. She went to the Cambridgeshire home of Alice Watts, stayed but a few days, then returned to London ill. In another version she says that she 'left Bushey abruptly' for London and became ill after fainting and falling from the top of the stairs in Mrs Dodds' house.[52] The illness itself was variously attributed by Emily to overwork, bronchitis, influenza, a fall down stairs, homesickness, and living in big cities. Her recollections of the chronology of events after the 'beginning' of her illness are more consistent. While she was ill in London during the summer of 1902, the Crompton-Roberts moved Emily from Mrs Dodds' to their home in Belgravia. There she lay for six weeks, 'scarcely caring which way things went . . . It was all a confused horrible nightmare of Doctors & nurses', who came and went across the hay-strewn stones of Belgrave Square.[53] She suffered from intense headaches, could not sit up without vomiting, and lapsed into a state of apathy. Mrs Crompton-Roberts and Mildred waited patiently for her recovery. Others—the Redden family, the curator of the Westminster School, Mr Ford, and the mother of her St Ives friend, Noel—all made enquiries at Number Sixteen. When, after a month and a half, she began to show some signs of improvement, the Crompton-Roberts moved her 'to a con-valescent home by the sea'. But the nausea and headaches worsened, seemingly aggravated by the smell of newly painted walls, the glare of the sun on sea and sand, and the nurse in charge with whom Emily quar-relled. After several weeks of dodging the sun's glare under a copse of stunted willows, and fighting with the nurse, Emily feigned recovery and was released. She went directly to Noel's family home in Waybridge. There she 'collapsed like an empty bag'. The relapse that followed was 'worse', she wrote, 'than the original.'

News of Emily's condition reached the Carr sisters, probably by way of Mrs Crompton-Roberts, and brought Lizzie hurrying to England. By October she was in London, where Emily was back in the care of the Crompton-Roberts. During the three months of Lizzie's stay, Emily's headaches, bouts of vomiting, and irascibility—which intensified in the presence of a sister with whom she had never 'hit it off'—grew even worse. Lizzie, much distressed by her sister's illness, 'wished to read the Bible and pray' with her all day. She even engaged a curate to offer prayers in the local church. When she and her sister were alone, according to Emily, Lizzie 'cried & scolded' her for smoking and playing Patience. But before others, Lizzie pretended 'we were utterly devoted sisters kissing & fondling me, which I loathed.' Emily, who did not care if 'people thought me a crank', fought against her sister's 'pretended' devotion. Anxious to have Emily return to Victoria, Lizzie quarrelled with the Crompton-Roberts' doctor, who felt that his patient was too ill to make the long journey. But she was apparently well enough to travel short distances, so the sisters 'moved from one part of the country to another [sic]: Richmond, Hindhead—anywhere except London', antagonizing one another all the while. Lizzie took the brunt of Emily's maliciousness while pretending that all was well. Near breakdown herself, she became homesick. Late in December the situation was calmed somewhat by the appearance of their guardian, James Lawson, and by the intervention of the Crompton-Roberts' doctor. Both men agreed that Emily's recovery depended on 'complete rest, freedom from worry and exertion for at least one year', without her sister and without any activity such as painting.[54] They recommended that this period be spent in a sanatorium. Though glad to end the months of bickering, Emily was incensed at having to terminate her art studies. She had 'struggled tooth & nail to earn for this period of study away', and in the last year she had begun to make progress. Now she was being forced to submit to the humiliation of abandoning her studies and, even worse, of yielding to a long period of confinement in a sanatorium to recover her mental health.

At this time Emily learned through the Reddens that Sammy Blake, who had met and married a Canadian nurse while in South Africa, had returned to Europe. His marriage in ruins, he had just entered a Swiss sanatorium after suffering a breakdown.[55]

On the twelfth of January 1903 Emily and Lizzie boarded the train at Liverpool Street station and a few hours later disembarked at Colchester in Essex. From there they travelled by coach to the village of Nayland, then by open cart to the East Anglia Sanatorium. The weather was mild and drizzly and it was almost dark when their cart wound up the highest hill in the region and entered the gates of the new building. The staff, headed by Dr Jane Walker, had been notified that Miss Carr, of 44 Carr Street, Victoria, British Columbia, would be admitted that evening.[56] Her room had been prepared and a lukewarm stone pig placed in her bed. Emily and Lizzie said farewell and Lizzie took the cart back to Nayland, feeling happy at the prospect of returning home, and confident that her sister was now on the path to recovery—though she was concerned about what people would think of Emily's being left at the sanatorium ill and alone. She might also have been embarrassed by the doctors' diagnosis of Emily's malady—'hysteria'.[57] A common enough illness at the turn of the century, it nevertheless had 'a bad reputation' and carried 'a pejorative implication'. Most usual among women, hysteria

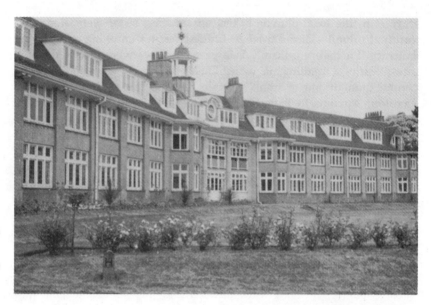

The East Anglia Sanatorium, 1970. Courtesy the Jane Walker Hospital, Nayland, Suffolk.

(from the Greek for uterus) earned for its victims a reputation for being 'highly impressionistic, suggestible, and narcissistic'. A hysterical woman, according to Carroll Smith-Rosenberg, was thought to be 'egocentric in the extreme, her involvement with others consistently superficial and tangential', and she was considered 'asexual and not uncommonly frigid'.[58]

Emily suffered from headaches, persistent vomiting, ennui, bouts of weeping, numbness, paralysis in one leg, and stuttered speech—typical symptoms of conversion reaction. Her 'hysterical' personality had manifested itself in other ways in keeping with this disease: in her sexual inhibitions with Mayo and others; in her obsession with taking revenge on those who did not think her up to their standard; in the insecurity she displayed among students and friends in London, St Ives, and Bushey; and finally in her occasional attention-getting behaviour. There can be little doubt that she had fallen victim to the classic form of conversion reaction, in which repressed anxieties are converted into physical symptoms.

Given that Emily's psychological development cannot be traced coherently—there are only hints, and Emily's no-doubt coloured recollections to go by—attempts to explain the causes of her psycho-neurosis must be speculative and ambiguous. Any explanation must, however, take into account the central role of sexual conflict in conversion reaction and therefore go back to the early episode in Emily's life that, by her own account, had a deep and painful effect on her: the brutal telling. Whatever happened between Emily and her father—perhaps unmentionable intimacies of conversation or gesture, perhaps something more or something less—its paramount place in her recollections suggests that before the event, and more so after, sex was a sensitive issue with her. The brutal telling could have had an element of incest. The psychological model of a 'hysterical woman' has often been predicated on an episode, probably fantasized, in which she is attacked by her father; the fantasy is the sublimation of the woman's incestuous feelings for her father. It could be that such feelings of sexual attraction became so severely repressed in Emily that years later, under the stressful situations that beset her in a foreign and not totally accepting environment, they manifested themselves as a neurasthenic impairment of her speech and limbs.

The East Anglia Sanatorium, still in use but now known as the Jane Walker Hospital and devoted solely to the care of the mentally handicapped, is a white T-shaped building of two stories, the first lighted by lead-glass windows and the second by a recessed balcony. On the ground floor, long corridors with creaky wooden floors lead to a bare institutional dining hall. A small chapel with a timbered ceiling stands close by the main building. The peaceful gardens are almost formal in front, where the high elevation offers a panorama of the rolling Suffolk countryside; in the rear they blend into woods, where narrow paths disclose well-placed wooden benches and the occasional gazebo.

In 1902 the institution was devoted primarily to the treatment of tuberculosis: the energetic Dr Jane Walker had been the first in England to experiment with open-air treatment for consumption. But it also admitted patients with other illnesses. As well as men and women with 'neurasthenia' and 'hysteria', there were some who suffered from syphilitic arthritis, dyspepsia, and appendicitis. Dr Walker spent considerable time at her Harley Street office in London but was not neglectful of her non-tubercular patients. She passed most weekends in the restful Suffolk landscape supervising her all-woman staff, tending to her patients, writing her many books on women's health care and tuberculosis, and testing the latest treatments. Emily was a recipient of the newest therapy for 'hysterics'.

For turn-of-the-century doctors, hysteria was the rubric for what would today be termed, among other things, neurasthenia, hypochondraiasis, depression, conversion reaction, or ambulatory schizophrenia. On the Continent an increasing level of sophistication in diagnosis and treatment was being achieved through the cumulative work of Charcot and Janet, then Breuer and Freud; but in Britain, very little was known about the condition. Patients complained of physical ailments—often severe headaches, loss of sensation in part or half of the body, and nausea—for which there seemed to be no physical origin. Confused, their doctors frequently submitted them to extraordinary diets, massage, electric shock treatment, blistering—even to amputation. Such 'cures', which usually had negative results, were naturally perturbing and exhausting to an already emotionally distressed patient.

A few months after Emily entered the sanatorium, a 'special nurse' arrived from London with Dr Walker one weekend. For six weeks she gave Emily 'a great deal of massage, a great deal of electricity and very heavy feeding'. The treatment, Emily wrote, was 'more or less experimental'.[59] This was hardly an understatement. In 1903 the effectiveness of electric shock treatment was still untested. The method of producing currents was 'rough and ready', with insufficient control over such factors as wave form, voltage, repetition frequency, pulse width, and pulse current.[60] Most turn-of-the-century doctors confined their experiments to animals, or at least few admitted to having experimented on humans. The shock treatments given to Emily may have reduced her respiration and heart beat and relaxed her muscles, but they were horrifying and nearly drove her 'mad'. They did nothing to stabilize her nerves, just as her diets—one limiting her to skim milk, another overfeeding her—failed to reduce her weight. Though she recalled having gained a little strength, the six-week experiment had left her 'nerves and spirit . . . in a jangle'.[61] Her apathy seemed, if anything, to increase. She had little interest in returning to her painting, little interest in people; in fact, little interest in anything at all.

These severe treatments must have been a last resort on Dr Walker's part. Most of her patients diagnosed as hysterics and neurasthenics were treated with 'careful diet, increased exercise—a good spin on a bicycle—or some absorbing mental work',[62] and pronounced cured after a few months. In Emily's case, recovery took fifteen. The severity of her treatment likely prolonged her confinement.

Though beautifully situated and comfortable, the East Anglia Sanatorium was not a happy place. There were frequent deaths, and despite the staff's attempt to be secretive, Emily usually learned about them. Sanatorium rules prohibited Emily from doing anything for herself; even thinking, especially about her art work, was forbidden. Yet within the dull routine of two meals in bed and one meal out, and an occasional stroll around the grounds, Emily found a niche for herself. She established close relationships with the resident physician, with whom she frequently enjoyed a cigarette, and nurses 'Hocky' and Miss Lovat. Apart from these three women, she 'detested the bulk of the bunch', including Dr Walker—towards whom, as usual, she let her feelings be known.[63] Emily's craving for attention, as well as her penchant for hurting those she hated, had not diminished. Attention and revenge were gained through her caricatures of, and silly rhymes about, the patients and staff. As in her Cornwall caricatures, Emily herself appeared in the parade of ridicule; in this case she was the pig-tailed, cigarette-smoking 'fat girl'.[64]

If Emily's craving for attention was not satisfied by her few friends or her comical sketches, her project of raising birds for Canada certainly was. Like her father, Emily was fascinated by birds. As a child and young woman she had raised eight ducklings, and kept a pet crow and a peacock. Since her first English spring in Goudhurst, she had been overwhelmed by English songbirds. As she had not known songsters in Canada, she decided to raise some for export. Encouraging the idea, Mildred Crompton-Roberts sent her the four volumes of Swaysland's *Familiar Wild Birds*.[65] On the thirteenth of March 1903 Emily stole a thrush nest. Later '2 nests of black-bonneted mauve-breasted chesty bull-finches' were taken.[66] She placed the birds and nests on a tray beside her bed and hand-fed them. When they could fly, she housed them in a wicker cage in her room. Not surprisingly, the birds for Canada became the concern of all. Walking patients gathered worms on their daily strolls around the twenty-five-acre estate. The gardener and the hospital staff also made contributions to the birds' food. In the centre of this activity was Emily, soon called 'Bird Mammy' by everyone in the sanatorium. She had frequent visitors to her room anxious to see the birds. But the attention was short-lived. After a few happy weeks, her medical treatment required her to abandon the project.[67]

Emily left the sanatorium on the seventeenth of March 1904, pronounced cured of her conversion reaction. But the personality traits associated with the illness—sexual fear, revenge-seeking, insecurity, and attention-getting behaviour—were to remain with her. Even the repressed anxieties of the brutal telling would emerge from time to time under conditions of stress and anxiety. These personality traits would diminish with age, lessening but not nullifying the possibility of another breakdown.

From the sanatorium Emily went directly to Bushey. She took rooms on the main High Street, but found John Whiteley's classes adjourned for the Easter break and her male friends departed. Though thought to be cured, she was hardly prepared to return to normal life. After the sheltered protection of the sanatorium, she nearly collapsed. She 'cried steadily for a fortnight for no reason at all'. Eventually the sanatorium's resident doctor came to Bushey and interested her in getting back to work. She wrote and illustrated 'long doggerel verses' about her life over the past fifteen months.[68] Having rid herself of some of her hostilities about the sanatorium, she recommenced classes under Whiteley at the beginning of April, and remained in them for three months. As soon as she had gained enough confidence to travel, she went up to London, stopping briefly at Mrs Dodds' to gather whatever she had left behind almost two years earlier. She did not visit her friends at Belgrave Square, or Mrs Redden, who had made several visits to the sanatorium and Bushey. 'Without good-byes', she 'slipped through London strait to Liverpool.' She was glad to be leaving the Old World and going home, but sad at her 'failures', her 'homesickness' and her 'shame and cowardice'.[69] Disappointed in England and the English and saddened that she had not learned half what she had set out to learn, she boarded a ship bound for Quebec.

4
Vancouver
1904-1910

Emily did not travel direct to Victoria after disembarking from the trans-atlantic steamer in Quebec City. She broke the journey in Toronto and passed two weeks there, suffering the late-summer heat and humidity among disagreeable hosts she never named. She also paused much closer to home. Leaving the CPR train at Ashcroft, B.C., she journeyed through sagebrush and grain fields for two days and two nights on the six-horse stagecoach of the British Columbia Express Company until she reached 150 Mile House in the Cariboo. There she was greeted by Edna Green, now Mrs Edward Carew-Gibson.[1] Now she was able to shake off her travel weariness and, though not yet home, renew her contact with her native province and some of the things she loved most. She made friends with the local Indians and 'jumped into a Mexican cowboy saddle and rode astride, loping over the whole country'; she also caught and tamed chipmunks and squirrels.[2] The sojourn with the Carew-Gibsons, which lasted two months, did much to ease her apprehensions about 'going home to face the people of my own town, a failure.'[3]

When Emily finally arrived in Victoria's inner harbour aboard the Canadian Pacific's new *Princess Victoria* on Christmas Eve, the small party that greeted her at the wharf found her greatly changed. Although she probably descended the gangplank wearing the same cape and plaid tam as when she had left five-and-a-half years earlier, she looked much older and certainly plumper. Fifteen months in the sanatorium, and the illness preceding it, had made her stout figure almost matronly and her once-handsome face pale, flabby, worn-out.

She had timed her arrival well. The candy-making, hamper-packing, turkey-stuffing, ginger-beering, and plum-pudding baking that had been occupying the Carr household for six weeks were over. Holly wreaths had been placed on the graves of their parents and brother Dick in Ross Bay Cemetery, and the Reformed Episcopal Church had been decorated with boughs of fir and cedar. There was nothing for Emily to do but enjoy a festive homecoming. She found her family had scarcely changed;

they had gone on living 'the old life in the old home'. Edith had lost some interest in the YWCA and was now a zealous member of the board of the Children's Protestant Orphanage. Devout Lizzie had given up the idea of becoming a missionary and was preparing to study physiotherapy in Seattle. Alice was preoccupied with her private school for pre-school children. Clara led an active social life in spite of having six children—two sons and four daughters. (The Nicholles lived on Government Street, two blocks away from the Carr house.) For their part, the sisters soon discovered that more than Emily's face and figure had altered. Having learned to smoke in England, Emily could restrain herself for no more than a week and finally dared to smoke a cigarette in her sisters' presence. Edith was shocked. She said that if Millie was to indulge in a habit so 'disgusting, unlady like [and] fast', it would have to be in the barn with the cow.[4] This was not all that disturbed her family. Emily frequently used 'the lesser swear words', such as 'D--M'; she played cards; she refused to attend church regularly; and finally she scandalized onlookers by riding astride, the first woman in Victoria to do so. In the eyes of her staid family she had returned from England a fat, fast, vulgar woman.

Victoria was changing in these early Edwardian years. To accommodate its many new residents, the city had expanded. The social columns of the *Colonist*—once reserved for guest lists of Government House functions, tea parties in the private gardens of Rockland Heights, and the happenings of the Victoria Hunt Club—were now filled with news of Victoria's Dancing Club, of lectures on Women's Suffrage, and of productions in Victoria's new theatres. The city's social activities had broadened, yet Emily soon found that as a thirty-three-year-old spinster, she was excluded from many of them. The Naturalist Club was for men only. The Married Ladies' Club, to which many of her former school friends now belonged, was out as well. Neither church nor charity oriented, and in any case not a joiner, there was little for her to do. Her closest sister, Alice, went round with young people who bored her. Her three best friends had left Victoria: Edna Green was living in the Cariboo; Ethel Warloch in South Africa; and the third, whom she never named, was nursing in San Francisco. Sophie Pemberton, her sketching partner in the early 1890s, was married and moved in a circle with which Emily had little in common. That left only Theresa Wylde, with whom Emily and Sophie had sketched and taken lessons in the old Roccabella mansion. But she was preparing to leave once again for study abroad. The two friends met happily in Theresa's Fort Street studio and indulged in art talk; they sketched together and even made plaster casts of each other's face. But this reunion was cut short when Theresa departed for London. Though she left Emily both her studio and her students, Emily felt she had lost the one close friend with whom she might have shared the feelings of guilt and depression she had brought back from England.

There was no question of her severe disappointment in her English sojourn. 'I had not learned very much,' she recalled, 'not half what I had

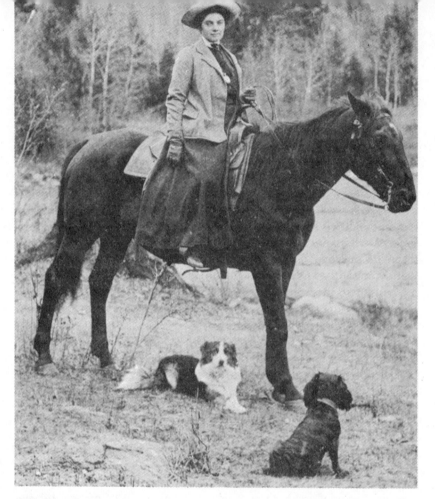

Emily in the
Cariboo, 1904.
Private collec-
tion.

intended to absorb once I got into the old country.' She also felt cheated
'by bad health & by circumstances.' She arrived in Victoria 'super-
sensitive', feeling that people were thinking 'poor thing [,] hoping so high
& getting so little.'[5] Her future as a single woman might not have been so
cheerless had she not been dedicated to a profession in which she considered herself a failure. Everything looked bleak. Even the studio in the
hayloft of the old barn gave her 'no joy'. While she was away it had been
rented to a minister and was now 'musty, sordid and horrible'.[6] 'I expect',
she later wrote, 'I was very cranky & disagreeable.' She was cured of her
limp and stutter but not yet completely well. As soon as the Christmas
festivities were over, she fled her sisters' critical eyes, their pity, and perhaps even her own irascibility. She went back to Ucluelet, to the Indians.
Klee Wyck among the Nootka would be free of the humiliations of Emily
Carr among the Victorians.

The winter season was not the ideal time to be sailing along the stormy
west coast of Vancouver Island—especially for one who suffered from
seasickness, as Emily did. Nor was Ucluelet in 1905 any happier than it
had been in 1898. A mood of apathy and defeat accompanied the damp,

biting cold that permeated every dwelling during that exceptionally cold winter. The sealing industry, which had been waning at the time of Emily's visit in 1898, was now dead. The absence of quotas and territorial fishing restrictions had resulted in overfishing, especially by the better-equipped white fishermen, and in an alarming decrease in the quantity of salmon. The drowning of the Reverend Melvyn Swartout the previous summer, and the departure of his assistant, Miss Armstrong, a year earlier, also had a dispiriting effect on the remote village.

For Emily the distressing conditions were incidental. She had come partly to slough off her own depression and partly to renew her identification with the natives. Among the children and elders, she found many who remembered her as the laughing Klee Wyck. She also made new friends with whom she could enjoy the kind of laughing, gesticulating conversations she had had before. She spent much of her time sketching the forest and Indian life around the village. Once again the children posed and once again she captured, in charcoal sketches, their chubby, shabbily clad figures. Braving the cold, she would hike to the Indian cemetery to paint in watercolour the tree-hung coffins. She felt 'weird' in this forested area, so different from Tregenna Wood. Also, she was fearful of 'the possibility of panthers taking her unaware from the rear.'[7] She could not have accomplished much in the cold, yet she returned to Victoria in mid-January much happier and better prepared to take over Theresa Wylde's art classes. She had not only renewed her contact with the Indians but had completed enough material to catch the attention of Arnold Watson, a reporter for the short-lived Victoria newspaper, the *Week*.

Emily had just dismissed a class of students and was about to make tea when he arrived. Though extremely diffident about being interviewed, she invited Watson to join her in a cup of tea. He asked her whether she was glad to be home again:

> Oh yes. You see this is my own country It has a grandeur of its own for anyone who appreciates the beautiful. England is pretty and—orderly. One misses the mountains and the woods. I do not mean to detract from the beauty of English scenery, but I suppose it is natural to prefer the scenes one has always been accustomed to. But I should like to import a Cornish cottage.[8]

Watson praised the village scenes of Cornwall that lined her studio walls. He then accompanied her home and discovered in her studio (either her father's former study or the hayloft)

> . . . many examples of her skill in black and white and sketches in two or three colours . . . The same class of work illustrating topics of general interest would, I am sure, earn her a place among the art contributors to the best periodicals.[9]

Watson's editor, Charles H. Lugrin, took the hint, and Emily was hired as a cartoonist for the *Week*. She was given political captions to illustrate and did this adequately, but in highly detailed sketches that were

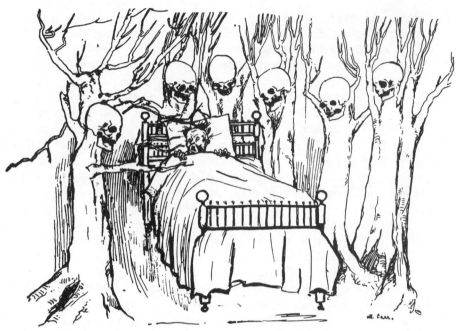

THE INARTISTIC ALDERMAN AND THE REALISTIC NIGHTMARE.

"Ye ghosts of all the dear old trees,
The oak, the elm, the ash,
Nightly those gentlemen go tease,
Who hew you down like trash."

'The Inartistic Alderman and the Realistic Nightmare', the *Week*, 3 June 1905. PABC.

unimaginative and in no way remarkable. Her work must have satisfied the editor, however: from the twenty-fifth of February to the seventeenth of November 1905, cartoons by 'E.M.C.' or 'M. Carr', as well as the occasional poem, were featured on the front page of the *Week*. (Having no middle name and possessing the same initials as Edith and Elizabeth, Emily sometimes used the initial letter of her nickname, Millie, when signing her pictures.)

Within two months of arriving home from London, Emily had been hired as a cartoonist and was teaching a large class of children. These minor successes must have tempered her feeling of coming back a failure. Yet as 1905 wore on, she did not find contentment in Victoria. It is likely that traces of humiliation remained, especially within the family circle of censorious sisters. Moreover, Victoria was a lonely place for her, now that Theresa Wylde had left. She made no new friends, and though her health had now returned to normal, she later recalled (perhaps romanticizing her relationship with Sammy Blake) that she was still 'bruised and deadened' from 'illness, England & love'. During the year Mayo Paddon married the girl with whom he had begun to walk in Beacon Hill Park shortly after returning from England. Emily saw herself firmly cast in the role of an old maid. As for Victoria itself, it still remained an artistic backwater. Despite the opinion of one visitor, who said he had never seen so many families occupied by literature and art, Victoria was still without an art gallery or even an art society.[10] There was no longer even an art display among the poultry and preserved fruit at the annual Saanichton Fall Fair. The fine-art events in Victoria for 1905 consisted of the exhibition of William Holman Hunt's painting, *The Light of the World*, and the visit of Miss Webly, an English miniature portraitist, who painted the Indians and the landscape around the city. When, on the recommendation of a Victoria friend at the end of the year, Emily was offered a teaching post in Vancouver, she did not hesitate to accept it. She had already been considering opening a studio in that city.

Despite its newness (it was incorporated in 1887), Vancouver already boasted an Art Association and a new exhibiting body, the Studio Club. The position, as instructor to the Vancouver Ladies' Art Club,[11] was only part-time, but it offered Emily an escape from the constrictions of Victoria, her family, and the lingering embarrassment of 'failure'. With what must have been a sense of relief, she gathered her plaster casts and paint boxes, her birds, squirrels, chipmunks, and newly acquired sheep dog, Billie, and moved across the Strait in January 1906. She found a temporary home with one of Clara's four daughters, Una, who was married to Frank W. Boultbee and lived on Melville Street in Vancouver's West End.

A few days after Emily left Victoria, Clara, Edith, Lizzie, and Alice trimmed Clara's drawing room with ivy and masses of white narcissus and gave a tea. Though the timing was probably coincidental, the tea might well have been a celebration of the departure of their sometimes difficult sister.

The spirit of optimism that gripped British Columbia in 1906 was nowhere more evident than in the city of Vancouver. For the past three decades the 'Liverpool of the Pacific' had opened the jaws of its harbour to shipping and receiving, canning and refining, and the shores of Burrard Inlet and False Creek were crowded with office buildings, docks, sawmills, grain silos, and packing houses.[12] There was the feeling that the wilderness of the province was finally beginning to pay back its hard-working pioneers. The Northwest Coast was no longer an 'uncivilized' land populated with 'lurking bands of Indians'. Vancouver residents were already leaving the ugly and polluted city for relaxation and recreation, escaping to the surrounding mountains and seashore. Sechelt Peninsula had become a summer resort, Buccaneer Bay a retreat for campers, and Indian Arm was dotted with fashionable cottages. Members of the Alpine Club of Canada and the British Columbia Mountaineers topped every peak within view of the harbour. The thousand-acre reserve in the city's centre, Stanley Park—where just two decades earlier the artist Thomas Mower Martin had wandered for days unable to find the lake hidden within its tangled forest—was dotted with rustic seats and summer houses and riddled with roads and paths. Electric tramlines connected Vancouver with outlying New Westminster, the Vancouver and

Lulu Island Railway took people to the fishing centre of Steveston; and the British Columbia Electric Railway provided a convenient link with the Fraser Valley communities. The Indian Reserve across the harbour to the north, previously ignored by all but missionaries, was now frequently visited by curio-seeking tourists. The Union Steamship Company's vessels took more adventurous Vancouverites to the now-popular Indian villages of Alert Bay and Campbell River on Cormorant and Vancouver Islands, or up the mainland coast to Skagway, Alaska.

During Emily's four and a half years in the harbour metropolis, Vancouver took on some big-city characteristics. Sarah Bernhardt, Pavlova, Mary Garden, Clara Butt, Nijinsky, and Paderewski all appeared at the Opera House on Granville Street. In the Hotel Vancouver's Oval Room one could observe the most sophisticated members of British Columbia society. Powell and Wharf Streets teemed with Chinese and Japanese immigrants who were the targets of rioters in 1907. Loggers and fishermen of every nationality could be found whooping it up on brawling Cordova Street. The lack of an established community dominated by an English colonial élite made the city much more easy-going and cosmopolitan than Victoria.

Despite the Art Association and the Studio Club, turn-of-the-century Vancouver had little time for art. It possessed a reputation for being a city where 'the quest for the dollar . . . [left] no time for the quest of the beautiful.'[13] Such English immigrant artists as Thomas Fripp and Percy Judge had survived on a trickle of students and commissions that came their way, but by 1906 Vancouver's burgeoning economy stimulated a clientele that sought not only art lessons but paintings for the walls of their Shaughnessy and West End homes. The practice of sketching and painting in watercolour was considered in Vancouver, as in Victoria, to be a gentlemanly pursuit for retired colonels and businessmen, a polite hobby for genteel ladies, and a healthy occupation for children. Emily sought to accommodate the growing interest in painting when she began her duties for the Vancouver Ladies' Art Club.

The situation was impossible from the start. Never a smart dresser, Emily felt dowdy before these well-dressed women, whom she referred to as 'middle age society dames'. The club was mainly a social organization; while some members were serious about their work, most were not. They 'dropped in at class at all hours', and 'one hussy always late would repose the model after we had already been working an hour.' Intolerant, as usual, of anyone who did not comply with her ways, Emily took their frivolity as a sacrilege and retaliated by giving harsh criticisms of their painting. 'You may look at my work if you wish,' one woman told her, 'but I do not care to take your criticisms, thank you.' After a month, Emily and the Vancouver Ladies' Art Club parted company.

Mrs Keith, the Victoria friend who had recommended Emily for the position, told her why she had not been successful: 'You wanted to make them work seriously & would not recognize they were a group of society ladies, killing time.' Emily had exaggerated their haughtiness, failing to

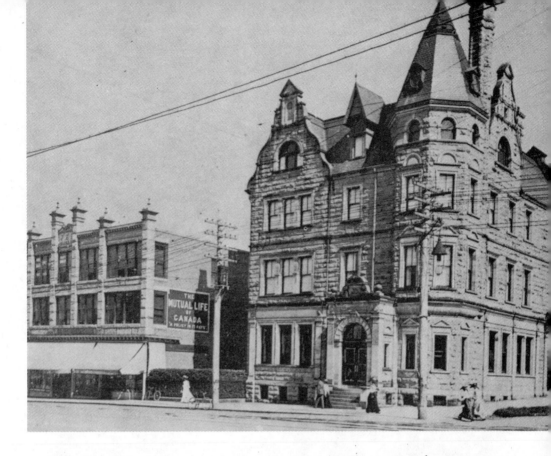

recognize their right to be serious or not as they pleased. She convinced herself that a major reason for her dismissal was that 'I did look horribly young for the post'—though at thirty-four, she must have been older than a few of the ladies.[14] She thought of herself as an ill-treated teacher, too young, too inexperienced, and too serious for the position. This was not a good beginning for her Vancouver career, but it showed Emily her limitations. After that, she recalled later, 'I kept away from adults as much as possible.' She decided to work with children, who were more pliable.

Only a few days after Emily's dismissal, the following advertisement appeared in the *News-Advertiser*: 'Miss M. Emily Carr, Classes in Drawing and Painting, Studio Room 6, Fee Block, next to the Bank of Montreal, Granville Street.'[15] Emily had taken two rooms on the second floor of the Fee Block, a new stone building at 570 Granville, between Dunsmuir and Pender. She shared the floor with business offices and the Men's Conservative Club. Her rooms, located above a jeweller-optician, became a classroom, an art-supply room, a kitchen, and the home of her animal menagerie. Emily found—and frequently changed—living quarters 'in one & another of the very miserable boarding houses' in the vicinity: Mrs Frame's Oakes on Burrard, Mrs Baker's Tea Kettle Inn on Dunsmuir, and a larger house at 1935 Granville.

Students arrived at the Fee Block studio in large numbers and Emily

The Fee Block (LEFT) on Granville Street, Vancouver, where Emily had a studio on the first floor (first window on the right). The building next to it, at Dunsmuir, is the Bank of Montreal (demolished). 1905. Courtesy Vancouver City Archives.

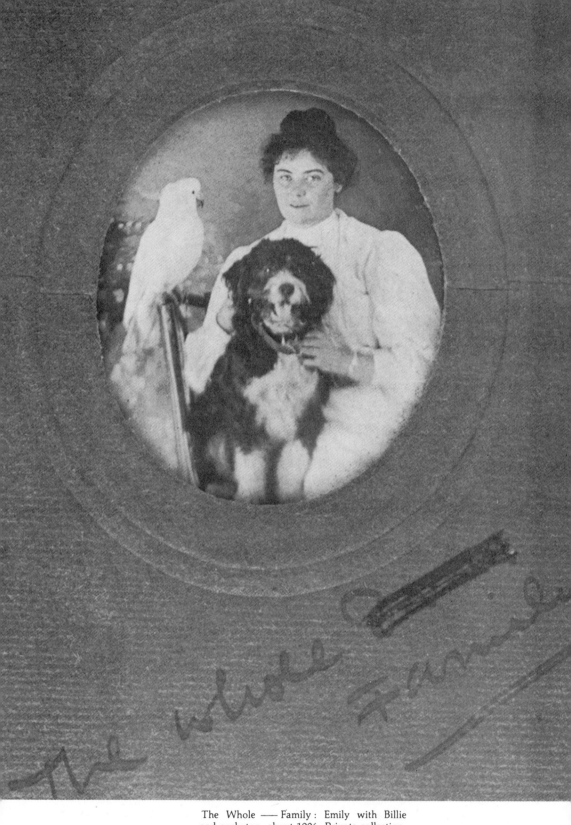

The Whole ——— Family : Emily with Billie
and cockatoo, about 1906. Private collection.

threw herself 'heart and soul' into her work. The children were responsive and almost immediately she made a success of teaching. Children raced up the long, uncarpeted marble stairs, past the glass offices of the Men's Conservative Club, past 'John', the smiling Chinese janitor, and into Miss Carr's studio, which was a wonderful place to be. There were inside window boxes bursting with flowers, and cages that rattled and squeaked with squirrels, chipmunks, raccoons, and bullfinches. Jane, the green-and-yellow Panama parrot, and Sally, the lemon-crested Australian cockatoo, added to the cacophony. Billie the sheep dog presided as patriarch. On special occasions the white rats, Peter and Peggy, were allowed to run up and down the long table, to the delight of the eight or ten children who guarded their rubbing-out bread from the omniverous creatures. And Miss Carr could be counted on for tea and cookies after every class.

The art lessons were as relaxed as the surroundings. Beginners found a sketch-pad and pencil before them and were asked to illustrate a nursery rhyme, or to sketch what they had seen on their way to school or what they had done on Sunday. The older children sat at easels and copied, in charcoal, Miss Carr's plaster casts of a hand, a foot, or a horse's head. If they remained, they advanced (as their teacher had before them) to paint still-life compositions in watercolour, and finally to draw from a posed model. Always 'the rooms teemed with life & laughter.'

When the warm weather came, the children gathered their folding camp stools, paper, and watercolour boxes and followed Miss Carr and Billie down Georgia Street, across the Coal Harbour Bridge, to the edge of Stanley Park. There they sat on the grassy banks of present-day Lost Lagoon, then a tidal inlet, and painted the scenes before them. Sometimes they sketched in the lanes of the residential West End, where there were interesting old stables, or on the high bank overlooking the CPR tracks and the harbour. But since sketching in back alleys and along railroad tracks brought complaints from parents, the usual spot was the park.[16]

Word of Emily's popularity spread quickly. Many of her pupils came from Miss Jessie Gordon's Neighbourhood House (later the Croften House School for Girls), and Miss Gordon, who had earlier refused Emily's application to teach art, asked her to give special classes in her school. Though many Gordon students may not have been very interested in art, they joined Miss Carr's class with enthusiasm because, in the words of one of them, it meant release from school on a sort of picnic. Some attended both Emily's Saturday-morning classes as well as those she gave in the school. Miss Carr was 'such fun'.[17] Her classes were 'always happy'; she sang, was 'very sloppy with the paint', and made everyone laugh.[18] Most of her pupils 'loved her and would not miss a class for anything.'[19] Emily did not confine their drawing to casts, still-life compositions, or models, but gave them freedom to express themselves. In her own work she was beginning to see things 'as being as well as doing', and she attempted to impart this insight to her pupils, one of

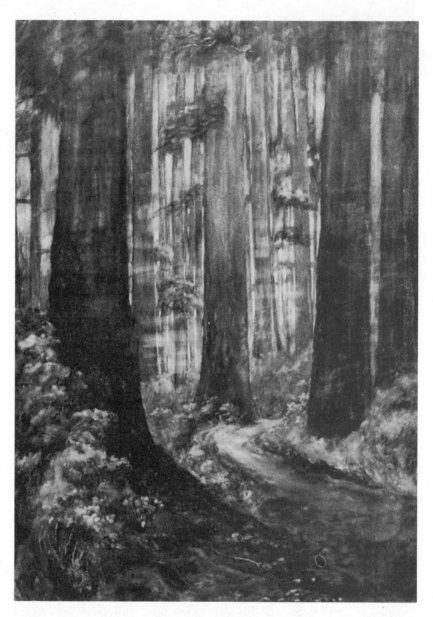

Untitled
(42.3.87), 1910.
Watercolour,
30 7/8 x
21 3/16. VAG.

whom recalled that Emily made her 'outlook bigger and seeing of nature different.'[20]

By the end of 1907 she had upwards of seventy-five pupils. (When the classes grew too large for her to manage, she hired a jovial Scotch girl called Belle as pupil-teacher.) There were also the classes in Miss Gordon's school, and Emily travelled weekly by the small ferry to North Vancouver, to teach at two more private schools there. The success of her teaching was followed by the local newspapers. In March 1907, just over a year after she had opened her Granville Street studio, the

Province reported that 'Miss Carr gave a most successful exhibition of her pupils' work.'[21] In April 1908 her studio was 'thronged with visitors', who saw more than 500 pieces on display.[22] Crowding the walls were 'clever compositions' in charcoal by the older students and competent black-and-white illustrations of 'The Old Woman Who Lived in a Shoe', 'Bluebeard', and other children's stories and rhymes by the younger children.[23] A reviewer in 1909 noted that the work of Miss Carr's students 'bore the stamp of individuality—all were original sketches, no copy work being shown'.[24]

Those years in Vancouver were among Emily's happiest, filled with 'joy, independence and lots of laughing'.[25] Everything 'was part of everything, not so much me and mine'.[26] As well as deriving much satisfaction from her students, Emily earned a comfortable living that, in 1909, allowed her to invest in the purchase of five city lots in the new Rosedale Hastings Townsite subdivision.[27] Yet her teaching cut severely into her painting time. Except for summer holidays, most of her work had to be done alongside her students, and a large number of inconsequential portraits and still-lifes were the result. She seldom had time to explore the wilderness, so readily accessible by rail or boat. When she did paint alone during the school term, it was usually in the nearby forest of Stanley Park, where the 'appalling solemnity, majesty & silence was the Holiest thing I ever felt.' Though she was beginning 'to see a glimmer of something beyond objectivity', Emily 'could not express it.'[28] She struggled fiercely with the trees, 'resentful at how tightly they sealed their secrets from me, resentful at my foolish art, humble & pleading before the great trees.' In one untitled wood interior, a watercolour (VAG, *42.3.87), she attempted to suggest the diffused light among the trees by rubbing out areas of paint. But this did little to make the trees less stiff or the atmosphere more holy. Emily's art was still captive to convention, which imposed a concern for detail, a striving for the picturesque, and the concocting of effects that had nothing to do with the forest as she now felt it. She later admitted that she was still 'looking for English compositions'.[29]

Emily's painting differed little from that of the Vancouver contemporaries with whom she first began to exhibit in the Studio Club in November 1906. Like them, she had been trained in an English academic school, and like them she was attempting to transfer English landscape conventions to British Columbia. Contrary to her later claim that her work was subjected to devastating criticism, her paintings received the same uncritical praise accorded to Percy Judge, Thomas Fripp, and other prominent Vancouver artists. Her portraits were described as 'quaint and pretty', her botanical drawings as 'charming', and reviewers seldom failed to notice her treatments of British Columbia's forest scenery.[30] But she did not, like Thomas Fripp, climb mountains to render their mist-covered peaks, nor did she offer a new perception of the landscape by blending the Japanese with the English landscape tradition, like another B.C. painter, Charles John Collings. Both in subject and in execution,

Emily's paintings did not depart from the restricted and conventional limits of the late-Victorian English watercolour school.

In June 1907 Alice had 'a spell of melancholy after cutting off a finger tip' and Emily suggested an Alaskan cruise to ease her nerves.[31] Alice agreed, and the pair departed from Seattle on the *Dolphin* in mid-summer. It was a splendid trip. Sailing between the islands and the mainland, the boat passed mile upon mile of wooded shore, snow-capped mountains that rose out of the sea, fiords that bit deep into the coast, bleak Indian villages, noisy fish canneries, and rowdy lumber camps. It stopped for a few hours in the colourful Kwakiutl village of Alert Bay, where Emily saw her first decorated community houses and totem poles. It then pushed further north, sailing past Bella Bella, Prince Rupert, Port Simpson, and up to Sitka on Baranof Island. There the *Dolphin* was greeted by a brass band composed of Indian children from the Mission School and by women selling brightly coloured baskets. Emily and Alice spent a week exploring the town. They saw the gold icons in St Michael's Orthodox Church, the Russian tea house, and the ruins of Baranof Castle. They climbed 3,200-foot Mount Verstovaia and became lost on their descent, despite the company of a Polish guide. They visited the dilapidated Indian settlement, where Emily purchased a tom-tom, a brow strap of bear's claws, a deer-hide, an eagle's leg, and a hollow bear's tooth through which she could whistle tunes. And in a wooded area behind Sitka they discovered 'Totem Walk', where totem poles of the Haida and Tlingit had been re-erected for the tourists. Emily painted the poles among the trees, the Russian bakery in the town, and a distant view of Sitka's harbour. After a week they sailed to Skagway, travelled on to Juneau, then sailed back down the coast to Seattle.

The three-week trip, which ended with Alice losing her suitcase, would have been little more than a relaxed holiday had Emily not painted the totem poles and met the Minneapolis artist, Theodore J. Richardson, at Sitka. Richardson had spent every summer since 1884 painting watercolours of the villages, totem poles, and tribal houses of the Alaskan Indians. He reputedly travelled to remote villages by canoe with Indians as guides and lived among them for weeks at a time. In studying the myths associated with the poles, and in recording them, he was preserving what he felt was a dying culture—and making a handsome living besides from the sale of his paintings in New York.[32]

Emily had several conversations with the sideburned, mustachioed Richardson in his small Sitka studio and was impressed by his work. Anxious to have his opinion of her Totem Walk watercolours, she showed him her paintings. Emily recalled that he told her 'his were not so good as mine', though an impartial comparison of their work at this time would have to find Richardson's far superior. With Richardson as a model and his flattery in her ear, Emily made a far-reaching decision. She had always loved the Indians; now in Sitka she conceived the idea of painting them and their totem poles. 'I shall come up every summer among the villages of B.C.,' she resolved, 'and I shall do all the totem poles & villages I can before they are a thing of the past.' Her painting now had a mission: to salvage what she perceived to be the dying heritage of the British Columbia Indians.

This was very much in Emily's mind when she returned to Vancouver at the end of the summer. She worked hard during the year: reopening her Granville Street studio in September, mounting a student exhibition in March, travelling inland to paint the landscape around Silver Creek at Hope during the Easter break, then returning to contribute to the Studio Club's exhibition in late April. When school terminated in June 1908 she boarded the Union Steamship's *Venture* and sailed some 150 miles up the coast to Alert Bay, where she stayed with missionaries, the Reverend and Mrs A.J. Hall.

Situated on the west side of Cormorant Island, Alert Bay was the gathering place for the Kwakiutl nation. Indians came and went, depositing their fish at the cannery, working for awhile in the sawmill, or surreptitiously meeting other bands for a now-illegal potlatch. Some lived in colossal broad-planked community houses that skirted the shore. The women trussed salmon on spindly pine frames, cleaned canoe-loads of fish at the water's edge, or picked berries in the forest; the men, less active while in the village, squatted against the houses in the sun or sought the shade under covered wooden platforms that extended from the boardwalk into the ocean. The variety of images here excited Emily: the colourful woollen shawls and cotton dresses of the Indian women who moved in and out of the brightly painted houses, decorated with huge spread-winged thunderbirds, and protruding multi-coloured beaks that opened to admit the inhabitants to a smoky-blue interior; totem poles, the newer ones covered with gaudy house paint and the older ones decorated with natural dyes and delicately faded; and behind all of this the thick luxuriant forest. Emily painted the community houses, the poles, and tree-hung coffins in the burial grounds; she even combined people, buildings, and landscape—subjects she had usually treated individually. Painting in watercolour, she worked 'like a camera', determined to be 'absolutely truthful & exact' because she was 'working for history'.[33] The necessity for speed and accuracy strengthened her technique, while the concentration on Indian motifs broadened her palette.

Emily made excursions to Alert Bay and Campbell River in both 1908 and 1909. She also travelled inland to paint the Indians at Lytton and the mountains around Hope, then up Howe Sound to sketch at Britannia Beach and across to Buccaneer Bay on the Sechelt Peninsula. During the summer of 1909 some of these places were also painted by Theresa Wylde, and it is probable that she visited them with Emily. Recently returned from study at the Slade School in London and exhibition at the Royal Academy, Wylde displayed in her painting a 'fearless manipulation of colours', as one reviewer would comment of a Wylde exhibition in Victoria in 1910.[34] Her influence on Emily can be seen in such works as *Salish Woman Weaving* (PABC), in which Emily employed brighter colours and gave less attention to detail; yet there is little hint of the expressionistic and almost mystical power of her later work. Her paintings at this time were still traditional: faithful and pleasing reproductions of picturesque scenes.

Though Emily's northern excursions were far from easy or comfortable—she had to travel by motor launch, stagecoach, and canoe, and put up with makeshift lodgings in a mission house or a tent—she was not visiting uncharted territory. Every steamship that sailed up the coast stopped at both Alert Bay and Campbell River, and scores of tourists disembarked to gaze at the poles and purchase curios from the Indians. Emily was presumably unaware that the need to record the rapidly decaying poles and houses around northern Vancouver Island—where Kwakiutl carvers like Billy Sewid and Charlie James were still carving poles and would pass their skill on to Mungo Martin—was not as urgent as in the Haida villages of the Queen Charlotte Islands or the Tsimshian villages of the adjacent mainland, where carving poles had virtually ceased in the 1880s.[35] However, Emily found her expeditions ambitious and rewarding enough. She undertook her task 'with terrific zest loving *the* people *the* place & Materials'. There were 'horrible smells' of smoking salmon, human waste, and rotting fish emanating from every corner of the villages; and the work was 'exhausting and the travel hard'. But odours and hard work did not 'gull' her like the 'Drunkin landladies' and the 'repellent hardness and suspicion' she found in Vancouver.[36]

While Emily had hurtful memories of her life in Vancouver, it seems clear that she hurt others. She became a founding member of the British Columbia Society of Fine Arts in 1908 and according to another member, Grace Judge, wanted to 'run the whole show'.[37] She insisted that a woman be elected to the hanging committee and was annoyed when the mild-mannered Miss Judge, not she, was chosen. She did not hesitate to criticize the work of fellow members as unreservedly as she had done three years before in the Vancouver Ladies' Art Club. Miss Judge recalled that Emily 'wouldn't be friendly', 'fought with everyone', 'had a hard time keeping friends', and 'enjoyed quarrelling'.[38]

Emily believed that the bolder approach she had taken in her painting isolated her even more from the artistic community. While she lacked the Royal Academy cachet that made Theresa Wylde's progressive work acceptable, there is little evidence to show that Emily's vivid colours were looked upon disapprovingly. The reviewers praised the 'strength and genuineness', the 'bold and striking' manner of her new work, which was still within the conventions of her fellow exhibitors.[39] Though Emily later recalled that she went 'her own way', and 'did not bother with the other artists and societies', she rarely failed to contribute work to the Society's exhibitions or attend on opening day. Nor was she as isolated from the artistic community as she led one to believe. Artists Theresa Wylde, Ann Batchelor, Margaret Wake, Statira Frame, and even Grace Judge were all entertained in her studio.

Emily's haughty quarrelsomeness was not all that created resentment

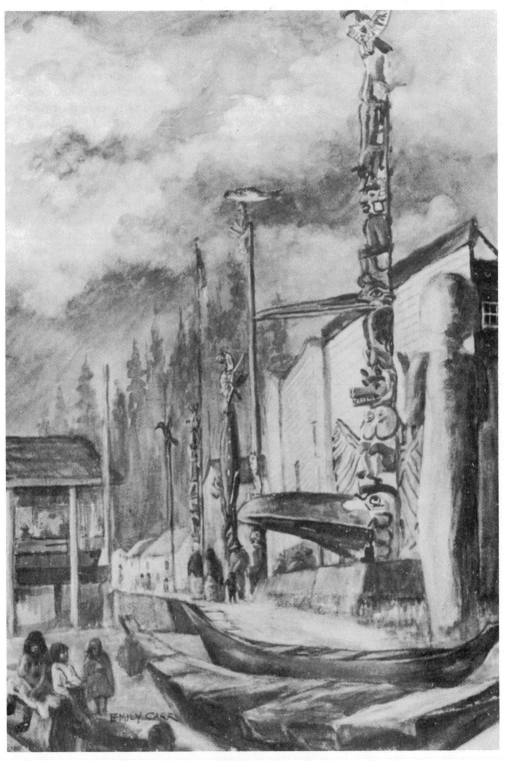

Canoes and Totems (Alert Bay), 1908. Watercolour, 22 x 15.
Collection Dr and Mrs Max Stern, Dominion Gallery, Montreal.

against her. She didn't care how she looked and thought it a big joke when one student found her scrubbing the studio floor dressed in her bathing suit.[40] The keeping of wild creatures—especially white rats—added to the image of eccentricity. When Emily's Indian pictures began to appear in public exhibitions after 1908, tales of her travels among the Indians began to make the rounds in Vancouver. The Indians had long been a motif for many British Columbia artists, and pictures of the easily accessible villages of Alert Bay and Campbell River were not uncommon in local exhibitions. Yet until now no woman had so openly talked about living with the Indians. This, not surprisingly, aroused some disapproval. One of her students 'could not understand how she could live among the Indians'; a fellow artist did not know 'how she could stay in the villages'.[41] Emily, who loved to shock, apparently did little to justify herself, for it was true that she preferred associating with Indians and animals. As she later wrote, 'it was as if everything hugged me' in the villages; in Vancouver 'as if everything hurt'.[42] Stranded by her temperament from the much-wanted consolation of mature friendships, she was lonely. Cheery students, her helpmate Belle, and the few artists who visited her studio did not provide adequate compensation. So Emily turned to Indians and animals and convinced herself that she preferred them.

Emily's companionship with animals not only fulfilled a lifelong need, but was a satisfying substitute for human relationships. Seldom was a summer trip made without Billie or her cockatoo Sally. And invariably she brought back 'some bit of wild life in tow': squirrels, raccoons, chipmunks, or a crow. In 1908, on her way to Buccaneer Bay to visit the Burnett family's summer camp, she bought a baby vulture, 'Uncle Tom', from the Indians for fifty cents.

> I had a little tent on a rock with thick bush all round. The cocatoo sat on the head of the bed. Billie slept under the bed. I was in it and 'Uncle Tom' the vulture slept under the floor of the tent. Wherever I went Uncle Tom was at my heels. When I went out sketching the cocatoo sat on my shoulder, the sketch sack was slung over the other & the sheep dog & vulture walked on each side. There was no meat to feed the vulture so we went down & dug clams & muscles for him. He grew into a great bird but he would not accept his freedom. I donated him to Stanley Park and when I used to go to see him he ran to me rejoicing.[43]

Of all of her creatures, the most rewarding companion was Billie. He was both a recipient and a provider of love during her four-and-a-half years in Vancouver. She wrote rather slangy verses that interpreted Billie's thoughts about studio life, summer excursions, and his feelings towards her, his 'Misses'. In 1909 Emily kept an illustrated calendar of his activities throughout the year. They included posing for the art students, attending the students' spring exhibition, accompanying 'Misses' to northern Indian villages, and getting his summer clip.[44] A framed poem called 'Bill' hung on Emily's studio wall. In her verses, laden with self-pity, Emily saw herself with 'no pa nor ma', no brothers, no aunts or

BILL.

BILLY AINT A BENCH DOG,
 BILLY AINT NO SPECIAL BREED
BILLY CANT BE JEST STYLED HANSOM,
 BUT HIS ONLY VICE IS GREED.

I AINT GOT NO PA NOR MA,
 I AINT GOT NO BROTHERS,
NEER A UNCLE OR A AUNT,
 I AINT GOT NO LOVERS.

KITH WHAT WANTS ME LIVES AWAY,
 KIN WHATS HERE DONT LIKE ME,
LIFE AINT JEST A COMFIE PLACE
 OFTEN SEEMS TO STRIKE ME.

WHEN I'M SITTIN' THINKIN'
 'DARN IT AINT IT DREAR'
BILLY UP AN WHIMPERS
 LICKS AWAY THE TEAR.

BILLY SAVVEYS HEARTACHE
 WHEEDLES IT AWAY
ENTERS IN WITH JOYOUS ZEST
 WHEN THE WORLD IS GAY.

BILLY SHARES THE LABOURS
 HOLDS HIS END UP FINE
DOES HIS DUTY FAIR AN SQUARE
 GOOD AS I DO MINE.

BILLIES JEST A BUNDLE.
 LOVE, AN FLEAS, AN' SMELL;
THINK 'ID CHANGE MY BILLIE
 FER THE THOROUGHBREDDEST SWEL

'DONT SAY ITS AG IN A DOG
 BOASTIN MILES OF PEDIGREE
I ONLY SAY MY OLD CUR BILL
 S' GOOD ENOUGH FER ME.
 SMOZ.

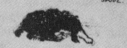

(LEFT) Emily's poem about Billie,
1909. Courtesy Exposition
Galleries, Vancouver.

(BELOW) *Billie*, 1909. Watercolour,
14 7/8 x 11 3/8. Courtesy Exposition Galleries, Vancouver.

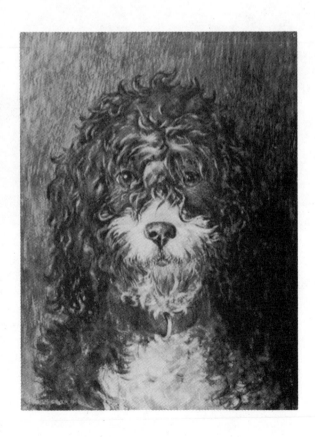

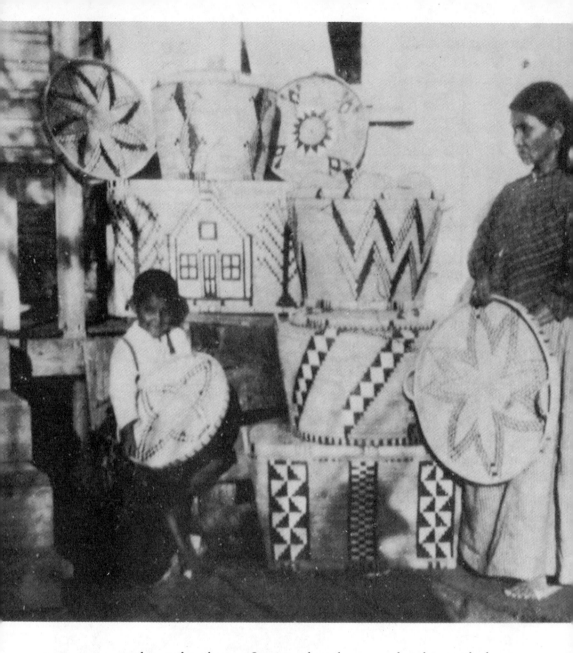

Sophie Frank, 1919. Private collection.

uncles, and no lovers. Sensing when she was sad and in need of comforting, 'Billy up an whimpers', and 'Licks away the tear'.[45] A now-aging sheep dog of doubtful pedigree gave her the two things she required in a relationship: loyal, undying affection and constant attention.

While among Emily's human contacts her students satisfied these needs intermittently, only one adult—Sophie Frank, a Squamish Indian of the Salish nation—came close to doing so unquestioningly and wholeheartedly. The long-braided, barefooted woman appeared at Emily's door the first week she was in her studio.[46] Sophie had canoed across the Inlet from the North Vancouver Reserve, where she lived, to sell her many-sized wild-cherry and red-cedar baskets in the city. Emily had no old clothes to exchange but asked Sophie, in broken Chinook, to save her a basket, for which she would pay later. Sophie insisted on leaving the basket with Emily in trust of later payment. The following month she returned and collected the old clothes that Emily had brought from Victoria. The 'deal', Emily recalled, 'was pleasing to us both' and 'cemented our ever friendship'.

Whenever she felt depressed she went across the Inlet to Sophie's modest house. There was always a new baby, often a dead one. Sophie— who saw only one of her twenty children live to the age of ten, whose husband drank heavily, and who often drank herself—was 'walled about by trouble'. Yet through it 'shone the serene childlike suniness of the Indian'. The friendship that developed between the two women transcended Emily's halting Chinook and Sophie's broken English. 'The chaff of life surrounding the Indian ignites so readily,' Emily wrote, and 'the tiniest, flimsy excuse sent us into bubbles of laughter.' They shared an unspoken religious feeling, so that Emily quite naturally joined Sophie when she performed acts of devotion. Sophie would put on her best skirt, 'a very full creation of loud plaid with bands of black velvet', then tie a bright yellow silk handkerchief over her head, fold her hands over the fringe of her big shawl, and walk to the bramble-covered graves of her deceased children, Emily accompanying her. Sophie was proud of the stones (each had cost a huge number of woven baskets) and patted them as lovingly as if 'the cold stone was a black haired, big eyed babe'. Then they would walk to the twin-spired Catholic church, cross themselves with holy water, kneel together in the silent, empty nave, and stare at the cheap lace and paper flowers, lighted by glowing candles, that decorated the altar. Emily was not Miss Carr, Millie, or even Emmie, but 'Sophie's E'mily', or 'My Friend, Emily the lady who goes all over to paint'.[47]

Emily also escaped her loneliness by spending weekends with her sisters in Victoria. She would leave Saturday evening after class, arrive early Sunday morning, and return to Vancouver on the midnight boat. These were peaceful visits, with long meals and much family reminiscing, and they were usually happy because Emily did not remain long enough to quarrel with Edith. When the boat pulled out of Victoria harbour to take her back to Vancouver at the end of the day, Emily never failed to have a 'hard cry'. At a safe distance she had feelings of tenderness for the women she found it so difficult to live with.

Alice, who continued to be Emily's favourite sister, began in 1910 to study French in order to accompany Emily on the next stage of her career: a year's study in France. 'Everyone said Paris was the top of art,' Emily later recalled, 'and I wanted to get the best teaching I knew.' She had probably been saving for the trip ever since Theresa Wylde had returned from England with her new style of painting. The artist and teacher Ann Batchelor, who recalled that Emily was 'hard to budge', made it easier for her to leave not only by encouraging her to make the journey but by offering to sublet her Granville studio for a good price

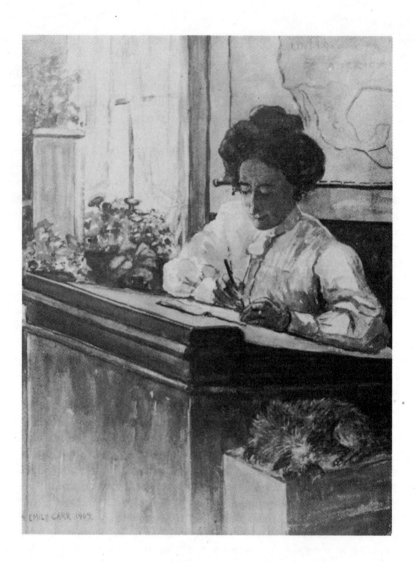

Alice Carr,
Sister of the
Artist, 1909.
Watercolour,
17 1/2 x 13 5/8
[sight]. Collec-
tion Mr and Mrs
W.G. Skinner.

and teach her students in her absence.[48] On the ninth of June, Ann and Emily held a joint exhibition and tea in the Granville studio and an art auction to raise supplemental money for Emily's trip. Though one person thought the auction was a 'rather pathetic affair', it was reported in the *Province,* and readers were told that everyone present 'took advantage of the opportunity of securing one or more pieces of her [Emily's] clever work.'[49] The article began:

> The friends of Miss Emily Carr are glad to know that she has recovered from her recent illness. Miss Carr intends to leave in a few weeks for a year's stay in Paris, where she will pursue her studies in art. During her absence her studio will be in charge of Miss Batchelor.

With her savings and auction earnings giving her enough money to be away for a year, Emily departed for France.

5
France
1910-1911

When Emily and Alice left Victoria on the eleventh of July 1910, they
were determined to see something of their own country before em-
barking from Quebec on the *Empress of Ireland*. The trip across Canada
by the CPR took them three weeks. They stopped first at Sicamous, B.C.,
then at Glacier House, where they climbed to the glacier and ice caves.
At Lake Louise in Alberta they fought off mosquitoes and attended to
Billie, who had sat on a wasp's nest, then was 'attacked' by a porcupine.
And in Banff they saw the sights by carriage. From Calgary they went to
Edmonton, where they spent a week with a friend Emily called Winnie.[1]
Billie remained in Winnie's care (Sally and Jane had been left with Lizzie,
'the lesser creatures given to one & another') and the women continued
their cross-Canada trek, returning to Calgary and making overnight
stops in Medicine Hat and Winnipeg. When they arrived at their destination, Quebec City, they were extremely disappointed not to find letters from home awaiting them. Nevertheless they set out to see the sights,
visiting antique shops and examining Quebec's monuments. When the
longed-for letters arrived, bringing news that 'pups, parrots and sisters'
were all well, their spirits rose and they continued their sightseeing with
lightened hearts. They made a pilgrimage to the shrine of Ste Anne de
Beaupré, visited nearby villages, and spent one day in a park where Alice
painted the wild flowers and Emily lay in the grass and read rustic love
tales. The twelve days in Quebec were relaxing, and gave Emily time to
gather her courage against seasickness and Alice an opportunity to prac-
tise her French.

On the twelfth of August they went to the Lower Town docks to board
the *Empress of Ireland* and found that their trunks had been shipped to
Liverpool three weeks before. It mattered little to Emily, who spent most
of the Atlantic crossing in her nightdress. Sea-healthy Alice delighted in
the eight-day voyage, despite her shortage of clothing. Arriving in Liverpool on the nineteenth, they located their trunks and, having several

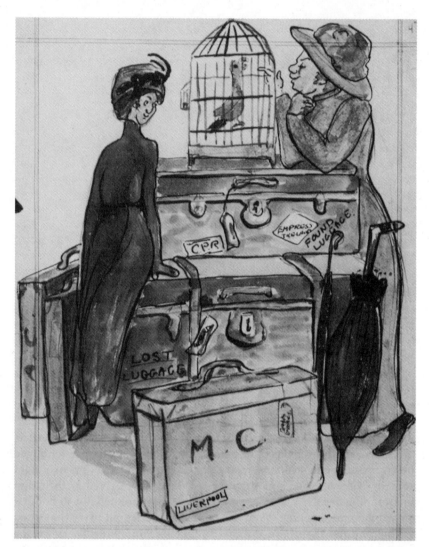

From a sketchbook:
'Liverpool Aug. 19. An So We Came To Liverpool, And Once On "Terra Firma" Again', 1910. Pen and ink and watercolour. PAC (C-96467).

hours before their train departed for London, they visited Cross's, the animal emporium. Over Alice's half-hearted protests, Emily bought an African Grey parrot, 'Rebecca', which was placed in a monstrous wedge-shaped box. When they boarded the London train Emily was in better spirits, as she had missed the company of a creature. After two nights in Mrs Dodds' Bulstrode Street house, and probably short visits with Mildred Crompton-Roberts and Marion Redden, Emily and Alice took the night-boat across the English Channel to Le Havre and there entrained for Paris.

As the train made its way through the French countryside, Emily braced herself in the corner of her seat and 'watched the villages glide by'. Her body still heaved with seasickness from the Channel crossing, but her 'spirit was thrilling wildly'. Just before she left Victoria a woman artist, whose name Emily never recorded, had given her a letter of introduction to an English artist who lived in Paris, Harry Gibb. The letter had meant little to Emily when she received it over a month before; but now, as the train pushed closer to Paris, it held exciting promise. Gibb would be her sole entrée into the art world and he suddenly became very important to her. As soon as she and Alice had settled in their flat in the Rue Campagne Première, Montparnasse, they set out for Gibb's studio on the Boulevard Raspail nearby.

The door was opened by a tall thin man, with a rosy complexion and bright blue eyes, who seemed to be about Emily's age. (At thirty-nine, he was a year older.) Emily produced the letter and she and Alice were invited into the studio overlooking a convent garden; here they met Gibb's wife Harriet, called Bridget, who was younger. Gibb immediately began talking about the contemporary art scene in Paris. For illustration he pointed to his own canvases: contorted figures wrestling on hot yellow sand; pot-bellied, big-buttocked, sagging-breasted women frozen in classical poses; nudes reclining in swirls of blue and yellow flowers; nudes dancing before muddy, abstract backgrounds. There were also still-life compositions and rank landscapes out of which leapt every kind of creature imaginable. Alice lowered her eyes. Emily was also taken unawares by this introduction to contemporary French painting. Though shocked by the distortion of the figures, she saw how 'flavourless, little, [and] unconvincing' conventional painting was compared with these pictures.[2] Her own work, described as bold by the Vancouver critics, seemed insipid compared with Gibb's canvases, with their startling variations on the human form and their pulsating colours. Unlike the Indians, who in their art distorted animals 'with meaning, for emphasis, and with great sincerity', this man had used distortion merely for reasons of design, intending 'to shock rather than convince'.[3] This revolted her, yet she was also fascinated because she had 'never imagined such things'. The 'rich, delicious juiciness in his colour', the 'interesting forms' of his still-life and landscape paintings, thrilled her.[4] While Emily looked in silent amazement, Gibb talked on, his words filling her with humility and embarrassment as she became aware of ideas and techniques—a whole world of painting—she knew nothing about. The only response she could muster at the end of that first meeting was in the form of an appeal: 'Please can you tell me where to start?'

It may have been a confusing introduction to modern art, but Emily had come to the right man. William Phelan 'Harry' Gibb had made his home in Paris long before Braque, Picasso, and Matisse had found their way to Vollard's Galerie Lafayette or Gertrude Stein had opened the door of her Rue de Fleurus apartment to entertain them on Saturday evenings. Dubbed the 'stray from the north of England', Gibb had sold Matisse's first picture, had exhibited with Bonnard, Seurat, and Manet, and been honoured by the Salon d'Automne by being elected a Sociétaire.[5] He had spent the greater part of his painting career working in the conservative English landscape tradition; only after study and travel in

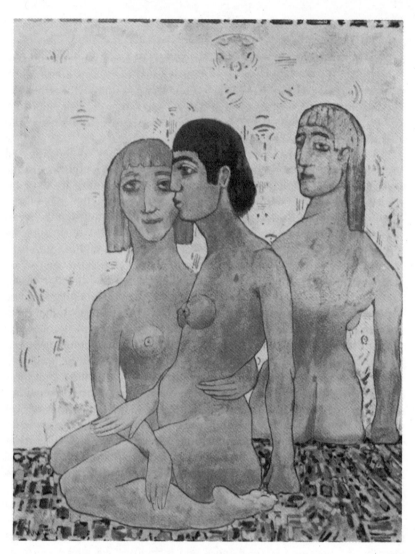

Phelan Gibb. *Three Graces*, about 1909. Oil on cardboard, 68 1/2 x 39. Lucy Wertheim Bequest Collection, Towner Art Gallery, Eastbourne, England.

Germany and France had he broken out of the academic mould. In England the art critic for the *Morning Post*, Robert Ross, praised his work; in Canada Sir William Van Horne bought it. But his painting made little public impact in Paris, though not for lack of connections in the Parisian art world. He could count Gertrude Stein, Braque, and Matisse as his closest friends, and almost every English-speaking artist in Paris among his acquaintances. He was known as 'a *real* personality', 'a man with something to say and who said it in no uncertain fashion'. A gifted mimic and raconteur, he entertained his friends with an 'unending fund of stories of his contemporaries in the art world of Paris'.[6] In many ways his personality outshone his art, though he was not a man without ideas. According to Gertrude Stein, he 'foresaw everything' in modern painting.[7] His ideas were an inspiration for many artists, yet they did little to raise his own art above the ordinary. His colours lacked the purity of Braque's, his lines the grace of Matisse's. He was incapable of making a painting 'a clear and complete work of art'. His pictures appeared as 'feeble copies of works of Braque and Matisse, instead of being their forerunners'.[8]

Gibb—who has been described as 'impetuous, self-willed dynamic'—alarmed Emily.[9] His 'queer twisted smile' disturbed her, his nudes revolted her, and his apparent indifference to his wife aroused her disapproval. Yet other things about him attracted her. She was intrigued by his way of life, observing as curiosities the set of colourful hand-moulded dishes from which he and Bridget ate; the solemn ritual with which they brewed a pot of coffee or made a salad dressing; their restrictive living quarters, which were confined to the studio and a tiny kitchen. And she was tremendously impressed by his intimate acquaintance with the Paris art world. Believing, correctly, that he could help her understand the precepts of the modern school, she hesitantly put the fate of her Paris sojourn in his hands.

Emily had intended to enrol in the Académie Julian, where Sophie Pemberton had distinguished herself. However Gibb insisted that she go to the less-expensive Académie Colarossi, where classes were not segregated as they were at the Julian; he felt that Emily would gain from seeing the stronger work of the male students.

The Colarossi occupied a series of rooms on the second floor of a squat building on the narrow Rue de la Grande Chaumière. Founded in the middle of the 1880s, it was reputable enough to have attracted Whistler, Rodin, Van Gogh, Gauguin, Modigliani, and Matisse, though little is known about it now. Like the many other accredited art schools in Paris, it probably offered three cours per day: the first from eight until noon; the second from one to five; the third from seven to ten. The instructors gave their 'crits' on Tuesdays and Thursdays. Not only was instruction provided for beginners as well as advanced students, but it was possible to work alone if one paid a daily fee for sketching privileges. Working conditions, however, were unpleasant. The small packed rooms were hot (when the stove overheated in the life class, even the nude model perspired) and filled with oppressive smells of perspiration, fresh paint, smoke, and often damp clothes. But Emily was not as bothered by this as by the things that made her feel 'shy and foolish'. At thirty-eight she was older than the other students; she was the only woman in the life class; and the language of instruction was French. When the instructor first 'waved and babbled' before her easel, Emily in desperation arranged for a French-speaking American to translate her crits in exchange for clean paint rags. As was to be expected, she was greatly embarrassed by the male nude model—probably the first she had seen, let alone drawn. She bravely tried to overcome her inhibition, but even the arrival in class of some 'grey haired kittens' who had 'nearly given up being wives & [were] looking for outlets' did not make her feel less uncomfortable. So after a few weeks she transferred to the clothed model class, which was 'less stuffy and exhausting'.

A unilingual woman from provincial Victoria who chose to study in Paris in 1910 had to have uncommon spirit and ambition, and not a little adventurousness. Yet Emily—living in the heart of the Latin Quarter of the French metropolis—donned a cloak of impenetrable conventionality for her sojourn there, and remained on the fringe of the revolutionary currents that existed around her. The Carrs joined the American Student Hostel Club, a pleasant rendezvous on the Boulevard Saint-Michel that offered lectures, visits to art exhibitions, conducted tours outside Paris, a lending library, and afternoon teas. They chose eating places that were patronized by safely familiar 'English and American misses'—a world apart from the Café de la Rotonde, which it would not have occurred to them to enter: where Trotsky played chess with Kandinsky; where Elya Ehrenburg sat all day writing poetry; and Modigliani, Braque, and Picasso met and argued loudly.[11] As for the famous centres of evening entertainment—the Cirque Médrano, the Concert-Maylo, the Gaîté-Montparnasse—or cultural events like the notorious Salon d'Automne, which exhibited the work of Matisse, Duchamp, Léger, and the decorative panels of Maurice Denis, we have to assume they escaped the sisters' interest or attention, since they are not mentioned in any of Emily's writings. Nor, even more surprisingly, is mention made of the Mareau-Nelaton collection, a legacy that gave the Louvre its first Impressionist paintings, though the Carrs did visit that museum.

After about a month, Emily left Colarossi's daytime classes, at Gibb's suggestion, and joined the private studio of the Scottish artist John Duncan Fergusson—to her great relief. Here 'the air was better' and she understood the lessons. She also enjoyed her cheerful instructor, who was one of the most interesting British artists in Paris. Like Harry Gibb, Fergusson had lived in Paris for several years. He too had been elected a Sociétaire of the Salon d'Automne, but he was more closely linked to the English-speaking community than Gibb; in fact, some looked upon him as its leader.[12] By choice he had few French artist friends and rarely went to Gertrude Stein's Saturday-evening soirées. Unlike Gibb, he was not hungry for recognition, having had two successful London exhibitions and the distinction of being singled out by an *International Studio* critic as a 'man who must go far'.[13] He had been influenced by the Fauves' violent colours and flat decorative motifs; by 1910, when Emily joined his class, his nudes and portraits were surging with rhythm and design. If she learned anything from him, it was how to see rhythm in nature; but she had little opportunity to absorb much. A few weeks after she began her lessons, Fergusson closed his studio and moved to the Atelier Blanche, which was probably run by a young British couple, the McLeans, who engaged a number of English-speaking critics.[14] Emily moved with Fergusson and was happy. However, though conditions at the Blanche seemed ideal, she was in hospital after only a few weeks.

At this time Emily had been in Paris for about three months. She felt she had been making some progress. She was certainly working hard, attending classes both day and night.[15] Though she continued to feel 'ignorant and silly' with the Gibbs, she and Alice often visited them and she always 'picked up some crumb of help'. In her enthusiasm to learn, to catch up to the moderns, to maximize her limited time in France, she drove herself. The strain of hard work was compounded by the worry of being so far behind the other students, the stifling working conditions, and the often unintelligible instruction in the ateliers. 'I began to feel myself going, going as I had in London.' She became 'nearly demented with headaches' and to Alice she was 'too hateful for words.' She attributed her illness in turn to measles, to the flu complicated by bronchitis, to jaundice, and to 'the close life rooms & the wear of the great city'. She later told a friend that she had suffered from 'measles with complications'.[16] However, the symptoms—headaches, irascibility, apathy, and nervous tension—were similar to those that preceded her 'hysteria' of eight years before. She was forced to discontinue her studies and enter the infirmary of the American Student Hostel.

The five-bed ward, with its noisy visitors, failed to soothe her headaches. She quickly pronounced the hospital abominable and begged Alice to take her home. But she had to stay there for six weeks. When she was released, she 'crept home weak as a cat.'

During the period of enforced idleness that followed, Emily sat by the French windows in her apartment watching the winter sparrows, the mattress-makers, the concierge flying out of her apartment nest at the sound of footsteps in the courtyard. Ordinary sounds became unusually interesting: a pass key turning in a lock, the door of the flat opposite swiftly opening and closing as one or another of her neighbour's lovers came and went; the landlady screaming for her cat Clarissa; an American music student practising the same notes over and over on her violin until Emily 'nearly went mad'; and at midnight every two weeks the clatter of the sewer crew pumping effluence from the apartment house through great hoses. Emily had the company of her parrot Rebecca, and probably because of her illness Alice was persuaded to consent to the purchase of another bird—this time a green parrot named 'Josephine'. However, even with her pets Emily was lonely; and the sparsely furnished apartment, with its primitive plumbing and little heat, added to her depression. When she was able to leave it she walked to the Montparnasse cemetery at the end of her street. There she sat on a bench in the winter sunshine, among the graves. She liked to go there because it was quiet.

After regaining her strength, Emily returned to the Atelier Blanche, but it was not long before she was in bed again. This time she attributed her illness to influenza caught from an Austrian student. She was back in the infirmary for another six weeks. This illness, which lingered on to early spring, was hard on Alice and 'most depressing for us both'. Emily despaired of making headway with her painting.

After the second hospitalization she had recovered sufficiently to take a month-long holiday for convalescence. Sweden was chosen, apparently so that Alice could study the Swedish school system. Cook's handled the travel arrangements, providing stopovers in Copenhagen, Hamburg, and Cologne. The two women visited public schools, where the high standard of domestic science and manual training departments impressed them, and time was passed at Langadraugh, a seaside resort where Emily took salt baths and recuperated. They also visited Emily's Vancouver friends, the 'Myrins', who now resided in Göteborg.

Emily and Alice returned to Paris in late April to find that Harry and Bridget Gibb were about to leave the city. They were not going far: the Ile-de-France village of Crécy-en-Brie, where Gibb intended to give an outdoor class in landscape painting, was only two hours from Paris by train. Emily decided to join the class at once. She loved the French countryside and was now wary of being 'cooped up in the city studios'. Above all, she wanted to study with Gibb. Her illness had made her forfeit his turn as critic at the Atelier Blanche, where the students considered him to be the best. 'Dour Harry Gibb,' she later wrote, 'had something I wanted.'

On the first of May, Alice and Emily made a day excursion from Paris to Crécy-en-Brie on the Grand Morin River. Emily was delighted by what she saw. The village was riddled with narrow cobblestone roads and winding canals. There was a sixteenth-century church, ancient mills, lindens, weeping willows, poplars, lilac, and the remnants of walled fortifications. It was arranged that when Emily returned to Crécy-en-Brie a week later, she would occupy a room with a tiny kitchen in the same house as the Gibbs. It overlooked the main street and, despite noises from the cobbled pavement, was very quiet. Alice decided to remain in Paris to continue her French lessons, but a room would be available for her on weekends.

When Emily arrived, Gibb was not there—he had been called back to Paris for a few days—but he had left instructions with his wife that Miss Carr was to begin sketching so that there would be work for him to criticize on his return. Emily chose not to paint in the quaint village. She explored instead the surrounding hills, where she found more villages, and farms with great grey stone barns and small cottages with earthen floors. These were usually the subjects of her oil sketches. But it was not only scenes for sketching that occupied her on these outings; there were also the French peasants. Their interest was attracted by Josephine, the green parrot, who would sit on the ring of Emily's sketching stool. Though unable to converse with them, Emily established a rapport by means of 'the international grin that goes so long a way', which had helped her gain the acceptance of the Indians at Ucluelet. Like them, the Ile-de-France peasants, who were even poorer, possessed dignity and a naive simplicity. Their acceptance of the very foreign Emily—they invited her into their homes, allowing her to share their simple life—gave her much satisfaction. Thus was her romantic identity with the Arcadian simplicity of those who lived on the land reinforced.

Awaiting Gibb's critique that first week, Emily had been 'sick with apprehension & nerves'. When Gibb returned from Paris, however, she found that she had worried in vain. He not only praised her colour sense but commended the way she put her paint on the canvas board. Sitting down on her stool before her easel, he took a fresh canvas and painted an entire sketch. Emily looked on, puzzled. He painted a scene that contained something more than the pastoral forms that lay before them.

It was not a copy of the woods & fields it was a realization of them. The colours were not matched. They were mixed with air. You went through space to meet reality.

Gibb had infused the scene with a quality of his own, revealing something inherent in it that was visible only to his imagination. He had given the woods and fields greater depth by juxtaposing warm colours with cool ones. That session with Gibb was a revelation for Emily. Everything before had been an ineffectual search for a technique that would express the power and feeling and visual excitement she had seen in the work of others, and that she longed to capture for herself.

Emily made progress and Gibb followed it with deep interest. His wife told her that he had never been 'so interested in any student's work'. Emily modestly thought this might have been because she was willing to destroy a sketch for the sake of experimenting, or because she worked unceasingly hard, but Gibb's interest was sincere. He told Emily that if she continued to improve she would undoubtedly become one of the great women painters of her day. Such praise gave her great joy.

Gibb and Bridget moved to St Efflam in Brittany in early June and Emily went with them. (Alice returned to Victoria.) Arriving in the lovely seaside resort before the start of the summer season, she was able to find inexpensive accommodation in Madame Pichodou's Hôtel de la Plage, a two-storey building across from the sweeping beach where the post coach stopped to change horses. The Gibbs took a suite of rooms in Madame Glass's more elegant Grand Hôtel.

With the change of environment, Emily established a new routine. By eight in the morning she was in the fields that rose behind the long beach. She worked there until noon, took lunch in the hotel, rested in her room, then prepared her materials and returned to the fields. At five o'clock she ate a packed supper, rested in the grass, did one more sketch, then returned in the dark to the hotel. Every afternoon Gibb climbed the hill to the fields behind St Efflam and gave Emily a lesson. Twice weekly he criticized her work at the hotel. His deep interest in her painting continued, as did Emily's regard for him as 'a splendid & inspiring critic'. Help also came from the more approachable Bridget Gibb, whom Gertrude Stein remembered as 'one of the pleasantest of the wives of a genius I have met'.[17] She 'read & thought & watched and had the knack of saying things' that gave Emily 'very many of the vital little sidelights on modern art.'[18]

The trio remained in St Efflam throughout the high season and into the early autumn. Emily was very happy. She had superb instruction, fresh sea air, good food, endless fields and farms to paint, the company of her two parrots, and a 'gesticulating, nodding, laughing acquaintance' with every peasant in the area.[19] 'I loved that country, and those people,' she wrote later. More important was the progress she was making under Gibb. She discovered that a painting could be more than an accurate transcription of visual fact. By using pure colours and simplifying forms, even by defying perspective, an artist could express something different. A picture could represent an artist's unique vision, an idea. To Emily this approach was thrilling. The freedom to experiment with colour, to defy the laws of form, released her from the limitations of her own mediocre draftsmanship and the drudgery of copying accurately. Once she left the bounds of conventionality there was the possibility of conveying another dimension of reality.

Emily's early attempts to do this often failed. Her juxtaposition of colours was crude, and broadly painted areas jarred with stippled patches. Frequently her bold approach was thwarted by her rigid perspective and conventional composition. While she did not yet possess the skill to explore her own vision fully, she was not without enthusiasm or a willingness to experiment. In †Autumn in France, painted while she was in St Efflam, she broke out with great exuberance, giving the hill behind the seaside village as much attention as the fields that swept before it. She did not allow the background to be lost in a haze of purple. Light fell evenly on all areas of the landscape; colour and brush strokes bound foreground to background. No longer copying the woods and fields, she had begun, like Gibb, to paint a realization of them.

Emily was anxious to see how her new style would suit the 'bigger material of the west'. She unpacked some Indian watercolour sketches she had brought with her from Canada and repainted them, incorporating 'the bigger methods' Gibb had taught her. She showed the results to Gibb. Aware that Picasso was using indigenous African art forms in his work, Gibb encouraged her experiments, assuring her that totem poles were entirely suitable subjects. This was important to Emily because her year in France was nearly over and she would soon be returning home to continue her mission of portraying the fast-disappearing Indian houses and poles.

She still had several weeks before her departure. She could have spent them with Gibb in Paris, but she had grown stale. Though she hated to leave him after four months of good work, she did.

There were several ways in which Emily could have heard of the New Zealand artist Frances Hodgkins and learned that she was at Concarneau. Her name might easily have been mentioned at the Colarossi, where, during the winter preceding Emily's arrival in Paris, Hodgkins had made a reputation as its first woman instructor. Emily could have seen Hodgkins' notice advertising her summer class at the Académie Grande-Chaumière, located next to the Colarossi.[20] Or Harry Gibb— who likely knew Hodgkins, at least by reputation—may have told Emily

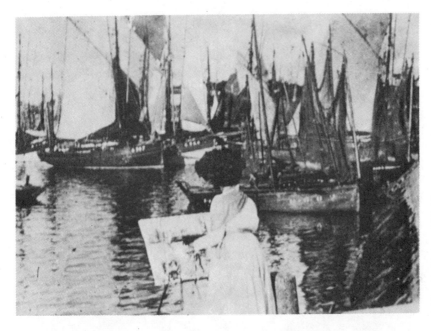

Frances Hodgkins painting in Concarneau, about 1911. Courtesy E.H. McCormick. Alexander Turnbull Library, Wellington, N.Z.

that she was teaching in Concarneau. In any case, Emily heard that there was 'a fine teacher of watercolour' summering and teaching in the Breton port. She packed her parrots in their wedge-shaped travelling boxes, gathered her work, and took the post coach and train to the much larger town of Concarneau.[21]

Years later Emily recalled that she had studied with 'an Australian woman' in Concarneau. It is curious that she never named her teacher and recorded so little about her. The opportunity for a friendship was certainly there. Emily was probably Frances Hodgkins' only student that autumn because her summer classes were over. As Hodgkins usually ate her evening meal with her students, she and Emily would have dined together in the pleasant quay-side café Hodgkins described in a letter home.[29] Over the fish soup, plates of crab, sardines, and veal, or the more exotic cock's crowns and frog's legs, the two women must have discovered that they had more in common than their plump figures, their age, their unrequited love, and their spinsterhood. They were both colonials and their painting careers paralleled one another remarkably. Frances began in the conservative parochial art community of Dunedin, New Zealand. She supported herself by teaching, painting, and illustrating and built up a local reputation with her portraits of the local Maoris. But like Victoria, Dunedin was not large enough to give her full scope. In 1901 she set out for Europe; she travelled widely on the Continent and studied in London, Cornwall, and Bushey. Then she went back to New Zealand with the intention of continuing her career. She now found its smallness and remoteness more oppressive than ever and in 1906 returned to Europe to 'learn what was being done in my chosen

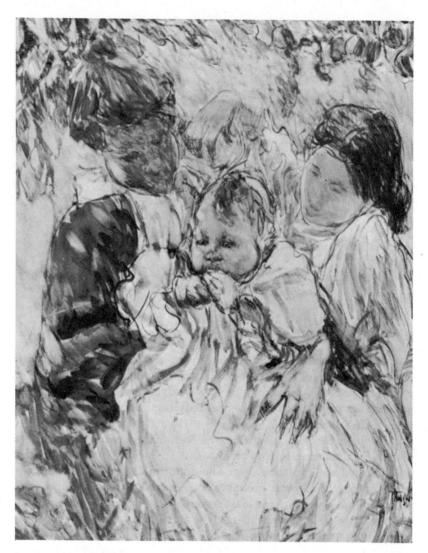

Frances
Hodgkins.
Summer,
about 1912.
Watercolour,
23 1/2 x 19 3/4.
Alexander Turn-
bull Library,
Wellington,
N.Z.

medium, and measure myself with the moderns'.[22] By 1908 she had settled in Paris, but after eighteen months she pronounced the city 'a deadly
place', where one needed 'great supplies of health & energy to face the
racket'.[23] When Emily met her, she had been living in Concarneau for
just over a year. There she had found 'the peace for which she craved, the
leisure to continue her work, cheap comfortable lodgings', and the
company of simple peasants and a few fellow artists.[24]

While these women shared similar backgrounds, were strongly out-
spoken, possessed an intuitive rather than an intellectual approach to
art, and reserved a great portion of their love for animals, they differed
on one point: loyalty to their native country. For Frances, Europe was
home and New Zealand was where she had been born. Though she had

strong family ties with her mother and sister, and possessed a somewhat romantic idea of the New Zealand Maoris (as did Emily of her Indians), these associations were fading. When Emily met her, she had turned her back on New Zealand. Europe was where she wanted to be, and in France she was beginning to establish a reputation for herself as a fine artist.

Emily hoped that the 'change of pace, teacher & medium' in Concarneau would give her work a new impetus, and it did. Concarneau was a great fishing port, the third largest in France, with many subjects to paint: boats anchored by the quay, lying on the beach with their red and grey nets swinging from their masts, or under sail in the bay. The Breton costume was another theme. Everyone wore cumbersome yellow wooden clogs and the women were clad in billowy aproned dresses and elegant lace head-dresses that rose in lattice funnels or winged out like a nun's coif. With such an abundance of sketching material, Emily probably had little desire to paint in the flat countryside surrounding the town. She lodged, as had most of Hodgkins' students, in the Grand Hôtel des Voyageurs in the centre of the new town. From there she could walk into the old fortified town in the middle of the harbour, the Ville Close, by crossing a drawbridge. On this island Emily found sail-makers in their lofts, washerwomen in open-walled wash houses, and tiny crooked cobblestoned streets that led always to the sea. Emily painted all these things under the guidance of her teacher.

An artist with 'an exuberant Late Impressionist technique', Frances Hodgkins was a brilliant watercolourist whose work displayed rhythmic spontaneity, original and imaginative colour harmonies, and superb draftsmanship.[25] Though she did not yet lean on the Fauves or the Cubists, she was aware of their existence and encouraged her students to keep an open mind towards their work. As a teacher she was 'stimulating'; some found her 'daring and courageous'.[26] She would seize a large brush and, standing well away from a student's easel, lash out with big decisive sweeps, working from the shoulder with her whole arm. 'Sometimes she let her pupils choose their own subjects, sometimes suggested something.' Criticism was sporadic, 'sometimes every day, at other times only once every three days.'[27] She insisted on only one thing: that her pupils work in watercolour.

Emily had been painting in oil since arriving in France. The change back to watercolour, the medium she used most frequently in Canada, was not retrograde. It did not mean a return to paler colours or to the academic approach of her earlier work. Under Hodgkins' guidance, Emily found that her Fauve palette could easily be obtained in this traditionally placid medium. She also found that some of Hodgkins' own colours were to her liking, particularly vert émeraude, cadmium, and French blues and yellow ochre. Colours were not all that Emily adopted from her teacher. The heavy broken line with which Hodgkins outlined her forms quickly became the structural basis for almost all Emily's Concarneau work. In *Bottle Girl, Concarneau* Emily departed radically

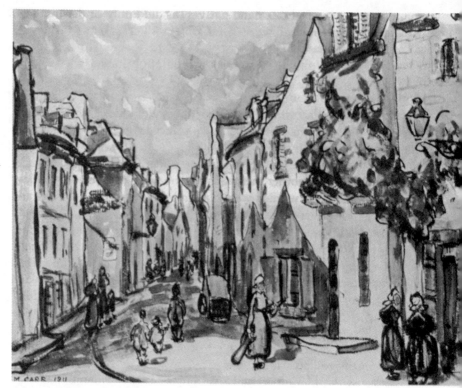

Street Scene, Brittany (Concarneau), 1911. Watercolour, 10 1/4 x 14 1/4. Collection Dr and Mrs Max Stern, Dominion Gallery, Montreal.

from the rigid perspective, the literal transcription, and the lack of unity evident in *Salish Woman Weaving*, painted just months before leaving Canada. And she was no longer hindered by the variety of brush strokes and sometimes uncertain juxtapositions of colours she had employed under Gibb. Feeling more at ease in the watercolour medium—and with Hodgkins' brilliant colours, unifying outline, unorthodox composition, and lucid style in mind—Emily painted *Brittany Coast* (showing a few boats in Concarneau's harbour) with an economy of brush stroke, a richness of colour, and an indifference to detail that reflected the influence of her teacher. She had taken the final step from the conservative camp to the modern by expressing, through colour and form, how she saw the land and sea around Concarneau.

The six weeks in the Breton port were a superb ending to Emily's fourteen-month sojourn in France. They were to be crowned by a memorable event that awaited her when she returned to Paris. After settling into the Hôtel de Chevreuse in Montparnasse, a few blocks from her former residence, she walked down the Champs Elyssés to the glass-covered Grand Palais. There she saw two of her paintings exhibited in the Salon d'Automne.

Since its inception in 1903, the Salon d'Automne had played a pioneering role in modern French painting by exhibiting the new forms of 'independent art'.[28] When, in 1905, it hung the works of Matisse, Vlaminck, Derain, Rouault, et al., they were immediately dubbed Les Fauves (the wild beasts). In this Salon of 1911, which introduced the Cubists, the furor among the press and public was similar to that of 1905. The Cubists' geometric patterns and their indifference to colour were thought to be no less outrageous than the Fauves' use of indigenous art forms and brilliant colours. Emily's name did not appear in any of the many newspapers and art journals that praised, or more frequently scorned, the contributions of the rebel Cubists. Compared with the paintings of Matisse, Jourdan, Léger, Rouault, and Vlaminck, her pictures, like most of the hundreds of other works displayed in the numerous rooms of the Salon, were unexceptionable; they would have been controversial only in the Salon of 1905.

Emily refers only vaguely to this event, but it is probable that Gibb, who was a Sociétaire, took some of her St Efflam paintings back to Paris with him in September and submitted them to the nineteen-person jury—which included John Fergusson. The acceptance of two paintings by Emily Carr—listed in the catalogue as *Le Collier* and *Le Paysage*— may well have been influenced by her two teachers. Nevertheless it was a personal triumph from which Emily would draw much satisfaction—and justification for her new style. Partly a Fauve herself, she had hung with the masters and rebels of modernism. With that accomplishment behind

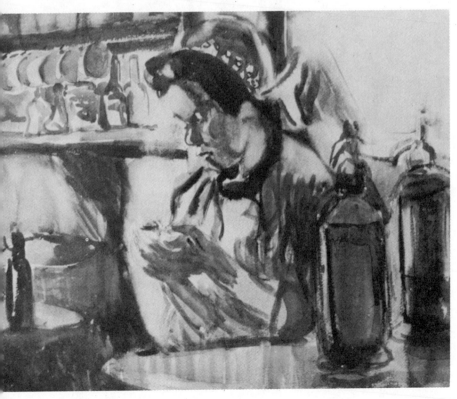

Bottle Girl, Concarneau, 1911. Watercolour, 10 3/8 x 14 1/4. Collection Dr and Mrs Max Stern, Dominion Gallery, Montreal.

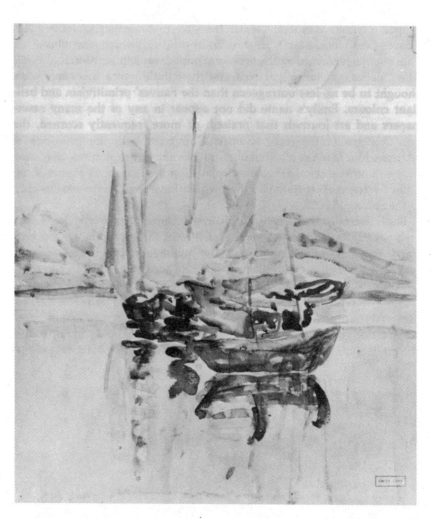

Brittany Coast,
1911. Water-
colour on paper,
12 5/8 x 11. Gift
of Major H.C.
Holmes, AGGV.

her she could face the seasickness of her voyage home, even the incom-
prehensions of her fellow Victorians, with aplomb.

Emily had other reasons to be pleased with herself. She had survived
the final months in France without Alice and without another breakdown in health. After the 'grinding plod, dampened by the dodging of illness', she had made a real advance in her painting. The sessions with
Harry Gibb had wakened her to an entirely different kind of art. But now
she was 'going back to the farthest edge of Canada', with 'all help from
art centres & art critics over'. She was proud of her breakthrough and
was prepared to show her family and fellow painters that this new art
made theirs anachronistic. Yet British Columbia 'had been proved unpaintable time & time again'. Would she, even though armed with
modernism, 'go home and drown in the unchartered sea of tremendous-
ness'?

6

Vancouver and the North

1911-1913

The products of Emily's study in France were first viewed by the group of family and friends who greeted her in Victoria. Emily remembered that those who 'had never taken much interest in my painting' reacted to it with embarrassed avoidance. 'When I unpacked my box there was dead silence among my sisters and my favourite friends.' They 'turned away and talked hard about something else.' There is nothing, she wrote, that hurts 'more than pity at your failure'.

Emily gave no public viewing of her work in Victoria. After spending the Christmas holiday with her family, she returned to Vancouver. She could not relocate in her old Granville Street studio, which Ann Batchelor had given up and a magazine distributor now occupied, nor did she return to her previous unbearable boarding-house living. Fresh from the ateliers of France, she now wanted to live and work in a studio.

While looking for a landlord tolerant of both animals and art students, Emily stayed in the West End home of Statira Frame, an artist and the mother of one of her former pupils, Molly. It was a pleasant and convenient arrangement. She spent the mornings painting with Statira in her attic studio. Evenings were passed sitting around the fireplace, where she entertained the family with stories of her experiences in France.[1] During the course of her three-week stay, Statira's husband William taught Emily how to make picture frames and Emily taught Statira much of what she had learned in France. Her student was most willing to be tutored. Statira gladly discarded her academic approach and adopted Emily's indifference to detail and her Fauve palette. By the time Emily had found a studio on the second floor of a rather small building across the Granville Bridge, at 1465 Broadway Street West, she had made her first conversion to the modern school.

Emily moved into her new quarters on the first of February 1912. By the end of the next month she was ready to stage a comprehensive exhibition of her new paintings. Seventy watercolours and oils, most of them painted in Brittany and all done in France, covered the walls of her Broadway atelier on Monday the twenty-fifth of March. Public curiosity, aroused by an advance notice in the *Province*, which assured its readers that the exhibition would be interesting, brought sixty people to her studio.[2] Two days later the showing was called 'a great success' by the *Saturday Sunset*, which reported that viewers were 'most enthusiastic over the "New School" in art'.[3] The *Province* followed up its pre-opening coverage by sending a reporter to Emily's studio to interview her. Excited, and apparently flattered, by the response of the public and the press, Emily chattered enthusiastically. She made it known from the beginning that she now aligned herself with those who, by the use of 'pure colour, more light' and 'a bold use of line . . . and an indifference to detail', were 'seeking the bigger things in nature'. In the studios of Paris, she told the reporter, there was 'a dissatisfaction with the greens and browns and actuality of a mere copy of nature.' By a proper juxtaposition of colours, an artist could get an effect of light that would reveal many things in nature never seen by the average person. 'A picture should be more than meets the eye of the ordinary observer, who sees only what he has been in the habit of looking for.'[4] Emily had assimilated not only the style, but also the vocabulary, of her teachers in France.

The reporter was startled by 'the riot of colour exhibited on the numerous half-yards of canvas.' The blues were 'so very blue, the yellows so unmitigated, the reds so aggressive, and the greens so verdant.' He did not understand her art, nor did he command the vocabulary to discuss it. Yet he justified Miss Carr's work to the public by acknowledging that her paintings had been hung in the Paris Salon and that she had 'met with the most favourable criticism from distinguished masters' in the French capital.[5] These accomplishments gave her work credibility and made it deserving of respect.

Emily was surprised and pleased by the interest in her exhibition. Some did not like her work; indeed, many viewers had gasped when they first encountered it. But several of her paintings were sold and students signed up for lessons.[6] The event, which introduced Fauvism to Vancouver, certainly did not elicit the violent response given Roger Fry's Post-Impressionist exhibition at London's Grafton Galleries two years earlier, but this could have been because fewer people in Vancouver really cared about art. Conservative painters like Grace Judge, who religiously adhered to the English landscape tradition, commented on how 'violently modern' Miss Carr had gone.[7] Yet Emily's advanced work did not mark for them the end of the old order of painting, as Fry's exhibition had done for English artists. Emily had been considered an oddity for some time, and no one was surprised that she had attached herself to this new mode of painting, in which they had no interest. There was only one exception to what might be called the passively respectful response to her solo exhibition. Nine days after it opened, an anonymous letter appeared in the columns of the *Province*, with the heading 'Against French Art'. Its author took umbrage with what Emily had said in the newspaper interview, as well as with the paintings that had crowded the walls of her studio. The major complaint had to do with Miss Carr's 'Vanity' in thinking she could 'eclipse the Almighty' by producing 'bizarre work' that was thought to be 'more satisfactory than nature itself'. Miss Carr 'had shown no inconsiderable talent in depicting the local scenery' before she had gone to France, and 'had she continued in these lines she might have become one of those of whom British Columbia could speak with pride.' The author regretted that she had now 'given up her inspiration' and exhibited 'nothing but the work of an excited and vitiated imagination.'[8]

Emily never took criticism lightly. If she had been waiting to spring upon the purveyors of conservatism, or those who were startled by her new work, or who had not provided the compliments she wished to hear, she now had an opportunity. Five days after the letter appeared, she struck back, using the same column:

> . . . Your correspondent states that the object of the new movement is to 'eclipse the work of the Almighty by the production of bizarre work', he is wrong, and has not even grasped the smallest principle of it. Art is art, nature is nature, you cannot improve on it. . . . Pictures should be inspired by nature, but made in the soul of the artist, no two individualities could behold the same thing and express it alike, either in words or in painting; it is the soul of the individual that counts. Extract the essence of your subject and paint yourself into it; forget the little petty things that don't count; try for the bigger side.
>
> The poor mere copyist has no chance, he is too busy worrying over the number of leaves on his tree, he forgets the big grand character of the whole, and the something that speaks, that vital something with no name he overlooks altogether though he may have exactly matched its colours locally, he has not allowed for the light and sunshine that is the whole glorious making of it. He has tried for the 'look' but forgotten the 'feel'.
>
> Contrary to my having 'given up my inspirations', I have only just found them, and I have tasted the joys of the new. I am a Westerner and I am going to extract all that I can to the best of my small ability out of the big glorious west. The new ideas are big and they fit this big land. As for the critics let them have their say. I do not say mine is the only way to paint. I only say it's the way that appeals to me; to people lacking imagination it could not appeal. With the warm kindly criticism of some of the best men in Paris still ringing in my ears, why should I bother over criticisms from those whose ideals and views have been stationary for the past twenty years? When the 'Paris Salon' has accepted and hung well two of my pictures, why be otherwise than amused at the criticisms of one who gives no name. . . .[9]

Emily concluded by extending a hearty invitation to anyone interested to come to her studio every Friday evening, beginning on the twelfth of April, to see the new work that gave her such joy.

This letter provided Emily with a chance to explain the intentions of the new school in her own words and gave her exhibition additional publicity, but in spite of the brave front of her response, she was hurt by the open letter, and by other unrecorded comments that presumably echoed its viewpoint. She was, of course, naïve if she expected Vancouver to provide sophisticated viewers who were willing to embrace the new and discard what was for them standard and orthodox. She had seen from the example of Gibb and the works of the Cubists, which had sent the critics to their battle stations the previous fall, that even in Paris the innovators had been criticized. Though she may have called these things to mind, her memory of the response to her exhibition was that it 'nearly broke my heart'.

The criticism might not have cut so deep had Emily not already felt slighted by another sector of the community, the Gordon Neighbourhood School for Girls. During her sojourn in France she had been replaced as instructor there by Margaret Wake, and was not rehired when she returned. She felt that her modern style had something to do with this. Though it is unlikely that the Misses Gordon would have relieved Miss Wake in the middle of the school year, replacing her with the less congenial Miss Carr, it appears that they were 'most disapproving of her new style'.[10] Whether or not they conveyed their disapproval to Emily, she had expected to be reappointed, and when she was not she felt slighted.

There were also difficulties with the hanging committee of the British Columbia Society of Fine Arts. Emily was a founding member and had been a regular contributor to exhibitions since its inception in 1909. She had already shown four of her new works at the Studio Club's 1912 spring show in March, but the Society was a conservative group, more concerned with standards than expression, and when she submitted ten pictures to the hanging committee for its spring exhibition in April of the same year, two were rejected by the jury. Emily responded by withdrawing all of her paintings and by writing a 'nasty' letter to the organization resigning her membership.[11] She continued to contribute works to the Studio Club, appearing in their autumn show that October, but it would be many years before she would be found among the ranks of the Society's exhibitors.

It is difficult to assess how seriously these rebuffs affected her. Certainly she was not without support: Statira Frame was a convert; Margaret Wake and Wake's life-long artist-companion, Ann Batchelor, were sympathetic; Emily's Friday-evening soirées *were* attended, presumably by sympathizers; and she did have students. Nevertheless her later autobiographical writings make of this period one of rejection. After 1912 she became highly sensitive to newspaper reviews, calling them 'newspaper slop',[12] and was wary of almost everyone, however sympathetic or interested, who viewed her work.

In spite of these distractions, Emily resumed the life-style of her former years in Vancouver: teaching art to children, acquiring more animals for her menagerie, visiting her sisters in Victoria and Sophie Frank on the North Vancouver Indian Reserve, and devoting what time was left to her painting. Never very far from her mind, during the winter and spring of 1912, was the challenge of applying her new technique to the totem poles and Indian houses of northern British Columbia. With the coming of summer, she made plans to visit Kwakiutl, Haida, and Tsimshian villages in northern British Columbia. She found out all she could about the availability of transportation and accommodation in remote areas. To ease transportation costs, she probably obtained free passage on the vessels and trains of the newly constructed Grand Trunk Pacific Railway.[13] To ensure independence, she equipped herself with a portable easel and camp stool, a bedroll of blankets, and a good supply of canned rations. After subletting her studio for six weeks to E. Wyly Grier, the Toronto portraitist, Emily and Billie boarded, in early July, a Grand Trunk Pacific vessel in Vancouver harbour.[14] The trip now before her was to be the most ambitious of any she had yet undertaken.

Once again Emily travelled to Alert Bay. There she made watercolour sketches of the totems and houses along the boardwalk and sketched in the cemetery at the south end of the village. She then asked William Halliday, the Scottish Indian agent, to take her and a young Indian girl (whom she likely befriended through her missionary hosts) on one of his visits to the less-frequented villages in the area. She travelled in his gas launch to the remote Kwakiutl villages of Tsatsisnukwomi, Mammlikoola, Karlukwees, and Guysadoms. Following this major sidetrip, she boarded the Grand Trunk Pacific steamer at Alert Bay and disembarked the following day at Port Essington at the mouth of the Skeena River. There she was met by her niece Emily English, whose husband managed the B.C. Packer's Balmoral Cannery on the north shore of the Ecstall River, near Port Essington. After spending about a week with her niece, Emily boarded the stern-wheeler, *Skeena*, and travelled 180 miles inland on the treacherous river to the white settlement of Hazelton, the distributing point for the Omineca gold fields. From there she made excursions to the Indian villages of Hagwilget across the river and Kispiox, further north on the Kispiox River. She then returned to the coast, travelling down the Skeena on *The Islander*, a paddle-wheel steamer, as far as Skeena Crossing (a point from which she had access to the Tsimshian village of Kitseguecla). There she boarded a train, and after making a stop at Kitwanga on the south bank of the Skeena, continued to Prince Rupert, the terminus. The steamer *Prince John* took her from Prince Rupert across Hecate Strait to the Queen Charlotte Islands, where she made the five-day tourist round trip, beginning at Masset in the north and sailing down the east coast of the Islands to Jedway in the south.[15] Not satisfied that she had seen enough, and not having had an opportunity to visit the more remote villages, she left the *Prince John* at Skidegate. There she found an Indian guide willing to take her by launch to the villages of Cumshewa on the north shore of Cumshewa Inlet, Skedans on the east coast of Louise Island, and Tanoo on Tanoo Island. From Skidegate she also travelled across Skidegate Inlet to the deserted village of Haina on Maude Island and through the narrow Skidegate channel to lovely Cha-atl, within sound of the breakers from the open ocean to the west. Returning to the northern coast of Graham Island, she made her base in the Indian village of Old Masset; from there she crossed Masset Harbour by canoe to Yan village on the west side and Ka-yang village on the east. She then travelled back to Prince Rupert on the *Prince John*, and sailed direct to Vancouver. She had been away for six weeks.

It was a momentous journey. Willing to leave the routes of the Grand Trunk Pacific's trains and steamers, to travel by canoe or gas launch, to sleep in a vacant schoolhouse or on the beach, Emily discovered villages she had never dreamed existed: some hung deep with moss, grown over with bracken, salal, and beach grass; others filled with weather-silvered totem poles and broad-beamed community houses; still others hugging white clam-shelled beaches or lost in dark green second-growth vegetation; dilapidated villages void of life except for a few old people too feeble to work in the fish canneries or on the fishing boats; and modern villages with gasoline street lamps, a brass band, native policemen, and baptized children. She found that the Indians too were diverse. Some were eager to adopt the ways of the white man, while others clung to what remained of their tradition. There were rich and poor Indians, the prosperous and the broken. Some were friendly, edging so close to her easel that her movements were hampered; others were hostile to the intrusive white. The Haida were known to treat newcomers with the greatest courtesy. When Emily was in Old Masset, she found the Indians kind and patient. She was taken in a canoe across Masset Harbour to Yan by an Indian woman, accompanied by her two children, who waited motionlessly in one of the deserted longhouses while Emily raced to sketch the poles before they were completely engulfed by the rolling mist.

On the other hand, the Tsimshian of the Skeena River greatly resented the white man. While they occasionally recounted legends to Emily, and 'crooned the tribal song or translated bits of history from their totem poles',[16] on the whole they were suspicious of white intruders, including Emily. Sometimes she met with 'surly behaviour' and twice she was greeted with 'a very threatening attitude and told to leave the village'.[17] The Tsimshian not only minded her intrusion but 'they were afraid that I was actually stealing the things that I was painting—the door of the house, the totem pole, or the gateway; that I was transferring it bodily to my paper and that it would disappear when I left.'[18] With 'a little tact & jollying', she could usually put them at their ease. She took care to let them observe her work, often making a duplicate sketch and giving it to them; before she departed from each village she held a little exhibition. (Some Indians left a potlatch to attend.) The Indians appreciated this courtesy and loved to look at her pictures 'right side and wrong'.[19]

The hostility Emily encountered in the villages of the Upper Skeena only strengthened her desire to make the white man more appreciative and understanding of the Indian culture. She knew that the Indians had no written language, that their totem carvings were their only permanent mode of expression. Seeing them rotting, being used for firewood, being destroyed by natives who were ashamed of their former 'paganistic' ways, she became more convinced than ever that it was important to record them.

Emily's dedication and determination were constantly put to the test. Camp life was often crude and uncomfortable. There was much 'weary tramping' along slippery slug-covered wooden planks, through head-high patches of stinging nettles and dense undergrowth. 'You have got to hold your nose against the smell of rotten fish, and you've got to have the "creeps" '—occasioned by nights of pitch darkness and queer noises when she 'hugged up to Billie's shaggy coat' and took comfort from the beat of his heart. Yet the difficulties were unavoidable and had their reward. Years later she would write rhapsodically of 'the pride of the Indian in his ancestors, and the pinch of the cold, raw damp of the west coast, and the smell and flavour of the wood smoke, and the sting of it in your eyes, and the awful torment of the mosquitoes, and the closeness of mother earth and the lonely brooding silence of the vast west'.[20]

It was on this trip that Emily made friends with Clara and William Russ, Haidas of Skidegate whom she wrote about in *Klee Wyck* as 'Louisa and Jimmie'.[21] In many ways the Russes were 'model' Indians. Their families were among the first to be baptized on the Queen Charlotte Islands. They were moderately prosperous and spoke good English; though influenced by the white settlers to the point of emulation, they were nonetheless proud of their Indian heritage. Emily travelled with them to villages accessible from Skidegate by boat. Ideal companions and guides and attentive hosts, they had endless patience, never urged her to hurry, and were always helpful. William erected a canopy when it rained so that Emily could continue working. He cleared the bush from around the base of the poles so that the lower figures were exposed for drawing. And once he caught a devil fish to break the monotony of Emily's canned rations. The Russes were not only accommodating guides; they also tutored Emily in many Indian customs. In the evenings, while sitting around a campfire in a deserted village, they would tell what she later called 'ghost stories'—legends relating to the carvings on the poles. Heard in these surroundings, with coffins perched on the tops of mortuary columns nearby and with poles leaning over her tent, these tales 'seemed very real'.

Emily learned on this trip how closely the Indians were linked not only to their traditions but to nature itself: their lives were regulated by the tides and seasons as well as by the myths that surrounded their guardian spirits. For her, an outsider, nature and tradition were memorably combined in 'the great stillness, the solemn old grey poles towering above the

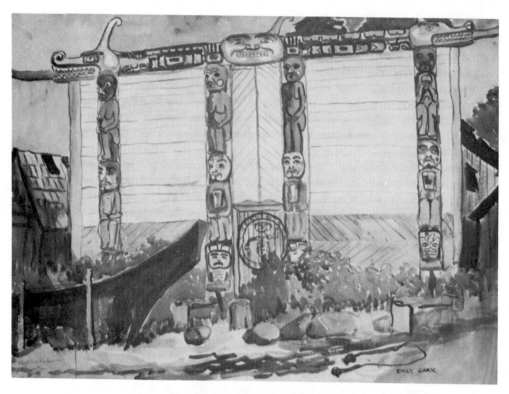

(ABOVE) *Tsatsisnukwomi Tribe, Klawatsis*, 1912.
Watercolour, 22 3/8 x 30 3/8. VAG.

(BELOW) Kwakiutl Village of Tsatsisnukwomi. (Note Emily's painting on the easel in the right-hand corner.) A photograph probably taken by Emily, 1912. BCPM.

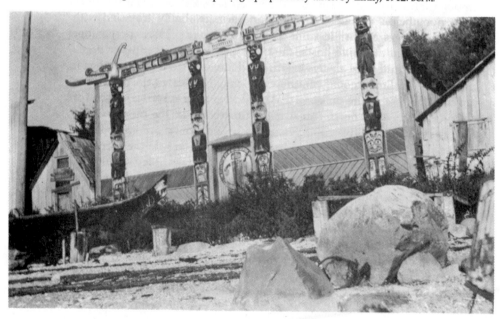

tent, the shorter mortuary columns crowded with their crested coffins, the water softly lapping the pebbly beach, & the sullen roar of the distant surf.' In these deserted villages she was able to experience the wholeness that she sought all her life: everything was part of everything else.

While Emily spent much of her time during those six weeks winning friends among the Indians, she was not dependent solely on them for transportation, lodging, and companionship. At the beginning of her trip the federal Indian agent provided transportation to the more remote Kwakiutl villages around Alert Bay. On the Skeena trip she enjoyed the hospitality of Emily English; further up the river, at Kispiox, she stayed with missionaries, the Reverend and Mrs Lee. During her first week on the Queen Charlotte Islands, she travelled in relative comfort on the *Prince John*. At Skidegate she stayed in the Methodist missionary's house, with a farm girl for company and 'to avoid scandal'.[22] When she travelled with the Russes to Cumshewa, Skedans, and Tanoo, she was accompanied by the missionary's pretty daughter, who was replaced by the farm girl when she went to Cha-atl. At Masset she had been assisted by acquaintances of another niece, Lillian Nicholles, who had taught school there the previous year. There were probably other whites who helped and accompanied her, but Emily does not mention them. Her later oral and written recollections seldom mention that she had relatives in the north, or that she was dependent on missionaries and government officials for her accommodation and transportation. Nowhere does she say that her major travel expenses were absorbed by the Grand Trunk Pacific Railway Company. Emily became well known for having lived among the Indians, for having made her travels without financial assistance, and she chose not to qualify this reputation.

The artistic side of this expedition took an unexpected turn. Emily soon found that it was impossible to paint the 'bigger, freer work' she had done in France. In the interests of her objective—to record all the poles and community houses in northern British Columbia—she had to work accurately. She 'stuck religiously to the facts',[23] doing what she had learned not to do and what she had lectured against—painting what she saw rather than how she felt about what she saw. The need for accuracy, and the hurried conditions under which she worked—private boat hire was not cheap, so speed was essential—seldom allowed her to go beyond mere recording. She often depicted a pole in isolation, or added a few trees in silhouette. Her field sketches of village sites, like *Tsatsisnukwomi Tribe, Klawatsis*, are more complete, incorporating logs, rocks, and foliage, but there is little relationship of foreground to background, as there is in her St Efflam oils and Concarneau watercolours. Gone was the chance to experiment. 'Working for history' meant the 'big' statement she had longed to make was not appropriate—though she later admitted that on this occasion she 'hugged the historical side too close'.

The recording was not always easy. It was usually impossible to capture all the figures on a sixty- or seventy-foot pole from a single location. Emily would beat down the beach grass or salal at the base of the pole

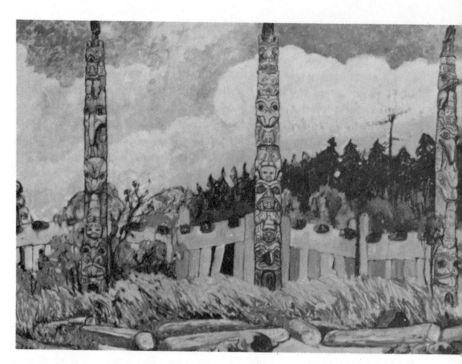

Tanoo, Q.C. Islands, 1913. Oil on canvas, 43 1/2 x 67 1/4. PABC.

and paint the lower figures at close range. Moving from one spot to another made it difficult to maintain the proportions of the figures but enabled her to represent all of them. A photograph of Emily painting at Tanoo shows head-high beach grass, while her canvas of the same scene exposes the poles virtually to their base. She had not only recorded the sections of poles crowded by foliage, but occasionally reconstructed a house from its remains. Because she was making a historical record, she felt she had to do more than capture the present; she sometimes had to reconstruct the past.

Emily believed that in recording the entire pole she was exceeding the capabilities of the camera. Yet that instrument, which she publicly denounced as a soulless machine, was of great assistance to her. Though she denied ever working from photographs, the ones she took or had taken for her on this trip enabled her to check the accuracy of her often-hurried watercolour sketches when making finished oils and watercolours in the studio.[24]

While the necessity for speed and accuracy left little time for experimentation, Emily was satisfied with what she accomplished on her 1912 trip. She had set out to record as many poles as possible. By the end of six weeks she had amassed a large collection of paintings and sketches of poles and longhouses from the Skeena River Valley, the Queen Charlotte Islands, and the remote villages around Alert Bay.

When Emily returned from the north in early September, the newspapers welcomed her home. One said that it was 'a matter for congratulations that an artist of Miss Carr's ability should have undertaken to make a record for posterity of these things of grandeur, of an age that is passing.'[25] It was hoped that she would once again 'allow her friends the privilege of seeing sketches of some of the remote corners of the north-land.'[26] The Vancouver public did not have to wait long. Emily contributed several field sketches, as well as a few finished works, to the Studio Club's exhibition that October. Her 'most weird and wonderful creations of Kispiox and Ktsukit [sic] villages' were thought to be 'perhaps the most striking series in the hall.'[27] Another viewer noted that Miss Carr's paintings scarcely fitted into the category of ordinary pictures; they 'might well find a place in a public gallery, where they would be a valuable memorial' to the Indians.[28]

Emily, of course, agreed. After all, she had made her collection 'for history'. But there were no public galleries in Vancouver to purchase or even exhibit her collection. Furthermore, there is no evidence that the Grand Trunk Pacific purchased any of her work. In Victoria, however, the provincial government was adding a new wing to its parliament buildings that would contain a Legislative Library and, it was said, an art gallery. Emily envisaged a place for her work there and wrote that autumn to Henry Esson Young, Minister of Education and Provincial Secretary, who was responsible for the new building. She told him that she had been working for some time on a collection of paintings of Indian

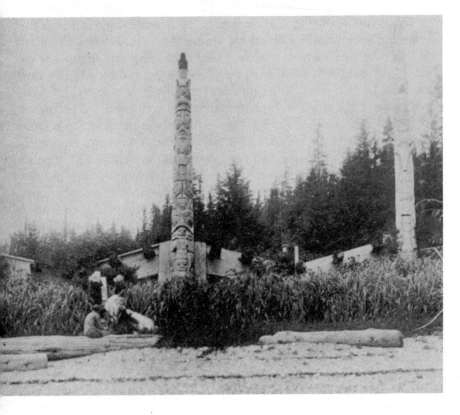

Emily Carr at Tanoo, Queen Charlotte Islands, with Clara Russ and the missionary's daughter, 1912. BCPM.

totem poles and villages of British Columbia. Since the Indians were no longer carving poles, she considered her collection valuable. She hoped her paintings might find a home in the room she understood was being set aside for pictures in the new building. She also asked for financial assistance 'to complete the work as the expense of travelling round . . . off the beaten track is heavy.'[29]

Emily had written to the right man. Young had greatly encouraged the collection of ethnological material for the province since 1907, when he had taken office in the Richard McBride government. He had asked government employees in the north to report village sites and had used the services of Dr C.F. Newcombe—a semi-retired doctor, botanist, and ethnologist—who, being well acquainted with the northern Indian villages, was able to acquire a fine collection of Indian curios and totem poles for the Provincial Museum. But Young looked upon the painting of artefacts rather differently from collecting them. Miss Carr's work, he felt, belonged in an art gallery, not a museum. Though only a month before receiving Emily's letter he had told the Island Arts and Crafts Society that plans had been drawn up for the inclusion of an art gallery in the new library, he now assured Emily that it would be 'some time' before it would be established.[30] About her request for financial support, he said nothing. Curious to know what this woman had accumulated, and thinking of a possible contributor to the collection he had already begun for the gallery, he asked Dr Newcombe to call on her and assess the anthropological value of her work.

Several weeks later, in mid-December, Newcombe travelled to Vancouver and visited Emily's Broadway studio. Apart from a few oil paintings, the work he viewed was, as Emily told him, 'still in the sketch condition'.[31] Yet Newcombe must have been impressed by what he saw because he bought three of her pictures for himself. Moreover, he compared some of her work with photographs and concluded, according to Emily, that the 'sketches gave a clearer interpretation than the photographs'. In one case he found, to her delight, that his own photograph, taken after Emily's drawing had been made, did not show all the pole. Emily, of course, had painted it in its entirety. Newcombe gave her the impression that he greatly appreciated her work—and he probably did. Yet about its suitability for the new library, he felt somewhat different. In his report on 'Miss Carr's collection of paintings of Indian Totem Poles' of January 1913, made to the curator of the Provincial Museum, Francis Kermode, he said that in most cases the carvings had been 'faithfully drawn, and would be of use in obtaining information as to clan legends and for illustrating this feature of Indian characteristics.' Her drawings of the poles on the Skeena River—where few good, large-sized photographs had been taken—were of 'especial value'. However, the paintings were 'too brilliant and vivid to be true to the actual conditions of the coast villages.' Moreover, the artist had used 'no standard of comparative size'; a short Haida burial pole appeared as large in one picture as a much taller house pole in another. In very few instances did she in-

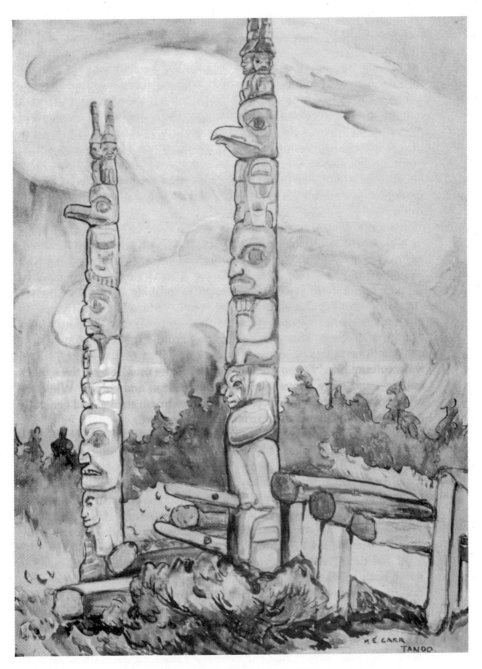

Tanoo, 1912. Watercolour, 30 5/16 x 21 7/8. VAG.

clude any Indians—only the poles and some of the houses. It bothered Newcombe that if the paintings were viewed at close range, one could see that the materials used had been 'laid on with a heavy hand' (shades of her French training!); only at a distance did he find that the colours blended and the roughness vanished. Without recommending that the government purchase any of the work, he suggested Miss Carr as a painter of decorative wall panels similar to those used in the museums of Brooklyn and New York City. 'If the colours could be toned down in new copies and if certain details of size and accuracy were corrected under proper supervision', and if an attempt was made 'to throw more life into the scenes illustrated', then Newcombe seemed to favour her engagement to decorate the new library or to finish a set of pictures for its walls.[32]

It is not known whether Emily received a copy of Newcombe's report or was informed by him of its contents. However, after the anthropologist's visit substantial changes became evident in her finished oils and watercolours. She used a much larger format for such canvases as †House Front-Gold Harbour—perhaps to provide a suitable size for decorative wall paintings. She frequently added Indian figures to otherwise deserted villages (an attempt to 'throw more life' into scenes illustrated?). Trees, logs, and beach grass around the poles convey their realistic proportions. Compared with her summer field sketches, studio watercolours like *Tanoo are more controlled—usually by a thick bold outline—and more conventional in composition and colour. While the oil paintings possess stronger colours, a looser brush stroke, and generally no outline, they are unadventurous in composition.

The friendly sympathy of Newcombe may have led Emily to believe that a commission would be forthcoming, but none came. However, a friendship with him developed. Through the winter of 1912-13, and for many years thereafter, she made use of his considerable knowledge of the Indians; and it was probably through him that she met and corresponded with other anthropologists, such as G.T. Emmons and Philip Drucker.[33] She also received a commission from Newcombe personally and became friendly with his son William.

At the time Newcombe viewed her paintings, Emily had decided to move back to Victoria. During the previous summer the Carr property had been divided into lots; some were put on the market and five, including the Carr house, were divided among the sisters. By Christmas, Emily had drawn up plans for an apartment building on her lot, which faced Simcoe Street and was just around the corner from the Carr house on Government Street. She had continued teaching during her last year in Vancouver, but without the Gordon School appointment and with the beginning of the pre-war depression effectively reducing the number of her students, she had more time for painting. As well as working hard translating her summer sketches and watercolours into finished paintings, she deepened her knowledge of the Indians by frequenting the City of Vancouver Museum, where she studied their displayed artefacts, and by reading ethnological works such as Charles Hill-Tout's *The Home of the Salish and Dené*.[34] When she could not find what she wanted to know in books, she wrote to her new friend Dr Newcombe in Victoria. This intense period of painting and study culminated in April 1913.

That month Emily rented the Drummond Hall on Pender Street and held a week-long exhibition of her Indian paintings. It was tiring. She not only attended the exhibition each day, from one in the afternoon until ten in the evening, but gave two public lectures. Nearly two hundred sketches, watercolours, and oils lined the walls of the rooms. They represented fourteen years of Emily's excursions: to Ucluelet in 1898 and 1905; to Alaska in 1907, where she was first inspired to record the totem poles; to Alert Bay and Campbell River; to interior villages like Lytton, visited before her French sojourn; and finally her ambitious northern trip of 1912. Viewers were doubtless overwhelmed, not just by the quantity of these works but by their exotic subject matter: the rich variety of totem poles that included the chunky stacked figures of the Tsimshian, the dramatic poles of the Kwakiutl, and the more simply carved ones of the Haida; paintings of 'dead boxes' nestled in cedar trees around Ucluelet, of natives, and of broad-planked, broken-down community houses. Attached to many of them were such mysterious place-names as Cha-atl, Etedsu, and Kispiox.

Paralleling the diverse artistic styles of West Coast Indian art was the stylistic development of the artist who had recorded it. Viewers saw minute watercolour paintings of the Songhees Reserve, timid pencil sketches of the villages around Ucluelet—all done when Emily had been uncertain how to record her subject. The monotony of the highly romantic watercolour interpretations of totems at Sitka and the smoke-filled villages of Alert Bay and Campbell River, painted after England, was occasionally relieved by the red skirt of a Salish woman weaving—an example of Emily's flirtation with brighter colours. Yet the real break with her traditional training was only evident in her works painted after France: the watercolour field sketches—wild in colour and bold in composition; the studio oils—immense in size and rich in thick, vivid daubs of pigment.

For those whose interest was quickened by what they saw, Emily provided an explanation of her mission. The lecture combined what she had gleaned from the pages of Hill-Tout's book and learned from Newcombe with what she herself had experienced. In her 'Lecture on Totems' Emily discussed the technique of carving and erecting the poles, the legends they expressed and the Indians who carved them, as well as her associations with the inhabitants of the villages she had visited. Her talk showed a deep understanding of the Indian people and an even deeper empathy with them. She had, of course, learned the elementary facts of their customs from books, but she now knew and could relate something more than the facts. She spoke of the Indians' 'sensitivity to ridicule', their 'quiet dignity', and their ability to read a person's character quickly; of their attachment to guardian spirits, to nature, and to their old ways—a subject that would be eloquently woven into her later *Klee Wyck* stories. She was probably nervous and in all likelihood read her lecture. Nothing emerged of the storyteller who had so thoroughly entertained her English friends. The theme of the lecture, and indeed the reason for the paintings and their exhibition, was stated in the opening lines: 'These poles are fast becoming extinct; every year sees some of their number fall, rotted with age; & bought & carried off to museums in various parts of the world others alas are burned down for firewood.'[35]

Only the *Province* reviewed the exhibition and lecture, but it did so with great enthusiasm. Nothing was said of Emily's artistic development, culminating in the vivid style that had so startled some visitors to her spring exhibition a year earlier. Without commenting on the artistic merits of the show, the reviewer called it 'a very valuable record of a passing race'.[36]

'A passing race.' Emily had used that same phrase in her letter to Dr Young: the totems she painted were 'real art treasures of a passing race'.[37] Already some of the things she had recorded were gone. Emily spoke in her lecture of the move of the Songhees from Victoria Harbour and of one small canvas of the former reserve that showed 'a phase of Indian life which has now passed into history'.[38] Almost that same month the Kitsilano band was removed from the south shore of Burrard Inlet to the more remote Howe Sound. As a record of the 'vanishing' Indian, the exhibition could not have been more timely.

This was Emily's farewell to Vancouver. Just weeks after the exhibition closed, her studio-apartment was approaching completion. She moved 'down to Victoria—for good'.

7

Chrysalis

1913-1927

Running a small apartment house seemed like a splendid idea at first. The building and its location had many attractions: two rentable suites to pay taxes, mortgage, domestic help, and living expenses; an apartment, accessible by a back stairway, containing a studio with a great north window; a large private garden behind; sister Alice's schoolhouse and the Carr family house within a stone's throw; Beacon Hill Park at the property's edge; and the Dallas Road cliffs and beach within a few blocks. Everything would be just right for the artist-rentier.

The construction of the Simcoe Street apartment house began in the spring of 1913. Emily had strong ideas about the building. To maximize the size of the back garden she insisted, against Edith's advice, on building close to the street. She had drawn up her own plans, but the architect-builder found them impractical. He and Emily disagreed repeatedly and construction faltered. It was not until the autumn that a classified advertisement reading, 'Flat, furnished or unfurnished, heated, three rooms, bath, garden', appeared in the *Colonist* to launch Emily on her career as a landlady.[1]

'Hill House', as Emily called the apartment because of its proximity to Beacon Hill (the name 'House of All Sorts' was a later literary invention), began its life at a bad time. Strikes, high unemployment, and the flagging economy of 1913 were only a prelude to the depression and inflation that lasted through most of the Great War years. Apartment owners like Emily could charge only minimal rent—if there were tenants to be found. Adjustments had to be made. In 1914 Emily divided her upstairs apartment into suites; in 1916 she converted them into rooms for boarders; and in 1918 she moved out of the building altogether, putting up a tent for herself in the back garden and cooking in a lean-to. But even with these adaptations, Emily found that the rents from her suites and rooms did not cover expenses. To save money she not only took on the job of landscaping the small front garden, but planted a large vegetable and fruit garden in the vacant lot adjoining hers so that she could have produce to sell. From 1915 she raised chickens and rabbits, also for profit.

Life in 1913 was no easier for the rest of the Carr family. Clara's husband, Jack, had left her and she had to manage on her own.[2] Alice was living in quarters she had built onto her one-room school on St Andrew's Street. She later found a position as governess-teacher with the family of the architect Alexander Hennell, newly arrived from England, and lived with the Hennells until 1922, leaving her schoolhouse to Edith and Lizzie, who moved into it in 1914. They returned to the Carr house a year later and became landladies themselves. With no money for maintenance, they let the house become shabby and the garden, which had been the pride of Richard Carr, grow wild. Lizzie, a trained physiotherapist, found employment in Seattle at the Children's Orthopedic Hospital; during the war she worked in Victoria at the Resthaven Private Hospital. Edith, who had given lessons at home in 'applied arts', discontinued her teaching but bred canaries for a small profit until her death in 1919.

The trying circumstances of the Carr women were far from uncommon during the 1913 depression and the Great War, which brought about the financial collapse of many established Victoria families. Few women were equipped to earn their living or were prepared to take even low-paying positions in banks and stores or with the government. The Carr sisters had been confident and comfortable on the $50,000 their father had left them, but Dick's and Emily's illnesses and two depressions had depleted their capital. Their kind guardian-lawyer, James Lawson, was blamed for the reduction of their inheritance, but in fact it was mostly due to the vagaries of health and market cycles. Their only asset, the tract of James Bay land left to them by their father, dropped in value during the depression. They were now among the genteel poor of Victoria.

Emily hoped that the occasional sale of a painting might add to her rental income. Shortly after moving into her apartment, she held an open-house exhibition in the studio, and in October she showed nine watercolours and oils painted in France and northern British Columbia at the Island Arts and Crafts exhibition. The reaction was mixed, though Emily's memory of it was not. A 'great many people' came to her open house and some of her pictures sold. Dr Newcombe himself bought eight or nine, and Mrs Dennis Harris and Mrs Hamilton Burns, the daughters of Sir James Douglas and Senator W.J. Macdonald, urged the provincial government to buy one or more of her canvases.[3] The open house had been mostly for friends, but the Arts and Crafts exhibition that followed put Emily's work squarely before the Victoria press and public.

The *Victoria Times* noncommittally reported that Miss Carr's pictures of totems were 'highly decorative' and attracted 'a great deal of comment'. The French pictures elicited a more positive reaction: 'excellent in composition', they showed 'the artist's post-impressionist style in its least aggressive form'.[4] The *Colonist's* reviewer made no secret of disliking

Emily's pictures. 'What is one to say of her work,' he asked, 'except that it is unlike anything that has ever been in Victoria before?' He granted that it was clever, that the drawing was beyond reproach, the composition excellent. But the colours! Even the most patriotic Irishman never saw grass as green as Miss Carr had pictured it in Brittany and Alert Bay. And the blues, yellows, and reds were just as blinding as the greens. Dismissing these colours (of a 'higher key than is vouchsafed to ordinary mortals to perceive') as an aberration, he remembered with surprising fondness Miss Carr's earlier work 'when it was signalized by quiet, sombre tints and beautiful nuances of colour'. He hoped that 'this attack of neo or post impressionism' would not permanently affect her colour sense.[5]

Emily's nine paintings probably overpowered, in both size and colour, the subdued and dainty landscapes of Beacon Hill Park that were the Arts and Crafts Society's stock in trade. Her work was undoubtedly aggressive and disturbing to Victorians, who liked stability and clung to standards that were anachronistic even in Britain. But though Emily was contemptuous of the 'tinkling teacups, tinkling conversation and little tinkling landscapes' of the Arts and Crafts set, acceptance was important to her.[6] It meant sales, and certainly prestige with childhood acquaintances and especially her sisters. Even though she already knew the conservatism of the city and its cultivated strata, she expected people to like her new mode, and some apparently did. Not only did C.F. Newcombe make purchases and Mrs Harris and Mrs Burns champion her work with the government, but people began to tell Emily that she was 'wise to paint these Indian places & totem poles because one day they would be valuable'; and, she later remembered, 'they even began to say that the modern style suited Indian stuff.'

Occupied with supervising her apartment house during the summer of 1913, Emily made no excursion north. She had plenty of sketching material from previous trips, however, and for a few months she worked hard in her new studio. But in 1914 she produced only a few canvases. That summer she constructed—legend has it with her own hands and the help of only one man—a summer cottage on property she had purchased the previous year.[7] (It was at Shoal Bay, where as a child she had passed five summers with Edna Green's family.) By 1915 she had stored most of her Indian work in the basement of the apartment house and was painting only on Sundays. By 1916 the big studio, where she had dreamed of painting so many fine pictures, was used as a sitting-dining room by the boarders. She was now unable to work in the studio without fear of discovery; being caught at her easel before she could throw the dust sheet over her painting was tantamount to being caught in her bath tub. She had always detested having someone at her shoulder while she worked; the worry that a boarder or a tenant might appear at any moment made it difficult for her to concentrate. If this happened her thoughts either 'stuck like mice paralyzed with fear in the corners or else they scampered clean off & never came back.'

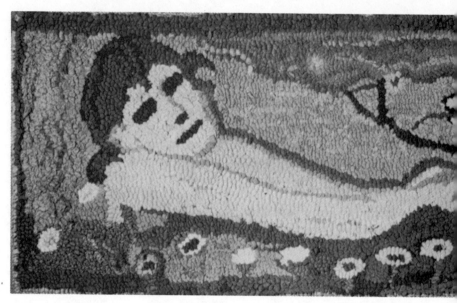

Adam and Eve
Rug, 1920s.
Approx. 20 x
74 1/2. Made
for Lizzie (who
did not like it).
PABC.

The struggle to maintain a dominant place for her painting after 1913 was short. Disappointed that neither the Grand Trunk Pacific nor the provincial government had purchased her collection, feeling alienated from the largely conservative artistic community, and with no money or time to undertake a lengthy excursion north, she discontinued her mission to record the houses and totems of the West Coast Indians. What little painting she did after 1913 was done within walking distance of Hill House—in Beacon Hill Park and along the Dallas Road cliffs—or during the summers at her cottage.

Though she was no longer painting Indian subjects, Emily did not forget about them. The Provincial Museum was not far from her home and she occasionally used its library and studied the Indian artefacts on display. She transcribed pages from the latest writings on West Coast Indians into her notebook;[8] she took a great interest in the meaning and precise forms of the crest symbols, copying these too. There was a practical purpose to these activities. From about 1915 she used the crest symbols as motifs for rag and hooked rugs, which she made from old clothes and, later, from discarded army blankets. She claimed that the inspiration for rug-making had come from seeing the Indian women 'squatted on the earth floor, weaving cedar fibre or tatters of old cloth into a mat'.[9] Though she had seen these tasks performed as early as 1898 in Ucluelet, it is more likely that she was inspired to emulate them by her friend and supporter, Mrs Dennis Harris, who in 1913 established a School of Handicraft and Design in Victoria and promoted a revival of interest in arts and crafts. By 1915 the Island Arts and Crafts exhibitions included almost as many craft entries as paintings. In the autumn of 1916 Emily joined the contributors by submitting 'three handsome mats

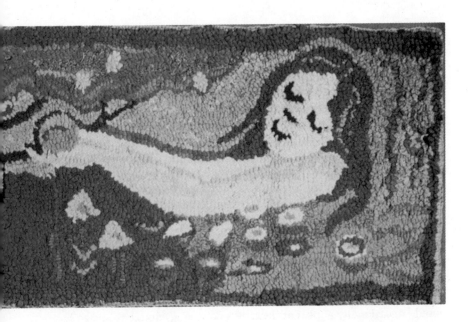

[hooked rugs] in Indian totem design', to quote the *Colonist*.[10] Thus she kept her interest in the Indians alive not only by learning more about their art and mythology but by making Indian-related handicrafts. She even made money from their sale.

Until 1913 everything in Emily's life had been subservient to her art. Not only had she become psychologically and spiritually dependent on it for self-expression, but it enabled her to confront herself without feelings of guilt or inferiority. Her art and her life had become inseparable. Even her sexuality had been sublimated into work, which on the one hand had caused illness to the point of a breakdown but on the other had justified her very being. She had elevated it into a historic mission. After 1913, however, when she became a landlady, the harmony of life, art, and mission was disrupted. At the age of forty-one Emily was thrown into a world of adults and their problems of money, alcohol, sex, and drugs. Suddenly she was dominated by other people's motivations, not her own.

Emily discovered almost immediately that running an apartment house was unpleasant. 'I loathed being a landlady.' There were the worries about what was going to go wrong next, keeping the suites occupied, broken leases, unpaid rent, incompatible tenants. The period during the First World War, when all the decent men seemed to have gone overseas while 'the miserable no-goods flocked into town', was the worst.

When Emily took boarders in 1916, the situation deteriorated. She kept the first floor—Lower East and Lower West—as rental suites, but converted the upstairs—her own suite and a smaller apartment she called the Doll's House—into a boarding house for ladies. She moved her bedroom to the attic, which was reached from what had formerly been her studio by a narrow stair, and decorated it with two giant spread-winged eagles and a border of frogs in the Indian motif on the underside of the roof. She converted her studio into an attractive sitting-dining room by scattering her hooked rugs on the floor, hanging her French and Indian pictures on the walls, and moving a huge leather-topped table—said to have been from British Columbia's first legislature—into an alcove under high windows overlooking Beacon Hill Park. She bought brightly coloured dishes, made attractive salads, and cooked hot curry and garlic dishes. In the spring and summer, flowers from the garden made the great dining table a mass of colour, and in the winter a high glass globe filled with goldfish provided an accent. (The fishbowl was removed when fish was served.) The atmosphere, one boarder recalled, was 'very nice and very interesting'.[11] In 1921, when Emily traded an English bobtail puppy and thirty-five dollars for a Javanese monkey she called Woo, the dining room became more lively.[12] During mealtimes Woo was chained to the far end of the dining table; her little black hand would occasionally appear at the table's edge long enough to steal a scrap of food from an unsuspecting boarder. Emily herself was often the centre of amusement, always ready with a quick reply to any complaint about the cooking that she—or a maid, when she could afford one—had prepared. To one near-sighted boarder, reluctant to eat a lumpy chocolate pudding, Emily said, 'Don't you like nuts?'[13] Such levity was a welcome contrast to her frequent bouts of temper or studied indifference.

Every kind of woman passed through the boarding house: 'decayed English Gentlewomen, Business women, teachers, students, busy bodies, gluttons'. By the early 1920s Emily tired of women and opened her rooms to bachelors. The problems were similar, however, and the battle continued.

It was nothing for a tenant to indulge in drugs, common-law living, or alcohol. A single summer in Miss Carr's house presented one young boarder with a surprising miscellany of loose living.[14] Emily raged 'at the injustice and hatefulness of it all'. When her rage subsided, she hardened. She lost much of the joviality that had prompted the Ucluelet natives to call her Klee Wyck and her Vancouver students to find her such fun. Cultivating a 'landlady face', which was 'not soft, not glad, not sorry, just blank', she allowed her natural mistrust to deepen; she became suspicious of everyone and, as usual, was seldom forgiving.[15] She performed the apartment chores grudgingly, taunted her tenants, and abused anyone who crossed her.

Much of the paranoia that had accompanied the public side of Emily's activities as an artist was transferred to her management of the apartment house. She found peculiarities and any show of independence in her tenants difficult to tolerate. When they rearranged the furniture, she felt hurt that they did not appreciate her way of doing things. Complaints about leaky faucets, or about any aspect of the house, were taken

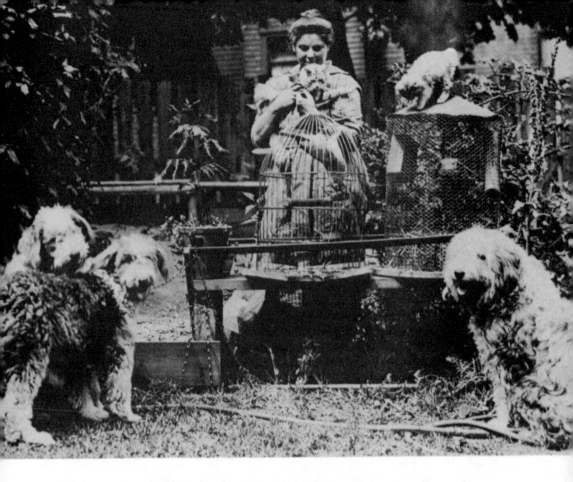

personally. Occasionally she derived satisfaction from portraying to the odd understanding and friendly tenant the quirks of the others; however, this was rare. Even though she was insatiably curious about them, her feelings 'amounted in most cases to plain hate'. One tenant who became a close friend showed how unpopular she was as a landlady by cheering when she heard that Emily had been pushed into the coal bin by a fellow tenant. Finding him stoking *her* furnace, Emily had plucked the glasses from his face and angrily trampled them into the basement floor. 'It was about time,' remarked Emily's friend of the incident, 'that somebody pushed her around; she had been pushing us around long enough.' Such confrontations, though usually less violent, 'happened all the time'.[16]

In order to forestall her tenants' criticism, as well as to mitigate her own intolerance of them, Emily ruled the house with force. When her feelings reached their highest pitch of hatred, she would pull the fuses and turn off the water, then seek refuge in her attic bedroom. As a result, she became alienated from everyone in the house.

For most tenants Hill House was a stepping stone to somewhere else; for Emily it was a permanent millstone. Had the apartment been financed through a company, she might well have let it go during the long economic doldrums, but she took out a mortgage for $5,000 from Alice

'Prince Pumkin, Lady Loo, Young Jimmey, Adolphs the cat, Kitten, Chipmonk, and parrot & self in garden at 646 Simcoe St.', 1918. PABC.

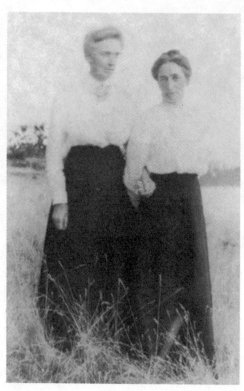

Edith and Lizzie, about 1918. Private collection.

in April 1913 and foreclosure would only have transferred the burden to her sister. Emily could have converted her lot adjoining Hill House into cash to pay off her mortgage, but she was advised by her lawyer not to sell her property during the Great War depression. Feeling financially trapped, she resented her dependence on the tenants and was jealous of their freedom to pick up and leave—an advantage of tenancy that she herself had often abused in England and Vancouver.

Things might not have been so bad during the Great War years had Emily received some sympathy from her sisters for her painting and her landlady chores. She recalled that 'one was noisey in her condemnation, one sulkily silent, one indifferent to every kind of Art.'[17] She yearned for their approval; but approval, for a style of painting they did not understand, was not forthcoming. Apparently Lizzie was particularly unsympathetic. Emily complained that she never missed an occasion to scoff at her more modern work. She credited her younger sister only with being able to cook, train a dog, and garter up her stockings well.

Emily's closest sister, Alice, not only failed to approve of her sister's painting, but disappointed her in another way. Emily had hoped that Alice would live with her and perhaps share in the duties of running the apartment house. But when Alice moved to the living quarters built onto her school and later took a teacher-governess position with the Hennells in Oak Bay, Emily was distraught. Alice acquired 'a tremendous infatuation' for the family, particularly for its head, and dropped her sister 'like a red hot coal'.[18] Even though Alice was not far away, Emily missed her terribly. She gave in to 'a bitter engrossing jealousy that warped everything in life'. Without support from Alice, who often took her side against Lizzie and Edith, the relationship with her sisters was even harder to bear. 'It was frequently thrust upon me that I had always been different from the rest.' It is questionable whether they showed disapproval of her careers as artist and landlady as openly as she later recalled. One friend described Emily's sisters as 'most undemonstrative', but eager to help if anything of consequence happened to one of them.[19] Nevertheless, feeling or imagining that they looked down on her, Emily grew more bitter and more guilt-ridden. The death of Edith in December 1919 did not ease the pressure. Emily was remorseful that things had not gone better between the two of them. Clara had died in January of the same year and Lizzie now became the head of the family.

Though Emily was resentful of her sisters, it was Alice who, in 1915, lowered the rate of interest on the mortgage she held from 7 to 6 per cent and moved its due date from 1916 to 1918. This enabled Emily to close the already half-empty apartment house and leave Victoria during the autumn of 1916, escaping to California.

She spent eight months in the San Francisco Bay area. Relatively cheap living quarters were found in a student residence near the University at Berkeley. Emily shared a community kitchen with 'young bubbling . . . girls who were going to be lawyers & doctors & teachers', and had a bed-sitting room to herself. She found employment with 'the Raventis', a couple who had 'a shop for basketry & fancy things' in San Francisco. They had been contracted by the decorator of the St Francis Hotel to provide lanterns and banners for the new ballroom and Emily was hired to help paint the decorations. The job was not entirely pleasant. Emily and another employee, working in an empty store in Chinatown, were pressed for time. There was no electricity in the shop, so work during the evening was impossible. Matters worsened when Emily's co-worker tired and left the completion of the decorations to her. 'It was a strange foreign experience' working alone in the heart of the not-so-savoury Chinatown, Emily recalled. But she finished the job and was surprised at how 'very beautiful' the lanterns and banners looked in the massive ballroom.

Though her second stay in San Francisco seems to have provided an uneventful respite from her cares as a landlady, and perhaps even allowed for some painting, one thing occurred that was out of the ordinary: a reunion with Mayo Paddon. It was 'funny how I ran into him again,' Emily wrote later, perhaps suppressing the fact that it was not a chance meeting. She said she had been shopping in San Francisco, had spent all of her money, and found herself stranded in front of a real-estate office with no fare to return to her residence across the Bay in Berkeley. 'I looked up & there on a board was Martyn's name.' She marched into the office and asked to see Paddon, to be told he was engaged. She scribbled 'Emily' on a card and sent it in to him. Within a few minutes 'out bounded Martyn, eyes puffy'. He of course lent her a dollar.[20]

Emily knew that Paddon had married a Victoria girl only months after her return from England in 1905. But did she know that Mayo was now separated from his wife and was most unhappy in spite of being financially successful? If she did, and expected something to materialize after their meeting, she did not say so. Paddon told her that she had made a great mistake in not marrying him, but there is nothing to indicate that he showed any interest in renewing his suit, or that they met again during her stay in San Francisco. However, every Christmas thereafter Emily received a pressed flower from him—without a note. She remained convinced that 'without love' marriage to him 'would have been hell', as she 'could not have made him happy'.[21]

Emily returned to Victoria in June 1917 much refreshed and rejuvenated. It was at this time that she began her 'Bobtail Kennel' and took a position as a cartoonist.

The idea of establishing a bobtail sheep-dog kennel had long been maturing in Emily's mind. Her loyal dog Billie was half-bobtail, and to that half she attributed the heart, instincts, and intelligence that filled him with 'loyalty, loveableness, wisdom, courage and kindness'. When Billie died, aged sixteen, before Emily went to San Francisco, his death 'left such a blank that the Bobtail kennel idea, which had been rooting in me those many years, blossomed.'[22] Obtaining a female from a prairie farm and a sire from a Victoria butcher, she began her enterprise. From 1917 until 1921 she 'aimed at producing healthy, intelligent working stock and selling puppies at a price the man of moderate means could afford.'[23] After the war there was a good demand among sheep- and cattle-men for working dogs and she met it by raising some 350 bobtail puppies within four years. It was an immense undertaking. She transported the dogs' food from the butcher in the Public Market to her home in a wicker pram. The dogs helped too by carrying a portion of it themselves in saddlebags strapped to their backs. She then prepared the food in great pots on the basement stove. Other chores included coping with distemper, which often resulted in early-morning 'drowning horrors' on the Dallas Road beach.[24] However, she usually enjoyed the work. She received great pleasure from the 'adoring Bobtail devotion' of the dogs, from their company on Beacon Hill, and their dependence on her.[25] Most were pedigree and Emily showed them in local dog shows as well as at the Pacific National Exhibition in Vancouver. She joined dog and kennel organizations and became, in a short time, greatly respected among other breeders and owners. But the work was exhausting and the upkeep of the kennels expensive. When, in 1921, she sold a large piece of her Simcoe Street lot, there was no longer enough room for the dogs to run and the kennel was disbanded.[26] She kept only one dog, Adam.

As well as starting up the dog kennel after returning from San Francisco, Emily became a cartoonist for the Vancouver-based *Western*

Woman's Weekly. She contributed a cartoon to almost every issue of the rather feminist newspaper during its two-year existence.[27] The paper believed that 'the natural steps towards unity would be a Women's Party'.[28] Seeking to express its views, Emily submitted cartoons that advocated equal pay for women, women's suffrage, pensions for mothers, an act to protect deserted wives, the appointment of women judges in the courts, and the election of women to parliament. Some of the material, like the problems of apartment living and the difficulties of finding dependable part-time help, was drawn from her own landlady experiences. The sketches depicting men as stupid and women as foolishly vain expressed long-held grudges. Emily may have been stating not so much a feminist viewpoint as merely her own. Drawing pen-and-ink sketches with accompanying verse that mocked human folly had long been a pastime, and the *Western Woman's Weekly* provided yet another outlet for nagging prejudices. The sketches were different in style from those she had done for the *Week* twelve years earlier. Gone was her concern for detail; indeed, the drawings were crude and childish, both in thought and execution.

Occasionally the *Western Woman's Weekly* carried a feature story on a local artist. In February 1918 Emily was singled out for the 'Artists and Their Doings' column. An accompanying photograph showed a rather heavy-looking Emily standing in the midst of her English sheep dogs, her cats, and a caged cockatoo. There was nothing in the story to suggest that she had been painting less or had put aside the Indian motif: 'She regards her paintings of B.C. Indians, their villages and their totem-poles as the serious work of her life.' The writer hoped that a collection that rivalled that of Paul Kane would 'eventually become a national possession', as it was a 'worthy tribute to the Indians she loves so well.'[29]

In 1918 Emily was still seen as a painter solely devoted to preserving, on canvas and paper, the Indian totem poles and houses. Yet since 1914 she had been painting landscapes almost exclusively. When the war ended and the economic situation in Victoria improved, Emily began to devote considerably more time to her art. In 1918 she discontinued her boarding house, moved back into her apartment-studio, and employed domestic help. In the autumn of the following year she sold the Oak Bay cottage for $1,200—making a profit of $200. When Edith died, she left the family home to Lizzie and two lots to be divided among her three remaining sisters. The lots were eventually sold and Emily, in accordance with Edith's will, received half of the amount while Alice and Lizzie each received a quarter. In 1921 Emily sold the lot adjoining Hill House, and the revenue further diminished the mortgage that Alice held. In 1923 Alice relieved her of the burden altogether by cancelling it.

In 1920 Emily began, once again, to travel during the summer months. However, the renewed excursions did not take her to the remote Indian villages of northern British Columbia. She had kept her interest in the Indians alive by continuing to weave their symbols into her rugs; but, with no prospect of selling her collection, recording the totem poles and houses was a mission she did not intend to take up again. In the summer of 1920 she returned to the west coast of Vancouver Island. She travelled to Ahousat, an island some twenty miles north of Ucluelet, where the Reverend and Mrs Ross lived at the mission station. Large parts of two summers were passed with the missionaries and their son Bill, who boarded with Emily during the winters. She devoted her time there to painting the landscape. Armed with 'her paints, canvases, sandwiches, waterbottle & dog', she was taken by Bill in his canoe to various painting spots. He remembered her as 'a nice old duck', though his parents were unable to comprehend this woman they considered 'queer and looney'.[30] Following the summers in Ahousat, Emily visited the Okanagan, but was taken ill there and spent most of her holiday in bed. Other painting excursions at this time took her to points north of Victoria on Vancouver Island, to Sproat Lake, and to friends' summer homes at Duncan and Cowichan Bay.[31] In the autumn of 1923 Emily underwent a 'serious operation', which she said was on her spine, though a friend recalled that it was a not-altogether-successful operation on her gall bladder.[32] This illness kept her in bed for part of the winter of 1923, yet by the summer of 1924 she was away once again, painting 'hard all the while'.[33]

It is difficult to discuss fully the work that resulted from these excursions in the early 1920s. The few known examples show that her pictures were now small in scale compared with her pre-1914 canvases; that she was painting out-of-doors in oil rather than watercolour; that she was giving less attention to details; and that she was primarily concerned with painting the landscape. In †Along the Cliff—Beacon Hill, 1919, Emily explored the shape and the structure of the cliff and the logs, beach, and rocks below it. She was after something that she had attempted to bring to her landscape paintings in France: a realization of the underlying structure of the landscape as colour and light. Her experiments were not confined to summer holidays. From about 1919, while Alice was living on Sylvan Lane with the Hennells, Emily used Alice's schoolhouse for a studio. It was there that Mortimer Lamb, a Vancouver mining engineer and promoter of the Ontario Group of Seven, viewed her new landscape and pre-1913 Indian paintings in the autumn of 1921.

Lamb had been told of Emily's 'admirable' collection of paintings by Sophie Pemberton (now Mrs Deane-Drummond), her childhood sketching partner.[34] On visiting the schoolhouse Lamb was 'greatly impressed' by the landscape paintings that dominated the walls of the classroom. He asked Emily's permission to write an article on her work for the Studio. She did not seem to disapprove and gave him for illustration the only photographs of her work she possessed—some 'exceedingly poor snap shots' of her pre-1914 Indian paintings.[35] Lamb wrote to Eric Brown, the director of the National Gallery of Canada in Ottawa:

. . . I was exceedingly interested in the pictures, which are not only

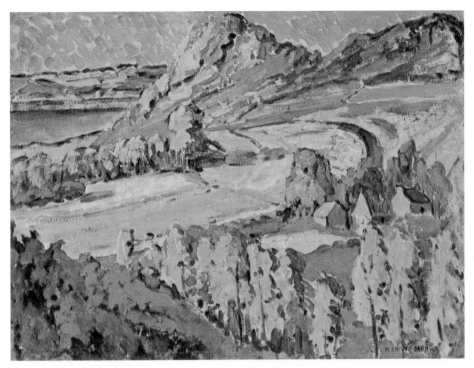

I—*Autumn in France* (St Efflame), 1911. Oil on board, 19 3/4 x 26. Courtesy VAG. NGC.

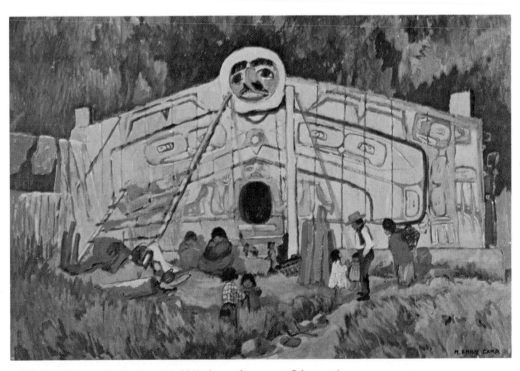

II—*House Front—Gold Harbour*, about 1912. Oil on card, 21 1/4 x 36 1/8. VAG.

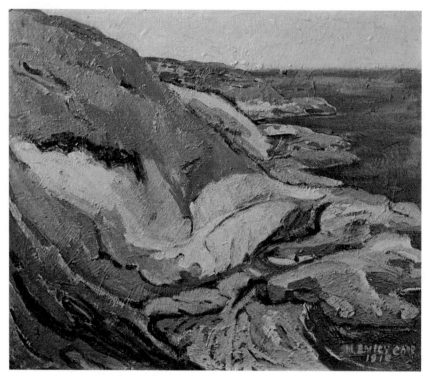

III—*Along the Cliff—Beacon Hill,* 1919. Oil on board, 15 x 17 3/4. Private collection.

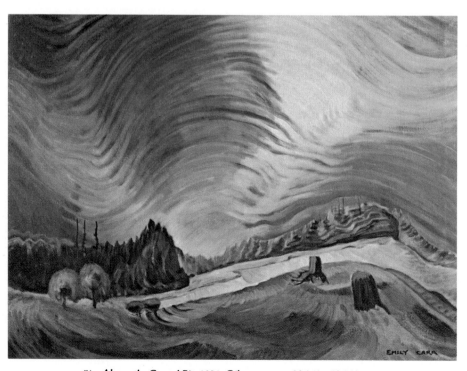

IV—*Above the Gravel Pit,* 1936. Oil on canvas, 30 1/4 x 40 1/4. VAG.

highly meritorious from an artistic standpoint, being fine in colour and broad and vigorous in treatment, but possess a real value from an antropological [sic] aspect. They represent, in the main, Indian villages, totems, and ceremonies, on the Queen Charlotte Islands, and the northwest coast of British Columbia; and were painted by Miss Carr some years ago, before many of the totems had been acquired by collectors.

Miss Carr assures me that the respective representations were done with the utmost fidelity to material facts; and it is therefore all the more extraordinary that she had been able to impress her work with an undoubted pictorial charm.

She will only sell the pictures as a collection, and it seems to me very desirable that they should be purchased by either the Dominion or the Provincial Governments. Do you think the National Gallery would be interested in this matter? If so, I shall be glad to arrange for photographs to be sent to you, although the photographs Miss Carr possesses are rather poor and do not give any sort of adequate idea of the pictorial merits of her pictures.[36]

Brown—who did not, it seems, receive any photographs—replied that he was not interested in purchasing an entire collection. He felt that the paintings sounded as though they 'would be more interesting to a Provincial or National Museum than to the National Gallery', and he forwarded the letter to the Indian Archaeological Department of the National Museum in Ottawa and thought no more of the Victoria artist.[37] Lamb did not proceed with the *Studio* article, but instead wrote several letters about Emily to A.Y. Jackson of the Group of Seven. The response was similar.[38]

Only months before receiving Lamb's letter, Brown had made a lecture tour of western Canada. He had, in fact, spoken at the Girls' Central School in Victoria, shown lantern slides of the paintings of central-Canadian artists, and called for a wider recognition of the country's artists. It is not known if he heard of Emily on this visit, but he did not contact her. His tour seemed to be a promotion of the National Gallery and the Group of Seven, rather than a mission to discover and assist new artists.

Brown made another western tour the next year, but again expressed little interest in local artists, reflecting the Gallery's apparent indifference to artists outside central Canada. In 1924 Emily missed yet another opportunity for national recognition when the National Gallery, in organizing pictures for the Wembly Exhibition in England, neglected to solicit submissions from the Island Arts and Crafts Society, with which Emily had exhibited that very year. Brown's oversight, attributed to a lack of time, did not go unnoticed.[40] British Columbia artists joined an angry Mortimer Lamb in demanding that the National Gallery adopt a 'nation wide policy' in art. 'The work of at least one or two British Columbia artists,' Lamb wrote in the *Province*, would 'command respectful attention anywhere'. Lamb had in mind particularly 'the expressive paintings of Indian villages and settlements by Miss Carr of Victoria.'[41] Lamb's open letter to Brown, the organizer of the submissions

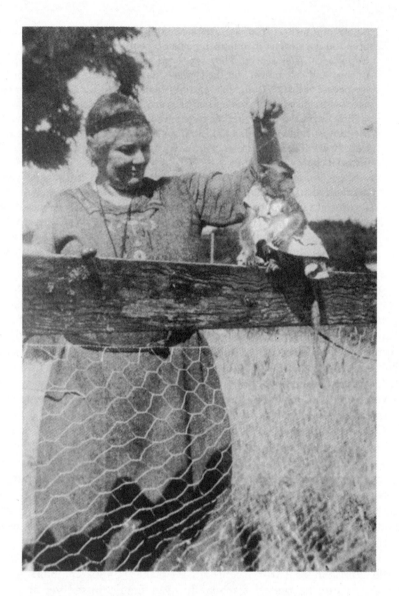

Emily with Woo, mid-1920s. Private collection.

to the Wembly Exhibition, had little effect, however. The National Gallery continued to neglect western and Maritime artists.

Although ignored by Ottawa, Emily did make the acquaintance of two artists who proved to be a tremendous influence in developing her attitude towards the landscape. In the early twenties she met Viola and Ambrose Patterson, young art teachers from the University of Washington in Seattle. After walking in Beacon Hill Park they discovered Hill House on Simcoe Street and saw a sign in the window indicating that room and board were offered. They entered the small fenced front garden, walked around the west side of the house to the back, then climbed the long wooden exterior stairs past the first landing to the second floor. They had found an ideal location for their weekend visits to Victoria. At the same time they met Emily, who 'loved to talk painting' and was 'literally starved for contact'.[42]

The artist-teachers had much in common with Emily. Ambrose Patterson had lived in Paris from 1903 to 1908, had attended the Académie Colarossi, and had been elected an associate of the Salon d'Automne. Viola Patterson had studied painting in the same city with the acclaimed artist and teacher, André L'Hôte. Their talk was of painting, of Emily's early expeditions to the Indian villages, of student days in Paris. While Emily entertained the Pattersons with stories of her travels and studies, they talked to her about their enthusiasm for the landscape of the Pacific Northwest. The Pattersons believed that their study abroad had been necessary, but felt that Seattle was now sufficiently sophisticated—having, since 1914, the Cornish School of Applied and Allied Arts and, since 1918, a School of Painting and Design at the University of Washington—to provide artists with both training and patronage. It was time too, they felt, that West Coast artists turned away from memorializing the countryside of Brittany and Provence and began painting the landscape around them.

Emily had long believed these things. But she had been painting the local landscape only sporadically throughout the 1910s, more consistently after 1919. As a subject it remained a second alternative to the region's natives and their artefacts. As stated in the 1918 *Western Woman's Weekly* article, her real mission was to record the Indian totems for history. After she met the Pattersons, however, she sought like them to develop in the modern idiom an art that would reveal the uniqueness of the West Coast vegetation.

The Pattersons were frequent paying guests at Hill House from the early 1920s until the late 1930s. Summers they would sit with Emily in 'the orchard with the animals about'; the winters found the three around the studio's Franklin stove 'with the monkey in his [sic] red flannel dress closest to the fire.' Emily was 'rather like her little dogs, snappy and cranky.' And though she bore 'a chip on her shoulder', they found her 'a warm if sometimes caustic friend.' Viola Patterson also remembered Emily's almost belligerent attitude, which appeared to say, 'I can make it on my own and don't need any assistance from you.'[43]

But Emily did need help and guidance. She had already received some abroad, and now the Pattersons gave her the encouragement she needed to do more painting, to transfer more of her energy from the house to her art, and to adapt her modern style to the landscape. She received help too from Jan Gordon's *Modern French Painters*, which the Pattersons probably recommended.[44] From January through March 1924 Emily studied and put into practice many of the ideas expressed in this book. A chapter on Cézanne particularly impressed her. Cézanne was 'trying to destroy the illusion of the *picturesque*, and to build up in its place a sentiment for the pictorial,' Gordon wrote. 'The ruined cottage, the old peasant woman, the blasted oak [and, Emily might have added, the

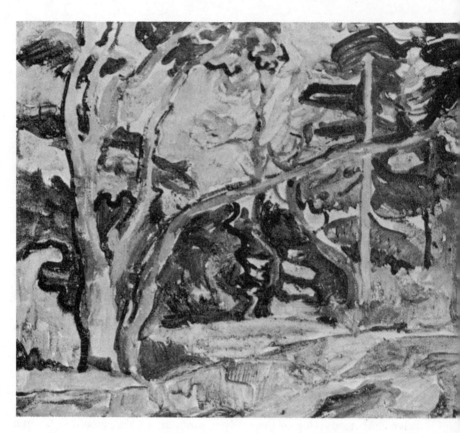

Deciduous Forest, about 1926. Oil, watercolour, and chalk on board, 15 3/8 x 18 3/4. The Art Emporium.

broken-down community houses and totem poles] . . . form the staple subject-matter of second-rate painters.'[45] Cézanne's work, on the other hand, was 'based upon the idea that the artist's first and most important task is to create . . . [a] sensation of rhythmical movement of lines and ordered sensations of depth.' He should not attempt 'to get an accurate imitation', but should blend space sensations with rhythmical pattern.[46]

These passages, all meticulously underscored in Emily's copy, partly expressed what she had learned from Gibb eleven years before, but that old habits and new missions had led her to abandon. Most important, they stressed the need to suppress the search for romantic associations, which had surely been part of the attractiveness of the Indians and their decaying relics. What Cézanne, through Gordon, now told her to do was to depart from both the imitation and the sentimental associations of the picturesque. Significant too was Cézanne's belief that all great art was experimental, and that 'the value of a work may be almost judged by the depth of experiment attempted in it.'[47]

With the writings of Gordon and conversations with the Pattersons fresh in her mind, Emily now 'quit convention to the wind' in her painting. She painted the wild-armed arbutus, the scraggy underbrush, the sweeping conifers in *Deciduous Forest* with no thought for detail, perspective, or even medium. Less controlled than the earlier *Along the Cliff—Beacon Hill, Deciduous Forest* is a celebration of the process of painting. Emily used oil, watercolour, and chalk. She experimented not only by mixing mediums, but by making her response as uncontrived, as devoid of preconceived ideas and techniques, as possible. Through her willingness to feel, to react spontaneously, she discovered that there was a rhythmic order in the chaos of nature. Asked at the time what he was striving for in his painting, Ambrose Patterson replied: 'to forget everything . . . and just go to it with utmost abandon.'[48] Whether Emily had learned this from him or not, she was doing just that. From the mid-1920s the landscape became much more for her than a silhouetted backdrop for community houses and totem poles; she now began to see and portray its rhythm, its structure, and its colour.

When Emily wrote to a friend in 1924 that she did not 'give a whoop' if the public liked her work or not, and that she was painting to satisfy her own ideals, she was not exaggerating.[49] She was no longer merely painting the British Columbia landscape in the French way; she was attempting to give it something of her own feeling and experience. The few paintings that remain from this period have many characteristics of her mature work. While *Deciduous Forest* shows her spontaneity and early discovery of rhythm in nature, *Twisted Branch* foreshadows her later convention of throwing the viewer into the midst of a tree or a forest. Neither the base nor the top of the tree nor any of its periphery is visible. However, the twisting, tortured limbs, the straight, powerful trunk, and the weightless foliage convey to the viewer a vivid representation of the whole.

Impressed by these new works, the Pattersons urged Emily to exhibit them. In April 1924 she submitted four paintings to the annual Pacific Northwest exhibition in Seattle. If she had any doubts about the merits of her new experimental work, they must have dissolved when one of her contributions, *Macaulay Point*, won second honourable mention.[50] Her confidence sufficiently restored, she contributed, after an eleven-year hiatus, to the exhibition of the Island Arts and Crafts Society, which she found more open to modernism than it had been in 1913. The *Colonist* noted 'a striking number of oils in the impressionistic school', which were exhibited alongside Emily's work comprising early Indian and French paintings as well as some recent experimental landscapes. Her Indian totem watercolours were described in terms of the 'bold originality' with which they suggested 'the primitive and horrific superstition of the aborigine'. Her most striking painting was thought to be *Arbutus Trees—Esquimalt*, with 'its branches tortured . . . by the sunlight which fires the twisted stems'.[51]

Thus Emily returned, in 1924, to public life as an artist. She not only began contributing regularly to both the Victoria and Seattle art societies, but one painting, *By the Shore*, found its way to the 48th Annual Exhibition of the San Francisco Art Association at the California

Palace of the Legion of Honor.[52] Contact through these exhibitions with Seattle artists like Kenneth Callahan—who, like the Pattersons, was concerned with developing a regional landscape art—soon became evident in Emily's work. Her rhythmic style, for example, was closely aligned to Callahan's and Viola Patterson's. Moreover, she was included by the Seattle artists in their regionalist movement. The 'prominent artist of Victoria', as one Seattle newspaper called Emily, was invited by the Seattle Fine Arts Society to be a member of the jury for the exhibition in 1925.[53] After 1924 she had more Seattle weekend visitors at Hill House, including J.H. Hatch Jr, Edward Ford, and Glenn Hughes.

Emily's Seattle success did not go unnoticed by Vancouver's artists, who were also contributing to the same exhibitions in Seattle. They thought of her, as did her Victoria contemporaries,[54] primarily as a painter of the Indians, and it was her Indian work that Vancouver's British Columbia Art League (of which Mortimer Lamb was an influential member) invited her to exhibit in 1926 and to lecture on.[55] Emily replied to the invitation by saying that 'she would gladly lend some landscapes, all expenses to be met by the League, but could not undertake Exhibition of Indian stuff nor lecture'. In response to this discouraging reply, the League's secretary was instructed to send 'thanks and regrets'.[56]

Had Emily agreed to exhibit and lecture for the Art League she would have found that Vancouver and its cultural community had changed considerably since she had left in 1913. The year, 1926, was something of a landmark. In the summer Frederick H. Varley, a member of the Group of Seven, arrived to begin a job as instructor in painting at the recently founded Vancouver School of Applied and Decorative Art. Newly hired for the design staff was J.W.G. (Jock) Macdonald, an Edinburgh-trained artist and teacher. They joined the already resident Charles Scott, director of the school and an excellent Glasgow-trained painter, and Grace Melvin, a design instructor, also from Glasgow. Although conservative artists like Thomas Fripp were still very active on the scene, some, like the English-trained W.P. Weston, had shifted their style radically in the mid-twenties. The whole group, led by Varley, were painting the British Columbia landscape with religious reverence and in a heroic mould. The British Columbia Society of Fine Arts, of which Emily had been a founding member in 1909, had also changed considerably. It now displayed a more eclectic attitude towards painting and welcomed representations of various schools into its exhibitions. The Palette and Chisel Club, like the Art League, brought mostly modernist artists together for exhibition.

While Emily was not prepared to exhume her Indian work from the basement of her house and dress it up suitably for exhibition at the Art League, and while she may have felt that as it had been done fourteen years before it was no longer part of her current artistic concerns, she was still sufficiently interested in her Indian pictures to invite Marius Barbeau to view them that autumn. The ethnologist from Ottawa's

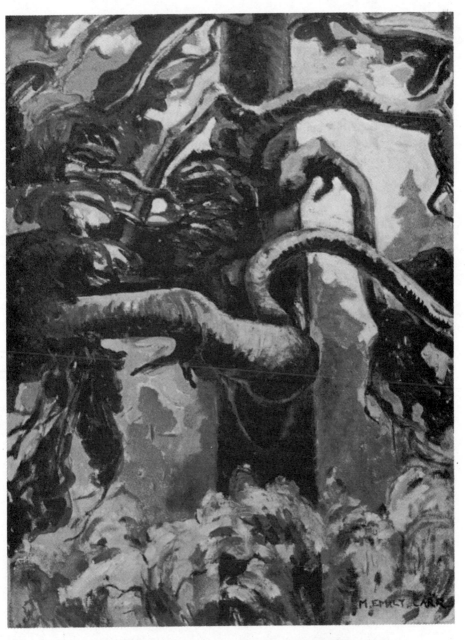

Twisted Branch, about 1924. Oil on canvas, 26 3/4 x 20 1/2. (Photo: Charlotte Rosshandler) Collection of Justin and Elizabeth Lang, Montreal.

Victoria Memorial Museum was giving four lectures on West Coast Indian art at the University of British Columbia. In them he made 'a strong appeal to Canadian painters . . . to use the remnants of native art as themes for their works. . . . The best we can hope for now is to preserve the remnants within our borders, not only from foreign collectors but from ravages of Indian frenzy.'[57] Barbeau's appeal for the art of a race that he felt possessed a greater love of beauty and grandeur than the white man was soon made known to Emily. A Vancouver friend forwarded to her the *Province*'s commentary on his first two lectures. She responded by writing to Barbeau immediately:

> . . . I am wondering if you are coming to Victoria I hope so very much as I would like to hear those lectures *immensely*. I am very interested in the Indians & have made a very large collection of paintings of their villages & totem poles going up North many years before they were taken away living among them & painting in their villages. If you do come to Victoria I would be very pleased if you would care to come to my home and see the collection it might be of interest to you would you phone me. My phone no. is 2866R and my house is only a few blocks from the CPR wharf and the Empress hotel. Walk out Gov street south to Simcoe St 4 blocks, turn to the left, up Simcoe. I am the last house on Simcoe & my studio upstairs No of house 646 Simcoe.
> Hoping I shall have the pleasure of meeting you.[58]

Barbeau replied in writing to Emily's invitation but did not visit her at this time.[59] It seemed that Emily had lost yet another opportunity to interest a government official in her collection of Indian paintings.

If Barbeau had visited Emily that autumn in Victoria he would have seen more than her Indian pictures and hooked rugs with Indian symbols. In 1925 she had contributed pottery, decorated with Indian motifs, to the craft section of the Island Arts and Crafts exhibition.[60] She had taken a course in clay modelling at the Westminster School of Art in 1900 and had admired Harry Gibb's handmade pottery in 1910, but did not produce any herself until about 1924. That year John Kyle, the director of technical education for the public schools in Victoria, arranged for a demonstration of the use of local blue clay. Two Victoria women, Mrs Catherine Lothian and Mrs Margaret Grute, took up Kyle's suggestion to use the local clay for pottery and adapt Indian designs to it. Local pottery-making was thus popularized. Tobacco jars, candlesticks, and other objects created from local clay and decorated with Indian motifs first appeared at the 1924 Island Arts and Crafts exhibition. The next few years witnessed a great blossoming of handmade pottery, all from local clay and much of it decorated with Indian designs. This flurry of pottery-making coincided with Emily's meeting Mrs Kate Mather, a craftswoman who operated a summer gift shop in Banff and wintered in Victoria. When Mrs Mather occupied the lower suite of Hill House in the autumn of 1924, she asked Emily to make 'Indian pottery' for her to sell.[61] Her prompting, and the promise of a commercial outlet, gave Emily the impetus she needed to begin.

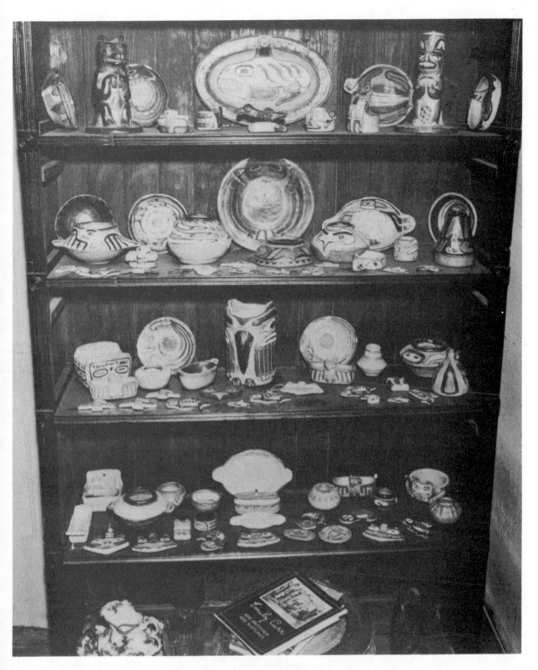

Emily's curio pottery displayed in Kate
Mather's home. Courtesy Mrs Charles S. Band.

She dug the blue clay from the Dallas Road cliffs, or from a construction site, then transported it home in her wicker pram. She ground the clay, ran it through a sieve, mixed it with a little fine sand, then kneaded it with a rolling pin until it became plastic. She then shaped by hand a wide array of objects and put them into her homemade backyard kiln for firing. This primitive oven was difficult to use because she had neither a damper nor temperature control: she had to regulate the fire by hand, keeping alert to sudden temperature changes and the danger of fire. The process took twelve to fourteen hours and every moment was 'agony, suspense, sweat'.[62] After the firing, and a cooling period of twenty-four hours, the pottery was painted with enamel paint mixed with sand to dull the gloss.

The one-bake clay was brittle and, as pottery, inferior both technically and aesthetically. Emily made no pretence about its value. She churned out hundreds of 'stupid objects, the kind that tourists pick up,'[63] feeling guilty about 'prostituting' Indian art by adapting it to pottery (a convention never known to the Northwest Coast natives). Though she prided herself on keeping the Indian designs pure, she took such liberties as perching ravens and frogs on candlesticks, bells, and ashtrays.

The miniature totems, pots, flower jars, plates, and plaques were marketed from 1925 in Victoria, Vancouver, and Banff. In 1927 Emily's curios also found their way to a Toronto arts-and-crafts sale, a craft exhibition at the Château Laurier in Ottawa, and a 'Produced in Canada' show in Peterborough; in 1928 to the Canadian Handicraft Guild's shop in Montreal; and in 1930 to the CPR's Handicraft Festival in Calgary, where Emily won a red ribbon. For several winters after 1924 she held pottery exhibitions at Hill House. People were invited for studio evenings, at which the pottery was displayed in a special room she had fitted with shelves she painted black. Kate Mather recalled that she hardly sold enough to pay for the evening's tea and cookies.[64] Almost everywhere else, however, the pottery sold well. An article on 'Women Potters and Indian Themes' in *Maclean's Magazine* (March 1927) claimed that Miss Carr's unglazed pottery had 'an instant appeal'; it was so popular she could not meet the demand.[65]

Emily felt that Kate Mather did not possess a '*real* understanding of painting' but certainly knew something about marketing.[66] She not only encouraged Emily to begin making commercial pottery but submitted her work to craft exhibitions across the country. In 1928, after she moved to Toronto and gave up marketing her friend's pottery, Emily was lost. She did not mind the making, but she hated the selling. She continued to hold sales in her home, but without the enthusiasm and support of Mrs Mather her interest soon faded. While she was involved in this enterprise, she occasionally had a helper in the person of young Carol Williams.

Carol Dennise Williams had come to Victoria from Toronto in the early 1920s with her parents, Captain Norman and Lenore Williams, and her brother Brock.[67] Carol was a pupil at Queen Margaret's School in

Duncan, forty miles north of Victoria, in September 1921. Emily probably met her and her brother in 1922, when the children were summer boarders at Alice's school.[68] Emily often lunched with Lizzie and Alice there, though her sisters considered her smoking and swearing a bad influence on the children. To Emily's surprise, Carol defended her against her sisters' criticism. It was, Emily later wrote, 'love at first sight'; almost immediately Carol became 'fearfully loyal'.[69] The two soon found that they shared a similar admiration for 'creatures'.[70] Emily, who had opened another kennel in 1923—this time for much smaller Belgian griffons—taught the child all she knew about dogs. Carol wanted to be an artist like Emily, who gave her painting lessons, often on the Dallas Road cliffs. Alongside her young pupil, Emily was herself spurred on to paint more. Eventually Carol stayed with Emily, not Alice, when her parents summered in central Canada. The middle-aged woman and young girl not only painted together on the cliffs but made several sketching trips to the island of Westholme, some sixty miles north of Victoria, which Captain Williams had bought around 1920, and to the area of the nearby community of Chemainus.

It is not surprising that the autocrat of Hill House unfolded in the company of a school girl. Emily's most harmonious relationships had seldom been with her peers, from whom she usually isolated herself; they had been with younger fellow students, her own pupils, the peasant folk in France, and the West Coast Indians. Since becoming a landlady in 1913, there had been little opportunity for Emily's child-self to receive satisfaction. A childhood relationship was perpetuated with her sisters, but it was filled with bitterness and guilt. Neighbourhood children did visit her house, especially in the spring when a litter of puppies was to be seen, but none except Carol Williams was embraced.

Emily quickly became dependent on the girl's unswerving admiration, which was a marvellous buffer against her sisters' criticism. She had found in Carol an outlet for her love, reserved until now for her animals. Carol for her part discovered a wonderful friend who taught her much about nature and painting, yet could slip as easily as she herself into childhood fantasy. The two often assumed imaginary characters for the entire day and neither would flinch for a moment from her impersonation. For Emily this make-believe reawakened her child-self; for Carol it provided a flight into the world of fantasy that she dearly loved. So close did they become, so attracted was Emily by 'the freshness and ardour of her mind and her affectionate nature', that she asked Carol's mother if she could adopt the child as her own. Mrs Williams, naturally taken aback, declined.[71] She did, however, allow Carol to call Emily 'Mom'. Emily responded by giving Carol the pet name 'Baboo' (because she had always wanted a daughter *and* a baboon!). The intimate friendship lasted until Carol moved to Ontario in 1926, but letters, Mother's-Day flowers, and visits kept the mother-daughter relationship alive until Emily's death. Though Carol's departure, and her subsequent marriage to Bill Pearson, robbed the relationship of its intensity, it was never forgotten by Emily—who cherished it so much that she shared it with few people—or by Carol, who wrote of it years later in *Emily Carr As I Knew Her*.[72]

In 1926, when Emily turned fifty-five, she had been in Victoria for thirteen years. Her autobiographical writings portray this time—which she called her 'blue period', her 'bitter years'—as one of trouble, despair, rejection, and testing, in which her brushes lay idle and she was quite alone.

So it appeared to her in recollection, but the facts make this picture seem exaggerated. For her painting, it was a time of growth and discovery. We know that after 1914 Emily painted less, but in 1919 her work entered an experimental phase that would eventually carry her to her self-confident peak as an artist. While there was a degree of rejection—or lack of sympathy—when she exhibited her work locally at the beginning of the period, approval and interest did come to her; and at its end she was on the eve of recognition from a far-away centre—Ottawa. In her personal life her relations with people declined and her appearance deteriorated. Most of her neighbours who knew her in the 1920s remember her peering from the upstairs window of Hill House 'dressed in outlandish clothes and with a stogie in her mouth', or walking her dogs on the Beacon Hill cliffs and chatting to them as she went along, or pushing a pram-load of clay from some construction site to her apartment house.[73] Yet anti-social traits did not overtake her completely: she was capable of inspiring the love of a child and of making some new and important adult friendships. Though she did submit to loneliness, discouragement, anger, and frustration in this period, she was not debilitated by these feelings. Through several years of economic stress—particularly during the war—she summoned the will power to keep a roof over her head by engaging in a multitude of activities not related to her beloved painting. In these, as in the painting she did accomplish, she was both energetic and creative.

8

Discovery
and Its Effects
1927-1929

In late August 1927 Eric Brown, the director of the National Gallery of Canada, and his wife Maud, travelled to British Columbia on their third western tour in six years. They visited the major Prairie cities, stopped briefly in the Rocky Mountains to attend the opening of the Scottish Highland Festival at the Banff Springs Hotel, then pushed on to Vancouver. There they visited Varley in his Lynn Valley cottage, and met with other artists before boarding the Canadian Pacific steamer for Victoria. The purpose of Brown's trip was fourfold. He intended to study 'the art demands and progress of art throughout the country'; to lecture on modern art; and to arrange, as he had on earlier visits in 1921 and 1922, for further National Gallery travelling exhibitions.[1] Brown also hoped to finish making selections for an exhibition of West Coast Indian art that he had been preparing with the National Museum in Ottawa since the previous December. This was intended to 'mingle for the first time the art work of the Canadian West Coast tribes' with that of the 'more sophisticated [modern] artists in an endeavour to analyse their relationships to one another.'[2]

The exhibition arose from interest in the efforts of the Royal Ontario Museum and the National Museum in the mid-1920s to purchase and restore many of the deteriorating totem poles of northern British Columbia. Three years earlier, in 1924, Marius Barbeau had commissioned the American artist W. Langdon Kihn to accompany him on a field trip to the villages of the Upper Skeena for the purpose of recording the Indians and their poles. The work of Kihn, who had previously painted Indian themes in southwestern British Columbia, was thought to reveal the 'aesthetic potentialities' of Northwest Coast Indian art.[3] Barbeau recalled that Kihn's success—referring to the recent purchase of his Indian collection by F.N. Southam of Montreal—made it easy for him to induce central-Canadian artists to extend their activities to the Northwest.[4] In 1926 A.Y. Jackson and Edwin Holgate accompanied

Barbeau to the Upper Skeena, and the following year Pegi Nicol, Annie Savage, and Florence Wyle were sketching in the same region. The Exhibition of Canadian West Coast Art, Native, and Modern, sponsored by the National Museum and the National Gallery, was the apotheosis of this artistic and anthropological concern. Museum and art-gallery officials hoped that West Coast Indian artefacts would now become recognized 'as one of the most valuable of Canada's artistic productions'.[5]

In February 1927 Barbeau, a co-ordinator of the exhibition, had written to G.R. Grieg of the Art Gallery of Toronto about the contributors. The Euro-Canadian paintings that were to serve as a background to the Indian artefacts had been chosen; they would be displayed alongside over forty of Langdon Kihn's totem-pole paintings and Indian portraits, a small number of canvases by Edwin Holgate and A.Y. Jackson, and—'to add a touch of the eastern range of the Rockies'—the landscape paintings of Lawren Harris, J.E.H. MacDonald, and F.H. Varley. Barbeau added that there was still the work of one artist to be considered:

> Miss Emily Carr of Victoria has made interesting paintings in which the West Coast scenery and totem poles are included. Mr. Mortimer Lamb communicated favourably of their quality. Mr. Eric Brown is to see them during the summer and we will know whether they are worth while.[6]

It was with this in mind, shortly after arriving in Victoria and settling into the Empress Hotel, that Brown telephoned Miss Carr. He identified himself as the director of the National Gallery of Canada and asked if he might view her Indian pictures. Emily later recalled that she had never heard of the National Gallery and was initially hostile. 'I don't think that is possible,' she snapped, adding that all her pictures were stored in the basement. Brown quietly persisted until she agreed to see him.

Eric and Maud Brown walked from the Empress Hotel to Hill House. They easily located the apartment block on Simcoe Street, climbed the back stairs to the second landing, entered the small enclosed porch, and knocked on the door. The woman who greeted them was very short, very round, and very cautious, Maud Brown remembered. Introductions were made, then the Browns followed Emily along the narrow hall that led to the studio. The walls were covered with vividly coloured oil landscape paintings. Though probably her recent oil sketches, Emily assured Brown that they had all been painted in France. She directed their attention to the hooked rugs on the floor and to the pottery on the long leather-topped dining table. Brown was mildly impressed by her souvenir crafts, but told her that it was the Indian paintings he had come to see. After some prodding, Emily led him into a room off the studio. Here Brown found what he had come for: the walls were covered with sketches, watercolours, and oil paintings of totem poles, Indian villages, and portraits of the Indians themselves. Brown was overwhelmed. Not only had he found a vast collection, towering over that of Kihn's, but the work was 'powerful and original'.[7]

The three passed what remained of the afternoon in the back garden under the apple tree. The dogs—Adam, Eve, Moses, and Joseph—as well as the monkey Woo, drew much of the Browns' attention. So too did Emily. They soon discovered that she possessed an unending fund of stories of her travels among the Indians. They 'enjoyed her humour, her quickness of repartee and her own special peculiarities.' They were greatly impressed by her 'genuine love of the Indian', and very concerned when she told them that 'she had stopped painting because nobody understood her work.'[8] Brown assured Emily that her paintings would be appreciated in eastern Canada. He told her about a group of artists in Toronto, the Group of Seven, who, like her, were defying public opinion and the artistic establishment. He spoke of F.B. Housser, a writer who was a friend of the artists, and of his recently published book, *A Canadian Art Movement* (1926), which told of the Group and its struggle. By the end of the afternoon the Browns had sufficiently impressed Emily to secure from her a promise to send a number of her Indian paintings to the Exhibition of Canadian West Coast Art.

Eric Brown left Hill House with a great sense of accomplishment, for he had made a discovery. He had found more than another contributor to the exhibition: he had encountered an artist who had painted more of the West Coast Indians than any other person. If he had any regrets about not having pursued Mortimer Lamb's suggestion to consider her work in 1921, he did not reveal them. The following evening, at a public lecture in Victoria, he spoke as though he had never previously heard of Emily Carr. 'You have here in Victoria one of the most interesting painters in the whole of Canada,' he told a small audience gathered in the auditorium of the Girls' Central School. Her work, he said, was 'as good as anything that is being done in the country.'[9]

Brown was not patronizing the conservative Victorians. En route to Ottawa two days later, he wrote his assistant, Harry McCurry, about Miss Carr of Victoria, who 'has been painting fine stuff among the Indians for 20 years & is laughed at by the good early Victorians for her pains.' He was 'much impressed by her ability as an artist and by her vision' and astounded that she had been doing this work, unknown to him and to the rest of Canada, for so many years. He had 'put her on the map' by his words of praise to the locals. He told McCurry about his invitation to Miss Carr 'to send a collection to our Indian West Coast show' and instructed him to have the CPR contact her and arrange for shipping, because he did not think that she was 'a fast mover'.[10] Brown also wrote Barbeau, who was making his way down the Skeena, that he had been 'favourably impressed' with the Victoria artist's work. He may also have suggested that Barbeau visit her on his return south, as Barbeau replied that, after completing his lectures in Vancouver in late October, he would visit Miss Carr. Barbeau added that he had just seen four of her pictures at Hazelton, and judged them to be 'certainly from a genuine artist'.[11] When Brown arrived in Winnipeg on the last leg of his journey, he was still ebullient about Emily and her work. Walter J. Phillips remembered him 'blowing into our house . . . full of this new painter that he'd discovered.'[12] Barbeau, having just visited Emily, wrote to A.Y. Jackson that her work 'has proved the greatest possible find to Mr. Brown & ourselves.'[13]

Brown requested from Emily, and received, an autobiographical letter containing a dramatic story that made his discovery all the more important. Her references to hardship and rebuffs, her rejection by the West, were quite in keeping with the low opinion he already had of the artistic climate in Victoria and Vancouver. An awkwardly typewritten page and a half (she was learning to type at the Sprott-Shaw Business School), filled with typos and makeshift spellings, the letter was Emilys autobiographical canon:

M. Emily Carr, born in Victoria of English parents. On leaving high school I went to San Francisco and became a student of the Mark Hopkins school of Art. After three years in San Francisco I returned to Victoria, taught childrens classes and saved strenuously to go to England. I attended the old Westminster school of art there. But after the free wild life of the West, London, wilted the very life out of me, so I went down to Cornwall and studied in the open, also to the Bushey studios. Returning again to Westminsters School, I broke down completely; wrestled three years with a desperate illness, then returned to Canada and started all over again, working and saving this time with paris in view. Teaching in Vancouver and very successful with childrens classes, I was asked to teach in the art club and made a complete failure, their comblaint being, 'that I could not realize that they were just amusing themselves and tried to make the ladies work in earnest,' so they dismissed me, I was glad.

In 1911 I went to Paris with a letter of introduction to a Modern painter of scotch birth Harry Gibb, this man opened my eyes to the joyousness of the new school. At that time he was being bitterly criticised.

By his advice I became a student at the Colorissy (don't know how to spell it) studio one of the schools where the men and women worked together, this he felt would make my work stronger, and may be one reason that I have heard strangers discussing my work say 'that chaps'. I could not stand the airlessness of the life rooms for long the Doctors stating as they had done London that, 'there was something about those big cities, that those Canadiens from their big spaces couldent stand, it was just like putting a pine tree in a pot.' So I left Paris and joined outdoor classes under Mr. Gibb who was then in Britanny. When my money was spent I returned to Canada, but they hated and ridiculed my newer work, the first exhibition in my own studio, made them angry the schools where I had taught would not have me back.

When I sent to an exhibition they dishonoured my work in every way, putting it behind things, unders shelves, or on the ceiling. My friends begged me to go back to my old way of painting, but I had tasted the joys of a bigger way it would have been impossible had I wanted to, which I did not. When ever I could afford it I went up north among the Indians and the woods and forgot all about everything in the joy of those lonely wonderful places, I decided to try to make as good a representative collection of those old villages and wonderful totem poles as I could, for the love of the people, and the love of the places, and the love of the art, whether any body liked them or not I did not care a bean.

I painted them to please myself in my own way, but also I stuck rigidly to fact because I knew I was painting history. The war came, I had a living to make of course nobody wanted to buy my pictures I'd never tried to paint to please them anyway. So I did horrible things like taking boarders to make a living, and the very little time I had for painting I tried to paint in the despised adorable joyous modern way. The last two years I have taken up the pottery, adapting and utilizing my Indian designs for it a much pleasanter livelihood than catering to peoples appetites . . . . [14]

Emily's theme of struggle and rejection, later embellished and enlarged upon in her autobiographical writings, evoked sympathy and even approval: the myth that it was somehow beneficial for artists to live and work in deprived and hostile conditions was widely accepted. Emily herself embraced this doctrine when she wrote of one of her trials as 'all part of what I had to go through, part of my training.' Canadians in the 1920s were particularly sympathetic to struggle stories; part of the success of the Group of Seven was due to the fact that they had been cast, by themselves and their supporters, in the role of abused but heroic artists. Emily may well have been influenced by what she now read of the Group and their triumph over an uncomprehending public. She had bought F.B. Housser's *A Canadian Art Movement*, recommended by Brown. In it she read Housser's exaggerated account of the Group's struggle 'against the entire press of the country and the opinion of those whose word was accepted as authoritative in Canada on questions of art.'[15] As she read, she mentally transferred the Group's reported adversities to herself. She associated critical reviews of their work— appearing in the *Montreal Star* and Toronto's *Saturday Night*— with the negative reaction she remembered receiving from the Vancouver *Province* and the Victoria *Colonist*. People who ridiculed the Group's work could be identified with the old tabbies who tinkled teacups at the Island Arts and Crafts exhibitions. The dispute between the Group and the academic painters of the Royal Canadian Academy and the Ontario Society of Artists was analogous to her difficulties with the conservative art societies of British Columbia.

Emily could also identify herself with the Group's ideals. Housser wrote that they believed a distinctive Canadian art could be developed through 'a direct contact with Nature itself'.[16] J.E.H. MacDonald and Lawren Harris set down 'their own reactions' to the Canadian North, forgetting the 'rules which they felt hindered this natural expression. . . . The seductive influence of so-called old masters and old schools and modern European artists' was not for the Group: their treatment and technique were derived from the northern-Ontario wilderness itself.[17]

Though the Group had its roots in commercial Art Nouveau, nor- thern-European Expressionism, and the American regionalist movement, they and their supporters believed, and wanted others to believe, that they were creating a wholly indigenous Canadian art. Their belief in an art that grew out of the land, rather than in the academies, corresponded to ideas Emily had expressed in 1912 and attempted to put into practice after meeting the Pattersons in the early 1920s. Since England, she had recognized a profound difference between the hazy English atmosphere and the clear Canadian one, between undulating paddocked meadows and thick tangled forests. Ever since France, she had been intent upon applying the new ideas she had acquired there to 'this big land' of British Columbia.[18] More recently, through the Pattersons and her Seattle acquaintances, she had made contact with others who were also concerned with creating an indigenous landscape art of the Northwest Coast. Having long conceived of herself as a westerner, she had never given a thought to an art that could be called Canadian. But when she met Brown and read Housser, she became filled with the Group of Seven's aspirations for the creation of a new Canadian art.

Unconsciously disproving Brown's impression that she was 'not a fast mover', Emily labelled, priced, and crated (with the help of a carpenter) twenty-seven watercolours and eleven oil paintings within two weeks of her September-twelfth meeting with Brown. When Marius Barbeau visited her a month later, her pictures had arrived safely in Ottawa and she was preparing to travel east for the opening of the exhibition, as Brown had offered her a return CNR pass from Vancouver to Ottawa. Her sisters urged her to make the trip and offered to tend her creatures and the apartment house while she was away. Excited, especially at the prospect of meeting the Group in Vancouver and Toronto and viewing their works, Emily left Victoria on the eighth of November.

She stopped in Vancouver long enough to dispose of twelve Belgian griffon dogs and to make her first acquaintance with a member of the Group, F.H. Varley, who had been residing there for a year. She visited him at the Vancouver School of Applied and Decorative Art, where he was teaching, then accompanied him to his Lynn Valley home across the harbour. Her response to Varley's work was favourable. She found the sketches 'most delightful'. They were 'appealingly Canadian' and offered 'a new delineation of a great country'.[19]

Once Emily found herself sitting idle on the train bound for Toronto, her misanthropic tendencies rose to the surface and she committed her dislike of her fellow passengers to a journal she began for the trip. The only other woman in the car was too religious, her husband had a voice like a gramophone, and the porter after Winnipeg was a 'grumpy old nigger' who looked 'exactly like "Woo" but not so pretty or cuddlesome'. Later another woman joined her car, but she too annoyed Emily. She laughed in a strange manner and made 'no secret to the whole car' of 'what "undies" ' she was wearing. A few old men looked foolish as they surreptitiously ate out of their lunch boxes—while Emily munched openly on the peanut-butter sandwiches and apples she had brought with her. But her exasperation vanished when she arrived in Toronto early Sunday morning, the thirteenth of November. She went straight to Kate

Mather's and received a warm welcome. After spending the day with Kate and her son Dick, she booked into her hotel—the Tuxedo on Sherbourne Street—and prepared to meet the Group. Varley had wired ahead an introduction, and arrangements had been made for Miss Buell, of the Women's Art Association, to take her around to the artists' studios.

A.Y. Jackson, the first artist Emily visited, lived in the Studio Building on Severn Street where he, J.E.H. MacDonald, and Lawren Harris worked. Fourteen or fifteen young students were gathered to meet her in Jackson's studio. They had tea, and sweets were passed around on the tops of cake tins. Carl Schaefer—then a student—has recalled that Emily 'appeared jolly and so pleased to meet us', and was 'enthusiastic about what was going on in Toronto'.[20] She viewed Jackson's three canvases of Indian villages in the Upper Skeena and felt they had something her work lacked: rhythm and poetry. So impressed was she by Jackson's Indian pictures that she felt 'a little as if beaten at my own game'. She consoled herself, however, with the thought that 'perhaps his haven't quite the love in them of the people and the country that mine have.'[21] The following day she visited Arthur Lismer's garden studio. His painting had the same rhythm as Jackson's but more poetry. He was 'going on to higher and bigger things', with more 'sweep and rhythm' of the lines, stronger colours, simpler forms.[22] Two days later, under a bleak November sky, she picked her way through the slush of Severn Street and climbed the Studio Building stairs to the third floor to call on Lawren Harris. On that day her ideas about art wholly changed.

Emily had been anxious for the meeting. Harris's *Above Lake Superior*, as reproduced in Housser's book, had impressed her as 'an austere formal picture of great depth and dignity'. Now she hoped to see more. Miss Buell, her guide, led her into the bare, grey-walled studio. The distinguished-looking grey-haired artist greeted her kindly, in a quiet and gentlemanly manner. Emily sat down on his sofa, and as he pulled out painting after painting for her to see, she hardly said a word. She was 'like a dumbfounded fool', leaving Miss Buell to do all the talking. Nothing she had seen before—in England, in France, any-where—had touched her so deeply, 'right to the very core'. Gibb's work in Paris had been strange and new, but Harris's was 'a revelation [,] a getting outside of oneself and finding a new self in a place you did not know existed.' His pictures were a radical departure from the prettiness of England and the modernity of France. They struck deep 'into the vast lovely soul of Canada; they plumbed to her depths, climbed her heights and floated into her spaces.' On Thursday, the seventeenth of November 1927, she had an epiphany.

Back in her hotel room she could not sleep. 'Two things had hold of me with a double clutch. Canada and Art. They were tossing me round & tearing me.' Between bursts of crying, she wrote in the journal she had begun a week earlier: 'Oh, God, what have I seen? Where have I been? Something has spoken to the very soul of me, wonderful, mighty, not of

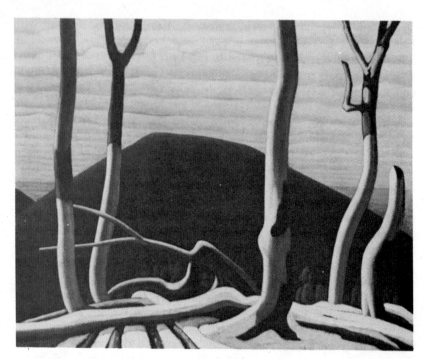

Lawren Harris. *Above Lake Superior,* about 1922. Oil on canvas, 48 x 60. Courtesy L.S.H. Holdings. Art Gallery of Ontario, Toronto. Gift from the Reuben and Kate Leonard Canadian Fund, 1929.

this world.' Harris was 'rising into serene, uplifted planes, above the swirl into holy places.'[23] She had always felt nearer to God in the landscape than under the nose of Bishop Cridge. The 'something that speaks, that vital something with no name', of which she had written in 1912, had been 'sometimes almost within reach but never quite.'[24] The discovery that Harris had not only found God in the vastness of the northern wilderness but had shown Him in his work stirred her deeply. His triumph made her feel that 'perhaps I shall find God here, the God I've longed and hunted for and failed to find.'[25] Giddy with the excitement of discovery, exhausted with trying to define whatever it was in Harris's pictures that had spoken to her that afternoon, she tried to sleep—without much success. What she had seen and felt in Harris's studio was 'surging through my whole being, the wonder of it all, like a great river rushing on, dark and turbulent, and rushing and irresistible, and carrying me away on its wild swirl like a helpless little bundle of wreckage.' A wreckage she was the next day—limp, spent, and exhausted.

Harris had invited her to return and she intended to do so—alone, this time—but she would have to put off another visit until she came back from Ottawa. The few days she had left in Toronto were already booked: by Miss Buell for visits to the studio of J.E.H. MacDonald, another member of the Group, and F.B. Housser and his artist-wife Bess; Sunday for going to the Toronto Art Gallery with the Mathers; and Monday, her last day in Toronto, for a visit to the home of Carol

Williams Pearson, who now lived with her husband Bill on a farm outside the city. The MacDonald visit was an anticlimax. He was away teaching and his son Thoreau showed his father's pictures, which Emily enjoyed, 'but without thrill'.[26] The Housser visit, on the other hand, was a delight and she found Mr Housser to be one of the Group in spirit.

At 1:30 p.m. on Monday, the twenty-first of November, Emily was off to Ottawa after missing the train to Carol's. Irritated by her mistake, and finding the Ottawa train stifling and smelly, she was in a vile mood by the time she arrived in the capital city. 'The acid virgin behind the desk' at the YWCA 'looked me up & down; decided she could give me a room.' Emily took the room, but stayed only one night.

Before moving to Bromley Hall the next day, she went down Metcalf Street to the Victoria Memorial Museum, where both the National Gallery and the National Museum were housed. She was given a royal welcome by Brown, Barbeau, and McCurry, and by other participants in the West Coast show who were helping to set it up: Edwin Holgate, Pegi Nicol, and Arthur Lismer. In the thirteen days that preceded the opening of the exhibition, Emily was teaed, dined, and taken for drives by her new friends. There were long talks in the Browns' charming flat about art, Paris, England, and the Browns' religion, Christian Science. There were evenings in Barbeau's house, where he 'beat a great Indian drum and sang some Indian songs that were very touching and real.'[27] There were pleasant afternoons in the National Gallery, where Emily sketched the Indian artefacts that were being set up for the exhibition. Using their motifs, she designed the cover for the exhibition catalogue†. She moved in with the Barbeaus and their two 'dear' young children, a grateful guest in their house on McLaren Street whose atmosphere was 'delightful'.[28] It was a happy time. She was meeting all the 'worthwhiles', the 'people who really count and are shaping a nation.'[29]

On a snowy fifth of December, the Exhibition of Canadian West Coast Art opened. Several rooms of the Victoria Museum were illuminated when Emily and the Barbeaus arrived in a cab. Inside, on the second floor, native art was juxtaposed with modern portrayals of the people and the land. Haida totems stood next to the village scenes of Edwin Holgate, A.Y. Jackson, and Walter J. Phillips; stiff-necked Indian portraits by Pegi Nicol and Langdon Kihn overlooked Tsimshian masks and kerfed boxes; cedar-bark capes and spruce-root hats hung beside panoramic views of the Rockies by Lawren Harris and F.H. Varley. No paintings bridged the gap between native and modern more completely than Emily Carr's. Her village scenes of beached canoes at Alert Bay, deserted community houses on the Queen Charlotte Islands, and Tsimshian poles straggling along the banks of the Skeena River provided an evocative setting for the native artefacts. The totem symbols worked into her hooked rugs and painted on her clay pottery echoed those painted on the Kwakiutl storage boxes, carved on the Haida paddles, and woven into the Chilkat blankets.

The opening, as Emily recalled it, was 'a fizzle'.[30] Invitations had not

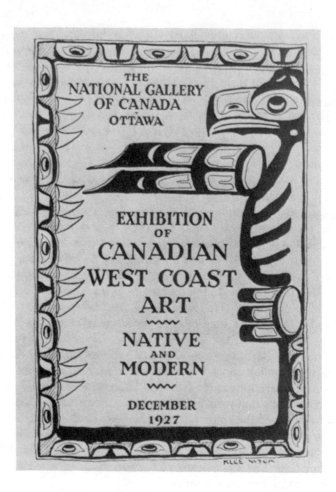

THE
NATIONAL GALLERY
OF CANADA
OTTAWA

EXHIBITION
OF
CANADIAN
WEST COAST
ART
〜〜〜
NATIVE
AND
MODERN
〜〜〜
DECEMBER
1927

Catalogue cover designed by Emily. Black and white. Courtesy VAG. NGC.

been sent to the usual gallery members, only to a handful of artists and the museum and gallery staff in the building. Emily stood in her black satin dress and nervously pulled her white elbow-length gloves off and on.[31] The Browns, embarrassed by the small turnout, were 'a trifle too forced in their gay humour'.[32] Marius Barbeau was hurt by the poor reception arrangements made by the Gallery and could only remark at the conclusion, 'Well that's over. Now we'll go on to the next job.'[33]

Some people said grand things to Emily about her work and she wondered, in her usual suspicious way, if they were really being sincere. She had only copied the Indian motifs; it was the Indians, not she, who deserved the credit for creating the wonderful forms. Comparison of her work with that of the Group's was a different matter. She had to admit that her paintings were not as good in workmanship. Their rhythmic landscapes and full-volumed poles made hers look stiff. Their cool tones made her vivid colours appear garish. As she wrote years later, her work after France was 'B.C. done Frankish, not real B.C. sombreness'.[34] But, as usual, she compensated for these shortcomings: 'I knew the people and

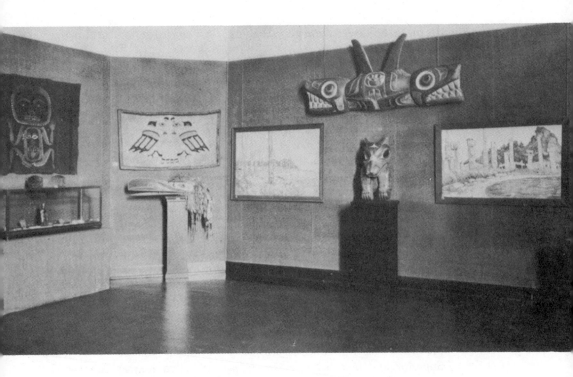

Exhibition of Canadian West Coast Art, the National Gallery of Canada, 1927. The top photograph shows a hooked rug, *Yan, Queen Charlotte Islands*, and *Skedans, Queen Charlotte Islands* by Emily Carr. Courtesy VAG. NGC. The bottom photograph shows two rooms of the exhibition with three paintings by Emily Carr on the right: *Old Village Guyasdoms, Tanoo, Q.C. Islands*, and *Indian Village, Alert Bay*. Courtesy VAG. NGC.

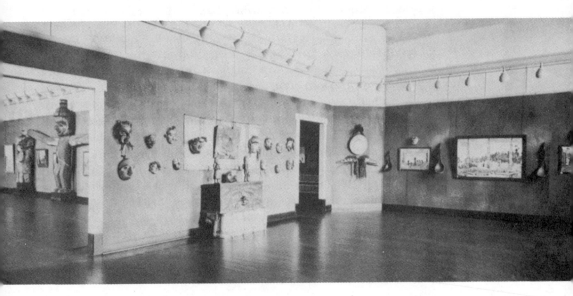

the places & I loved them more than people who had gone west and given them a swift look over.'

A few days after the opening, Emily was in Montreal. Once again the artists were responsive. Annie Savage, who had participated in the exhibition, took her to Holgate's studio, where she saw more of his totem-pole paintings. The highlight of her Montreal visit, however, was the Royal Canadian Academy exhibition at the Art Association of Montreal. There Emily had an opportunity to study some of the Group's work, leisurely and alone. She was critically appreciative of Mac-Donald's *Solemn Land*, Jackson's *Autumn in Algoma*, and Lismer's *Happy Isles*. She found Frank Carmichael's work 'a *little* pretty and too soft', and A.J. Casson's cold and uncompromising.[35] But Harris's *Mountain Forms* was unsurpassingly beautiful. The great cone, the spiritual light rising from behind it, then moving across the canvas, stirred her deeply. Every other picture paled in comparison.

Leaving Montreal, Emily stopped in Ottawa only long enough to phone the Barbeaus, then went on to Toronto and to Carol Pearson's farm, where she spent three days. Her last four days in the city provided a memorable climax to her trip. In Ottawa and Montreal the work of Lawren Harris had haunted her, and she had returned to Toronto expressly to see him once again: to get another look at *Above Lake Superior* and to talk about painting. She called him as soon as she arrived. He not only made an appointment to see her at his studio, but invited her to dine at his home that evening. They talked little. Harris played a symphony on his orthophonic and Emily—absorbing the glorious sounds that filled the room, along with his paintings—was carried off into another world.

Two days later she was once again sitting on the sofa in Harris's large grey studio, looking at *Above Lake Superior* and revelling in the other canvases he brought out for viewing. Sensing her enthusiasm, Harris talked a great deal about his work. He showed her the different ingredients he put into his paint to give his colour vibration and explained the technique of rubbing raw linseed oil into the canvas before applying the paint. But most important, he discussed his religion and how it was linked closely to his art.

Harris's beliefs, growing out of an appreciation of the transcendentalism of Ralph Waldo Emerson and an interest in Eastern and occult writing, found their ultimate expression in theosophy, which professed a direct, mystical apprehension of God.[36] It became for him a means of directing both his life and his art towards spiritual fulfilment. Harris sought to show the 'inner sense of order, proportion, and rightness, and the universal rhythmic flow and balance' in nature by reducing its diverse forms to cones and spheres and by employing dramatic lighting effects—an elusive glow radiating from behind the landscape, or shafts of light penetrating the heavens.[37] Art, he felt, was not a product of the intellect or the result of academic training, but the intuitive response of the artist to a higher spirit.

Emily found much of what Harris told her about his interpretation of theosophy appealing: the role of the artist as teacher and high priest; the call to create a new Canadian art; and especially the artist's relationship to God through nature. She had long ceased to be satisfied by conventional religion and had not attended the Reformed Episcopal Church of her family regularly since her return from England in 1904. Harris's ability to convey the spirituality of nature in his painting impressed her greatly, and she was open to any teaching that would enable her to achieve his level of consciousness. She wanted to get hold of something in his work that hers lacked—the 'bigness lying behind it'. She did not want to paint like him. Their temperaments—his 'calm' and hers all 'turbulence and eruption'—prohibited that. But Emily felt that, given a chance, she too could bring the Divine spirit of nature into her painting. She longed to return to her totems and 'wrestle something out for myself, to look for things I did not know of before, and to feel and strive and earnestly try to be true and sincere to the country and to myself.'[38] Aware of the great impression his work and his ideas had made on Emily, Harris encouraged her to find her own way in expressing her material.

The meeting in Harris's studio, on the thirteenth of December, was by sheer coincidence Emily's fifty-sixth birthday and it was 'a wonderful birthday treat'.[39] In retrospect it became much more than that to her. Not only had she found a person whose painting she admired, who was sympathetic to her difficulties, but through Harris she was moved to explore the spiritual significance of her own work. 'I guess that long talk in Lawren Harris's studio was the pivot on which turned my entire life.'

Lismer and Jackson returned to Toronto from the West Coast Exhibition in Ottawa filled with enthusiasm for Emily's work. Though they felt that her knowledge of contemporary art was poor, they told her that she 'had got the spirit of the country and the people more than the others who had been there.'[40] They now recognized her as the 'new type of artist' about whom Fred Housser had written. She, like them, had exchanged 'the velvet coat and flowing tie' of the studio artist, in the words of Housser, for the attire of the 'bushwhacker and prospector' who 'paddles, portages and makes camp; sleeps in the out-of-doors under the stars; climbs mountains with his sketch box on his back.'[41] They thought that Emily had not only accomplished this without National Gallery patronage or CNR passes—she never revealed to anyone the assistance she received from the Grand Trunk Pacific in 1912—but had preceded them by several years. In 1907, when Emily first painted the totems in Alaska, Jackson had not yet travelled to Georgian Bay, nor Tom Thomson to Algonquin Park. In 1908, when she had spent the first of many summers at Alert Bay, Lawren Harris was in the Middle East making illustrations for *Harper's Magazine*. By September 1913, when Arthur Lismer became the last member of the Group to discover the North, Emily had held her huge solo exhibition in Vancouver, showing over 200 works of totem poles and houses in Sitka, the Queen Charlotte Islands, the Skeena River, and the west coast of Vancouver Island. Harris, Lismer, Jackson, and MacDonald were immensely impressed by this fifty-six-year-old woman who had not only discovered the North long before them, but had done so travelling with bedroll and pack, by canoe and on foot. As Harris said many years later, Emily had been pursuing the same aim as the Group, but alone, unfortified by understanding companions.[42]

Emily's stay in Toronto was the highlight of her first trip east. As well as the three memorable visits with Harris, there had been parties at the Houssers', lunches with Miss Buell, and dinner with Kate Mather. For her birthday Emily received 'three home letters with the dearest wishes from the girls', which helped to suppress her pangs of homesickness. She was so happy that she even attempted to buy a new dress to wear to Harris's. After viewing her ample figure in one store's multiple mirrors, and seeing 'fat in all the places it was not wanted', she returned to her 'old raggy black', content that she had done her duty by making the effort.

The evening after this third meeting with Harris, Emily left Toronto, having spent the day scrambling about the bookshops in search of the four books he had recommended. (Clive Bell's *Art* and P.D. Ouspensky's theosophical tome, *Tertium Organum*, were all she could find.) On her trip west, she alternated knitting with reading.

Almost six weeks after her departure, on the twenty-first of December, Emily returned to her sisters, dogs, and monkey. It had been a momentous trip that made the year 1927 her *annus mirabilis*. Her work had been raised to national recognition; she had met the major artists in Canadian painting and linked herself to the nucleus of Canadian art. She could now project her westernness into their Canadianness and share their ambition to create a new art for Canada and their quest for an artistic expression of the essence of the land. She had already diminished her sense of failure and non-acceptance by linking her 'rebuffs' to theirs, and was all the more justified in doing so because the Group now accepted her as one of them. The leading members—Harris, Jackson, Lismer, and MacDonald—had embraced her fully and she was ecstatic. She had found a group of artists whose work, though it went beyond her own, had inspired her to emulation and achievement. One of them, Harris, even promised to watch, prod, and encourage her, as Gibb had done before. This thrilled her because she empathized with him most. 'I seem to *know* and feel what he has to say.'

Emily was also gratified that the National Gallery and the National Museum had jointly recognized her Indian work. The goal of her painting since 1907 had been the portrayal of the Indian totem pole, and though she had turned to the landscape during the last thirteen years, she was now inspired to go back to the totem motif. But now she would paint this subject matter differently, with less regard for history and cold fact. 'Next time I paint Indians,' she had pledged in Toronto, 'I'm going off on a tangent tear.'[43]

After Christmas festivities with Lizzie and Alice—and two weeks of cleaning house both inside and out, satisfying tenants' complaints, and nursing sick dogs—Emily began to paint. Though there was no respite from the usual intrusions, she devised a way of partitioning off her studio to give her privacy while she painted. Feeling more secure behind the partition, she pulled out some pre-1913 Indian sketches and plunged into work. Encouragement for this bout of painting was not long in coming from her eastern friends. She received a letter from Eric Brown telling her of the great success of the West Coast Exhibition, which had moved to Toronto, and expressing pleasure in her return to painting. 'You are at the very height of your powers,' he wrote; with renewed interest and public appreciation 'you will do lovely things.'[44] He was looking forward to the time when she, Varley, and others would start a West Coast group. The same day a letter arrived from Marius Barbeau confirming the success of the show in Toronto. People greatly liked her work and, more important to Emily, Barbeau had heard Harris—who had just seen her paintings for the first time—remark that they showed 'the greatest familiarity with the subject and the best understanding.'[45] Days later a letter from Harris himself arrived. It was a 'wonderful letter', she wrote to Barbeau. Harris 'really liked my stuff & found something worth while in it.'[46] Harris had told her that her work was more impressive than Lismer had led him to believe. As for criticism, he could offer none: 'I feel you have found a way of your own wonderfully suited to the Indian spirit, Indian feeling for life and nature.'[47] As if to reassure her that her paintings were more than a copying of Indian forms and designs, he added that they were works of art in their own right.

The ensuing correspondence with Harris marked for Emily the first real exchange of thoughts about her painting she had ever had. In her letters to him she clarified her aims and beliefs. Harris's replies were sympathetic, encouraging, suggestive, and gave her much-needed support. He advised her not to let her bouts of depression and feelings of isolation interfere with her task: 'when we enter the stream of creative life—then we are on our own—have to find self reliance—achieve conviction—learn to accept—and begin to see a supreme logic behind the inner struggle.'[48] Harris assured her that he was looking forward to her new work—a unique experience for Emily.

The National Gallery, Marius Barbeau, and the National Museum all purchased her paintings in the spring of 1928.[49] Barbeau included *The Totem Pole of the Bear and the Moon* as an illustration in his novel based on Indian legends, *The Downfall of Temlaham* (1928). (Emily was paid a token fee.) The Canadian Handicraft Guild bought three boxes of her pottery and two hooked rugs to sell in their Montreal store. In addition, shipments of her souvenir pottery were requested for sale at the West Coast Exhibition in Toronto, and in Montreal when it moved to that city in March. Brown included some of her pictures in the Canadian Annual at the National Gallery and Barbeau suggested that they could also be exhibited at the Canadian National Exhibition in Toronto that summer.

The press was enthusiastic about the National Gallery's discovery. When the West Coast Exhibition was in Toronto, Emily was featured in the *Toronto Star Weekly*. Muriel Brewster's lengthy article, 'Some Ladies Prefer Indians', made Emily's northern journeys sound as prodigious as the Group's. Emily had been 'lost, strayed, ship-wrecked and starved' as she drifted from village to village during the summers when she recorded Indian villages and totem poles. For this effort she had received no appreciation in her native province. When her paintings were exhibited, they were 'scorned, laughed at and hidden away'. She had 'lost faith in herself as a painter', Brewster continued, until the National Gallery invited her to contribute to their West Coast Exhibition.[50] Emily's story of rejection, told to the director of the National Gallery only months earlier, now became widely known, as did her reputation of using Indian themes for her subject matter.

That winter and spring her letters to her eastern friends were full of work and enthusiasm. As she wrote to Brown:

> Have just had an orgie of canvas making. I make even the wooden stretchers, mitre the corners & then stretch & prepare raw canvas. I have made 15 dandi ones. seems a shame to paint on them. I am hard at work, I find that the best plan is to get buisy early, before the disturbances of the day begin, have been at my easle at 6 a.m. most mornings this week.[51]

Charles Scott, from the Vancouver School of Art, went to see her and she proudly reported his amazement at how much she had accomplished.

Emily was thrilled to be working on the Indian material again but was in need of new subject matter. She wrote to her old friend, William Halliday, at Alert Bay to ask about conditions there. Of her Haida friends, Clara and William Russ, she requested travel assistance in the Queen Charlotte Islands. Barbeau was also importuned for a list of interesting Nass River villages. 'I just thirst to get back,' she wrote to Barbeau; she wanted 'to get the feel of the places again', even if the poles were gone.[52]

The Russes offered to take Emily to points on the Queen Charlotte Islands for a relatively inexpensive twelve dollars a day. Barbeau urged her to revisit the Skeena, where he felt she would find the best poles, and advised her to contact Walter E. Walker, director of the Arrandale Cannery, who had offered to oblige his friends and artists. Brown was also helpful, securing a rail and boat pass from the CNR to ease her expenses. By the end of March 1928 she had her plans well laid for a six-week trip to Alert Bay, the Skeena and Nass valleys, and the Queen Charlotte Islands. With cash from sales of her pictures and pottery, with the CNR pass, and the encouragement of her eastern friends, she set out in late June 1928 on her most ambitious journey.

Emily had always felt that it was necessary to wrestle with the elements in order to get the feel of the North. But she seemed to do little else that summer. During the first half of her trip, in villages around

Alert Bay and the Skeena, she had only one really fine day. It had ceased to rain by the time she left the Skeena and reached the Nass, but the mosquitoes emerged from the bogs and 'were *simply fearful*', making work 'a torment'.[53] In the Queen Charlotte Islands the rain returned and it poured unceasingly. Conditions were hardly favourable to good sketching as she worked in broken-down Indian grave and community houses, clad, when it was not raining, in hot and uncomfortable clothing for protection against the mosquitoes.

Emily had hoped to find her best material in the Queen Charlottes. Fond memories of travelling with Clara and William Russ to the forsaken villages of Cumshewa, Skedans, and Tanoo had made her save those islands for the end of her trip. But everything seemed to go wrong. She arrived at the height of the fishing season and William Russ was unable to fulfil his promise to take her sketching in his boat. Another Indian guide was found—likely through her niece, Emily English, whose husband was now managing the South Bay Cannery in the Charlottes. Had the trip been completed, Emily might not have begrudged the fifty-dollar cost, but on the first day, just off Skedans, a terrible storm hit them. She became ill and asked to be landed on the beach, where she attempted to dry her clothing under her tent fly. Her Indian guide went back in the dinghy for his niece and nephew and left the gas launch dead in the water while they struggled ashore. As it drifted towards the rocks the party watched in dismay—Emily for her dog Ginger Pop, still on board, and the Indians for their boat. A few hours later a Norwegian seiner picked them up and saved the boat. Forced onto the stormy sea once again, Emily was desperately sick; she lay sprawled on her back on top of the fish hatch until two men carried her to the captain's bunk. At Cumshewa she left the seiner and was reunited with Ginger Pop. She spent the night in a Japanese scow and the following day caught a fish-packer back to the South Bay Cannery. She had neither time nor money to return to those villages—whose poles, she felt, were 'more sober and desolate and tragic' than the poles on the mainland.[54] Having done little work, she left the Charlottes a few days later.

Though weather permitted Emily access to those villages on the Nass River where Barbeau had assured her she would find some of the finest specimens of Northwest Indian art, getting upriver at the height of the fishing season was no easy task. She had to spend almost a week at Walter Walker's Arrandale Cannery waiting for transportation. The Walkers were most obliging: there was tea and a chat in the afternoons, cheap meals in the mess hall, and a pleasant cottage for sleeping. But there was no sketching to be done. Finally Walker freed Fred McKay and his boat from cannery work to take her to Greenville, a new village with no poles but within easy reach of the old villages of Gittex and Angedar.[55] Emily passed most of a week walking around the swampy village and refining her mosquito armour: thick duck pantalettes to protect her legs, two sets of gloves for her hands, and a broad-brimmed hat with a cheese-cloth veil, complete with sewn-in glasses. Recently

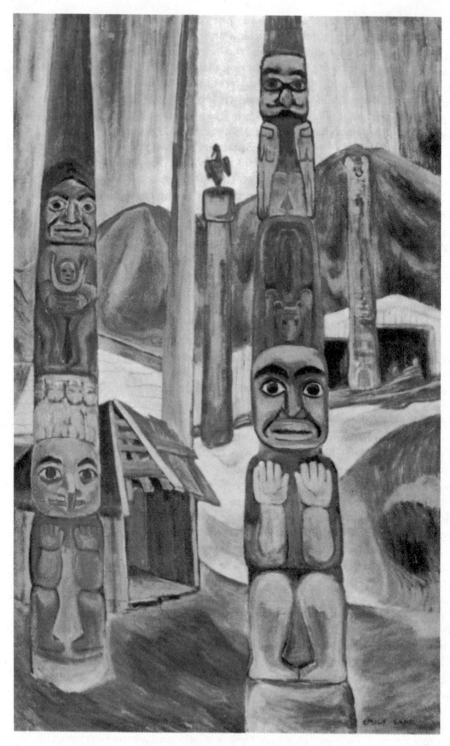

Corner of Kitwancool Village, 1928. Oil on canvas, 43 3/4 x 27.
Collection Dr and Mrs Max Stern, Dominion Gallery, Montreal.

ravaged by fire, Greenville offered no sketching subjects of interest to Emily. Nor was there much company. Its only inhabitants during the fishing season were a pack of half-starved dogs and an elderly native couple who lived at the opposite end of the village from her schoolhouse home. The old man, Lazareth, grudgingly took her to the deserted village sites across the river in his rowboat. He waited in the middle of the river, to escape the mosquitoes, while Emily, dressed in her outlandish costume, pushed her way through the beach grass and stinging nettles to Gittex and Angedar, where it took only a day to sketch the poles she had waited a week to get to.

When Emily had made her Skeena trip in 1912 she had been anxious to see the poles at Kitwancool, a village lying fifteen miles north of Kitwanga, but had been warned against travelling there because the native inhabitants were notoriously unfriendly.[56] Now at Kitwanga again, she was offered transportation to Kitwancool and did not hesitate to accept.

> I went in on a wagon with the chief & his son & was very well treated. It is an awful waggon road took 7 hours & nearly bumped the life out of me. The heat & dust were terrific there were 4 indian men (one just returning from jail). I went in for two days & got held up for 5 by a terriffic storm it poured rain & hail for 4 days which made working *very difficult*. I crawled into little grave houses which were clammy cold & leaky & always in the wrong spot to get the right view. I was particularly sorry not to do some better stuff there as the poles are very lovely they are in shocking repair but the carving is so tenderly done with great expression. I slept out the first night but after the storm the Indians gave me a corner of their house it was a huge log affair very clean just one enormous room. The chief & his wife & son had one corner a married daughter & her husband & 3 children another & I had mine. Was given a table & a chair & I had my own bed & hung my tent fly across the corner. While the weather stormed there were good fires & it was cosy & I was much interested in it all. They were a fine bunch, kind clean & dignified. There were two babies hanging up from the rafters in cradles which everyone shoved as they passed & kept rocking. I was struck with the great resemblance of the women to the carved faces on the poles they might have been family portraits & probably some were. I worked in a broken down community house which gave scanty shelter & was shared by some dozen Indian horses who took all the dry spots & left me the leaks. I shall get some stuff out of my sketches but do wish I'd had fair weather.[57]

Though 'in shocking repair', the poles in Kitwancool were perhaps her greatest find. Many had fallen to the ground and were overgrown with grass and fireweed; some tottered backwards or forwards; only a few stood proudly erect. But together they comprised the greatest number in any village she visited that summer. In Skidegate and Masset, in the Charlottes, where Emily had found some of her finest material in 1912, there was not a single high pole left. In Alert Bay, only three poles remained. In the Skeena the federal government had attempted to restore some poles by applying a heavy coat of grey preservative paint, but this diminished their subtlety and made them less interesting. Decay, pilferage, and export through the burgeoning curio trade had not been offset by new work. Though some carving was still being done—especially in the Kwakiutl villages of the south—the new poles seemed superficial and meaningless. Emily felt the Indian was now 'carving to please the tourist and to make money for himself, not to express the glory of his tribe.'[58]

She was witnessing a more advanced stage of the acculturation of the Indian she had noted in 1912. Though the Indian population was still declining rapidly, teachers claimed that the enrolment in their Indian schools was at an all-time high and the clergy boasted that there were few heathens among British Columbia's Indian population.[59] The Indians were absorbing the white man's way of life, partly out of emulation, partly for survival. Emily noted the change in her Queen Charlotte friends, Clara and William Russ. They now lived in a new house, purchased their goods from a mail-order catalogue, and were too busy earning their livelihood during her summer visit to fulfil their promise of transportation assistance. It was in Clara's mother, the friendly pipe-smoking Mrs Brown, that Emily found the traditional Indian, the Indian of her childhood. Elderly natives often disappointed her, however. The old couple in Greenville treated her with indifference; she had received more attention from the pack of half-starved dogs that roamed the village.

On this 1928 excursion, Emily was more prepared than ever before to live among the Indians. She chose to sleep in their villages rather than in the mission houses. She travelled to the remote villages without a white companion. (Six-pound Ginger Pop was her only protection.) Yet while she was more adventurous, more eager to meet the Indians, they were less eager to meet her. She quickly discovered that she was no longer a novelty to them. Whites were now either mistrusted or simply ignored. Unable to find much evidence of the Indian she had long idealized, Emily turned to the deserted villages. There, among the dilapidated poles, she sensed the carver's intense feeling for his culture, his relationship to his emblems and to nature. When she sat before the 'Totem Mother' in Kitwancool, she saw the 'strange, wild beauty' that was carved deep into the pole.[60] The intensity, the power, the spirit that Emily had seen and felt in the mountain paintings of Lawren Harris she also perceived in the totem poles of northern British Columbia, and she was determined to inject those qualities into her paintings of them.

In many ways the trip was unsuccessful. She had failed to visit three of the most interesting villages on the Queen Charlotte Islands; she had spent about half of her six-week journey merely waiting for transportation from one point to another; and the poor weather conditions and tormenting mosquitoes had made sketching sometimes impossible. Yet she did get to Kitwancool on the Upper Skeena, and painting the poles there was a great accomplishment. Emily showed that even at a portly fifty-six she had the fortitude and the conviction of her mission to enable her to endure the arduous month and a half. She wrote to Brown

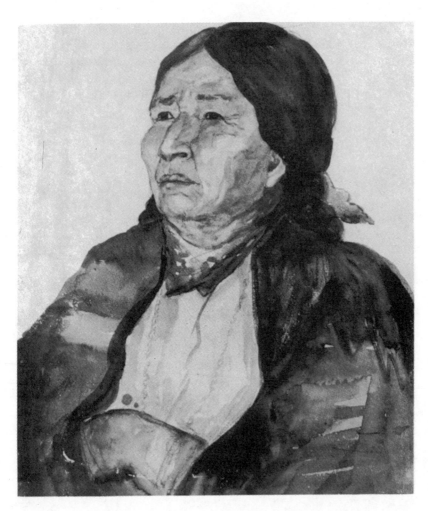

Mrs. Douse, Chieftainess of Kitwancool, 1928. Water- colour, 12 5/8 x 11. Newcombe Collection, PABC.

that in spite of all the difficulties she had had 'a great trip with some good spots, some bad, some exciting, and some trying.' Regardless of bad weather and insects, she had accumulated 'a bunch of work to keep me busy this winter,' though thirty large watercolours and a few oils she made from her sketches were not enough to keep her occupied all winter.[61] She was forced once again to work from her 1912 sketches.

Having brought order to the house and garden after her six-week absence, Emily proceeded to translate her watercolour sketches into oil paintings when Mark Tobey arrived in Victoria. She had met the handsome, copper-haired artist in the mid-twenties at the Pacific Northwest exhibition in Seattle. In 1922, at the age of thirty-two, he had begun teaching at Seattle's progressive Cornish School of Art, but when he realized that there was more to see and learn, he travelled to Europe and the Far East. It was shortly after he returned from this trip, in 1928, that

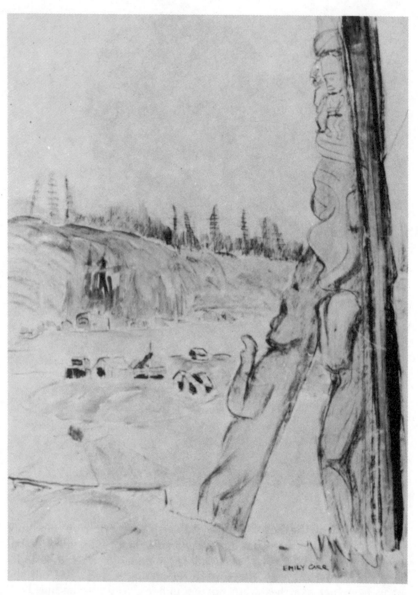

EMILY CARR

Kitwancool. Inscribed: 'Kitwancool rough sketch canvas owned by Hart House Toronto', 1928. Watercolour, 30 x 22. PABC.

Tobey asked Emily if she could get a class together for him to teach in Victoria; his fee would be fifteen dollars a head for six lessons. Emily invited him to stay with her and let him use her studio to give a class that she herself attended. She also arranged for him to use the studio of the Victoria artist and teacher, Ina D.D. Uhthoff, who enrolled in the class herself and gained a new vision from it. 'That was where art changed its face in Victoria,' she later recalled, as 'abstractionism took the place of realism under the guidance of Mark Tobey.'[62] His series of lessons did little to tear Victoria's artists away from their staunch traditionalism, but Tobey's presence helped Uhthoff and had an immense effect on Emily.

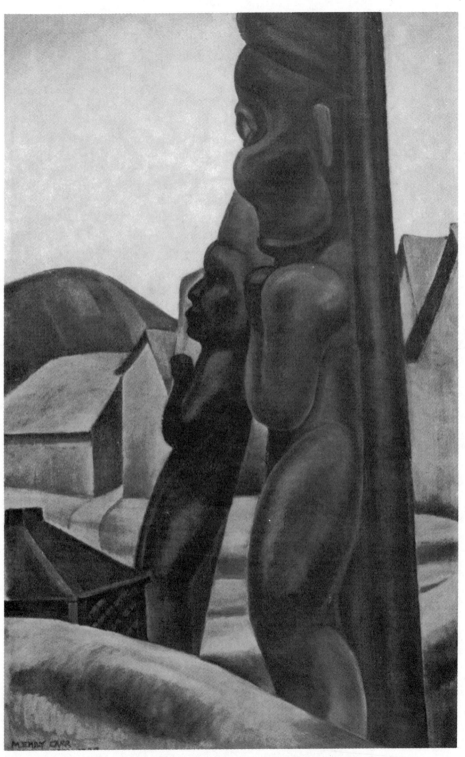

Kitwancool Totems, 1928. Oil on canvas, 41 1/2 x 26 7/8 [sight]. HH.

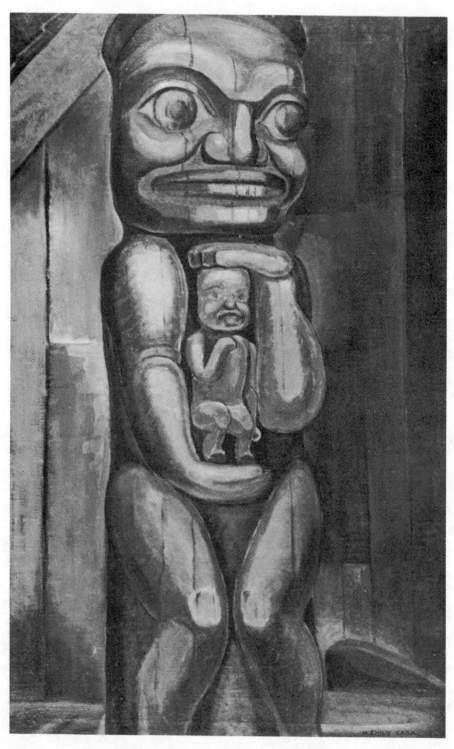

Totem Mother, Kitwancool, 1928. Oil on canvas, 43 x 27. VAG.

After his three-week visit, Emily wrote to Eric Brown about Tobey, praising him: 'He is a man who interests me very much.' She found him 'very modern and very keen', a 'good talker', and one of the best teachers she had encountered; she had received 'a tremendous lot of help from his criticisms'.[63] Indeed, the assistance Emily received from Tobey that autumn, and over the next two years, cannot be overestimated. Though Emily's junior by twenty years, Tobey had already worked as an illustrator, charcoal portraitist, decorator, and caricaturist. He also had a reputation for being one of the most dynamic teachers then living in the United States. When he arrived in Victoria, having recently returned from France, he was infected by the Cubism of Braque and Picasso and was anxious to work out this approach for himself. He attempted to explain and impart it to Emily—no easy task. Her work had little feeling for form, volume, or light. As Tobey recalled:

> I had to battle with her to teach her form as I knew it relative to the principles used by El Greco, Rembrant [sic] and all those associated with the conventions relating to Leonardo's discourses. She was painting a little in an impressionistic way which she had learned in Europe and painting ash trays etc. with Indian designs.[64]

Emily had many fine times with Tobey and many discussions about painting. She allowed him to paint her portrait.[65] They took early-morning walks on the Dallas Road cliffs and had late-night chats and cups of Postum around the studio fireplace. Tobey likely told her about his commitment to the Bahá'i Faith and how it, like theosophy for Lawren Harris, had influenced his art. He encouraged her to pep up her work by using greater contrasts, exaggerating light and shade, and watching the relation of one rhythm to the next. He also showed her how to cast an interior light across the canvas and around each object. After arguments and discussions, she learned how to do all of these things— though it was a struggle.

This was an important time in Emily's career. In 1928, the year she met Tobey, she had just made a momentous trip to the North after being inspired by the Group of Seven to paint a new kind of art. She had renewed her affinity with the totem and, more than ever before, per-ceived its spiritual qualities. She had come to realize while in Toronto that she would have to learn something about planes, cubes, and volume, about the spaciousness she knew her painting lacked. It would have been difficult for Emily to work these things out alone. She was a slow learner, stubborn and set in her ways. She had tried that summer to imbue her painting with something of the Group's rhythm, form, and light, but the results—as in *Corner of Kitwancool Village*—had not been promising. Only a dynamic man like Tobey, a well-seasoned artist-teacher in whom she had confidence as a painter, could help her. Tobey could battle with her, push her to advance, and he did.

He also had an understanding of Emily's subject, the Indian motif, and this was crucial to her development. He was a long-time collector of

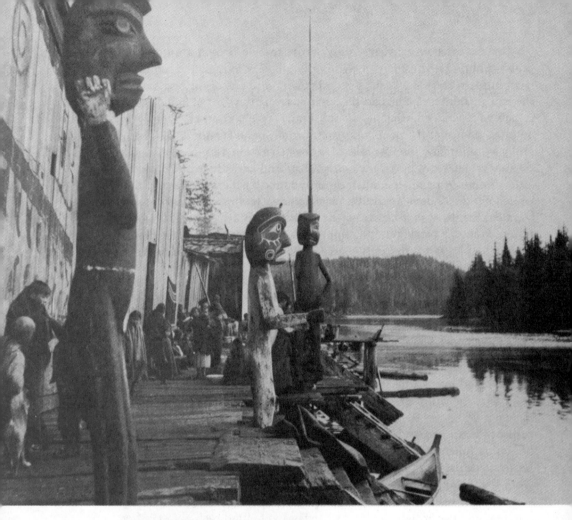

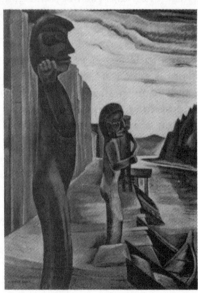

(ABOVE) Blunden Harbour, 1901.
Photograph by C.F. Newcombe.
BCPM.

(LEFT) *Blunden Harbour*, about
1930. Oil on canvas, 51 x 37.
Courtesy VAG. NGC. (Reproduced
in colour as Plate V.)

Northwest Coast Indian art; in fact, this interest alone might have brought them together. Tobey probably saw how his principles were embodied in the totem's sculptured lines and realized the endless possibilities of this motif for the study of volume and form. A carved pole—the Kwakiutl pole excepted—was never untrue to the original shape of the tree; yet the dramatic contrast of protruding and recessed shapes gave it the illusion of being greater in diameter than it was. The superimposed figures on the pole emphasized its verticality, height, and thickness. Added to this was an inner tension that seemed to expand, or to press against, the surface of the raised areas. Also, movement was conveyed by the tense dramatic poses of the interlocking figures.[66]

Though Emily may have been aware of these qualities, she did not begin to express them in her painting until after the three-week session with Tobey in 1928. When she painted *Totem Mother, the figure that had impressed her so much at Kitwancool, she was able to exaggerate its height and width and emphasize its inner volume. She knew that the small figure made the larger appear greater in comparison, that by stressing the relief of the larger figure's eyebrows, mouth, and cheeks, and by exaggerating the size of the head, she could enhance its wild beauty. She was now approaching the point of being able to portray her subjects as expressions of an omnipotent spirit. She was within reach of fulfilling a new aim, which was not merely to show a collection of objects in a landscape but to create figures whose palpable qualities of power and meaning lent them an awesome significance.

Emily's emblematic portrayal of the totem pole reached a high point in †Blunden Harbour, painted in 1930. It is ironic that she had never been there. Ever short of material from which to work, she borrowed from William Newcombe a photograph of the Kwakiutl village located in a bay off the mainland coast that had been taken by his father in 1901.[67] In transferring the scene onto canvas, she eliminated details in the photograph—the people, the logs in the water, the deciduous trees behind the buildings, and the paintings on the house-fronts. To give an aura of drama, she exaggerated the height of the distant hills and the thrust of the wharf, added clouds, and increased the height and the volume of the poles. Showing her mastery of another skill that Tobey had taught her, she gave the light a definite source, allowing it to rise from behind the mountains and move around, imbuing every object in the picture with a blue/white glow, so that the brown poles, the grey wharf, the blue/green hills and water possess a marvellous luminosity. The effect is almost surrealistic. The poles themselves are stark figures in a setting that is rich in the play of colour and form. Haunting sentinels, they express Emily's vision of the power which she felt resided in the totem pole. *Blunden Harbour* is among the truly memorable images of Canadian painting.

Emily left little record of her work with Tobey, who recalled making several visits to Hill House. Though she seldom referred to the relationship, there can be little doubt that she became very dependent on it. In return for his criticism, she was willing to allow him the use of her studio when she went east in March 1930. (Emily later complained to a friend that he used all her paints and brushes.)[68] Nevertheless, eager for his help, she sent him five dollars for his boat fare later that year. Tobey took three weeks to reply to the invitation. Always annoyed by slow correspondents, Emily told him not to bother to come. He did not.[69]

With this break, Emily lost perhaps her most stimulating teacher, as well as the friendship of a man who was to become one of the great American painters of the century. Because his actions did not comply with her expectations, she cut him off. She referred to him thereafter as a spineless creature. The man who had taught her how to link her feelings to her art, who had wrestled her away from her housework (which he saw was interfering with her painting) and galvanized her creative drive as not even Lawren Harris had done, was cast aside. Years later, referring to her rejection, Tobey said he did not know why she had turned against him 'with a fury'.[70]

Emily's new work, inspired by the Group of Seven and developed under the effective guidance of Mark Tobey, reached central Canada in the spring of 1929 when two of her paintings—*Skidigate* and *Totems, Kitwancool*—were included in the Annual of the Ontario Society of Artists. Though they evoked little public response, Lawren Harris was ebullient. He wrote Emily that it was as if 'your ideas, visions, feelings were coming to precise expression.'[71]

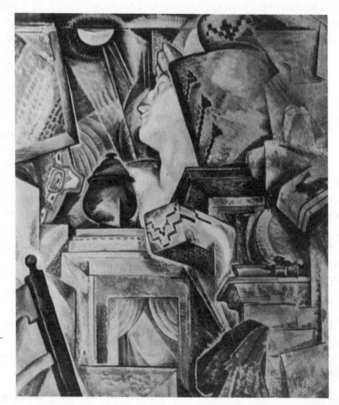

Mark Tobey.
Emily Carr's Studio, 1928.
Oil on canvas,
29 3/4 x 24 3/4.
Collection Mr
Loren Juul,
Washington.
Seattle Art
Museum.

9
Spirit and the Land
1929-1933

In 1929 Lawren Harris suggested to Emily that she leave her Indian subject matter for a year and seek to express the spirit of British Columbia 'in the exotic landscape of the island and coast.' He reminded her that the totem pole was 'a work of art in its own right', and that it was 'very difficult to use it in another form of art.'[1] Perhaps as a result of Harris's letters, Emily admitted that 'while working on the Indian stuff . . . I was copying the Indian idiom instead of expressing my own findings.'[2] She continued to paint totem poles into the early 1930s, and returned to them a few years before she died, but by 1929 she had become, through Harris's encouragement, more deeply interested in the woods, where she was 'finding something that was peculiarly my own.'[3]

Learning to express her own vision of the forest was not an easy task. Emily perceived the wilderness in two contrasting ways. One grew out of a European fear of it; the other was rooted in her conception of the special relationship Indians had with it. She thought that Indians imbued the forest with spiritual significance and drew virtues from it, believing themselves to be part of nature under one supernatural being. This, of course, was both an oversimplification and an exaggeration. The Northwest Coast Indians were not so much people of the forest as of the shore; they lived not in the midst of the forest but on its fringes. However, Emily's belief that they, unlike the white man, accepted the forest and communed with it, was a hedge against her fear of it. Her early forest-interior paintings linked the sense of mystery and fear with a formalized suggestion of the presence of God: in *The Cathedral, Stanley Park*, painted in 1909, the interior of the coniferous forest evokes the nave of a Gothic cathedral. Though Emily's perception of the forest as essentially fearful remained unchanged, her attempt to come to terms with it was cut short when the portrayal of the natives and their artefacts began to absorb her interest. Largely through the influence of Viola and Ambrose Patterson, she came to feel that an indigenous Northwest Coast art,

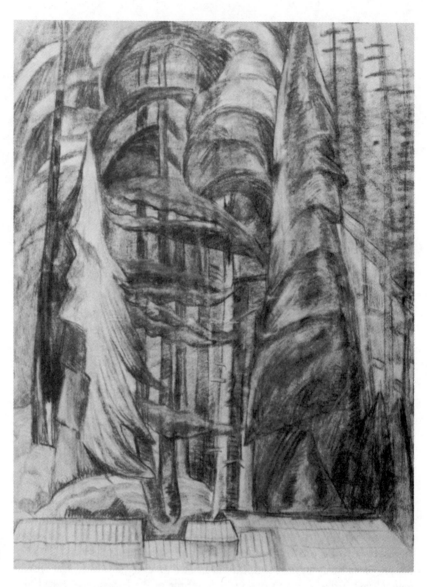

Nootka
(42.3.118), 1929.
Charcoal, 28 3/8
x 21 3/16. VAG.

growing out of the inspiration of the landscape, could be created; and by the early 1920s she was painting the landscape around Victoria. Immediately after her 'discovery' by the National Gallery in 1927, Emily abandoned her landscape painting and returned to the Indian motif. Then in 1929—her interest in the wilderness as a subject renewed by Harris and Tobey and the Group's passion for it—she took the practical, energetic step that had served her aspirations many times before: she embarked in early May on another excursion.

Nootka, on the southern tip of Nootka Island off the west coast of Vancouver Island, was the point from which she chose to explore the forest landscape. She reached the outpost by train, travelling up the east

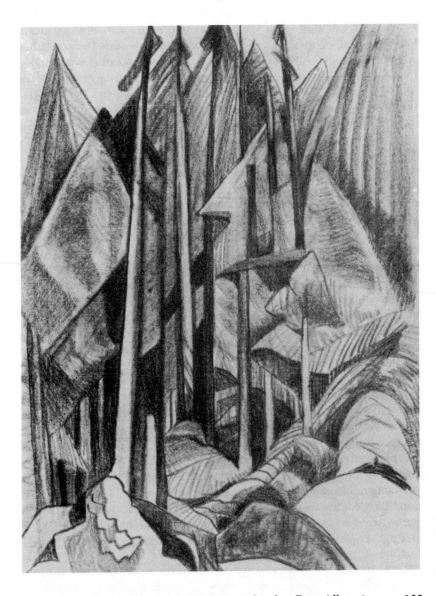

Nootka
(42.3.124), 1929.
Charcoal, 24 1/2
x 18 13/16. VAG.

coast of Vancouver Island, then cutting inland to Port Alberni, some 100 miles north of Victoria. There she boarded a steamer that took her 40 miles down narrow Alberni Inlet and Trevor Channel to the Pacific, turned north, and sailed a further 95 miles up the west coast to Nootka. It was not the fastest means of transportation because the steamer made frequent stops, depositing people and goods at the white-washed gabled cannery houses clustered around San Mateo Bay, the 'grey & forsaken & broken shacks' at Kildonan cannery, and at other west-coast settlements, like Ucluelet, where Emily had first painted the Indians over thirty years before. Passengers included businessmen, Japanese and Indian workers returning to their villages, as well as tourists. There were enough of them to encourage a pianist and a banjo player to produce 'ear-splitting' music that brought uniformed officers, stewards, and high-heeled young ladies to the dance floor.⁴ They had a merry time and the weather was good— at least until the boat arrived at Nootka. There the pouring rain made the woods dark and heavy-scented, the thick moss like water-filled sponges, and the plank walk in front of the long row of white-trimmed red houses slippery. The weather eventually cleared and Emily began to explore the area. She hiked to the entrance of Friendly Cove and sketched Bert Fish's lighthouse perched on a rocky promontory; she climbed a high cliff and portrayed the village from there; and she pushed through the dense woods to sketch the one-room Indian church and the broad and sprawling house that belonged to Captain Jack. She also drew the bulky canoes lying on the beach, and her hotel, which sat on worm-eaten piles and hung in space over the water. Behind most of these subjects loomed the forest. Emily stylized the trees. Cedars swept and drooped; pines thrust their boughs stiffly towards the sky; Douglas firs balanced their foliage on the pinnacle of their tall stick-like trunks; while other trees, less recognizable, were merely drawn as triangles, or faded into zig-zagging lines. By defining each form, and consciously smelling, hearing, and feeling the forest as she did so, Emily hoped she would cease to be overwhelmed or frightened by it and, more important, that she would become one with nature and God.

Back in Victoria she began to rework some of her sketches on canvas and produced one of her most celebrated paintings, †Indian Church. For this stylized interpretation of the church and the woods at Nootka, she eliminated the outbuildings, added crosses from an adjacent cemetery, elongated and simplified the church itself, and exaggerated the height and density of the surrounding vegetation. A fragile and awkward symbol of Christian faith, the church stands bravely against an over-whelming outgrowth of towering natural forms; while the white building is in stark contrast with the rich green tapestry of formalized plastic shapes behind it, each strives upwards towards heaven. The painting is a striking image that synthesizes Emily's concern with the spiritual qualities of the Indians and of nature.

Eager for another chance to explore the dense woods of the west coast, Emily left Victoria again in mid-August. She took the *Princess Maquinna* from the dock at the foot of Belville Street in Victoria and sailed up the west coast of the Island to Port Renfrew, some 60 miles north of the city. When she arrived at the small fishing and lumbering community, it was barely light. She walked past the charred ruins of Godman's Hotel, past the cannery that no longer canned, the box factory that no longer boxed, to the new hotel. Though accommodation was modest, as it had been at Nootka, Emily was overjoyed 'to be able to feel the sting of the fresh salt spray, to smell seaweed & clam flats, to see the canoe bobbing on the waves.'⁵ She was even more impressed by the dense forest that had so overwhelmed Richard Carr on his voyage around Vancouver Island in 1879. Attempting some verse, she wrote that she wanted to feel 'The

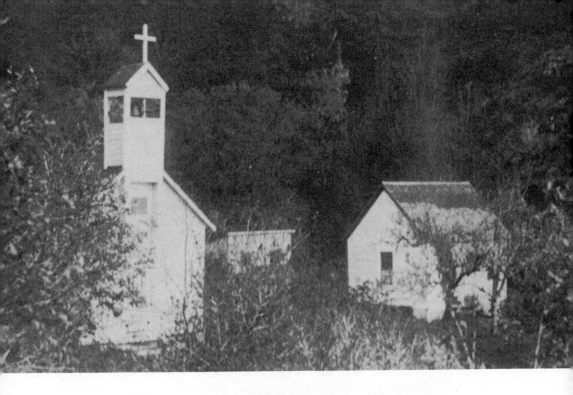

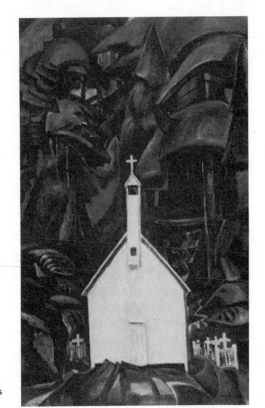

(ABOVE) Church, Friendly
Cove, about 1930. BCPM.

(RIGHT) *Indian Church*,
1929. Oil on canvas,
42 3/4 x 27 1/8. Art
Gallery of Ontario,
Toronto. Bequest of
Charles S. Band, 1970.
(Reproduced in colour as
Plate VI.)

reality of growth and life and / light, and the sweetness of Mother / Nature, the nearness of God, / the unity of the universe, / peace, content.' She sketched the trees in charcoal, trying to reveal their 'organized orderly / form'.[6] She knew that the Indians, in stylizing their figures, had reduced their animals and mythical creatures to the barest minimum, walking the thin line between representation and design. In the process they were pushed to the utmost stylization. Attempting to find a common denominator for the forest and to refine the forms without losing the representation of trees, underbrush, and background, Emily reduced the trees to geometric shapes. The trunks are vertical tapering columns, the foliage full-volumed triangles, chevrons, or diamonds, while the foreground underbrush rises and falls in curving mounds. She allowed the patches of penetrating light to fall chaotically over the volumed surfaces. The forest, thus reduced, is fragmented; form jars against form, light is reflected as through a prism. Yet there is a harmony of shapes, of crowding, of reflecting light, and of pushing upward.

These sketches must have satisfied Emily, for they were the basis for her monumental canvas *Grey, in which she attempted to symbolize God through nature and to elicit from her viewer a strong emotional response, similar to the one she had experienced while viewing Harris's work. Using a cool, neutral palette of browns and greys, and reducing the forest almost to the point where the shapes no longer resemble their life models, she unified the surging growth into one beautiful structural whole. In Grey—which is made haunting and dramatic by the light that pulsates from within the central cone-shaped tree—Emily formalized her experience of fear and loneliness in the forest, as well as her sense of an omnipotent being: a horrific God dwelling in a terrifying primordial wilderness. It is a theatrical piece, not born out of an immediate experience but contrived in her studio. In its use of dramatic effects it is no different from Blunden Harbour, which she would paint only months later from a photograph, but it was the 'highest' thing she was capable of at the time and she was 'quite excited over its doing'.[7] Emily later felt that it was static, and said that while painting it she had been 'thinking more of effect than spirit'. Grey showed 'the difference between a play and real life'.[8] Compared with what was to come in the next few years, it undoubtedly did.

On the first of April 1930 the Colonist announced that 'Miss Carr left last Saturday for Toronto, Ottawa, Montreal and Washington in each of which cities some of her pictures are being shown in the next week or two.'[9] Emily made the trip to attend her first solo exhibition in eastern Canada—at the CNR's Sparks Street ticket office in Ottawa in May—yet the reporter went on to single out the April exhibition with the Group of Seven at the Art Gallery of Toronto as the high point. This was not the first time Emily's pictures had hung alongside the Group's. Some members of the Group had participated with her in the 1927 West Coast Exhibition; in the Canadian Annuals at the National Gallery in Ottawa

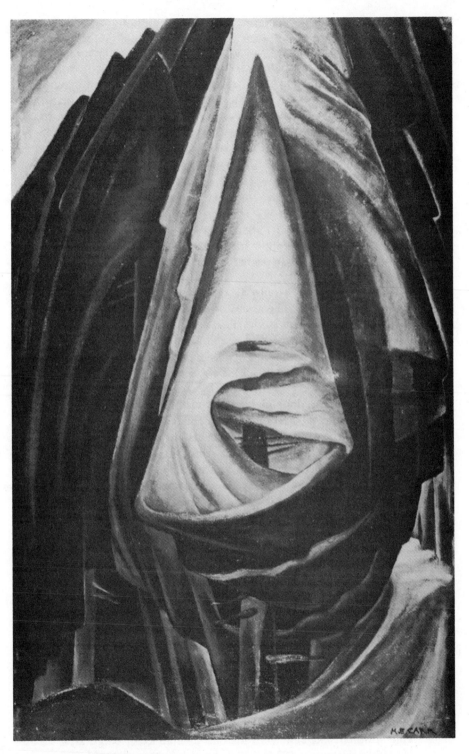

Grey, 1929-30. Oil on canvas, 43 3/4 x 27 1/4. Mrs Charles S. Band.

in 1928 and January-February 1930; in the Ontario Society of Artists exhibitions in Toronto in 1929 and March 1930; and in the Exhibition of Paintings by Contemporary Canadian Artists at the Corcoran Galleries, Washington (where both the Group *and* Emily were called poster artists), in March. But the Toronto show was different from its predecessors because the Group, not a gallery director or a committee, had invited Emily to exhibit with them—a gesture that proved she had been accepted by the artists who had inspired her three years earlier.

Much about this trip to eastern Canada differed from that of 1927. Artists who had met Emily previously now found her happier and more confident. She did not complain so much about artistic rejection in British Columbia, but spoke of the 'miracle' that had happened: at last she had met people.[10] Nor was she as shy, or as reluctant to express her opinion on matters of art. She boldly told a *Morning Citizen* reporter in Ottawa that Canada wanted for its art 'something strong, big, dignified and spiritual that shall make her artists better for doing it and her people better for seeing it.'[11]

Emily's friends in Toronto, Ottawa, and Montreal helped to reinforce her new confidence. There was another meeting with young Ontario artists in A.Y. Jackson's studio. Fred and Bess Housser gave parties in her honour. Encouragement and enthusiasm came from Arthur Lismer. Doris Spiers took Emily and her Belgian griffon, Koko, for drives and listened while she talked 'in a little soft English voice' of feeling still very much misunderstood as an artist by her fellow Victorians.[12] Lawren Harris opened the door of his great restful studio and engaged her in further intimate talks about art and life. In Ottawa, Marius Barbeau invited her to be a guest once again in his home.

Harris advised Emily to visit the spring exhibitions in New York City. Eager to follow his advice, and bolstered by her new-found confidence, she contacted an old Victoria acquaintance, Nell Cozier, and her husband, who lived in Long Island, and they offered Emily the hospitality of their home, as well as their companionship while sightseeing in New York.[13] Emily took the overnight train from Toronto.

She rarely recalled her two-week American sojourn and included it in her autobiography only on the insistence of Harris. Fear of what 'great cities'—London and Paris—had done to her kept her on Long Island for the greater part of the trip.[14] It was not until the last few days that Emily ventured into Manhattan (probably alone), registered at the Martha Washington Hotel, and set out to visit some galleries. She immediately found the city disagreeable—'like living in an egg-beater', as she told one friend.[15] The elevator rides that were necessary to reach top-floor galleries spoiled her pleasure in the pictures, while the quietly pretentious air of the galleries themselves made her feel uncomfortable. Moreover, she was afraid that what she was encountering might confuse her, unsettle the line she had chosen to take in her work, or even throw her into an emotional state similar to the one she had experienced after viewing Harris's paintings in 1927. If it had not been for an accidental meeting

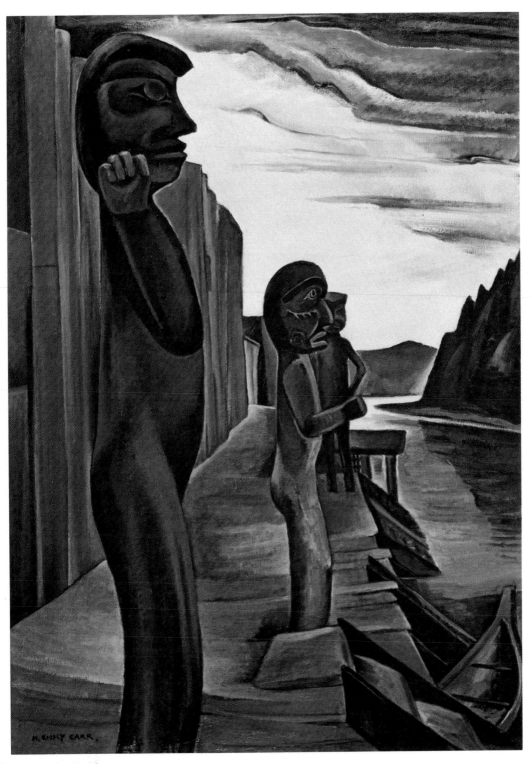

v—*Blunden Harbour,* about 1930. (After cleaning in 1979.)
Oil on canvas, 51 x 37. Courtesy VAG. NGC.

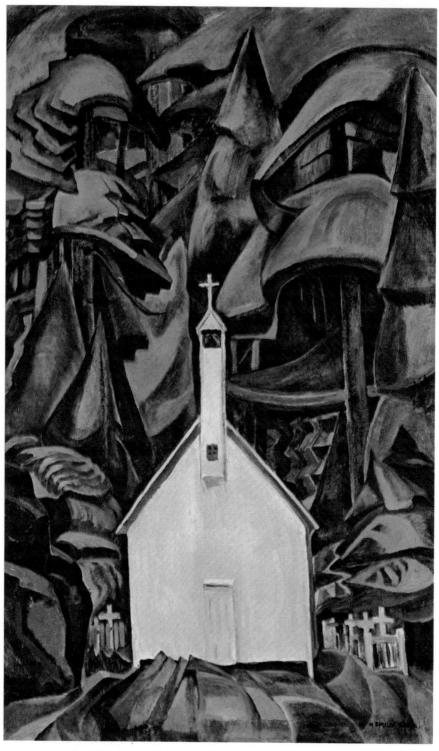

VI—*Indian Church*, 1929. Oil on canvas, 42 3/4 x 27 1/8. (Photo: Larry Ostrom)
Art Gallery of Ontario, Toronto. Bequest of Charles S. Band, 1970.

with Arthur Lismer at the Roerich Gallery, Emily might have seen very little. Lismer invited her to join his party on their gallery tour and Emily accepted gladly. Feeling secure in his hands—Lismer even instructed elevator operators to make descents as smoothly as possible—she now enjoyed herself. With his guidance she saw paintings by Kandinsky, Braque, Duchamp, and Archipenko at the John Becker and De Haube galleries. She was introduced to the artist Georgia O'Keeffe and her work at An American Place, the gallery of O'Keeffe's husband, Alfred Stieglitz. O'Keeffe's *Lawrence Pine Tree, with Stars* remained in Emily's memory and later moved her to find and note in her journal D.H. Lawrence's description of a pine tree in St Mawr, which had inspired it.[16]

On her last day in the city Emily took advantage of a letter of introduction from Harris to visit, on her own, Katherine Drier, an artist, art connoisseur, and collector. Emily was thus privileged to view, in a luxurious setting, one of the great private collections of modern painting in the United States, embracing a vast range of art from the School of Paris to German Expressionism, Russian Constructivism, Italian Futurism, and the American moderns. Drier was excited by a recent acquisition, Franz Marc's *Deer in Forest*, which may have inspired a charcoal sketch, a watercolour, and an oil painting that Emily executed only months later.[17] Yet her vague recollection of her New York visit, recalled some ten years later, showed that she was not affected by much of what she saw. Most of the paintings had nothing to do with her own development, and Emily made little effort to come to terms with them. More memorable than this side trip were the hours she had passed in conversation with Lawren Harris.

Harris did more than repeat what Emily had already gleaned from Ouspensky and Bell; as in 1927, he told her how his religion, theosophy, had affected his life, how it had facilitated his higher experience of God and nature. He opened 'the rich cupboards of his heart stored with art knowledge' and told her things she had never dreamed of. His knowledge of art, life, and religion was rich 'with his own perception [,] his inner struggles [,] his bigness [,] his love of lovely things'.[18] Once again Harris assured Emily that she too could link up (as he would have put it) with the informing spirit, and create as a direct result of that experience.

After Emily returned to Victoria from the East, the correspondence between Simcoe and Severn Streets quickened. 'If you feel like uncorking any time,' Harris wrote, 'do so.'[19] Emily did. She questioned, argued, and demanded further explanations and answers about Harris's religion. She believed theosophy's God was in essence the same as her less-complex 'God in all', but its abstinence from prayer and its denial of Christ were difficult for her to accept. Harris answered her queries patiently. He was 'always *very lovely* to me, as though I was a venerable old dame due respect instead of a good stepping on.'[20] Sometimes his thoughts wandered to his own problems—by 1932 he had virtually quit painting—but more often they had to do with Emily. Stand on your own, he urged, for 'you and you alone have a vision, the feeling for what you want and

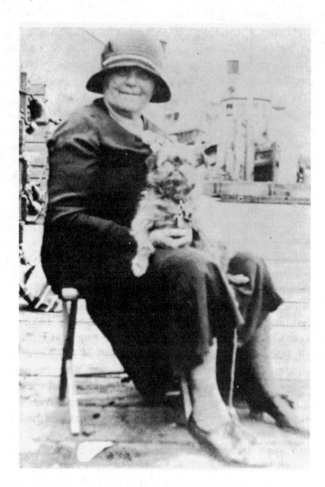

Emily about to set off on a day's sketching trip to Kapoor, north of Victoria. Photograph taken by Nan Cheney in the summer of 1930. Courtesy Mrs Cheney and the Special Collections Library, University of British Columbia.

therefore nobody can help you directly—for no one sees what you see and how you see. Don't look back, look ahead, know a new life in your art is yours, is close, is a real fulfillment for you.'[21]

After 1930 the cultivating, the refining of her relationship with God through experiencing nature became an obsession. Though Harris insisted that Emily stand alone and work things out for herself, she could not. She experimented with a variety of philosophies and religions, confident that they would bring her closer to seeing and feeling God. She adopted Harris's phrases—like 'God made manifest' and 'the informing spirit'—as if the very writing of them in her journals would usher her into a higher experience. Attempting to cleanse her body as well as her thoughts, she fasted on orange-juice and egg diets.[22] She also read and found comfort in the 'so understandable' poems of Walt Whitman and the essays of Ralph Waldo Emerson.[23]

Fred Housser had given her a copy of Whitman's *Leaves of Grass* in 1930. 'Song of Myself', 'A Song of the Rolling Earth', and 'Song of the Open Road' Emily read 'to cheer up on', to realize 'growth and immortality', and to communicate with all living things.[24] She 'learned heaps of him by heart' (ignoring the 'fleshy' parts) during morning and evening walks with the dogs on Beacon Hill. Whitman's optimism and assurance 'hit the spot every time'.[25] Emerson's early essay *Nature*, probably recommended by Harris and Housser, was also read, transcribed, and absorbed for the possibility it offered of a higher experience of God through nature.

Though never a joiner, Emily sought guidance through one of the many 'psychological' cults in Victoria which, like theosophy, held pantheistic ideas of God. Unity had become, during the Depression, an anti-materialistic alternative to Christianity, and the New York metaphysician, educator, and author, Walter Newell Weston, drew unprecedented congregations to the Unity Centre in Victoria. Emily was frequently among them. Though she hated Weston's monotonous voice, and entered the church only after the 'screeching' soloist had performed, she rarely missed a Sunday-morning service or a Thursday-evening faith healing when Weston spoke at the Centre. One series of lectures that impressed her more than any other was on the work of the famous Father Divine. The self-appointed Black Messiah, formerly a gardener named George Baker, became known in the early 1930s for his five-second faith healings, his ostentatious banquets, his feeding of Harlem's poor, and above all for giving Blacks a sense of dignity. His preaching on the brotherhood of man brought many conversions and a multitude of followers willing to sacrifice their wages for his cause. So much was Emily impressed by Weston's account of the Black Messiah, so much did she want 'to experience a wonderful healing', that she petitioned members of the Unity Centre to bring him to Victoria.[26] Her enthusiasm was not shared by all, however, nor were sufficient funds forthcoming to bring him to that city.

Emily heard other religious enthusiasts who came to Victoria, such as Harry Gaze, who in May 1931 spoke on 'Applied Psychology' in a series of five lectures dealing with meditation and 'absolute communion with the divine'.[27] In the fall of the same year Emily also attended a series of lectures on the New Cycle Philosophy at the Empress Hotel. The Australian-born lecturer, Christina Killen, offered 'the student with unlimited mind' a means of uniting 'with a Higher Order of Being'.[28] The formula for doing so was easy to grasp: by setting up vibrations, an individual could contact the 'living Energy' inherent in all matter.[29] A tree, to use Killen's example, 'though apparently at rest', was 'alive [,] vibrating all the time'. The energy within its trunk, branches, stems, and leaves was 'never still for an instant'; it was 'continually sending itself through the tree'.[30] The human mind was an open receptacle for these energy vibrations, contact with which was tantamount to linking up with God and the universe.

In 1934 there were other preachers, like Raja Singh, who seemed to offer a deeper experience of God and nature. A deputy secretary of the Indian Christian Mission Society, whom a Victoria paper described as 'a brilliant, interesting, and deeply spiritual speaker', Singh came to Victoria in January 1934.[31] During his two-week visit to the city he held forth on 'India's Challenge to Christianity', 'Mahatma Gandhi', and 'Oriental Views of Christian Life'. Emily attended every lecture and rally and at each one was carried away by 'his great clear voice'; his simple, easy-to-grasp ideas; his humble invitation to prayer; and his ability to 'take you right in front of God' in a few simple sentences. She even invited him to dinner. When he arrived hatless and without an umbrella, in a great downpour of rain, his wet condition only added to the merriment of the evening. He told Emily of his work among Eurasian orphans and was greatly admired. In the space of two weeks 'Uncle Raja', as she called the much younger man, was added to the 'remembrance garden' deep in her heart.[32] For a brief time he replaced Harris as a father image, which Harris had become over the past seven years. Singh returned to Victoria only once a few months later. Emily was camping on the outskirts of the city, but she hitchhiked into town to hear him preach. She never mentioned him again in her journals, probably because he had failed to answer a letter that 'needed answering'.

The New Cycle and Applied Psychology lectures, Weston's talks at the Unity Centre, Emily's acquaintance with Raja Singh, the writings of Whitman and Emerson, as well as numerous other books—such as *In Tune with the Infinite* by Ralph Waldo Trine—were all avenues in her search for a deeper experience of the informing spirit and for the means by which she could be raised into another dimension of being. While Emily never embraced any of these doctrines fully, each lecture, sermon, and book not only confirmed her feeling that God could be found in nature, but convinced her that communion with Him through her art could elevate her soul to a oneness with the divine universe.

On the nineteenth of August 1930, with the poems of Whitman and the essays of Emerson in her sketch satchel, Emily sailed from Vancouver on the *Cardena* to the northeast coast of Vancouver Island to paint the forests and poles in the remote Koskimo villages around Quatsino Sound and Queen Charlotte Strait. It was an arduous trip, as always. Emily no longer travelled with her bedroll and tent fly; but the hotel room at Port Hardy—with its 'cigarette stinks', dead flowers, and the stench of someone who had been 'drunk sick behind the bureau'—was hardly an improvement.[33] There was the usual stress on her nerves and temper of waiting for an Indian guide to take her in his boat to out-of-the-way villages. (She wrote one friend that she was having 'awfully bad luck' with transportation.)[34] On the ocean she was ill with splitting headaches and nausea from 'rough churning on the sea'.[35] Most of the villages she visited were abandoned by the native fishermen out of season; the totems and stray-animal pets were left to her alone. She made charcoal and watercolour sketches of the landscape and poles, and in one Koskimo village painted three stray yellow-eyed cats amidst a sea of tangled underbrush. But it was the forest that commanded most interest. 'What do these forests make you feel?' Emily asked in her notebook, then went on to describe the trees' weight and density, their crowded orderliness, their profound solemnity yet uplifting joyousness, their growth and expansion, the sense of God's presence among them—and the creepy feeling she had when she walked in their dense undergrowth.[36]

Emily returned to Victoria in mid-September. During the autumn and winter she tried to recapture what she had seen and felt. She got out her typewriter, thought back to her summer in the forest, and commenced to describe 'its looks and feeling and thoughts'.[37] Day excursions to the woods in Esquimalt and nearby Beacon Hill Park helped to recall the vegetation in Port Hardy. Remembering Georgia O'Keeffe's painting, *Lawrence Pine Tree, with Stars*, Emily turned to the Lawrence passage that described it. The 'passionless, non-phallic column, rising in the shadows of the pre-sexual world', Lawrence wrote, was 'strange', 'never sympathetic', hedging 'one in with the aroma and the power and the slight horror of the pre-sexual primeval world.'[38] Without commenting on the sexual imagery, Emily wrote in her journal that this interpretation was clever but not *her* experience of pines. They might be sad, but they were 'never cruel or indifferent'.[39] However, she found it difficult to recreate her forest experience of the previous summer. She returned to her sketches of Indian totem poles and worked several into canvases. But the forest dominated; it was omnipotent. In *Strangled by Growth*, a Koskimo pole—representing D'Sonoqua, the Wild Woman of the Woods—is smothered by twisted ribbons of green and yellow foliage. Up until 1929 her totem poles had always dominated the underbrush and the trees; now the converse was often true.

Emily sought to broaden her vision and her rendering of the forest by reading art books that she had borrowed from friends and found in the Provincial Library. She learned from Mary Cecil Allen's *Painters of the Modern Mind* (1929) that the function of the artist is to translate 'the images of the seen world into other terms', to remove them into 'another sphere of being' by attaching 'another meaning to them', rather than making them 'unrecognizable as images'.[40] Allen wrote that this could be accomplished by the use of rhythm—of line, colour, light, and shade. Emily read, recorded, and then underscored as she discovered how rhythm could be achieved by creating a 'dynamic design which uses combinations of straight lines and curves to produce slow or sudden movements in the pattern', by reducing nature 'to a rhythmic series of light and dark patches representing not light and shade but the varying depth of colour in objects', and by studying the colour and line transitions binding one movement to another.[41] Rhythm thus gave the objects in a painting a 'synthesis so closely knit and so organic that it obliterates the impression of the several parts of movements and presents one complete living structure.'[42] Emily read more about rhythm in A.M. Berry's chapter on 'Movement and Rhythm' in *Animals in Art* (1929). She underscored a passage in which Berry wrote that 'a rhythmic impulse of growth, a definite and ordered movement' was to be observed 'throughout nature'.[43]

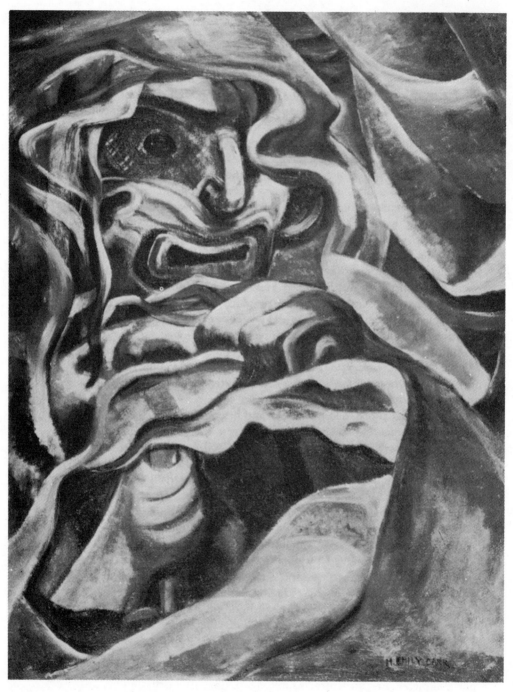

Strangled by Growth, 1931. Oil on canvas, 25 x 19. VAG.

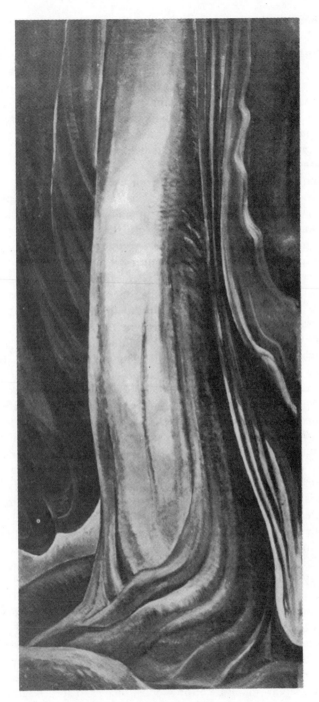

Tree, 1931. Oil on canvas, 50 3/4 x 22. VAG.

This was the kind of artistic description that struck a sympathetic chord in Emily. Until now her forests had been lifeless. Tobey had told her that her work was too monotonous and lacking in contrasts. She herself complained to Harris that it was 'dull, heavy and static'.[44] Reading Allen and Berry not only reinforced her previous ideas of volume and form, of tension and structure, of reducing an object to its barest essence in order to reveal its spirit, and of using nature as a source for that inspiration; the books also impressed on her the concept of rhythm, of the unity of part to whole, of balance and transition in movement and colour.

Another book Emily learned from was Horace Shipp's study of the British artist Lawrence Atkinson: *The New Art* (1929). Shipp explained how Atkinson relied on his subconscious to explore the structure and relationship of planes and masses, the directions of growth and movement in every object.[45] The reproductions of Atkinson's drawings and sculptures in Shipp's book impressed Emily deeply, as had Georgia O'Keeffe's 'Jack-in-the-Pulpit' flower series, which she had seen the previous spring. They enabled her to paint the monumental canvas, *Tree. Like O'Keeffe, Emily did not paint the entire subject. She thrust her observer against the trunk, leaving the greatest portion of the cedar out of the painting. She attempted to imbue it with life and movement by applying what she had read in Allen's book and had seen in the works of O'Keeffe and Atkinson. She juxtaposed light and dark colours, and achieved a rhythmic balance between the slowly curving ascending lines of the trunk and the falling draperies of the background foliage. She imbued the trunk, as she had the totem poles earlier, with an inner tension that pressed against its surface, giving it a far greater diameter than its measurable one. *Tree* is a tremendous celebration of life; one expects it to thrust even further upwards and expand even further outwards. Yet this canvas, completed in the early spring of 1931, did not satisfy Emily. She longed to go into the woods and explore further 'the pervading direction, the pervading rhythm, the dominant, recurring forms, the dominant colour'. 'Oh, Spring!' she wrote that winter, 'I want to go out and feel you and get inspiration.' The chance for 'fresh contacts' and 'more vital searching' had to wait until Harry Gaze completed his lectures at the end of May.[46]

In June 1931 Emily rented a cottage at the Goldstream Flats, a great primordial stand of timber that some foresighted person had preserved as a wilderness in 1912. Lying only eight miles north of Victoria, the Flats are between two hills, so that the sun comes in late and disappears early. A river churns noisily as it bursts under fallen logs and over flat stones. There are vine maples, cotton woods, pines and spruce, all of great age and heavily mossed. But the outstanding feature is the massive red-cedar trees, with their 'heavy sweeping bows drooping with a fern-like gesture layer upon layer of bluey green'.

For some time Emily 'had been feeling the necessity of doing large

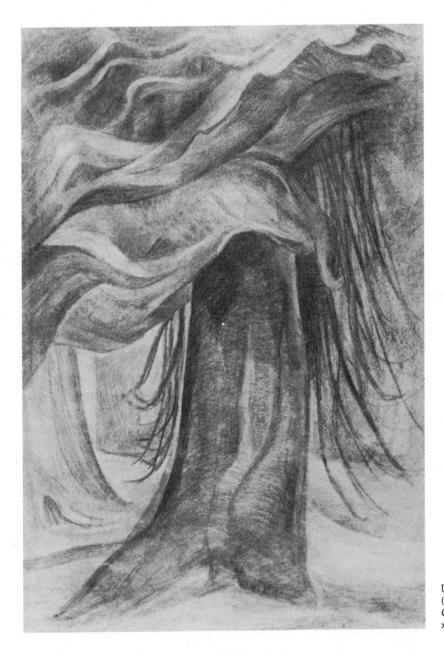

Untitled
(42.3.115), 1931.
Charcoal, 35 1/8
x 23 1/2. VAG.

sketches [so] as to get the sweep and freedom of these great tree forms.' She took large 35-by-23-inch sheets of Manila paper and armed with charcoal, a folding sketching board, a camp stool, and accompanied by her dogs, she walked the short distance from her cottage to the woods. There she sat among the cedars, 'staring, staring, staring—half lost, learning a new language or rather the same language in a different dialect.'[47] Again she committed her thoughts to a notebook. 'What is that vital thing the woods contain, possess, that you want?' she asked; she then 'endeavoured to commune & come as close to God' as possible, 'to feel the power of his presence' in everything about her.[48] Thinking of what she had read in Shipp and Allen—how Allen had stressed the movement, the mood, the recurring forms and the unity of part to whole—Emily set to work. Though she was using a larger format, she did not attempt to include more of the forest but sketched single trees, often only their trunks and lower branches. The realistic composition that emerged from these sketches is uncannily similar to that of her 1909-10 Stanley Park forest interiors, though the sweep of the boughs is more decisive, the form of the trunks more exaggerated. These charcoal sketches—some done on full sheets, others on half—are devoid of both the exaggerated volume and the flatness that had characterized Emily's work since 1928. These trees have soft, pulsating, internal rhythm instead of the earlier geometric stiffness. Dramatic effects—rays of light and solid, bulky forms—are avoided. These works are also less complex than her forest sketches of the previous two summers. In Goldstream's predominantly cedar forest there was no underbrush and few small trees. Though it rained for a good deal of the trip, this did not hinder her. The rain only made the boughs droop more rhythmically, the colours appear more intense, and the air heavier with the scent of moist earth and cedar.

The charcoal sketches done at Goldstream are finished works in themselves. They breathe and move. Though more realistic than the charcoal sketches Emily did at Nootka and Port Renfrew, they are no less spiritual. They mark the beginning of her independence from the heavy, static compositions she had formerly produced under the influence of Tobey and Harris. However, the studio canvases she painted from her Goldstream sketches do not have their spontaneity. †*Forest, British Columbia* relies on earlier conventions: the forest possesses the same awesome, eerie light as the post-1927 forest and totem pictures; the foliage hangs in great heavy curtains, as if suspended in the air rather than from the tree's trunk; the colours—deep purple, blues, and an amazing variety of greens—intentionally or not make the setting surreal.

In September Emily was back in the woods, this time as the guest of Mrs McVicker, a former antique dealer she had known in Victoria, who was now living on a farm at Metchosin. Though Emily wrote in her journals that her hostess 'frazzeled me out with her constant grumbling', she did manage to do some sketching.[49] In fact it was probably the Metchosin woods that inspired *The Little Pine*—a canvas that is less awesome than her previous studio work. Many of the conventions in this painting are old: the rocky foreground rising and falling in a horizontal wave, the sky's curving shafts of light, as well as the mature, triangular, background trees leaning towards the centre of the picture. But to these now-familiar characteristics Emily added movement and a wider range of colour and allowed the young trees in the middle ground to open from their triangular encasements. However, the unity she was after evaded her because the horizontal foreground, the shafts of light, and the

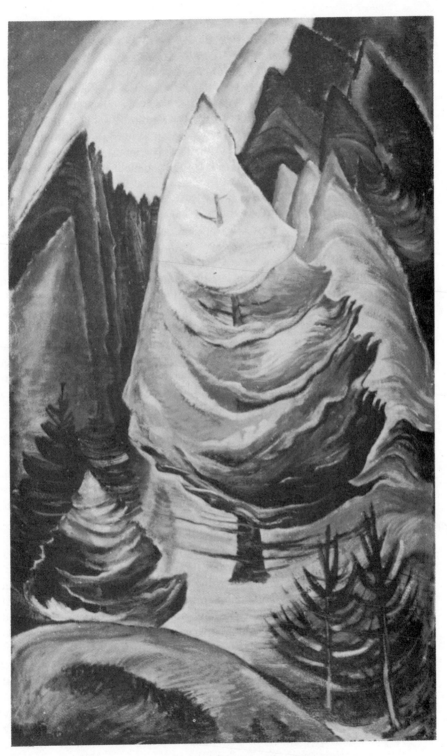

The Little Pine, 1931. Oil on canvas, 43 15/16 x 27 1/16. VAG.

middle-ground trees are unconnected by either colour or movement.

In December 1931 Emily sent six paintings to Lawren Harris for inclusion in the Group of Seven's annual exhibition at the Art Gallery of Toronto. Four were forest interiors painted during the past year. Harris's response was encouraging and perceptive. 'It's a thrilling attempt you have begun,' he wrote a few weeks after receiving the paintings. 'You're just beginning a deeper search into the fundamental life in trees and forest and nature in the deepest, most secret moods and meanings.' *The Little Pine* was favoured by all of her eastern friends, but it was the tree-trunk pictures like *Tree* that Harris thought opened 'a new furrow' in her work.[50]

The spring of 1932 found Emily back among the trees, in May at a hunting lodge on Braden Mountain in Metchosin and in June at a cottage in Cedar Hill. By this time her thinking had been expanded by the New Cycle and Applied Psychology lectures and the ideas of Atkinson and Allen. Realizing that she had to dig deeper to express the forest as one breathing, growing, moving whole, Emily embarked on her most vigorous attempt to go beyond the nineteenth- and early twentieth-century artistic vision of the forest, to break with Atkinson's simplification of forms and the distinct volumetric styles of Harris and Tobey. On this trip she took with her two aids that she thought would assist her in deepening her perception of the forest and in attaining a level of consciousness where she would be at one with God and nature and able to create through His inspiration: a little notebook in which to describe her subjects and a new medium she had adopted for sketching.

As early as 1929 Emily had expressed her thoughts of the forest at Nootka and Port Renfrew in prose and verse. Since girlhood she had written couplets or rhyming verses, accompanied by pen-and-ink sketches, to commemorate special occasions. Prose fragments recording Indian legends were first written in 1912 and short stories in 1926, when she began a short-story correspondence course with the Palmer Institute of Authorship in California. These stories, drawn mostly from her travels among the Indians—along with an article, 'Canadian West Coast Indian Art', which appeared in the *McGill News* in 1929, and her journals (begun in 1927)—showed Emily's interest in, and facility for, expressing herself in prose. 'Trying to find equivalents for things in words' helped to find 'equivalents in painting,' Emily wrote in 1930.[51] It was with this in mind that she now opened her notebook and asked herself: 'What attracted you to this particular subject?' 'Why do you want to paint it?' 'What is its core, the thing you are trying to express?'[52] Answering these questions 'from myself to myself', she forced herself to analyse form, the direction of movement, and colour, and the central idea to be expressed.[53]

Another aid on this sketching trip, one that she had not previously employed, was the new medium of oil and turpentine. Though wanting to combine the quickness of sketching in watercolour with the intensity that is possible with oils, Emily did not want the burden of carrying supplies for both watercolours and oils into the forest. She discovered that by combining generous amounts of turpentine with oil paint, then applying the mixture with broad-bristle brushes to Manila paper, she could obtain the freshness and delicacy of watercolour (which she had most often used for her sketches). And this new medium was far superior: it dried immediately, like watercolour; one did not have to wait before adding other tints; and, unlike watercolour, its colour intensity did not diminish when it dried. The advantages over oil were even greater. Oil was slow; the oil-on-paper medium was quick. Oil colours had to be built up on the canvas gradually, whereas this medium could be applied to paper freely and quickly. It was also economical. Emily purchased 'oil-strong tinting colours' in pound tins of house paint from Ross's Paint Store and found them much less expensive than imported tubes of oil paint. Also, the Manila paper was not as expensive as canvas.[54] She was thus free 'to slash away because material scarcely counts. You use just can paint, and there's no loss with failures.'[55] The oil-on-paper sketches, which Emily turned out in great numbers, were initially intended to lead to studio canvases. She began by using only turpentine and black paint; gradually a little white, then blue, brown, and green were added for highlights; soon she was employing the whole spectrum of forest colours and producing finished pieces in oil on paper. Though she never exhibited her 'papers' without fearing they might look 'tuppancy among all the canvases', many people found them more alive.[56]

Emily's claim that she learned a lot about 'freedom and *direction*' from her oil-on-paper medium was certainly valid.[57] Her most satisfactory work—whether French landscapes, the Indian villages of northern British Columbia, or the woods surrounding Victoria—had always been done out-of-doors, where she was directly in touch with her subject and free from intrusions and reminders of household chores. With the new medium, painting *en plein air* unleashed her greatest asset as an artist: spontaneity. It allowed her to lose self-awareness and gradually forget many of her conventional ideas of the forest, and helped her to depart from the flat, static poster style of Tobey and Harris. In one black-and-white oil-on-paper sketch (Untitled, VAG,*42.3.160), Emily was able to suggest the movement and form of a young pine tree with only a few slashing strokes of the brush. By using the paper as another colour, she made the light come from within the tree rather than from behind it. The surreal elements in *Tree* and *Forest, British Columbia* are no longer present. Heaviness and exaggerated volume give way to a lyrical weightlessness. No longer able move so easily among trees, rocks, and salal, one is caught in the forest's midst where the underbrush chokes, the trees grow irregularly, and 'each seed according to its own kind [is] expanding, bursting, pushing its way upward towards the light and air.'[58] In these early oil-on-paper sketches Emily was deriving her forms from the forest, not imposing them. She was entering 'into the life of the trees', realizing her relationship to them and understanding 'their language, unspoken, unwritten talk'.[59] At the same time she was plunging her viewer into the chaos of the west-coast rain forest and conveying a new vision of it.

Emily also produced oil-on-paper sketches in the studio as an intermediary stage between charcoal drawings and a finished canvas. By reworking her ideas in this medium, she could more easily transfer the vitality of her on-the-spot sketches to such canvases as *Forest* (VAG, 42.3.13). After 1932 she seldom returned to contriving dramatic effects in her studio canvases.

Early in 1933 Emily sent a batch of her black-and-white oil-on-paper sketches to Lawren Harris. He had been watching the unfolding of her forest-interior ideas keenly and was now amazed to discover yet another development in her work. As one of his friends recalled, 'Lawren was raving about what that woman has!'[60] He communicated his excitement in a letter: 'Personally I do not feel that your sketches are subject to criticism.' This new work was 'so unusually individual and so saturated with what you are after [,] perhaps more so than you realize.'[61] Other comments were forthcoming when Harris passed them to Bess Housser. She invited Harris, A.Y. Jackson, Yvonne McKague, and several others to join in a group criticism one evening. Bess noted the comments and passed them on to Emily. They ranged from pronouncing one work 'a Humdinger' to warning her that another verged on being 'a flat screen of decoration'.[62] But none of the remarks could alter the positive encouragement Emily had already received from Harris, who felt the sketches were more alive than her finished oils. 'Golly, you can do it Emily—don't let anything put you off, delay or hinder you . . . Even if you come through with one out of three or four endeavours, it will hit the mark. . . . More power to you.'[63]

It was true that Emily missed the mark more often than she hit it in her early oil-on-paper experiments, but she was developing her own expression, her own vocabulary, and no one knew it better than Harris—except perhaps Emily herself. She was now communing with nature, as she had long wished to do. She now felt that God was speaking to her, that she was 'only a channel for the pouring through of that which *is* something.'[64] But she was still far from her goal, which was to engage and transform the elements in the forest so that they expressed one idea: God's presence in all matter.

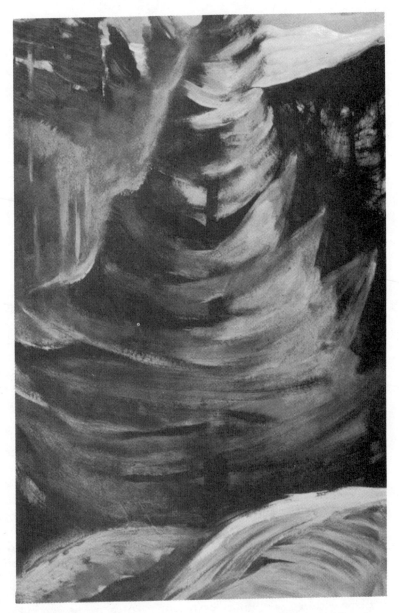

Untitled (42.3.160), about 1932. Oil on paper sketch, 18 1/16 x 11 3/4. VAG.

10
New Friends at Home
1930-1934

In the early thirties Emily was productive as an artist, and her reputation was growing, but she was still very much a landlady concerned with the daily chores of running her house, dealing with tenants' complaints, and balancing the budget at the end of the month. Sundays were passed with Lizzie and Alice in the old family home or at Alice's schoolhouse. Though Emily had discontinued her griffon kennels in the late twenties, she still had numerous dogs, which she exercised morning and evening along the Dallas Road cliffs. She also had Woo, a cage full of chipmunks, and a cat.

Bolstered by the support of her eastern friends, Emily became a frequent contributor to Northwest Coast exhibitions. But even acceptance by the National Gallery of Canada and the Group of Seven did not ensure a favourable reception at home. She received a poor review in the *Vancouver Sun* in February 1928 when she exhibited with the Vancouver Palette and Chisel Club. Brown, who had seen the clipping, wrote that he was 'not surprised you don't show much of your work there.'[1] Since the founding of the Vancouver School of Applied and Decorative Art in 1928, that city was not unfamiliar with modernism, but a reporter reviewing the British Columbia Society of Fine Arts Exhibition of 1929 wrote that he found Miss Carr's several 'eminently striking pictures . . . rather bewildering'—perhaps, he continued sarcastically, because 'I was not adopted in my childhood by an Indian tribe,' or because 'I have not the opportunity Miss Carr had enjoyed of becoming thoroughly imbued with the aboriginal way of looking at things.'[2] The praise of her eastern friends could not make up for such comments, and Emily did not exhibit with the Society again for years. Apart from selling a few paintings at Spencer's department store and at the Vanderpant Galleries, she turned her back on Vancouver (though she exhibited occasionally with her old friend Statira Frame at the Palette and Chisel Club). She even declined an invitation to exhibit and lecture at the recently established Vancouver Art Gallery for the reason that they were always 'wrangly & squabbly'.[3]

While Emily spurned Vancouver, she continued to show in Seattle and Victoria, where newspaper criticism was less harsh. In 1929 she was asked to judge the Annual Exhibition of Northwest Artists in Seattle. In the autumn of 1930 she was among the exhibitors. The critics, familiar with her work since 1924, were overwhelmed by the 'radical change in her style'.[4] Interest was so great that the Art Institute of Seattle offered her a room in the Gallery and she accepted. The ensuing exhibition— Emily's first solo in the United States—took place in December 1930; but even there the reception was mixed. One critic wrote that her paintings had 'a peculiar strength', which prompted 'either praise or condemnation for their originality.'[5] Another agreed, saying that 'you are either widely enthusiastic about them or you shake your head dubiously and mumble something about nightmares done in oils.'[6] There was criticism of the 'weird shades of green, electric blues, dull grays and browns', the 'complete lack of life and movement', and the 'static' totem poles.[7] Emily herself was concerned about their lifelessness, the lack of contrasting colour and movement in paintings like *Grey*. She complained to Harris about the reviews, and though he assured her that 'you can't ever expect much more—except from artists and folks that have a real creative bent', she knew that much of the criticism was not unjustified and this depressed her.[8] Nevertheless the following year she was back among the ranks of the Northwest Artists exhibitors and even captured first prize for the watercolour *Zunoqua*.

Ironically it was in Victoria, the bastion of the Island Arts and Crafts Society, that western praise for her post-1927 work could be depended on. Yet this did not appease Emily, who thought that whenever the public and the reviewers reacted favourably, it was because they liked the eastern 'kick-up' over her work, not the work itself.[9] There was some truth in this. After 1927 the Victoria press certainly guarded itself against criticizing a recognized artist in their midst. Eric Brown's Victoria lecture praising her work in the autumn of 1927 was followed in 1928 by the *Colonist*'s reprint of Muriel Brewster's *Star Weekly* article, written during the West Coast Exhibition of 1927. Victorians read that Miss Carr's 'remarkable paintings of Indian villages' were 'occupying the most important space' in the exhibition. And though the West had ignored her, now 'after twenty years of artistic labor' she was 'being recognized by Canadians and by her fellow artists as an outstanding figure in a definite field of Canadian art.'[10] A month later the *Colonist*'s readers were told that the director of the National Gallery thought Miss Carr's conception of art was 'as big as Canada itself'. The local reporter added that it appeared she had 'placed Victoria on the map, artistically.'[11] The reviewers of the Island Arts and Crafts Society, where Emily's work dominated the oils section of the Society's exhibitions from 1928, were no less respectful. Though many were undoubtedly puzzled by her new work, little adverse criticism appeared. Two articles in the *Colonist* about the Society's 1928 exhibition, which introduced Emily's full-volumed Indian pictures, were largely devoted to her contributions. Discussion of these paintings—obviously an outgrowth of a conversation with Emily—not only praised them as being historically important but recognized their value in showing 'the spiritual side of the aborigine'.[12] Though less perceptive than the Seattle reviews, the comments of her Victoria critics were certainly more pleasing. Emily continued to condemn the Society, but rarely did she fail to contribute to its annuals after 1928.

Conservative Victoria regarded Emily's paintings of rain forests and remote Indian villages politely but without comprehension. Nevertheless, her native city was the scene of one of the high points of her career when she was not only given a solo exhibition under the best local auspices, but revealed publicly her gift in another medium: words.

In late February 1930 Emily was visited by Katherine Pinkerton, a writer from the United States, and another sojourner, Lodewyk Bosch, a young Dutch artist-critic. The pair were 'staggered' when their eyes fell on her powerful forest and totem canvases. They had expected to find delicate watercolours that were the stock in trade of the Island Arts and Crafts Society. Instead they found work that 'spoke to us, soul to soul, spirit to spirit'. They were amazed to learn, undoubtedly from Emily, that people did not like her work because it was not 'nicely' painted, because the subjects of her pictures were 'strange totem poles, Indian houses, etc'. Eager to assist a painter who in Europe 'would have been acclaimed as one of the greatest artists of her day', they prompted the Victoria Branch of the Women's Canadian Club to invite Emily to speak at their next meeting.[13] Emily would thus join the ranks of Nellie McClung, Arthur Lismer, Lady Tweedsmuir, and other personages who had addressed the club in the Crystal Gardens. Arrangements were also made by Bosch and Pinkerton for an exhibition. Bosch hung some fifty paintings representing Emily's earlier and recent work, while Pinkerton used all her tact to persuade Emily to give a talk. Emily consented, but almost backed out at the last minute because of a domestic crisis. On the third of March, the day before the event, Woo, taking advantage of Emily's preoccupation with her speech writing, stole a tube of yellow paint and ate it.

> All day I hung over my monkey. I washed inside as far down as I could reach with gasoline rags. I gave emetics and physic. Woo submitted, pocketed the physic in her cheeks and spat it out later. She lay across a hot bottle in my lap.[14]

Woo recovered only hours before 'a lady in a swell car' called for the unusually well-dressed Emily and her griffon, Ginger Pop, and drove the short distance from Hill House to the Crystal Gardens. After a general meeting in the concert hall, Emily mounted the platform and, trembling, turned to face the 500 'Club Potentates' who were seated on wooden chairs arranged in semi-circles. Ginger Pop was placed in the lace, satin and fur lap of the president, Mrs P.B. Scurrah. Grabbing the edge of the reading desk for support, Emily began. Her nervous voice was too soft to reach those at the back of the hall. Several women called 'Louder!' The president waved. At this, Ginger Pop leapt from her plush lap and darted to Emily's feet, thawing both the audience and Emily. As she looked down and caught the eye of her dog, she found 'all the voice I needed'.[15]

Emily had had only a week to prepare her address, yet it did not suffer from lack of forethought. Drawing lightly on some personal experiences, and on years of thinking about art and the creative process, she made an 'eloquent plea for a more tolerant and sympathetic view of modern art', in the words of the *Colonist*.[16]

'I hate like poison to talk,' Emily began. 'Artists talk in paint—words do not come easily. But I have put my hate in my pocket because I know many of you cordially detest "Modern Art".' Not only did her words appear to come easily, but they elucidated some difficult concepts as she shared her deeply held beliefs with her audience of clubwomen. Referring to painting in the nineteenth century and the influence of the camera on it, she pointed out the camera's limitations: it cannot comment, select, or feel.

> The camera has no mind.
> We may copy some thing as faithfully as the camera, but unless we bring to our picture something additional—something creative—something of ourselves—our picture does not live. It is but a poor copy of unfelt nature. We look at it and straightway we forget it because we have brought nothing to it. We have no new experience.
> Creative Art is 'fresh seeing'.

Defending 'distortion', she cited the Old Masters who, in stylizing their depictions of 'the dear, queer old saints', had enabled their spirit to shine through.

On modern painting, she expressed an idea that had transformed her own work not so long before:

> The beauty concealed in modern art consists more in the building up of a structural, unified, beautiful whole—an enveloped idea—a spiritual unity—a forgetting of the individual objects in the building up of the whole.

She paid generous tribute to the Group of Seven, who had 'burst themselves free, blazed the trail, stood the abuse and lived up to their convictions'.

On Canadian painting, she said:

> Canada wants something strong, big, dignified, and spiritual that shall make her artists better for doing it and her people better for seeing it. And we artists need the people at our back, not to throw cold water over us or to starve us with their cold, clammy silence, but to give us their sympathy and support.

Then, making a veiled reference to her role as a rejected and misunderstood artist, she said:

> I tell you it is better to be a street-sweeper or a char or a boarding-house keeper than to lower your standard. These may spoil your temper, but they need not dwarf your soul.

There was an impassioned reply to the charge of some that the West was unpaintable and its forests monotonous:

> Oh, just let them open their eyes and look! It isn't pretty. It's only just magnificent, tremendous. The oldest art of our West, the art of the Indians, is in spirit very modern, full of liveness and vitality. They went far and got so many of the very things that we modern artists are striving for today.

She ended by making her plea—but not for 'my own pictures. . . . They are before you to like or to dislike as you please. . . . The plea that I make to you is for a more tolerant attitude towards the bigger vision of Creative Art . . .'[17]

All through the address, Ginger Pop sat at Emily's feet, his body taut, his nose held high, and his whiskers and beard sticking out like an aggressive old man's. Only at the conclusion, when Emily was thanked and presented with an armful of daffodils, did he move from his post. Hearty applause followed. The meeting adjourned and Emily and a few club members walked over to the Empress lounge for tea. A dish of cream was found for Ginger Pop. Emily, delighting in the attention given her dog and in the warm reception to her talk, was satisfied for once. The *Colonist* gave a lengthy resumé of the lecture, and made an honest, though clumsy, attempt to describe her pictures. As a result, the lower floor of the Crystal Gardens where the paintings were hung had many visitors during the few days the gallery was open. It 'was never without its little group of visitors', who expressed surprise and admiration for Emily's work. Mortimer Lamb, who came from Vancouver, said he would like to have the show moved to his city. Another visitor, a Mrs Tooker, wanted it for Berkeley, California. The 'unusually big attendance' constituted 'something in the nature of a record in the club annals.'[18] Even Emily, usually critical of newspaper reviews and public receptions, felt that she had 'made a hit'.[19]

The exhibition and address not only gave Emily an opportunity to restate her artistic beliefs and to sway Victoria's conservative public; it allowed her to meet like-minded souls who revered, as she did, the modern school. Though suspicious of Bosch, the sophisticated European whom many thought decadent—he wore his heavy, straight black hair in a pompadour—she was probably overwhelmed by, and grateful for, a flattering article he wrote in the *Colonist* prior to the exhibition. He invited her to his Fort Street studio, but her admiration diminished when she found him painting a still-life from paper flowers. She dismissed Bosch the artist as a fraud, especially when he later outraged her with an exposition of the phallic imagery of her totem poles.

Emily took more seriously two Victoria artists, Max Maynard and Jack Shadbolt. Maynard, a young school teacher, was an admirer of the English landscape artist, Paul Nash, and much impressed by the paintings of the Group of Seven, which he had discovered by reading Housser's *A Canadian Art Movement*. He had already seen isolated examples of Emily's work in the 1928 and 1929 Island Arts and Crafts exhibition, in which he himself had been a participant, but not until her solo exhibition at the Crystal Gardens did he see 'whole walls of her sweeping canvases'. Filled with enthusiasm, he took Victoria High School principal Ira Dilworth—who would become, more than a decade later, Emily's literary collaborator, trustee, and confidant—and a high-school art teacher and sculptor, Earle Clarke, to see the work of an artist who he felt was 'a real genius'. However, they did not share the young man's enthusiasm for Emily's work. Dilworth joked openly as he viewed the paintings, and Maynard found himself defending them. All the while 'a little old lady, wearing a shapeless dress almost reaching her heavy oxfords and an Aunt-Maryish hat looked on from a distance.' When his friends departed and Maynard was alone, the woman advanced and asked his name. When he in turn asked hers, she replied, 'Miss Emily Carr'.[20]

Maynard was the vital force in a small group of talented young men who called themselves the Fossils and often gathered at Ira Dilworth's on Thursday evenings to read poetry, listen to music, and discuss art and literature. One of them, Frederick Brand, remembered Max as 'a stimulus to us all' and another, Jack Shadbolt, spoke of him as one of his mentors.[21] One by one Maynard took his friends—Brand, Shadbolt, and John Macdonald—to Emily's studio. On Brand's first visit Emily's manner was stiff; 'she showed her canvases grudgingly, as though the integrity of her art were threatened, and she remained aloof during the whole "interview".'[22] Macdonald remembered their hostess as being austere and frightening.[23] The same austerity and aloofness greeted Maynard and Shadbolt, who saw in Miss Carr a splendid audience for their youthful enthusiasms about art and its history. But they made Emily feel ignorant and uncomfortable as they confidently expounded their ideas and flaunted their jargon. She did not know 'the history of Art and the things that are written about their men', nor was she familiar with or interested in art technique.[24] (In 1933 she asked a friend to explain egg tempera.)[25] 'She never said a great deal,' Shadbolt recalled, 'but let us chatter away.'[26] Unimpressed and unamused, Emily silently cursed them for being 'so bloated with their own conceit'.[27]

Maynard and Shadbolt, who visited Emily several times over the next few years, shared her reverence for the British Columbia coastal landscape; indeed, they recognized the need for a new interpretation of landscape and found this more often in her work than in that of Paul Nash or the Group. 'Under the image of her brooding, visceral and vaulted interior spaces of the rain forest', Shadbolt's interest in tree forms grew 'into something compelling'.[28] The titles of some of Maynard's

forest sketches—*Dancing Trees, Tree Forms,* and *Rhythmic Roots*—
could easily have been used by Emily.[29] Emily resented the young men's
dedication to 'her' forests and their verbal fluency in analysing and
dissecting them. She felt threatened, not flattered, by these disciples.
They were young; they had caught the fever of the British Columbia
landscape; they were, as one Victoria critic put it, painting 'living' trees
and 'the essence of the landscape'.[30] They admired Emily, were under her
spell, yet she remained distant and critical. They were 'despicable cads';
she 'never did care for those two'; 'they came to me, not I to them'.[31]
Jack, she feared, wanted her 'Indian designs for his beastly commercial
. . . daubs'.[32] Maynard took her ideas and, twisting them a little,
paraded them as his own. She once accused him of tacking one of her
sketches on the wall and copying it over and over. Many of Maynard's
sketches did have elements of her tree and log forms. Like all young
artists, he was strongly influenced by others, especially Carr and Harris.
Shadbolt was only slightly less under her influence, which dominated his
forest scenes and at the same time enriched them.

Occasionally Emily's fear subsided and she would decide that she had
an obligation to give out ideas for others to improve on and carry further. At such times she would invite Maynard to her studio for a critique
of her most recent work. But his criticism usually 'wasn't worth a sniff'.[33]
She expressed her indignation sarcastically to a friend: 'These square
hind jaws of Max seem to absolutely dent me. . . . I think his
judgement in art rotten too. . . . He always likes my very worst
things'; he 'pulls out some sick duck of a canvas and never sees anything I
know is good.' She seldom acknowledged his comments but lay back and
let him 'prance on top with boots on'.[34]

Maynard, who visited Emily more frequently than the other young
men, quickly became aware of her fear and jealousy but was undeterred.
He also came to see that, though she easily identified with Indians,
French peasants, and animals, and was greatly impressed by the
Establishment—like the National Gallery and the Group of Seven—she
had very little time for much younger practitioners like Shadbolt and
himself who were working not only in her artistic territory but on her
home ground as well. Nevertheless, Maynard's admiration of her work
was unshakeable in spite of her less than friendly behaviour to him,
which decades later caused him to say that she was 'a bitch and all her
greatness did not make up or substitute for her haughtiness.'[35] The New
York sculptor, Ronald Bladen, then a young student of Maynard's,
recalled Emily's presence as being 'so strong that you either went with it
or ran away from it.'[36]

Edythe Hembroff was one artist who became a close friend of Emily's
but was little influenced by her work. A contemporary and friend of
Maynard and Shadbolt, she met Emily in the summer of 1930, not
through her high-spirited friends but as the result of an overture from
Emily herself. After reading in a newspaper that the young woman had
recently returned from art studies in France, Emily phoned and invited

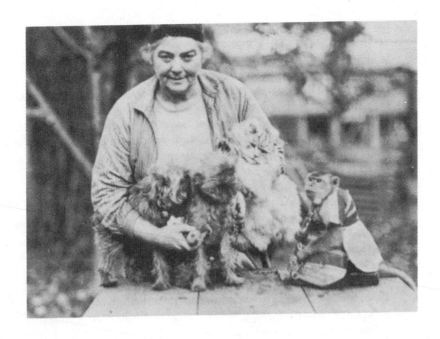

(ABOVE) 'Mom and family'—Emily with two griffon
dogs, cat, and Woo, mid-1930s. Private collection.

(BELOW) Emily with Woo, mid-1930s. Private collection.

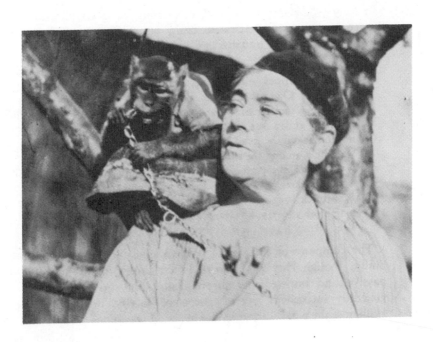

her to tea. Hembroff was 'attracted to her at once'. Emily's 'melodious voice with soft English undertones', her 'pleasant round face with fine contemplative grey eyes piquantly pulled up at the corners', her 'headband stretched across her forehead in a heavy arc and unruly wisps of hair tufted out over each ear', were all observed and remembered from that first visit.[37] The two women soon found that they 'had common grounds of purpose and experience; were of compatible temperaments.'[38] But there were notable differences between them. Edythe Hembroff was twenty-three, well dressed, and attractive. Unlike Emily, she had enjoyed the moral support of her family for her art. Though Hembroff was a practising artist, Emily felt that she strove for 'the Artistic setting' rather than for 'Art itself'.[39] Nevertheless Emily gave her 'crits' of her work, sympathized with her rejections from hanging committees, and cheered her rare victories. Above all, she set Hembroff—who, as a portraitist, posed no threat and did not encroach on her artistic territory—against the more successful Shadbolt and Maynard. When Maynard won the Beatrice Stone medal at the Vancouver Art Gallery in 1936, Emily advised Hembroff not to 'give them the satisfaction of letting them know that *their* recognition . . . is of the least importance.'[40]

Until the first of her long absences from Victoria in November 1932, Hembroff was a frequent visitor to Emily's studio. During the winter of 1931-2 they practised Hembroff's genre—figure-drawing and portraiture. Though Emily was not keen, they engaged a child model (plucked from Alice's school) or painted one another or themselves. When preparing for a portrait by Hembroff, Emily revealed a streak of vanity by putting on her best black dress, with a bolero jacket, and pinning a cameo broach at her throat.

In May 1932 Hembroff accompanied Emily to an abandoned cabin on Braden Mountain in Metchosin. Emily described their life there to Nan Cheney, a painter she had met in Ottawa in 1927:

> Edythe Hembroff and I are rusticating among ants, verdure and wood ticks. It's glorious, exhilarating, soothing, ticklesome and inspiring all at once. . . . Our cabin is log and very old. Two rooms and a passage connecting same with a door each end and cyclone whipping through down the gulley. We are 1000 ft. above sea level and everywhere are hills not too heavily wooded but that you can scramble over them. There is a waterhole among the bullrushes and we have to carry the water a long way. In fact, everything is primitive and completely inconvenient. There's a junk cookstove which we ignore and cook splendid meals over a huge open brick fireplace in the other room. A huge black iron kettle and a mammoth steel frypan are our choicest possessions. We sketch all day and sleep all night. I get up at six a.m. and go out onto the hills . . . .[41]

The company of the young woman must have been refreshing for Emily, though Hembroff worried that Emily might have found her passive and boring.[42] Hembroff trod lightly to avoid conflict and generally succeeded. If Emily expected to find in her another Carol Williams, she was disappointed. Hembroff was older, she did not possess the childish spontaneity of Emily's earlier sketching partner, nor was she passionately fond of Emily's creatures. But Edythe Hembroff admired Emily greatly—though not in Carol Williams' uncritical way—and did much to promote her painting in Victoria. Indeed, she 'acquired a sense of mission to bring E.C. out of obscurity and local neglect.'[43] In 1931 she suggested to the Island Arts and Crafts—without success—that it buy one of Emily's works. She and Brand then approached Victoria's women's clubs and individuals for contributions to raise money for the purchase of *Kispiox Totems* for presentation to the British Columbia Archives. This time the response was gratifying. The painting was ceremoniously presented to the government and afterwards a 'pink tea' was held at the Empress Hotel.[44] The money Emily received, $166, went towards the purchase of her van, 'The Elephant'.

In 1932 Maynard became vice-president of the Island Arts and Crafts Society on condition that one room of its annual show be devoted to modern art. For the autumn exhibition, under Maynard's direction, the 'moderns' were given a 'small poor' room of their own in the Belmont Building.[45] The exhibitors included Emily, Maynard, Shadbolt, Hembroff, Ina D.D. Uhthoff, and Ronald Bladen. Maynard even wrote a 'rousing document' entitled 'The Modern Point of View', which was available to all who ventured into the room.[46] The *Colonist* acknowledged that 'a room devoted entirely to modern work' was included in the show, but did not attempt to discuss it.[47] The *Times* added that it was significant for the exponents of the modern school to have their own exhibition space and singled out the work of Miss Carr for special mention.[48] Maynard recalled that there were sympathetic viewers among members and patrons, but as 'nobody had any clear sense of what was going on in the arts', there was little understanding.[49] The event that Emily saw as 'a step' turned out to be a concession to Maynard and was not repeated the following year when he was no longer vice-president.[50] Having a Modern Room at all had been a small triumph for the painters who exhibited in it, but modernism had not yet crossed the Strait—nor would it for years to come.

For the past year Emily had been thinking about creating a permanent place for exhibitions in Hill House. Her plan was idealistic and naïve. She wanted a gallery where modern and conservative painting could be exhibited with equal respect, and a place where children's classes, lectures, and discussions could be held. She had, after all, opened her house to small exhibitions of her pottery and paintings several times in the past and had plenty of space. There were four good sized rooms across the front of the house for hanging' and the studio could be used for talks on art, music, and photography. Perhaps the Beacon Hill Park authorities could take over the building. She would remain in the house, occupying the upper suites and acting as a built-in director-curator-caretaker. Though she could not 'give' the building, she would donate much of her free time and even use her 'old Indian Junk as a standby' for exhibition.[51]

Lying conveniently adjacent to the park, the 'Beacon Hill Galleries' would be 'a warm quiet nook to drop into on those dull winter days' when no band played in the park. During the summer it would attract tourists who frequently asked, 'Is there no picture gallery in Victoria?'[52] On Saturday mornings it would be open to children, on Sundays to everyone, and during the week to those willing to pay a small entrance fee. Above all it would 'induce the growth and better understanding of art among our citizens', Emily wrote in a letter she circulated, 'especially if short talks were added.'[53]

At first it looked as if the venture might succeed. The park superintendent was approached and, according to Emily, 'the scheme interested him greatly'—provided that the necessary funds did not come out of his budget.[54] As evidence of the house's suitability, Emily installed a connecting door between the vacant lower flats. She filled their four front rooms with her Indian totem pictures, the rather conservative landscape paintings of her old friend Mrs Annie Bullen, the watercolours of the 'gifted Chinese student' Lee Nam, and the portraits of the young Robin Watt. She sent out a letter of invitation to a meeting at Hill House, and on the fourteenth of December 1932 forty citizens gathered, including representatives of the city council, her 'Modern Room' allies, contributors to the purchase of *Kispiox Totems*, as well as a few members of the Island Arts and Crafts Society and a reporter from the *Colonist*. In an article headed 'People's Gallery Plan is Under Consideration', the *Colonist* reported that 'Miss Carr explained her reasons for making the suggestion.'[55] 'There would seem,' she began, 'to be a further need for more exhibition space than that offered by the annual Island Arts and Crafts Society.' Victoria needed a place 'that touches all classes, all Nationalities, all colors', one that would benefit 'boys who have asked for membership to the existing club in Victoria and been refused', one that would allow workers hitherto banned from the existing society's exhibitions to 'feel comfortable'. 'It would be a place for those who do know something about Art' as well as 'those who do not, . . . a place one could sit and rest and look at pictures' of all types, 'conservative-progressive-oriental-children's'. Above all, it would be a place 'for the spirit of art to grow in. . . . It would not take very much money to start simply and happily,' she continued; 'we don't need a stone edifice and liveried attendants, rooms full of priceless pictures and the wrangle and worry of trying to be able to boast that we have the *most magnificent gallery in all Canada.*' However, it did need the financial aid of 'the many clubs and societies of Victoria' and 'moral support and mothering'.[56]

When Emily concluded her speech, an alderman, representing the mayor, 'expressed appreciation at Miss Carr's views and the enthusiasm which she had shown in the cause of art for the people.' There was 'a lengthy discussion'. Jack Shadbolt, who chaired the informal proceedings, selected a committee, which included himself and Emily, 'to weigh all the arguments advanced and present some more specific proposal for the financing and administration' at a meeting to be held in the near future.[57] With that decided, the proceedings adjourned and all present viewed the exhibition, and no doubt enjoyed refreshments at Emily's expense.

The following day Emily informed Eric Brown that her 'scheme' had 'met with *good response*'. The people who came 'were pleased with the rooms and the exhibition' and it looked 'as though the idea may go through', provided that the estimated cost of $95 a month could be found to support it.[58] Brown replied enthusiastically. His gallery would 'do everything in its power to help it along by sending exhibitions and so on.'[59] The offer from the National Gallery director caused the idea to burgeon in many sceptical minds. Yet the need for a permanent gallery must have been reassessed even by Emily when, shortly before Christmas, she held an exhibition in her still-vacant lower suites. On the first day one person came; on the second, four; on the third, fourteen. Though by the New Year she told a friend that the gallery was 'not squashed yet', by early January the gulf between enthusiasm and support, pledges and donations, had widened.[60] It was the height of the Depression. Funds could not be raised through public institutions and few individuals were enthusiastic enough to commit their money to a non-profit organization. Some, like the Lieutenant-Governor, were willing to lend their moral and financial support only if a new fireproof building were constructed.[61] Others may have objected to Emily's dominant role in the project. She had a reputation for being bossy, and difficult to get along with, and some probably felt that she was temperamentally unsuited to the position of curator-director-caretaker. There were also problems among the artists themselves. The Island Arts and Crafts people saw the establishment of a gallery as a threat to their organization, and though initially enthusiastic, were now 'bucking' at the idea. Other artists 'wanted to make it purely a selling show' rather than an educational experience for the people.[62]

Edythe Hembroff felt that Emily had misconceived the interest of the public. The 'little people'—the butcher, coal man, and vegetable man— who had been curious about her work were not sufficiently interested or financially prepared to support the gallery plan.[63] Nor did many share Emily's resentment of the Island Arts and Crafts Society for being a social élite, for favouring traditional art, and for excluding orientals from its membership. Another incentive of Emily's—the wish to rid herself of a burdensome apartment house so that she could devote more time to art—was hers alone. The gallery idea was in large part based on Emily's own grudges and misjudgement.

On the eighteenth of January enthusiasts of the People's Gallery, now greatly diminished, gathered once again in her home. They were asked 'to determine what financial assistance could be assembled', and a committee that again included Emily was appointed to report on the matter a week later.[64] The final consensus was that 'it is inadvisable at this time to attempt to establish the proposed gallery', as there was no way to finance the idea.[65] Informing Brown the next day of her defeat, Emily seemed relieved. 'Now I'm glad after the two months wrestle & , waste of time and energy to throw myself back into work on my own things.'[66] A childish poem, 'Ideal', was written in commemoration.

Shortly after the failure of the People's Gallery, Jack Shadbolt, John Macdonald, Frederick Brand, Edythe Hembroff, and, later, Max Maynard all left Victoria. Emily grew kindlier towards Maynard and Shadbolt once they were no longer on her doorstep. When Shadbolt, and his friend John Macdonald, wrote to her from New York requesting that she send some sketches so that they could 'persuade one of the galleries . . . to stage an Emily Carr exhibition', she was pleasantly startled.[67] She did not send them any, but thereafter she became something of a proud patroness, speaking highly of Shadbolt to an uninterested Lawren Harris and asking after him. She came to respect Shadbolt and Maynard as the only artists besides herself who had really worked hard in Victoria and often wrote that she regretted no longer having them about. Thus two acquaintances—who at close range had been feared, envied, and fought with—entered Emily's good graces when she no longer had to meet them.

Edythe Hembroff and Fred Brand continued to popularize Emily's work. Now married and living in Vancouver, where Brand taught mathematics at the University of British Columbia, the pair sent several of her sketches to Gertrude Stein in Paris. They were returned a year later, unopened, with a characteristic note from Alice B. Toklas stating that Miss Stein was too busy driving an ambulance in Spain to concern herself with the Canadian woman's work.[68] More realistic and helpful to Emily were the shows organized by Brand and hung in the UBC library: two group exhibitions in March 1933 and February 1935. Brand gave introductory talks at the openings and wrote favourable critiques in the university newspaper.[69]

Emily also received encouragement for her work from Margaret Clay, a librarian friend, who submitted her painting *Vanquished* to the exhibition sponsored by the International Federation of Business and Professional Women at the Stedelijk Museum in Amsterdam. Though Miss Clay did not think 'the exhibition was a great success from an artistic point-of-view', Emily received 'many letters of appreciation from Europe as a result of it.'[70] In January 1933 *Saturday Night* published an article by Mortimer Lamb on her work that was strongly flattering and well informed. He praised her forest canvases for their 'organized and rhythmic design in which form, volume and colour contribute to produce an harmonic synthesis'.[71] Lamb was undoubtedly her most important western supporter, but Emily considered him 'a rather silly old man . . . with a great "blow" like a whale.'[72]

Emily had become dependent on the East for criticism and support for her work; she never missed an opportunity to cite approvingly the National Gallery and the Group of Seven, to the disadvantage of local societies and artists. But by 1934 she found that her relationship with eastern galleries and artists was deteriorating. She was not only without her young Victoria friends, but it seemed that she was losing the support of her eastern friends as well.

Some of her dealings with eastern Canada had been unsatisfactory from the start. The problems began with her first contribution to the West Coast Exhibition in 1927. Cheques from the sale of her pottery were slow to reach her and Emily complained that she lost money on the exchange she had to pay when she cashed them. When the exhibition moved from Ottawa to Toronto and then on to Montreal, there was some confusion about where her pottery was and what had been sold. In many cases she had not labelled the pieces according to the accompanying price list, and as a result the articles sometimes had more than one price. The return of her twenty-six watercolours was delayed. Initially Emily was 'only too pleased' to allow her paintings to stay in the East as long as the Gallery could make good use of them, but on a whim she changed her mind and demanded that 'my watercolours be sent home to me as soon as possible'.[73] The Gallery finally shipped them to her, but they had been badly packed and many arrived damaged. She sent them back to Ottawa for insurance evaluation, holding up their return further. Emily's complaints to the National Gallery's assistant director, Harry McCurry, were either ignored or elicited a scolding. The Gallery had no official responsibility for the sale or the disposal of her pottery, McCurry told her in 1928, adding that she should be thankful that the Gallery 'had brought her work before the Canadian public so that she could reach a wider field.'[74] But Marius Barbeau, usually neutral in such matters, agreed that there had been 'many delays and lack of sufficient explanation' in the handling of her work.[75]

Emily's patience with gallery officials was limited. She had never been good at keeping track of her paintings, or in tending to financial matters. When a borrower failed to give her a prompt account of sales or picture locations when she requested one, suspicion set in; she decided that she was somehow being cheated and friction developed. Emily liked 'to work & create'; exhibition arrangements were dismissed with an 'ugh'.[76]

In 1931 Emily complained to Nan Cheney that the National Gallery had 'never bothered to buy anything except those two or three old old original watercolours which they show as samples of my work & make me sick.'[77] It was true that for years the Gallery owned nothing more recent than three of her 1912 paintings. Her annoyance increased when Arthur Lismer, giving a slide lecture in Victoria on behalf of the National Gallery in 1932, showed only a 1912 watercolour by Emily. Even 'old Victoria', she wrote to Nan Cheney, 'was *actually indignant* at the rotton thing Ottawa put on the screen to represent my work.'[78]

Shortly after returning to Victoria from her 1927 visit to the East, Emily had complained to Barbeau that none of her eastern friends had written to her. Though letters from Brown and Harris followed within days, she was anticipating neglect, as usual. Her impatience, usually voiced, lost her many correspondents. By 1931 even Barbeau had 'not written for ages' and Emily concluded that there was 'someone else he is interested in probably'.[79] She declined the invitation of the National Gallery—extended by Charles Scott, a member of the provincial selec-

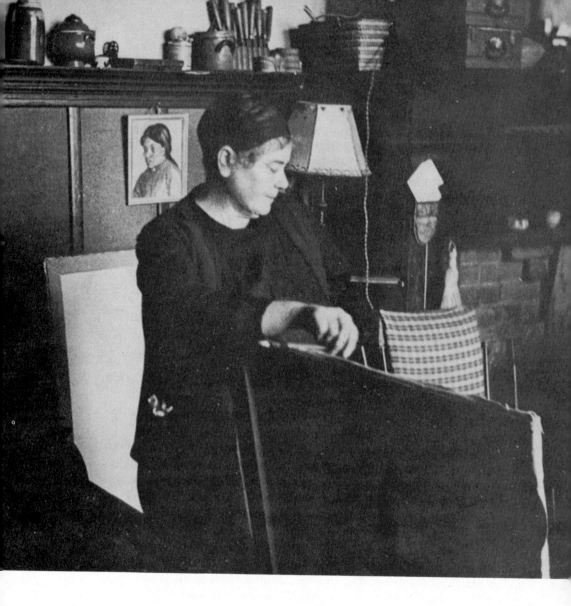

The four photographs of Emily that follow were taken in her
studio, with a flash, by H.U. Knight in October 1933. With
her was John Vanderpant, Vancouver photographer. VCA.

(a) Emily's portrait of Sophie is on the wall.
(b) With John Vanderpant. Note the chair suspended from the ceiling.
Tree hangs above the door.

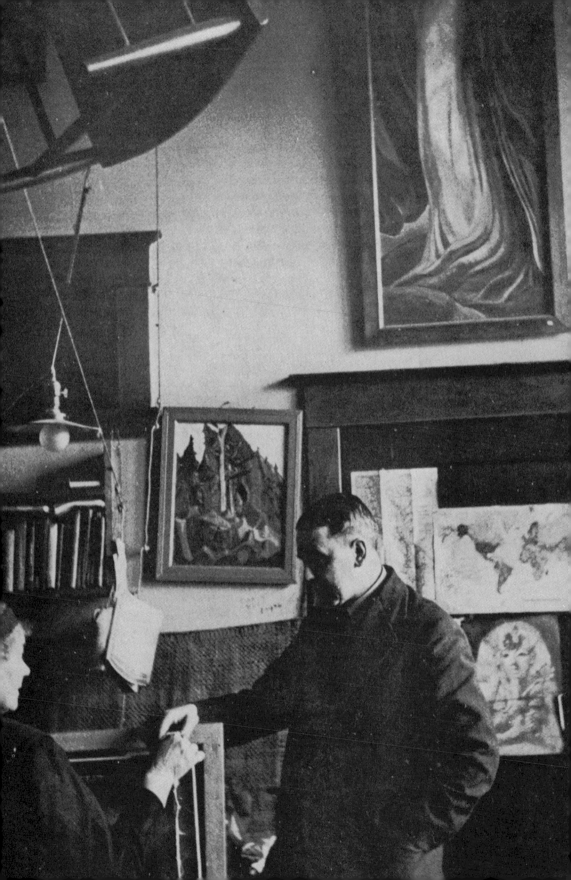

tion committee—to submit work for the annual exhibition of the Canadian Society of Painters in Watercolour in 1933. Only when Brown himself made the request by telegram did she agree to do so. In the next two years not one painting left her studio for an eastern exhibition. Gallery officials continued to include her work, but they managed to avoid her by submitting older paintings from local private and public collections. Her oil-on-paper sketches—which marked a breakthrough in her development, as well as in the changing perception of the western-Canadian landscape—did not reach Gallery officials in the East until 1935, four years after she had begun to work in that medium.

In October 1934 Emily wrote Brown 'straight from the shoulder'. She complained that the National Gallery had not 'purchased a single canvas' but continued to show her 'two miserable old watercolours done more than *twenty* years ago'; that it had failed to hang all the work she had sent East because, as she heard 'on pretty good authority', it was 'too modern'; and, finally, that the Gallery continued to delay returning her paintings from exhibitions. Though she assured Brown that she would always feel grateful to him for hauling her 'out of the slough of despair', she wanted him to know that it had been 'a harder uphill pull' from 1927 than most knew.[80] After this harsh missive, a certain aloofness existed between officials of the National Gallery and Emily. The following year she wrote to Nan Cheney that she had heard nothing from either the Browns or the Barbeaus.[81]

In some ways Emily did have her most difficult time after her 1927 'discovery'. She had been praised by eastern gallery officials and artists as a great undiscovered, unappreciated Canadian artist. There had been good press coverage for her contribution to the West Coast Exhibition, and sales of her pottery, hooked rugs, and paintings had been plentiful. Encouraging letters had followed and Brown had assured her that she could count on 'some public attention . . . in the future'.[82] Between 1927 and 1933 she contributed, as a result of Brown and other eastern supporters, to more than twenty-two exhibitions in eastern Canada and abroad. Yet the feedback was minimal and unsatisfying—singling out her work as the most individual in the exhibition or dismissing it as foreboding, even dull—and after 1928 both sales and letters declined. At a time when economic pressures were causing Emily to lower her apartment rents, and shipping and crating costs were soaring, the lack of satisfactory compensation made her efforts seem futile.

That there seemed to be little evident appreciation of her work, and less remuneration, was not really the fault of Canadian gallery officials. Emily's complaining letters did not help matters. The National Gallery, in spite of its fumbling, channelled her paintings to every possible show. Its purchase budget was severely limited after the Depression set in. It had other artists as well as Emily to consider; and, compared with her western contemporaries, she was treated far better than most. Her forest canvases of 1928-31 were a hindrance to her popularity because few eastern Canadians were familiar enough with that landscape to ap-

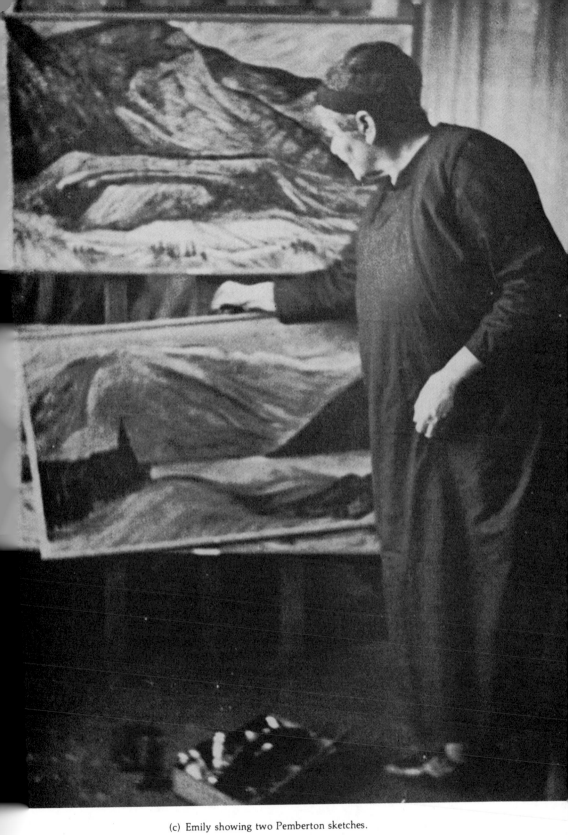

(c) Emily showing two Pemberton sketches.

preciate them. By 1930 many artists were turning away from the landscape motif and taking up figurative work and even abstract painting. As a latecomer to the landscape genre Emily was, in a sense, out-of-date. Even Lawren Harris, her staunchest supporter, remembered the time 'when a number of the canvases & sketches of Emily Carr did not appeal to me.' His dislike was not a 'matter of art so much as the fact that I was not conditioned to respond to the many phases of the British Columbia landscape & its moods.' He held 'a prejudice against the landscape & the air of the pacific slope—the lush growth, the opulent patterns', until he moved to Vancouver in 1940.[83] This prejudice, shared by many, was not conducive to sales or popularity.

Had difficulties with gallery officials been Emily's only problem, she might not have felt so hostile to the East, but this situation was exacerbated by deteriorating relations with those 'worth whiles' she had met in 1927, and again in 1930. Though initially glad to be identified with the Group, Emily soon realized that she was far from being one of them. Hearing of the 'eastern Artists going off in bunches, working, sharing each other's enthusiasms and perplexities', made her 'jealous, furiously jealous'.[84] 'Now I resented all the artists in the East pooling thoughts & sketching trips & I always alone.'[85] One by one she dismissed those easterners with whom she had established contact: A.Y. Jackson, Arthur Lismer, F.H. Varley, Bess and Fred Housser, and finally even Harris himself.

Though Emily had been moved by Jackson's work in 1927, she had never hit it off' with him after their initial meeting. She claimed that 'he despises me for a *woman* artist.'[86] Animosity mounted when, in 1932, she heard that he had given her work 'the black eye', calling it 'monstrous, uninteresting, dull etc'.[87] In his autobiography Jackson wrote that 'she sometimes saw slights where none was intended, leading her at times to be less than gracious.'[88] With Arthur Lismer, Emily got on splendidly at first. His visit to Victoria in 1932 was a red-letter day and she was 'tickled stiff' when he spent nearly all of his short visit with her. However, in 1933 she had sent some of her paper sketches back East for her friends' comments and Lismer sent his crit direct to her. His remarks were both flattering—he admired their feeling of power and courageous attack— and critical—he advised her to work on a smaller scale. After receiving this advice, her defences went up.[89] On Lismer's 1935 lecture-visit to Victoria, Emily referred to him as 'a leaky old blow bag'. She gave him some 'lip', and another of the Group was alienated.[90] Lismer, prepared for her now-famous cold shoulder, had asked a friend before arriving in the city if there was a boarding house near the park and beach where one could 'dodge the E. Carr's'.[91] He did not avoid her that time but on his next visit in 1937 he was successful: in Emily's words, 'Lismer did not look this way.'[92] Varley is said to have found her masculine and dirty and to have disliked her paintings.[93] 'What a fish he is,' Emily wrote to Nan Cheney.[94]

Not surprisingly, after 1933 she received little further attention from

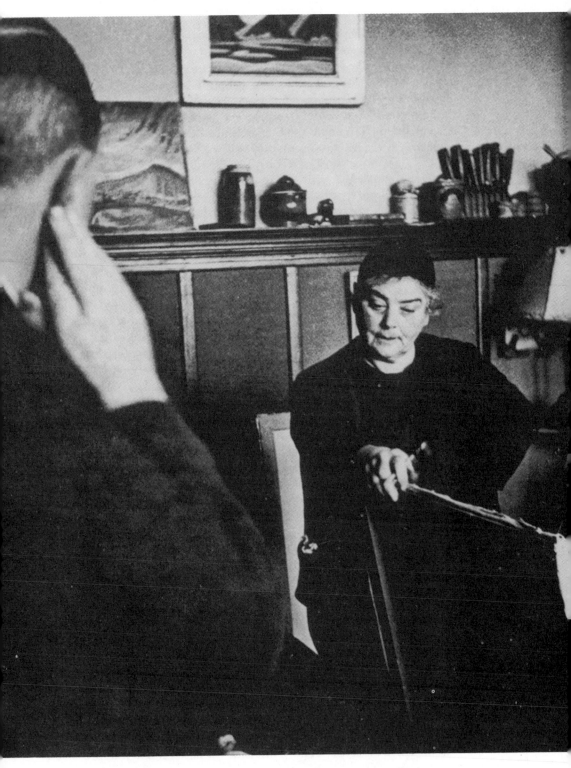

(d) The painting above Emily's head is an oil sketch by Lawren Harris—a gift from him—for *Bylot Island* (about 1930). With John Vanderpant.

these three men. 'What's the good of sending to exhibitions?' Emily wondered. 'First I sent it to get the crits of the men in the East, which were helpful. Now they don't give me any.'[95]

More unexpected were her cooling relations with Lawren Harris and Bess and Fred Housser, the three people who had introduced her to theosophy, Whitman, and Emerson. Harris especially had given her confidence and, after 1927, had become her mentor, the person she was never afraid to argue with. Her friendship with them took a new turn on her last eastern trip in November 1933.

Emily wanted to visit the important exhibition of painting at the Chicago World's Fair but arrived one day late. Though deeply disappointed, she forced herself to see the sights of the city and the Fair. Homesickness overcame her and she did not even finish out the week for which she had paid in advance. She wired Bess and Fred Housser that she was coming to them and left for Toronto.

They received her warmly. The Houssers' home, where Emily was a guest for nine days, was 'all books and pictures and lovely talks & people'. There were 'many delightful lunches, teas, dinners'.[96] She spent three long afternoons in Harris's studio and one evening at his home for dinner. She visited the inaugural Canadian Group of Painters exhibition—in which she herself was a participant—at the Art Gallery of Toronto. Though she found it interesting, she felt that the new group 'lacked the dignity and unity' of the Group of Seven, which it had replaced. She saw Jack Shadbolt, then teaching in Toronto, and reported that he was 'in fair spirits and as know-it-all as ever'.[97]

'It's a rare thing,' Emily recalled, 'to be in a company of doers instead of blown-out air cushions', and to be made to feel 'one of them and not a stranger from the far off West.'[98] Yet for all the attention she received, there were moments that made her loneliness in Chicago seem mild. Long discussions about theosophy with Harris and the Houssers tortured her. Their 'denial of the divinity of Christ', and their belief that He 'was *only a good man*', tore at the roots of her very being.[99] Their rejection of prayer, of Christ, of the Bible, led her to the edge of a frightening abyss. Emily talked 'straight and unafraid' with them into the small hours of the morning. The conversations took her 'for a brief spell to a higher place of thoughts and ideals', above the body, sex, colour, and creed.[100] She asked many questions and discovered there was much that she had misunderstood. Her friends patiently explained the reasons for their beliefs. Bess was 'dictorial', while Fred's talk was so deep that it 'nearly drowned me'.[101] Though the conversations were exhilarating, they were also agonizing. Attempting to think as they did, and being persuaded that their attitude to God opened 'a way for the artist to find himself an approach', Emily decided that in comparison with the pictures of the Canadian Group she had just seen, her work was greatly lacking.[102] It suddenly seemed to her that she had not caught the spirit of the western-Canadian landscape after all. This made her need for a new approach all the greater. As she had not been able to receive inspiration from the Chicago exhibition, a deeper understanding of theosophy became urgent. But it was so difficult to grasp! She had 'some bad days and sleepless nights'.[103] After one particular session with the Houssers and Harris, she ached 'with the awfulness of everything [and] cried out bitterly.'[104] She became 'stiff with horror' when she realized what their beliefs portended: no prayer, no Bible, no Christ, no solace, just 'a sort of endless voyage with God, always way way beyond catching up.'[105] One day the emotional strain became too much: she grabbed a broom, went outside, and swept snow. Further discussions eased the tension somewhat, but Emily left Toronto 'quite unconvinced that it was what I wanted'. Back in Victoria a few weeks later, she wrote Harris and told him she could not 'swallow some of the theosophy ideas'.[106]

Emily had been well schooled in the Bible's teachings and had always related to God through Christ. She could not accept the theosophist's claim to a direct and intuitive knowledge of God; the exclusion of prayer as a vehicle of worship seemed to offer a cold and remote form of religious experience. Theosophy was 'such a lot of queer man-made rigamorole' that spun her round in circles, made her giddy.[107] Her religion was 'weak & shaky in spots, vague & hungry too', but if she lost it, 'there'd be nothing, *nothing*.' That was 'too awful to contemplate!'[108] Fearful of losing all her cherished beliefs, she returned to the religion of her youth, to its atonement for sin, its prayer, its Christ, and its Bible.

It was at this time, shortly after her trip, that Emily met Raja Singh. His Christianity, tinged with the Eastern spiritualism that had attracted her to theosophy, filled the vacuum that had been created by her talks with Harris and Bess and fortified her long-held beliefs. 'Here a live Christ leads you to God',[109] she wrote of Singh's Christianity, and rejoiced at being free from the remote, mysterious God of theosophy.

Emily felt that her rejection of theosophy had hurt Harris, Bess, and Fred and caused a rift between them. If Harris was disappointed, he never said so to her. His letters were still filled with theosophy, yet he was glad that Emily had found something that would yield her 'the fullest inner life'.[110] Bess Housser was less conciliatory. Writing to 'Dearest Mom' (both Bess and Fred called her Mom), she said that she and Lawren and Fred 'must have been shocking' to make her feel like giving up their philosophy so abruptly. She invited Emily to write 'a good long letter telling me all about your experience and what it is doing to you', and ventured to ask, 'How does Whitman fit in now?'[111] Whitman remained. So too did Emily's belief in communing with God through nature. But she returned to her childhood Christianity for good.

The note of mockery in Bess's letter hurt Emily. Not wanting her friends to think that she was wholeheartedly in tune with theosophy when she was not, she had risked losing their friendship by telling them so. But other things besides Emily's break with theosophy chafed against their relationship. Emily thought his Arctic paintings, which she had seen on her trip, were 'dead and lifeless', though 'still beautiful in colour &

light'.[112] For the first time since they had met almost six years before, Emily and Lawren were out of step artistically. That breach was widened by Harris's persistent praise of *Indian Church*. Feeling that she had made great progress since that canvas had been completed in 1929, Emily was annoyed by his compliments. And something that happened the following year placed a barrier between them that was solid, impenetrable, insurmountable.

In July 1934 Bess Housser came West. She did not travel as far as Victoria and Emily, who had to go to Vancouver to see her, was disappointed. She had looked forward to having Bess in her flat and sharing her sketches with her. Emily arrived in Vancouver in an ill temper. She was irritated by Bess and sparks flew. Then the bomb was dropped: Bess planned to divorce Fred Housser and Lawren would end *his* marriage. She and Lawren had decided to marry.

Emily was shocked. She was not surprised so much by their mutual affection—Lawren had given her enough hints of that—as by what she thought of as the immorality and deceit that had surrounded it. Bess tried to put things in the best light by talking about 'higher love and non sex' and by insisting that Fred was in love with Yvonne McKague, a young painter whom he would later marry.[113] But Emily was unconvinced. Her moral code was deeply offended. 'They'd been living falsely,' she wrote. She felt that she 'could never quite trust them again.'[114] After Bess left, Emily wrote that 'the door of the jolly old Eastern friendship was banged to, leaving them one side & me the other.'[115]

The 'bust up', as Emily referred to the incident, left her without kinship in both art and religion.[116] More important, it deprived her of Harris. Mrs Harris had always been safely in the background. Bess—stronger, opinionated, and herself a painter—would be competition as Harris's wife. No longer would there be those quiet, uninterrupted talks in Harris's studio. Emily felt robbed. When the affair surfaced in Toronto, there was a scandal and the couple left eastern Canada permanently, moving first to New Hampshire, then to New Mexico, then to California. Emily had lost her greatest supporter. Even when, years later, Harris and Bess moved to Vancouver, it was impossible to restore the old relationship. Harris did not cease to write Emily, but his rare letters were light and superficial, with few helpful criticisms. As late as the 1940s Emily was calling Lawren and Bess 'intolerant people'; their theosophy was all 'rigarmoral'.[117] Bess was 'a poser' and a 'hypocrite'.[118] Harris had weakened and bent under her influence. She heard he was even asking Bess's advice in art matters, which was surprising, since 'Bess never ranked more than an amateur in art compared to Lawren.'[119]

Only days before Bess arrived in Vancouver with the 'whole story', Emily—whose ties with the East had weakened considerably—fortified herself by making a long-overdue decision. She wrote in her journal that for years she had been at the mercy of the East. 'Now they are torn away and I stand *alone* on my own perfectly good feet.' From now on her 'own soul' would be her critic and she would 'push with my own power, look with my own eyes'.[120] During the next few years, that is what she did.

11
Fruition
1934-1937

Throughout all the vicissitudes of her relations with friends and acquaintances, Emily had 'the girls'—her sisters—to fall back on. They saw much of each other throughout the year, and always celebrated birthdays and Christmas with gift-giving and dinners. Their relationship was cemented by tradition, common memories, affection, and blood; otherwise it would not have survived a steady round of wounding remarks, disagreements, and criticism. Lizzie and Alice were impatient with Emily and critical of her; she in turn criticized them and provoked them, sometimes deliberately. Emily could be objective about them in her journals and acknowledge that they were 'miles apart in temperament, in habits and likes',[1] but she was unable to tolerate their differences when they were together, and was most aggrieved by their apparent lack of interest in her work. Yet she often wrote of her sisters tenderly—they were so good and unselfish, 'the finest women ever'.[2] She couldn't imagine life without them. 'We love each other, we three; with all our differences we are very close.'[3]

After Edith died in 1919, her position of authority was inherited by Lizzie. Like Edith before her, Lizzie became a parental figure for Emily, a constant reminder of the guilt that still haunted her for disappointing her mother in failing to meet the standards of her sisters; as in childhood, Emily still measured herself poorly against them. This was enough to produce tension and to prompt little acts of rebellion, but the relationship underwent further strain when Emily began to suffer from deafness in her left ear in 1932. 'Elizabeth says I'm stupid clicks her tongue & shakes her head continuously at my *stupidity* because I am *deaf*.'[4] Emily's irritation was increased by Lizzie's virtuousness, by her Biblical verses written on scraps of paper and repeated when the moment was 'right', and by her 'small & mean & unjust God'.[5] Emily, who had a penchant for reliving childhood squabbles, wrote of Lizzie: 'She's the first person I ever remember quarrelling with.' It was 'a baby fight, I bit her arm; Mother tied me up to the verandah post it was dark . . . I was terrified of dark it was dreadful.' On another occasion she had scratched Lizzie's hand and could still 'feel the burning shame' of those two or three nail marks on the back of her sister's hand. 'How vile I was,' she wrote, referring to an incident of some fifty years before, 'and yet how *supremely* she could aggravate and go off with saintly air.'[6]

Emily complained that her sisters seldom came to her, but she visited them often. Every Sunday, ritualistically, she and Lizzie, who was still living in the old family home on Government Street, went to Alice's schoolhouse for dinner. (Sometimes they also went for lunch during the week.) Alice's pupils sat on each side of the schoolroom table on dictionaries and cushions. Lizzie and Alice were at the ends, where one carved and the other served vegetables. Alice's helpmate sat on her right and Emily sat on Lizzie's left. During the meals the children remained silent while the three sisters, Emily taking the lead, remembered when Father . . . The reminiscences were interrupted by Alice ordering the children not to chew so loudly, or by Lizzie objecting to Millie's table manners, her slang, or her smoking. When Emily deliberately unsettled Lizzie, Alice would restore peace by siding with Millie, who would then drift back into the past with, 'Do you remember when . . . ?'[7] These little flare-ups, which were so frequent that they almost became an accepted means of communication for the sisters, kept Emily in her childhood role as the youngest naughtiest child, and her sisters as superior parent figures.

But if her sisters treated Emily like a child, she played the role, which had many advantages. She could demand their attention and usually get it; she could depend on their protection; and she could indulge in mischievous acts—such as swearing—and always be excused. For Emily these expectations never changed, nor did her sisters' understanding of them.

Emily went to the schoolhouse whenever she required an ear for her apartment-house grudges. Alice seemed bored and indifferent to her complaints, saying little; if Lizzie happened to be there, she was vocal and sided with the opposing party. A squabble inevitably resulted. Sympathy for her complaints was important to Emily. When she did not get it from her sisters, she decided that they disapproved of her, thought her unable to cope. She would return home wishing she had not gone, regretting that she had shown some temper, brooding over the feeling that her sisters did not consider her successful either as a landlady or as an artist. She was the black sheep again and her defences mounted. But she thought nothing of trudging back to Alice's the following day, as if she got a neurotic satisfaction from confirming over and over her inferior position in the family circle.

Being conservative, and possessing the ideals of their parents, Lizzie and Alice had difficulty in considering painting as anything more than a relaxing hobby, a view that seemed to be confirmed by Emily's failure—

except when she was in Vancouver—to derive a supportive income from her art. Their lack of demonstrable interest, or their failure even to ask politely about her work when she returned from a sketching trip, was taken by Emily as disapproval and even contempt. Her frequent depressions at this time—'not much use to my fellow men either by working or being alive'—were blamed on the 'quiet ignoring of my work by my own folk'.[8] A friend has recalled that Lizzie and Alice 'hesitated to say anything about her pictures for fear of saying the wrong thing'; but their silence was the wrong thing too.[9] It was enough to make Emily believe that she was unappreciated, even ill-treated, by her sisters. Yet they were not entirely unsympathetic to her painting. While Emily was preparing for a solo exhibition in Edmonton in 1933, Alice visited her studio. She was known to prefer her sister's early watercolours, but as she examined the oil-on-paper sketches, she said: 'They're beautiful. No that's not quite it. They're wonderful.'[10] The approval of Lizzie was registered the next year, at one of Emily's At Homes, when she saw something she liked in Emily's work for the first time. In the same parental way they cared about everything she did, the sisters gave Emily real support in her career. They urged her to go East in 1927, agreeing to feed her animals and attend to the apartment chores during her absence. And according to Emily, they were 'quite keen and enthusiastic' over her decision to visit the Chicago World's Fair in 1933.[11] They even encouraged the purchase of her caravan. And though they rarely visited her while she was camping, they asked that she keep them informed of her well being daily by mail. One friend has recalled that 'Though they did not always understand her', they were 'devoted to her and immensely proud of her.'[12] Nevertheless, Emily remained convinced that her sisters were 'not the least interested'.[13] Even if this had been true, her attitude towards their own work was no different. As she grew older, Emily had little tolerance for children, and when she was at Alice's school the palms of her hands itched 'to smack their young hides'. Towards Lizzie's activities—visiting the sick and attending functions associated with the church—she was equally unsympathetic.

The Carr sisters were three very different women who loved one another dearly, who fretted over one another's well being but could not step beyond the family roles in which they were entrenched to take a wider interest in one another. Of the three, it was Emily who had the greatest need for company and reassurance. Alice had the Hennell family's letters and visits, Lizzie had a great number of old friends. Emily had fewer friends, especially after 1933, and her sisters became even more important to her. As her need for them grew with advancing age, their differences, and her inability to achieve a mature adjustment of her relationship with them, became increasingly apparent.

Considering all possibilities for companionship, Emily felt that she did not have a friend of her own age or generation; that she did not fit into the family, the church, or even into her own apartment house as a landlady. On perhaps little evidence she dismissed her younger women acquaintances for having 'disgusting love affairs'; the married ones 'leaked any personal news' to their husbands. Women her own age were boring, self-centred old maids, or grandmothers engrossed in their off-spring—and none of them was interested in painting. As for men, they could not be trusted.

Emily had cultivated a host of new friends since returning to the city in 1913. Few, however, came close to meeting her ideal of 'a friend person', someone '*really* nice and companionable' with whom she could freely share every thought.[14] She did not look to marriage as a panacea for lack of companionship: her observations of married couples in the apartment house persuaded her that such a union was a seesaw of fighting and saying horrid things to one another, then making up and feeling sorry. Lawren Harris had been a 'friend person', but by 1934 they had parted in art and in religion, and Emily strongly disapproved of his divorce and remarriage to Bess Housser. She maintained a sporadic correspondence with Lawren, and when he and Bess moved to Vancouver in 1940 his occasional visits were always welcomed. But after 1933 things were never the same. She had lost the one person to whom she could say anything.

One friend noted that Emily had 'an astonishingly large and wide circle of acquaintances', but she still thought of herself as a lonely person.[15] Sometimes she blamed her solitude on her art, feeling that 'artists are queer, they have to be alone a lot.'[16] In a rare moment of self-awareness she blamed herself: 'I'm always bursting forth making enemies instead of friends, whirling round in a muck of rage muddling everything & getting all wrought up.'[17] The result was always the same: she was regretful and solitary afterwards. Her defensive attitude and accompanying moods of quiet hostility were sometimes revealed publicly. A talk she gave for the Normal School Literary Society, for example, in the autumn of 1935 was one such occasion.

Emily was unforthcoming from the start. Dressed in a heavy tweed suit, a sweater, and scarf (she preferred to perspire rather than remove any of her clothing), she stood sullenly before her audience and proceeded to read her prepared speech. What followed was 'The Something Plus in a Work of Art.'[18] She gave the impression that she was either very nervous, and so not able to speak easily, or indifferent to her audience. When she flipped hurriedly through some oil-on-paper sket-ches mounted on an easel, curtly identifying each as trees or Indian totem poles, she fully expected her audience would be nonplussed. She made comments such as 'You won't like this one' as she passed from sketch to sketch. One student, who had frequently seen Emily walking and chatting to her dogs on Beacon Hill and who had looked forward to the lecture, left with the impression that 'Miss Carr really didn't care about us—probably because she had decided that we wouldn't care about her work.'[19] Yet Emily was struck by the hearty response of appreciation from the students and regretted her unfriendly attitude. 'I wished I had faced those young things more steadfastly,' she wrote, and 'looked at them more and tried to understand them better. She had not intended her animosity to be directed towards the students, but towards their teachers—three 'rather set stiffs' who, she felt, were not interested in painting or in the creative artist.[20] Believing they were against her, she decided to beat them to any demonstration of disapproval by showing that she did not care whether they liked her work or not.

Had Emily been alone with the students, she might have relaxed and been more confident. When Gerhart Ziegler and his friend Klaus, two young German acquaintances of the New York critic Katherine Drier, visited Emily in Victoria for two weeks in 1930, she treated them royally. They joined Emily on her Beacon Hill walks, allowed her to guide them on a day excursion to Goldstream, and listened while she read the poems of Walt Whitman. They understood little of art yet were eager to learn about British Columbia's forests and Indians during evening chats around the studio fire. Another young man who enjoyed a similar rapport was Philip Amsden, an English tenant who occupied the suite opposite Emily's from about 1929 to 1932. Though engaged in manual labour, Amsden had literary interests, and Emily, recognizing a fellow spirit, frequently invited him into her studio. Over cups of Postum they had long conversations about the work of Lawrence, Katherine Mansfield, and Walt Whitman. Emily reminded him pleasantly of an aunt in England and one summer, when he rented a cottage at Beecher Bay in Sooke, she was frequently his guest. 'I laid on the grass,' he recalled, 'while Miss Carr sketched.' Their friendship became even closer, if Amsden's surprising recollection is true that they rented and shared a cottage one spring.[21]

In this kind of relationship Emily could feel confident because she was the centre of attention and could guide the conversation. But the presence of an authority figure posed a threat and put her on the defensive, inhibiting her and preventing rapport. Her unfortunate Normal School talk was not an isolated incident. The year before, Varley had invited Emily to act as a judge at a student exhibition at the British Columbia College of Art and her behaviour had been similar. She pointedly ignored the students because she felt their work was appalling. However, it was the presence of the instructors that kept her from relaxing and giving the students' work more than a passing glance. She not only condemned the exhibits but later criticized the luncheon given for her at the Georgia Hotel. Thus she converted her uneasiness into hostility.

Emily was naturally less on the defensive at home than on alien ground. Though she complained that showing her work was a torture and discussing it with strangers was even worse, she gave many exhibitions. Visitors were put at a disadvantage from the moment they crossed the threshold of her studio. Emily suspended her chairs from the ceiling by ropes. She claimed that this gave her more workroom in the studio, and it certainly did; yet it was not without malice that she had devised a system whereby unwanted guests could not plant themselves on *her* chairs. She had to decide if she wished visitors to stay before she awarded them chairs, which she would lower by a pulley in the corner of the studio.

A major cause of Emily's loneliness was her penchant for striking out before being struck—notably displayed in her aggressive relationship with her boarders and tenants—and then being left alone feeling guilty for her action. In her relations with others, Emily was mainly concerned with how people reacted to her—whether or not they hurt her, made her feel stupid, or prompted feelings of insecurity and self-consciousness. So great was her involvement with her own feelings that she devoted little thought to others except as they affected her. There were three people, however, to whom she gave disinterested attention and sympathy at this time: Sophie Frank, Harold Cook, and Lee Nam.

Sophie Frank, who remained a friend after Emily left Vancouver, won Emily's deepest respect and affection by reason of her sheer misfortune— twenty-one dead children—and her simple trust. Something above their differences of ethnicity, environment, and religion—'something understandably higher'—bound the two women together.[22] Even after discovering that Sophie was an alcoholic, that she had a bad influence on the young girls in her North Vancouver village, and was reputed to be 'a woman of the street, the chattle of the lowest waterfront derelicts', Emily continued to regard her warmly. She was probably hurt by her friend's 'hideous' lying, especially about her prostitution, yet each Christmas a hamper went from Simcoe Street to Sophie's small house on the North Vancouver Salish Reserve.[23] Acquaintances were always asked to take something to Sophie if they were going to North Vancouver. And it was to Sophie that Emily dedicated her first book.

A similar friendship existed between Emily and the severely handicapped Harold Cook. She made frequent trips to see him at the Provincial Mental Home on the outskirts of Victoria. 'Cookie', as he was known to the other inmates, had lived with the missionaries in the Indian village of Kispiox and it was probably there that Emily met him. During her hour-long visits they talked about Indian villages they both knew and about animals. Emily read Harold her stories and he read to her from his 'autobiography' (which he was writing, kneeling at a chair, in a scribbler she supplied him with). She took a polite interest in his institutional job—polishing the brass spittoons—while he was 'fearfully interested' in her painting and treasured newspaper clippings about her, and the letters she wrote.[24]

Lee Nam, the Chinese artist for whom Emily gave exhibitions and whom she publicly supported in her 'People's Gallery' when he was refused membership in the Island Arts and Crafts Society, was also a friend. He expressed his admiration of Emily by showing an interest in taking lessons (he did not become her pupil), by always recognizing her best work, and by giving helpful critiques.

Emily identified herself with, yet felt superior to, each of these three people, whom she once referred to as 'a prostitute, a lunatic and a

Chinese artist'.[25] Like the students in San Francisco, St Ives, and Bushey who had come to her for mothering and guidance, they received protection and warmth from her. She could drop her defences with them and relax, confident that they would not criticize or judge her and knowing that these friendships were on her terms. Often feeling excluded and rejected herself, she befriended those she considered beneath her, while at the same time getting back at the Establishment and indulging herself with the love and attention that her charitable acts earned for her. These were her rather naïve motives and rewards.

Many of Emily's friends were both loved and hated, often used, then cast aside when she saw fit. When all was well and she received their help, sketches were given in appreciation and invitations for dinner and tea sent out. Flora Hamilton Burns has written that Emily had 'a great capacity for friendship'.[26] But she was always ready to criticize, and to retaliate for real or imagined grievances. Her letters had to be answered within a short time: she would not keep up a one-sided correspondence. Regular visits were expected; when these lapsed, she ruthlessly complained of one friend to another, or committed her grudges to her journals or letters. Her descriptions were vivid and cutting. One acquaintance had 'breath like a bad drain' and another—an excessive talker—was 'an old blow bag'.[27] Though overly critical, and always ready to sacrifice someone to protect her work, she knew that friends were indispensable to her. She took precautions to keep them apart lest they compare any resentments or intimacies she may have revealed. She even kept her close friendship with Carol Pearson secret from her later friends. Indeed, Carol was unknown to most of them until her book, *Emily Carr as I Knew Her*, appeared in 1953, eight years after Emily's death.

Emily's friends and acquaintances were usually old Victoria residents. The 'shy and retiring' William A. Newcombe was perhaps her most frequent visitor.[28] 'Willie', the son of Dr C.F. Newcombe, who had looked at Emily's work for the Provincial Museum in 1912, was Emily's handyman. Neighbours often saw him puttering around the gardens at Simcoe Street, and at her next house on Beckley Street, with Emily close at his heels, lecturing him on such topics as the importance of not letting himself go (he refused to acquire a set of false teeth).[29] He crated her pictures, made her frames, hung her At Home exhibitions, assisted with her moves, and ran errands to her camp sites. But he was much more than a handyman to Emily. He had acquired a broad knowledge of natural history from his father and became a first-rate naturalist. Although not university educated, he was assistant biologist at the Provincial Museum until professional jealousies prompted his dismissal in 1933 on a trumped-up charge of theft.[30] He shared with Emily an interest in nature and the Indians of the coast, and she admitted learning a great deal from him. (He gave a short talk on the Indians at her At Home in November 1928.) He lent her photographs taken by his father at the more remote villages, and it was from one of these that she painted

Blunden Harbour. Willie, like his father, brought anthropologists such as Erna Gunther—curator of the Washington State Museum and professor at the University of Washington—to Emily's studio to view her totem-pole paintings and to see her small collection of artefacts. Gunther was impressd by the 'anthropological excellence' of Emily's Indian paintings, as well as by her deep love for the natives.[31] She visited Emily often—she came to Victoria every two or three months—and Emily probably enjoyed seeing her but felt intimidated by Gunther's scholarly knowledge. The anthropologist was 'nice enough', Emily wrote, 'but noisy & self-opinionated'. Though there were many friendly conversations, Emily insisted that she would never 'think of talking . . . Indians or art' with Gunther because she would 'swamp you like an immense leak'.[32] The patient, long-suffering Willie Newcombe was easier to converse with. But even their friendship was not secure. No doubt in retaliation for her frequent abuse, Willie often stayed away, only to be called 'a swine' by Emily for ignoring her.[33]

During the 1930s several of Emily's friends were directly or indirectly involved in criticizing the short stories she had begun to write in the 1920s. The most constant of her 'listening ladies' was Flora Burns, who for years was the only person who knew that Emily was writing seriously.[34] Emily had been a contemporary and friend of Flora's mother. When she died in 1924, Flora, who worked in a bank, took her mother's place in Emily's life. Emily found this gentle, unselfish woman to be an inspiration, and Flora was more than charmed by her much older friend, with whom she was never bored. Flora remembers Emily as a born storyteller, with quick movements, lovely hands, a many-coloured voice, a mobile face, and large grey eyes that took in everything.[35] Flora spent many long afternoons and evenings in the studio listening to Emily stumble through her illegibly handwritten first drafts. In 1926 Flora enrolled with Emily in a correspondence course on the short story. 'Every week or two' during the course, Flora recalled, 'she would read me her latest story, ask for my criticism and compare it with that of the Palmer Institute. . . . With her spontaneous gifts of vivid writing and story telling she soon outstripped anything the Palmer Institute could teach her.'[36] As well as providing criticisms, Flora sent Emily's manuscripts—which were returned—to *Maclean's Magazine*, the *Atlantic Monthly*, the *Saturday Evening Post*, and the *Countryman*. She also urged Emily to send a story to the American-based International Correspondence Criticism Service and to enrol in Mrs E.B. Shaw's creative-writing course at Victoria College in the summer and autumn of 1934. Flora served not only as literary critic but as almost the sole intellectual stimulus for Emily, who normally read very little. She provided her with books like Shipp's *The New Art*, which complemented and broadened Emily's interest in spiritualism and art, and stressed to her the importance of developing her writing and painting simultaneously. She even suggested that one depended on the development of the other.

Flora Burns was Emily's only trusted critic until the spring of 1936 when she met Ruth Humphrey, a teacher of English at Victoria College. Though generally frightened of, and shy with, anyone who taught at a university, Emily agreed to trade a sketch for Miss Humphrey's crits. She soon found that Ruth was not, as anticipated, a severe critic. But Emily was not an easy pupil. She was 'impatient' and used 'very foul language'.[37] Her stories, like her letters and journals, were riddled with literary deviations: slang, such as 'dame', 'busted', and 'beastly'; garbled words, like 'flornity' for forlorn; and muddled syntax, illogical paragraphing, capricious punctuation, and wildly incorrect spelling. She was also verbose. First versions of her stories were 'more detailed, much fuller' than they needed to be and required paring down.[38] Emily responded to criticisms up to a point, and became proficient at 'cutting out the slop'.[39] Under Flora's and Ruth's guidance she saw her stories become more precise, less sentimental, and almost devoid of slang. After several visits from Ruth, she noted that writing was 'coming easier and I see more'.[40] Emily was not entirely submissive, however. While she knew that these women were 'well read and well educated in English', and saw herself as a 'know-nothing' in comparison, she felt that 'their way of expressing' was not 'my way', for they did not 'see with the same eye'.[41] Flora wanted 'too much sentiment', she complained, and Ruth's 'stripping' left the stories 'cold and humanless'.[42] Emily was aware that the mechanics of her writing was poor, yet she knew instinctively that if she were 'ultra-honest, ultra-true, some deep realizing of life' would compensate for her lack of training.[43] Though she firmly acknowledged that these two women were helping her, she resisted their academic niceties, feeling that she had to find her own form of expression.

Like most of Emily's friends, her listening ladies were usually kept apart. On one occasion, however, when Flora, Ruth, and Margaret Clay were invited for a group criticism, there was friction. Ruth and Flora were 'antipodes'. Emily scarcely knew when one or the other would 'strike a mine and blow up'.[44] When her critics revealed their own weaknesses in openly disagreeing about the merits or flaws of a story, this made it easier for Emily to resist having her impressions—'only obtainable by direct contact with the Indians and wild places'—blunted by academic convention.[45] Sometimes when they had finished going over a manuscript she rebelled because she thought their alterations had robbed it of her personal expression. She knew that her spelling, punctuation, and paragraphing needed attention, but she was crushed when her listening ladies changed words or altered meanings. 'If they'd only punctuate and let me be me,' she complained, 'and leave them at the best I can do.'[46] Their changes frequently made Emily realize how much she wanted to maintain her independence, which she had always fiercely upheld in her painting. When Emily sent Harris some of her stories in 1930, he had stressed that she should not be influenced by anyone else's advice. In her writing, as in her painting, there was a fine line between inspiration and emulation. Having strong faith in the truth as she saw it, in simplicity, and in success through hard work, she sometimes maintained her independence by finding fault and casting aside helpful suggestions. She could be overwhelmed by ideas, as when Lawren Harris was instructing her in theosophy, and allow herself to be engulfed by them. Then, swamped and almost suffocated, she would emerge with something worthwhile to use as her own. She possessed a knack for recognizing and assimilating the best advice of others.

Emily's father had been the first to kindle her interest in literature, although he was not a literary man. He gave her Scott's *Lady of the Lake*, and Emily claimed she memorized almost all of it. But she was not an avid reader. Generally she read a book only when someone lent or gave it to her. She read the simple stories, many of them about animals, in *Understudies* (1901) by Mary E. Wilkes, a New England writer, and she probably read Pauline Johnson's Indian legends, which were serialized in the *Province* during her stay in Vancouver. She admired the stories of D.H. Lawrence and Katherine Mansfield, which she was introduced to a few years after she had begun writing her own short stories, but she felt that Lawrence wrote mostly for effect and dealt with 'nothing but sex'. Dostoyevsky was 'beastly'.[47] Her tastes leaned towards the sentimental.

Emily's early stories often reflected the simple morals and the sentimentality of the soap operas she liked to listen to on the radio. (She enjoyed sharing the 'natural and clean' lives of the characters on such programs as *Vic and Sade* and *Ma Perkins*.)[48] Yet she would have denied that her writing had a sentimental or moral purpose. She wrote of her childhood because she found that many things became clearer to her after she had written about them. She came to understand her animals better after meeting them halfway in a No-man's-land she created, where animals and humans achieved complete harmony and understanding. Re-creating her visits to Indian villages enabled her to relive experiences that were not renewed after 1930 and that had begun to recede into the past. Writing became for her a way of coming to terms with her past.

Though a cheque from even one of the many publishers Ruth Humphrey and Flora Burns submitted her work to would have been welcomed, Emily wrote more for her bottom drawer than for the public. When she told Harris of her writing, he encouraged her, suggesting that it would give her 'another realm to live in'.[49] And it did. There was nothing more comforting than slipping into bed with a hot-water bottle at her feet, cushions at her back, a woolly shawl around her shoulders, an all-day-sucker in the form of a toffy blob in her hand. Then with a five-cent scribbler on her knees, a pencil in hand, and wire glasses on her nose, she would cast her mind back to all the animals she had known, to the Indian villages, and to the cow yard and garden of her childhood. The stories were first written in longhand, then set aside, then written over and over again in a much shorter form, and finally typed. Much effort was devoted to paring down sentences, to choosing the right word, and to reproducing a dialect—whether Indian, French, or Chinese— accurately. While Emily worried that she might be deluding herself about her capabilities as a writer—she took her writing no less seriously than

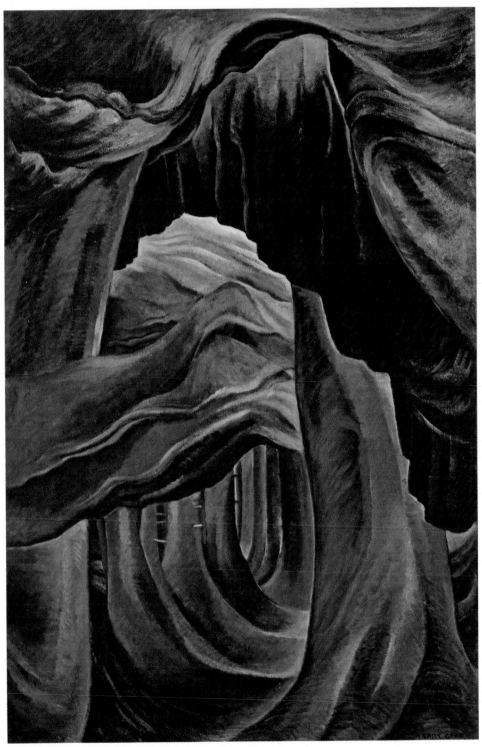

VII—*Forest, British Columbia*, about 1931. Oil on canvas, 51 x 34. (Photo: Michael Neill) VAG.

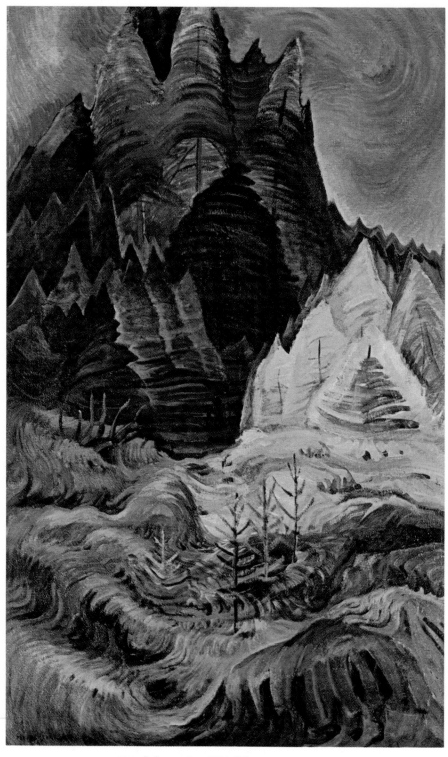

VIII—*Reforestation*, 1936. Oil on canvas, 44 x 27.
Courtesy The McMichael Canadian Collection, Kleinburg, Ontario.

her painting—her increasing ability to produce the 'real thing' in words carried her forward.

> I found writing helped painting as painting helped writing. It seemed to make things clearer in my own mind, trying to express them one way or another. It taught me to look deeper with a searching earnestness. I visualized my words and worded my 'seeings' and seemed to get a fuller understanding a deeper inlook. At first it was very difficult to find words & form sentences . . . there was a great deal of cutting down leaving out and selecting just as there was in painting. I went over and over and over disheartened at the crudity & illiteracy of my writing and then when I remembered all the miserably poor sketches I'd made I did not feel quite so bad.

Whatever the discouragements and self-doubts, writing was a deeply satisfying substitute for the companionship and intimate conversations Emily had always yearned for and seldom experienced with people. Though she claimed that writing was the second of her two occupations, by 1934 she sometimes wanted to write more than she wanted to paint.

When Emily painted *Grey* in 1929-30 she was interested in reducing the forms in nature to geometric solids. Then, when 'the world did not seem . . . to be quite so much on the run or quite so much alive', she had wanted 'to catch something and pin it down.'[50] In 1931, working at Goldstream among the cedars, she began to perceive the energy and movement in each individual object of nature. She realized that there was 'only *one* movement sweeping out into space' when she spent many afternoons during the autumn and winter of 1932-3 on the grassy cliffs of Dallas Road overlooking the sea. Working in charcoal and oil on paper, she was 'careful about the transition of one curve of direction into the next'. She continued to imbue each object with energy, but she now attempted to link one object to the next until the painting was a structural whole.

In June 1933 Emily visited her niece Lillian Rae and her family on their farm at Brackendale, north of Vancouver, and spent a happy week with them. (Sophie was living nearby and 'Lil' invited her over for lunch, with her Frank.) She then travelled to Lillooet. After a day of anguish and tears, when she had to arrange to have her feeble old dog Koko destroyed, she turned her mind to the surrounding mountains and 'plunged into work'.[51] From Lillooet she went to Seton and Anderson Lakes and then to Pemberton. The awesome mountains evoked a rush of invocations:

> Oh, you mountains, I am at your feet—humble, pleading! Speak to me in your wordless words! I claim my brotherhood to you. We are of the same substance for there is only one substance. God is all there is. There is one life, God life, that flows through all. He that formed me formed you. Oh, Father of all, raise my consciousness to that sense of oneness with the universal. Help me to express Thee.[52]

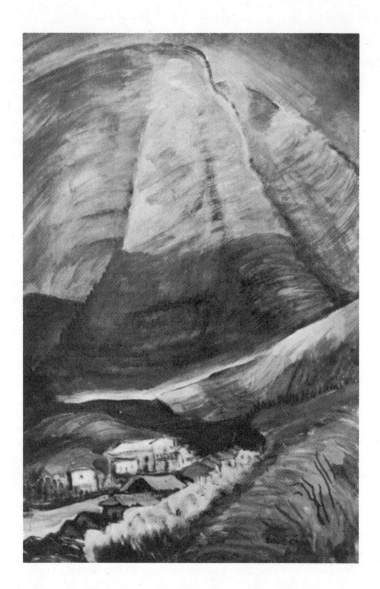

Houses Below Mountain, 1933. Oil on paper, 36 x 23 3/4. Collection Dr and Mrs Max Stern, Dominion Gallery, Montreal.

However, Emily found that the mountains 'crushed' upon the lakes; and the forest near Pemberton, through which she hiked for miles in order to obtain a particular view, was 'creepy'. She was overcome by 'a feeling of stifle, of being trapped, of oppression and depression, of foreboding and awe.'[53] This landscape alienated her, and as a result she was not able to perceive it as a unified whole. In her oil-on-paper sketch *Houses Below Mountain*, form jars against form, the mountain rises clumsily above the cluster of buildings. Only after she wrestled with her mountain subject in the studio did it sit solidly on the earth, harmonizing with the houses and foreground over which it towered. This canvas became *The Mountain*, which she finished in October 1933.

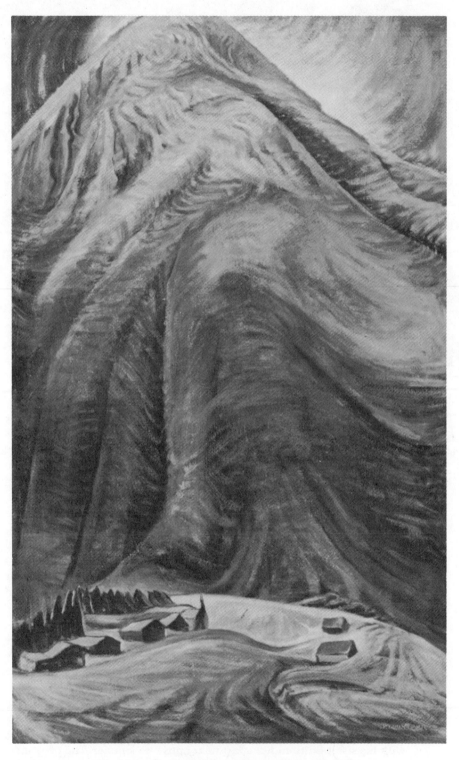

The Mountain, 1933. Oil on canvas, 43 3/4 x 27. Collection Dr and Mrs Max Stern, Dominion Gallery, Montreal.

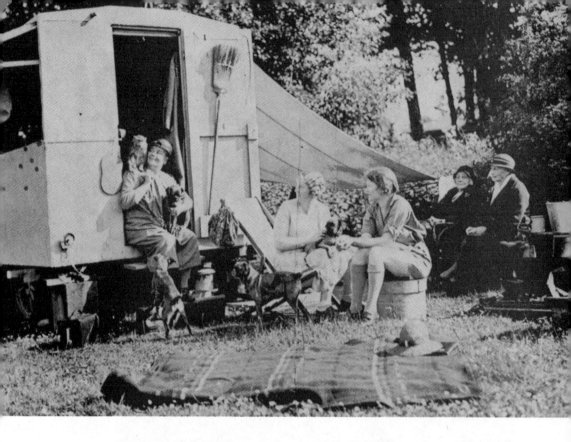

Emily and
'The Elephant'
visited by
Joyce Maynard
— sitting on
the box — and
the Morleys,
1934. PABC.

Before 1933, Emily's excursions to the wooded areas outside of Victoria—Metchosin, Cedar Hill, the Goldstream Flats, and the Sooke Hills—had been contingent on available accommodation. But the time required to make liveable an old shack, a friend's summer cottage, the upper storey of a garage, or a derelict hunting lodge was time stolen from her writing and painting. In 1933 Emily found a solution to this problem when she bought a caravan in which a man had hauled his family and possessions from Ontario to British Columbia. She paid for it with the $166 she had received for *Kispiox Totems* and fitted it with a bed, bookshelves, utensils, sleeping boxes for the animals, an oil stove, and canvas tarpaulin that could provide a cooking shelter. This vehicle—which she referred to as 'a hideous box I got cheap' and 'Noah's ark' (she being Mrs Noah)—was named 'The Elephant'.[54] Every spring and autumn she arranged to have it hauled to various wooded and seashore areas around Victoria. She rarely left the city during the summer because the forest was 'too leafy & ugly for a bit & ridden by yelling school age youngsters.'[55]

The first trip Emily undertook in her new semi-mobile studio was in the late summer of 1933. She chose to locate at the Goldstream Flats, where the aged cedars had made her conscious of the forest's rhythm two years earlier. As a companion for this maiden trip she permitted the mentally handicapped Henry Brand, the brother of Frederick, who lived with his sister Edith in her apartment house, to join her. The poor man-child—he was twenty—did not provide much company, hopping on one foot or fidgeting aimlessly, but Emily enjoyed herself. During the long evenings, after Henry had settled into his tent, she imagined the cedars stretching their boughs protectively over the van as she breathed in their intoxicating scent. On one occasion she slipped into a nondescript garment, crept down to the stream, and lay on the flat stones, letting the cold Malahat water ripple over her ample body. In the distance she could faintly hear Henry 'making strange sorts of noises and talking in his sleep'.[56] But this did not spoil her pleasure in the gurgling of the stream and the whispering firs and cedars. After giving herself a rubdown, she slipped between the sheets with a hot-water bottle at her toes, feeling like 'a million dollars'.[57]

Henry left at the end of the second week on account of the rain, but Emily was not entirely alone for the ten days remaining. She was joined for her nightly dips by Mrs 'Pop Shop', the woman who ran the nearby concession. On weekends less-welcome visitors invaded her camp. Picknickers gawked at her racing griffons, at the screeching Woo tugging on her chain from her hollow tree home, and of course at Emily, planted like a gipsy in the midst of her disorderly camp. Visits from friends who wanted a day in the country, while not unwelcome, took up her time on weekends. But during the week she was able to do some work 'of deep feeling'. She began 'to burrow under the surface, to sit still and let the woods push me rather than dicker with them' as never before. But even here she found it difficult to make a complete statement. 'The individual mighty trees stagger me,' she complained. 'I become engaged with the figures not the sum.'[58] Her attempt to portray the forest as one great rhythmic whole was abortive.

She had been inconvenienced by the rain. Moreover, during the past months she had broadened her subject matter to include sea and sky. She felt overpowered by Goldstream's immense trees rising starkly from the ground, which lacked underbrush and new growth. After Henry Brand left, she was frequently handicapped as well by her fear of the forest's solitude and by loneliness. 'I suppose I'm a coward,' she wrote one evening towards the end of her stay. 'I am not afraid exactly but it's creepy.'[59]

Despite occasional bouts of loneliness and fear, from 1933 to 1936— from the ages of sixty-two to sixty-five—Emily went to the forest more often. She claimed that she 'went back on the humans', finding companionship in the woods, which were 'so much more sensible than people steadier & more enduring'.[60] Protected from the disappointed reactions of friends, the censorious 'girls', the 'crits' of her listening ladies, and the distractions of tenants, she could concentrate her whole being on revealing her sense of the transcendental qualities of nature. Now she attained the height of her creativity, and what she felt was a true oneness with God and nature.

The Esquimalt Lagoon, Metchosin, Sooke, and Albert Head offered as subjects not only the familiar cathedral-like forests, with ghost flowers

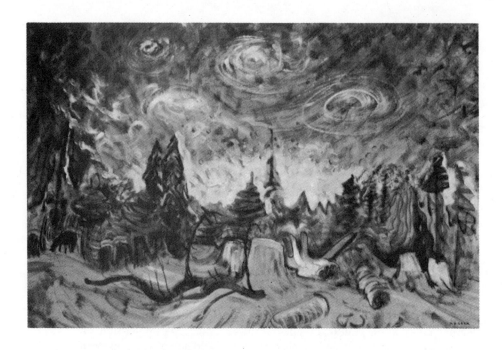

(ABOVE) *Stumps and Sky*, about 1934. Gouache on board, 23 x 35 1/2. Art Gallery of Ontario, Toronto. Gift from the Douglas M. Duncan Collection, 1970.

(BELOW) *Mrs. Jones Farm*, 1933. Oil on paper, 24 1/8 x 36 3/8. VAG.

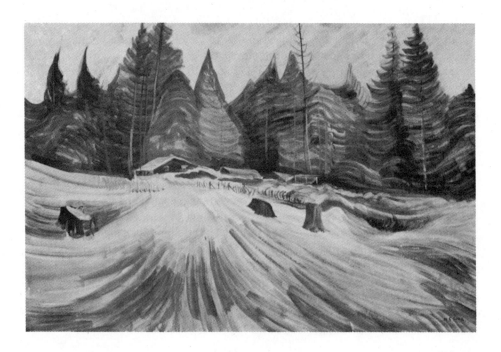

and red earth, but several other landscapes she had previously disregarded: the gaping caverns of gravel pits covered with dry, burnt prickly-grass; logged-over areas with exuberant second growth and tangled underbrush; a log-strewn seashore linked with a wide scoop of sea and an immense arching sky. Sitting on a camp stool before her subject, she would smoke a cigarette; occasionally she would sing a hymn—'Breathe on Me Breath of God' was a favourite—in her deep, soft voice. Feeling a 'divinity and oneness with the Creator' and relying on her intuition—which she believed to be the voice of God speaking within her—she would raise her gaze slightly above and just beyond her subject, so that it was out of focus.[61] Then, with her sketching-board on her lap and brush or charcoal in her hand, she would strike out with her arm and wrist and with curved or slashing motions make great sweeping strokes that included rising spirals, S-curves, and interlocking rings. All the elements previously defined separately were now powerfully fused to convey the internal push of growth, as in *Metchosin* and *Stumps and Sky.*[62] In *Mrs. Jones Farm*, background trees—their boughs curving up and down alternately—flow one into another, creating a definite rhythm. Each brush stroke merges with the next, each positive colour reflects the negative one adjacent to it. The whole painting moves and breathes. Emily wrote that the process of creating studio canvases from these field sketches was long and complex. Ideas had to be worked and reworked in further oil-on-paper sketches until she attained the seemingly spontaneous union of elements in canvases such as †*Reforestation* and †*Above the Gravel Pit*, both painted in 1936.

Seeing how close Emily was to dissolving form, outline, and what she called the organized chaos of growth, Lawren Harris now urged her to go all the way, 'to take the idea [movement in space] and extricate it from the representational'.[63] She hesitated, fearing that to reduce elements to their unintelligible essence would lead to mere decoration and design. She could have dissolved the forest images completely and used her vocabulary of curves and spirals and rings to define movement, light, and growth. But by doing this—as she wrote in reply to Harris—she would lose touch with nature. She preferred to cling to the earth.

From 1933 to 1936 Emily's paintings were magnificent expressions of herself and her attitude to nature and God. She had gradually overcome her fear of being alone in the forest and found herself able to rise, as never before, above herself into another realm of existence. She was painting her 'own vision now, thinking of no one else's approach, trying to express my own reactions.'[64] She still read books (Denman Ross's *A Theory of Pure Design* helped her at this time), and she attended spiritualist meetings, even though she had returned to the Christian faith of her youth. But she was now expressing her own ideas—sometimes with the aid of her unconscious. Dream visions of the universality of growth and movement in nature occasionally remained with her long enough to enable her to capture them on paper the following day. From 1933 to 1936 she watched her work gradually move towards the point

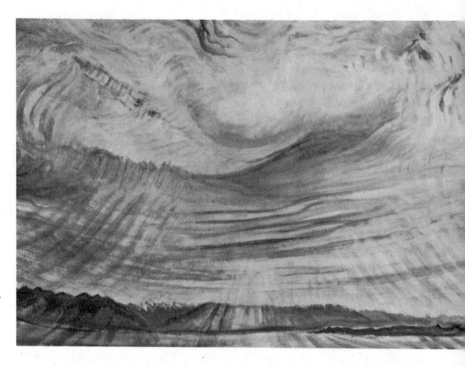

Sky, about 1935.
Oil on paper,
22 1/2 x 35.
Courtesy VAG.
NGC.

where it transcended paint, design, and pattern. On days when it was too wet to sketch, or in barren periods when the forest, shore, and sky did not speak to her, or when she needed a rest 'in preparation for a *mad* onslaught' of painting, she had her writing to turn to. 'These were the very happiest days of my life,' she wrote later.

In this period, when her greatest satisfactions came from the act of creating and from the feeling that she was expressing God and His nature in her work, Emily experienced contentment, and even moments of joy. As a result, she related to her non-painting environment more equably. By 1934 her apartment chores were less resented; they were seen as a necessary prelude to creativity. She found that her need to receive tokens of success—to have her work praised and exhibited and purchased—had diminished. 'Is one painting for the world?' she asked. 'Or is one just trying to get nearer to God and express that of him which is all things and fills all spaces?'[65] Emily did not in fact turn her back on humans or exhibitions. She continued to exhibit with the local art societies in Victoria and Vancouver. The Women's Art Association of Toronto gave her a solo exhibition of oil-on-paper sketches in November 1935. (A laudatory review by Graham McInnis in *Saturday Night* made her blush.)[66] She received many visitors, some of them strangers who wanted to see her work. She enjoyed concerts by the Hart House Quartet and visits from two of its members, Harry Adaskin and Boris Hambourg. She advertised a sketching class in the *Colonist* (26 June 1936) and a few months later wrote in her journal: 'My pupil is scrubbing away, making

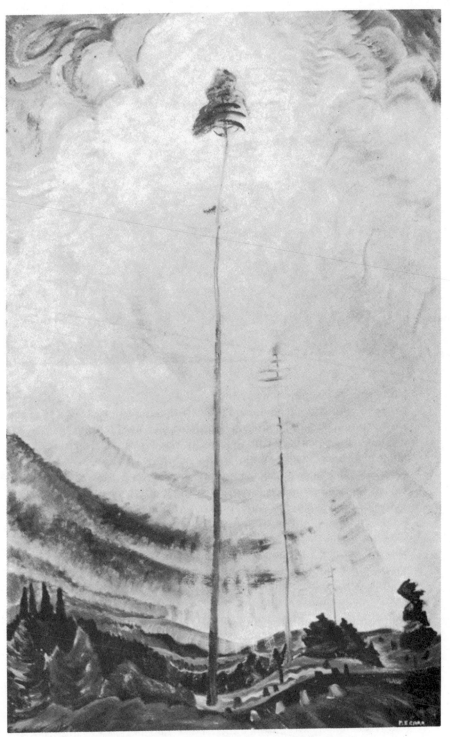

Scorned as Timber, Beloved of the Sky, 1935. Oil on canvas, 44 x 27. VAG.

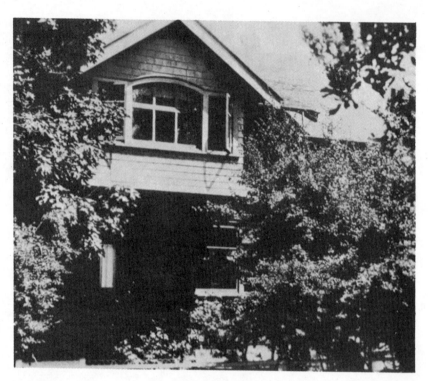

Emily's house on Beckley Street, mid-1930s. Private collection.

a blue sky, two sunny houses, and a bit of plum tree. She is happy. I am trying to get behind her eyes and poke them out into space.'[67] In 1934 she took a summer-school course in short-story writing, which she enjoyed, and gave a garden party for the twenty-odd students. (Her story, 'The Hully-up Paper', was chosen to be read—by Emily—at the closing exercises.) She entertained again that summer when a lower flat became vacant and she invited 'a smash of people' to see her work.[68] These At Homes—there were at least four from 1934 to 1936—meant much preparation, and fatigue afterwards, but Emily did not mind. 'People are kind to me and if my stuff gives them pleasure and helps them to see things a little I am happy.'[69] In this uncharacteristically tolerant and appreciative mood, she could adjust to what she thought of as eastern neglect. She realized that her earlier recognition had been abundant. Occasionally she even admitted that she had been 'wasteful of it, did not follow it up. . . . Praise embarrassed me so that I wanted to hide.' She continued: 'You've got to meet success half-way. I wanted it to come all the way, so we never shook hands.'[70]

This state of equilibrium between Emily's everyday life and her creativity was achieved when the aging process was beginning to make itself felt in stiff knees, a rheumatic hip, partial deafness, and 'troubles below the waistline, due to ructions in the liver.'[71] Her sisters, two and four years older, were also ailing. Alice had been suffering from increasing loss of sight since 1928 and early in 1935 Lizzie discovered that she had cancer of the breast. Illness, and approaching old age, gave the sisters a common ground of fear and need. Emily wrote in January 1936 that it was 'comforting' to know that two sisters could quickly be at the third's bedside 'if things were wrong'.[72]

In 1935 she found a sensible solution to one of her problems: she put Hill House up for sale. She wanted to be rid of the constant whitewashing of walls, the climb to her second-floor apartment, the constant struggles with the furnace and repairs. The Depression had lowered both rents and occupancies. Now twenty-two years old, Hill House was both 'out of date & out of repair'. Emily hated the thought of giving up the studio and garden but lacked funds to modernize the building. However, in the depressed real-estate market the house was impossible to sell; but she was able to arrange a trade whereby it was exchanged for a bungalow on Oscar Street, in the district of South Fairfield on the other side of Beacon Hill Park. She found a cottage for herself that she could rent for twelve dollars, and rented out the Oscar Street house for twenty-five dollars a month, which she herself collected.[73] The thirteen-dollar difference was an important part of her income.

Emily's new home was a brown-and-white shingle cottage on Beckley Street, at the western end of the James Bay district some distance from Hill House and the Carr properties. The move was accomplished with the help of Willie Newcombe, and by the beginning of March 1936 Emily, and what was left of her animals, had settled in. Much to the disapproval of her sisters, it was in a working-class neighbourhood of 'peaceful little streets with peaceful little gardens' of wallflowers in front and vegetables behind.[74] Emily had exchanged the sedateness of Simcoe and Government Streets and the lushness of Beacon Hill Park for a newer and drabber area that contained the almost treeless playing field of Macdonald Park, overgrown remnants of Senator Macdonald's Armadale estate, and an industrial wharf and harbour complex along the water's edge. Yet within her small lot, Emily soon made her mark. There was not much of a front garden, but she gave her dogs the run of the back one, which was shaded by an apple tree and plum and pear trees. Bantams were put in the chicken house, budgies in a home-made aviary on the large back porch, and the caged animals—squirrels and chipmunks—went into the crowded kitchen along with Woo, who was now kept in her own cage because the cottage had no basement. The interior of the house—large enough for Emily but not for her possessions—was made functional by Willie Newcombe, who constructed racks for her paintings and hung others on the walls amid the potted ferns and Indian artefacts. The bare floors were warmed by her woven rugs. The studio, 'the size of an aspirin box', was, as Emily wished, 'a quiet place to study and paint and die in.'[75]

Emily was now living alone for the first time. It was 'lonesome and drifting not to have any tenants to do for.'[76] Though she had seldom befriended her tenants, she was accustomed to hearing 'their bumps & their heavy feet', and had taken a nosey interest in their comings and goings.[77] Now there were no sounds but the squeaking of the chipmunk's wheel, the padded footsteps of her dogs and cats, Woo's rattling of the cage door, and her own shuffling from one room to the next. Alice and Lizzie, who lived five blocks or so up the hill, were not as accessible as before.

Lizzie went into hospital towards the end of July and died quietly on the third of August. Emily wrote: 'People say, "I want to remember Lizzie as last I saw her in life." But I love to remember her as last I saw her in death. Life had always seemed so full of frets and worries for her. . . . It was like being introduced to a new Lizzie, this radiant person in the coffin.'[78] Emily wept a great deal that summer, feeling regretful and guilty that she and Lizzie had never 'hit it off'.[79]

Though she made an autumn trip in her caravan, little work was accomplished. Back home she put off translating her sketches onto canvas for weeks. Signs that her own health was fragile became apparent when an increasingly gnawing pain in her chest developed into a full-fledged heart attack in early January 1937 and she was rushed to St Joseph's Hospital. 'It's a bit of a blow,' Emily wrote when she realized how ill she was.[80] For a month she lay thinking of the things she would be able to do and the ones she would have to forgo. She could only hope that her patience would endure.

Now began her life as an invalid.

Emily's illness robbed her of most of her animals. Realizing that she would no longer have the strength to tend to their needs, she asked Willie Newcombe to dispose of almost all her pets before she returned home, hoping that they had 'got more or less used to my not being there' during her absence. 'If they found out I had not gone but was just hiding,' she wrote, 'I could not face . . . to send them off.'[81] She hated to think of the 'empty boxes and baskets and perches' that would await her, of the life that would be 'so empty & bare & cold' without 'their warmth and love'. Cocky Do, her 'high stepping affectionate' bantam rooster, had died while she was in the hospital, but most of the other dogs, birds, chickens, and cats were found new homes.[82] Woo was taken to the monkey house in Vancouver's Stanley Park. (She lived on for a few years, seemingly content among her own kind.) This left only Pout, a griffon dog, and a few birds and chipmunks.

It was almost two weeks before news of Emily's illness reached the East. Flora Burns, her most loyal Victoria friend, realized late in January the seriousness of Emily's condition and the difficulty she would have in paying medical and hospital expenses. She wired her sister, Mrs Patricia Keir, in Montreal, who in turn informed Eric Brown of the National Gallery that Emily had been 'stricken with angina' and was in the hospital in serious condition. Mrs Keir hoped that Brown and his committee would 'feel that some immediate action should be taken to relieve Miss Carr from her critical financial position.'[83]

Brown responded to the news with effective aid. He wired the director

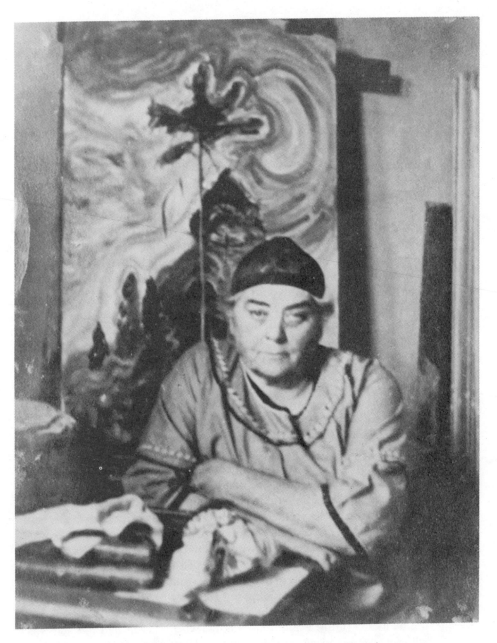

Emily, about 1936. The painting behind her is *Sunshine and Tumult*. PABC.

of the Vancouver Art Gallery, A.S. Grigsby, and asked him to visit Victoria and 'select 6 or 8 most interesting works and ask someone to arrange for shipment to National Gallery our expense.'[84] Grigsby entrusted the job to Eric Newton, the English art critic, who was visiting Vancouver and planning to go to Victoria to address the Canadian Women's Professional and Business Club.

Newton arrived in Victoria by way of Nanaimo, having encountered a fierce late-January snowstorm between Duncan and his destination. He went first to see Emily's paintings at Beckley Street. Willie Newcombe had tabulated, dated, and dusted Emily's paintings in preparation for the viewing, and he and Ruth Humphrey met Newton at the cottage. After ten minutes alone with the paintings Newton emerged from the studio to exclaim: 'This is *another* force of Nature', referring to the earlier snowstorm.[85] After seeing over 150 pictures, he chose eight. Willie shipped these—as well as four pictures Emily had selected before her illness for the London Coronation Exhibition to be held in May 1937—to Ottawa. Meanwhile, Emily lay in her hospital bed wondering if 'the queerness of the totems' would lead Newton 'off the track'.[86] She soon found out that they did not.

When Newton went to St Joseph's to visit her, he was 'very sympathetic and understanding' about her work.[87] 'What he had seen had impressed him very greatly . . . because it was honest and deep.' He urged her to get better, for 'those hands must not lie idle there when you can do things like that with them.'[88]

Not long after Newton's visit, Emily received from Lawren Harris her first cheque from picture sales. The $200 just about covered hospital expenses. Exhausted from the excitement of receiving the money, she was awake all night. More cheques arrived from the National Gallery, the Art Gallery of Toronto, the Vancouver Art Gallery, and many individuals—including Charles S. Band, Vincent Massey, H.S. Southam, and Isabel McLaughlin—rallied to help.[89] By mid-February, shortly before she was to leave the hospital, Emily told a friend that she had plenty of cash.[90] The attacks of pain were now less frequent and she was looking forward to being in the woods in the summer and hoping that 'by then I can kick the moon'.[91] By mid-April she had received close to $3,000 and was sitting up in bed painting again. The relief from financial worry was 'a big factor in aiding my recovery'.[92] So too were the many letters urging her to go on, the promises of support from galleries, and the plans for future exhibitions. Emily, who in 1933 had felt she was without friends and support, suddenly had both in plenty.

12
Writing and Ira
1937-1942

Emily had hoped to lead a 'fast life' again after her heart attack but found that she was a near-invalid.[1] To her stiff knees, rheumatic hip, swollen ankles, temperamental liver and gall bladder, partial deafness, and overweight were now added *angina pectoris* and cardiac asthma. One day a week had to be spent in bed, and other days she did not rise until eleven, well after the best light for painting had left her studio. She had to learn to shove, not lift; kneel, not stoop; take slow steps, not fast ones.

It was clear that Emily needed a housekeeper-maid-nurse, but finding someone who would stay with her was not easy and she embarked on a series of hirings and firings. The very thought of someone 'bossing me and my house' was intolerable to her.[2] Not surprisingly, Emily ended up doing most of the bossing. Girls of high-school age were usually in her service for only a few months. Emily's attitude to 'that class' of girl who wanted to be 'ladies-in-waiting and *sharers*' was no doubt the cause of their short employment.[3] Mistrustful, and angered by her incapabilities, she was impatient and quick-tempered. If a girl showed fear, Emily's annoyance increased. There were constant rows that sometimes ended in tears on both sides. Emily grumbled that whenever this happened, her employee had the advantage: 'they have only to dissolve into tears for me to soften to a pulp, no matter how they have angered me.'[4] Though she complained that the mere presence of a maid put her off her work, there was one compensation: the girl could also be a model when Emily was short of subjects to sketch.

Emily found the very youthfulness of her maids annoying. With their make-up and their boyfriends, they were a constant reminder of the hated 'ugliness of old age'. Being old was not bad if one stayed away from mirrors. Yet 'broken-down feet, bent knees, peering eyes, rheumatic knuckles, withered skin' were hard for her to tolerate.[5] When her maid Blanche was camping with her in Langford in 1939, the young girl was visited by her boy friend. From the bed where she had already spent a good deal of the sketching trip, Emily observed Blanche's Jimmy approaching in his shiny blue car—'complete with *radio*'—while Blanche paraded before the window in sky-blue slacks and a moiré silk bolero of royal blue. All the while 'dowdy old me lies in grey coarse blankets on a rusty spring cot'.[6] 'Blanche-Brainless', as Emily called her, was '*impossible* [,] a new lover [,] one & *two* letters from him *every day* to be answered & so filling her head she could think of *nothing* else'.[7] Two days after they returned to the city, Emily fired her.

Her patience, never great, was not only exasperated by her maids but heavily taxed by demands for exhibition loans. While picture sales lost their momentum after the early months of her illness, invitations to exhibit increased. Emily contributed to more exhibitions in 1937 than during any of the three previous years. Her energy and nerves were drained by crating and shipping pictures—with the help of Willie—then keeping track of their whereabouts and waiting for them to be returned; while the various inefficiencies of galleries maddened her. The Art Gallery of Toronto's Loan Society borrowed pictures in 1937, then failed to answer her letters; the National Gallery had a number of her paintings circulating in several exhibitions and did not return them promptly; the Canadian Group of Painters, to which Emily was elected in 1933, requested her contributions at the last minute; the Montreal Museum of Fine Arts offered her a solo exhibition then withdrew. Emily was further angered when she received little feedback after she had made her contributions.

Her new work—oil-on-paper forest and seashore landscapes—was being given widespread exposure. In March-April 1937 the Art Gallery of Toronto, motivated by the enthusiasm of Charles Band, gave Emily a solo exhibition of some twenty paintings. There was praise for the 'strong rhythmic movements', the 'intensity of her color', and her mastery 'at creating mood and atmosphere'. Referring to a recent Vincent Van Gogh exhibition at the Gallery, one critic felt that the two artists were 'both expressionists, and work, as far as one can judge, under the influence of deep and intense feelings.'[8] The comparison with Van Gogh, which was made frequently, was apt. The short brush strokes and shimmering light that created a unity of movement in such mid-1930s oil-on-paper sketches as *Stumps and Sky* called to mind Van Gogh's Provençal landscapes.[9] Yet the 'essentially Canadian' nature of Emily's work was recognized.[10]

In 1938 Emily sold the van and rented a cottage in a cow pasture near Telegraph Bay, where she 'chewed the cud peacefully with the rest of them'.[11] As it was July, it was too late to revel in the contrast of old and new growth. The smoke from distant forest fires clouded the usually clear atmosphere and the place was 'too close to town to be anything but meek.'[12] Yet 'the joy of being loose in the woods again was *terrific.*'[13] A few yards from the cottage door stood a row of tall pines, in front of which stood a group of 'grand red trunk arbutus very old & gnarled'. The

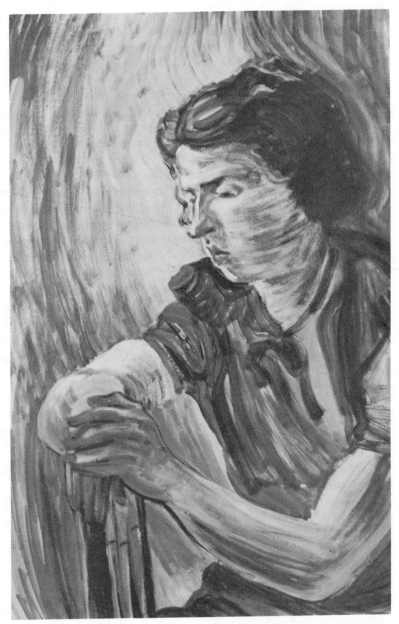

The Cook, about 1938. Oil on paper on wood panel, 34 x 22 1/2. Private collection.

path to the nearby beach was neither long nor hard, though Emily only once made it as far as the shore. On the whole it was a successful three weeks. The weather, while cold, remained dry, the cottage was comfortable, her health kept fair, and her maid Shirley 'fetched and carried and did not pester'.[14]

The National Gallery had organized a large exhibition of over 200 paintings and carvings, called 'A Century of Canadian Art', for the Tate Gallery, London, where it was displayed from the fifteenth of October to December 1938. Tom Thomson and Emily—who was represented by *Indian Church, B.C.*, *Totem Poles, B.C.*, *Sky*, and *Blunden Harbour*— were the two painters most frequently mentioned by the British critics. *Indian Church*, which Lawren Harris had long judged to be her finest painting, was cited in *The Times* as 'one of the most interesting pictures in the exhibition'.[15] It was probably Eric Newton (who had visited Emily the year before), writing in the *Manchester Guardian*, who described Emily's four paintings as 'utterly convincing and completely independent of any tradition'.[16] Newton also reviewed the exhibition for Canadians in the *Canadian Forum*. After remarking on the poster-like qualities of paintings by some of the Group of Seven, and paying tribute to the work of J.W. Morrice and David Milne, he turned his attention to Emily Carr

> who, unlike Milne, is at her best when she is working on a big scale. And her best is magnificent. If the word 'genius' (a word to be jealously guarded by the critic and used only on very special occasions) can be applied to any Canadian artist it can be applied to her. She belongs to no school. Her inspiration is derived from within herself. Living among the moist mountains and giant pines of British Columbia, a country climatically different from the rest of Canada, she has had to invent a new set of conventions, a personal style of her own. Where the Eastern Canadians have been content to stylise the outward pageantry of the landscape, she has symbolised its inner meaning, and in doing so has, as it were, humanised it. Her trees are more than trees: they are green giants, and slightly malevolent giants at that. The totem poles she often paints are haunted by the Indian deities they represent. Her art is not easy to describe, and indeed her power can hardly be felt in the four works shown in London. It happens that I saw over a hundred of her paintings when I was in Victoria. To see them was rather like reading an epic. Four short quotations cannot adequately represent the cumulative effect of the whole.[17]

When Eric Brown returned to Ottawa from the opening, he conveyed in a letter to Emily the 'fine impression your work made on the critics and discerning public'.[18] She was naturally pleased, but took pains not to become complacent from 'this honeyed stuff, this praise'.[19] The following year she was to fret that the praise and tributes might make her 'smug and stagnant'.[20]

The London triumph was overshadowed by another one closer to home. In the spring of 1937, after Emily had returned from hospital and was getting back on her feet, Eric Brown urged Nan Cheney, recently transplanted to Vancouver from Ottawa, to try to arrange a solo

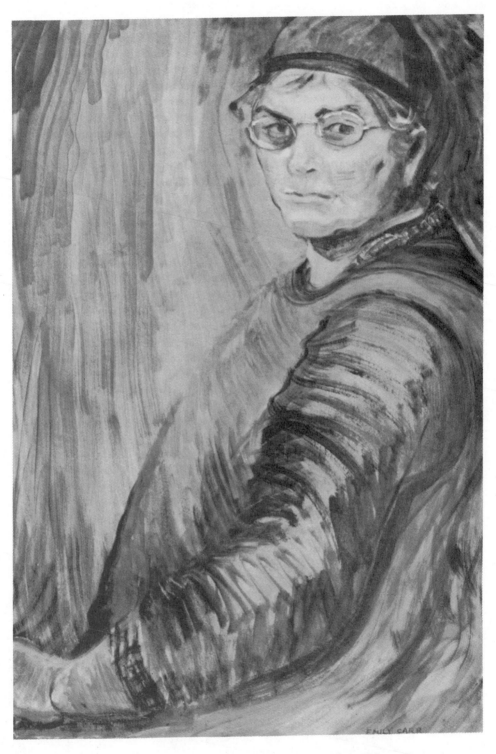

Self-Portrait, about 1938. Oil on paper, 34 x 23. (Photo: Salt-marche visual communication—Toronto) Private collection.

exhibition at the Vancouver Art Gallery. It was a slow and difficult task. Though interest in modern painting in the city had been kept alive by the Vancouver School of Art and the short-lived British Columbia College of Art, there was still a strong anti-modern element that extended to the founding members of the gallery on the board of directors. Nan Cheney, whose reputation was not unknown, was nevertheless able to persuade the gallery to take a chance. Thus in the summer of 1938 Emily received an invitation to exhibit twenty-five or thirty canvases that autumn.

She had no great hopes for the exhibition and was doubtful of public interest. She feared above all that Nan Cheney, who not only organized but hung the show, would be disappointed. The majority of the paintings were oil-on-paper sketches, framed without glass in quarter-round. A few were monumental forest interiors dating from the early 1930s. Most were recent and as rhythmic and lyrical as their titles: *Happy Wood, Swirl, Flung Beyond the Waves,* and *Upward Trend.* When the show opened on the evening of the twelfth of October the response was one of pleasure and surprise. A greater number of pictures were sold than in any previous one-person show at the gallery: eleven out of twenty-nine, a figure that astounded Emily. The reviews were generous and enthusiastic. One critic was surprised to find that she had 'abandoned the Indian totem poles, on which her earlier reputation had been based. . . . Although at first glance the pictures appear to be merely forest scenes, a closer study reveals forms, color and light which drive toward a fundamental conception of B.C. as a growing organism.'[21] She had not only recorded the forest, but 'penetrated into its silent life, partaken of its solitude'.[22] Others, like Vancouver artist Jock Macdonald, were moved to even greater praise. Macdonald wrote to McCurry at the National Gallery that she was 'undoubtedly the first artist in the country and a genius without question'. He saw in her sweeping forest canvases and sketches 'the first conscious expression of the rhythm of life, relating this rhythm to all nature, and definitely causing the observer of her work to be conscious of the fact that he or she is also related, even though there is no physical body represented.'[23]

Never before had Emily's paintings met with so overwhelmingly favourable a reception; never before had her interpretations of the spirit of the forest drawn such a positive response from British Columbians. Mrs Cheney reported to McCurry that the show was 'a tremendous success'; and that considering the gallery's small space and mustard-coloured walls, the paintings 'really looked awfully well'.[24] The success was continued at the University of British Columbia, where Hunter Lewis of the English Department arranged for the show to be hung in the faculty room in the Library. 'For the first time,' wrote a student, 'an artist had with amazing penetration made intellectually valid and aesthetically satisfying use of the British Columbia landscape.'[25] Whether or not this interest in Emily's work was stimulated by her success at the Tate, as Mrs Cheney suggested, the many viewers it attracted gave it their warm appreciation.[26]

Emily had decided that she would not go over to Vancouver for the opening, and she missed it. But four days later, having changed her mind about making the trip, she took the early-morning boat, unable to resist seeing her paintings in a larger area than her eight-by-ten-foot studio and anxious 'to get the effect of them hanging in a strange place'.[27] She spent three days in Vancouver and returned home exhausted, but thrilled by the response to her exhibition. At last the people most familiar with the B.C. landscape were seeing it through her eyes and accepting her vision of it; she 'had been able to make their own Western places speak to them'.[28]

This recognition came at a time when Emily was past sixty-five, in poor health, and with all the dreaded indispositions of old age fully upon her. The loss of strength and independence made it difficult for her to follow up her successes of 1937-8. Her solo exhibition in Vancouver had so impressed the gallery staff and public that they decided to make it an annual event; but preparing for it would be a burden. Not wanting to show 'old chestnuts',[29] Emily wondered if her health would permit another sketching trip. Would she be able to find a compatible maid-companion? Could she find a shack not too far from town and on level ground? Once there, would she be capable of walking the necessary distance to the woods or shore? Afterwards, would she have the strength to mount and frame her sketches? Could she ask Willie Newcombe once again to crate and ship them to Vancouver? Would there be the strength left to paint canvases from the paper sketches? And finally, would she find that she had become weak creatively as well as physically, that she was fizzling out as an artist? This was the question that disturbed her most because she felt she was still so far from her goal; there remained so much to be explored and expressed.

Although Emily had never had so much leisure, her uncertain health often forced her to spend many days in bed. Her normal routine of keeping three canvases on the go, and of devoting not more than two consecutive days to each, had to be broken. Now it took her three weeks instead of three days to prepare a dozen canvases for painting. Material for them, and for her paper sketches, was difficult to procure. The workmen at the lumber yard were 'such fools' and the 'little maid's ignorance of town and shopping colossal'.[30] The presence of a maid meant frequent interruptions when she painted. And if the girl happened to glance at an unfinished canvas, Emily felt that it had 'a *bad effect*', destroyed 'some half formed idea', left her stranded.[31]

Emily managed to slip through 1938 without a single visit to the hospital, but she continued to put on weight and to work too hard. She paid the consequences in March 1939 when a slight stroke hospitalized her for several weeks. Nevertheless by late spring she was back in the woods—this time among the sheep on a fifteen-acre farm in Langford. There was variety in the landscape. In front of the six-room cottage, which she named 'Rat Hall', there were woods, and in the back a logged-off clearing with great rocks covered with yellow-green moss.

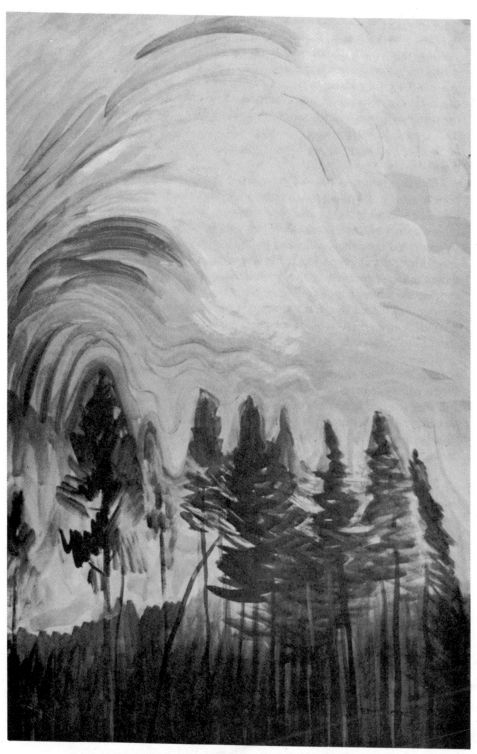

Young Pines and Sky, about 1939. Oil on paper, 34 5/8 x 22 3/8. VAG.

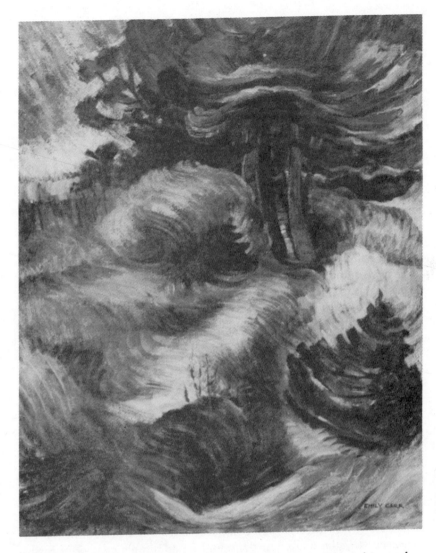

Most of her sketching was done from the cottage's two broad verandas. Though it is doubtful that she met the previous year's output of thirty oil-on-paper sketches, she had never camped in greater comfort. But neither on this excursion nor on two subsequent outings—a two-week camping trip to Craigflower Road in September and a trip to Metchosin the following May—did Emily have the freedom and solitude of her camping days in 'The Elephant'.

She made four sketching trips between 1938 and 1940, as well as occasional outings to Beacon Hill Park or nearby Macdonald Park. Not only was the number of trips reduced—from an average of two a year to one a year—but so was her output. Emily found it difficult to meet exhibition deadlines, especially when new work was required. She retained the spirit to paint and to develop, but the flesh was weak. Fewer sketching trips, less new work, and reduced hours of studio painting inevitably had their impact on her art.

Arthur Lismer visited Victoria in 1940 and noted in a letter to Charles Band that Emily's painting 'retained a high enough standard', that 'she could play any tune' she cared to, but he could find few 'high spots'.[32] During her 1941 solo exhibition in Vancouver Jack Shadbolt, who now had less contact with Emily, publicly praised her as 'our first significantly original painter', though he questioned her 'chemically doubtful colours' (she used house paint rather than imported oils for her oil-on-paper sketches). He noted 'occasional lapses' in her work. He wondered if she was not becoming 'a victim of her own formula'; if she had not 'given way to it'; indeed, if it was not ruling her to the point where she was now 'repeating old themes with less and less vigor'.[33] Shadbolt's critical remarks were not taken lightly by many of those who gathered at the Vancouver Art Gallery to hear his lecture on Emily's painting. Her public standing had by now been consolidated by four annual shows in her old home city of Vancouver and by reports of continual eastern success. Not surprisingly, the lecture nearly broke up when a member of the audience questioned Shadbolt's authority to speak on Miss Carr. According to the Vancouver Sun, 'A lively few minutes followed before quiet was restored,' enabling Shadbolt to conclude his talk.[34]

Shadbolt was not alone in criticizing the work shown in the 1941 exhibition. The Province's reviewer observed in Emily's painting jarring rhythms that were more disquieting than fascinating.[35] It is true that the work she did on the four sketching trips between 1938 and 1940 seldom reached the high standard of her earlier paintings. In *Young Pines and Sky there is less certainty of colour and little direction of movement: the horizon line is too well defined, prohibiting a smooth flow of energy from sky to earth. Emily had added more gasoline to her oils to obtain fluidity and this resulted in diluted colours and a too-loose handling of forms. In many paintings brush strokes sweeping from the foreground towards the centre lead to a dead point from which the eye cannot easily move. However, there are some fine works from this period. In †Forest Landscape (II) the diluted medium and an admirable control of forms and rhythms cohere in a fully realized study. Furthermore, Emily was capable of transferring the spontaneity of the oil-on-paper sketches onto canvas, as in *Tossed by the Wind. The play of warm and cool colours in this painting was 'more than just paint', she wrote a few years later; it possessed 'my love . . . and my heart.'[36]

The decline in the quality was more evident in her new totem canvases. Emily had returned to this theme in 1937 when an abundance of early Indian sketches provided ample material to be reworked onto canvas in her studio. Paintings like *A Skidigate Beaver Pole that were first shown in her 1940 Vancouver solo lack the strength of her 1927-31 Indian work. The poles are not fully moulded to emphasize the tense inner volume of the sculpture. They do not sit solidly on the earth but seem to float in a tumultuous sea of undergrowth. The static figures clash

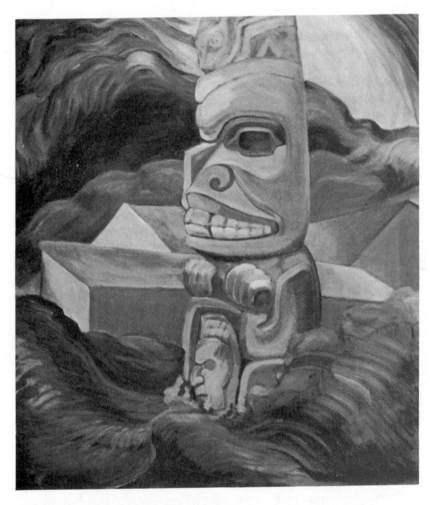

A Skidigate Beaver Pole, about 1940. Oil on canvas, 34 x 23. VAG.

with the buoyant life of the vegetation; unity of movement is absent.

Perhaps sensing the failure of many of her post-1937 paintings, Emily had frequent bouts of depression. She felt 'old and ugly, stupid and ungracious'. There were days when she did not want to be nice but to 'grouch and sulk and rip and snort.'[37]

With her strength failing, the forest less accessible, her animal menagerie reduced to a few birds and beasts, and the privacy of studio painting invaded by her maid, Emily found it difficult to live and work as before. She no longer could envision a future, and the present was merely a poor copy of the past. To escape it, she began to live in the past more and more through her writing.

While Emily still saw painting as her 'recognized job', and felt she should not be wasting her time 'trying to scribble', she could not keep from writing.[38] 'Things tease me inside till I tackle them.'[39] Moreover, writing did not demand as much physical exertion as painting. She could not always walk the short distance from the bedroom to the studio, but she could write 'among the pillows'.[40] Nor did writing require the same mental energy as painting. It was easy to drift back fifty years to the village of Ucluelet, whereas beginning a canvas when she had not adequately worked out its theme, or was short of material from which to paint, was almost traumatic. In writing there was no fear of producing sub-standard work, for as she had not published, she had no standard to maintain. Working on a regular basis had always been important to her. With painting, regularity was now impossible; but with her writing she could be sure of working one or two hours a day either in bed or, weather permitting, in the backyard hammock.

In her seventh decade writing became a pleasant fondling of the past for Emily. Remembering the things that had meant most to her in a position of ease was relaxing and comforting. She told an acquaintance that she wrote *Klee Wyck* 'for the pure joy of reliving and travelling among the places & people I love.'[41] The stories about her birds were written to console her for having had to give them up. The stories about her English bobtails, her monkey, the wild flowers of her childhood, were written for the same reasons. But her writing was not only a means of recreating happy memories; it gave her another satisfaction. 'I'll be even with them yet,' she said of her tenants, by 'using them for stories.' After 1936 she no longer had the burden of running the apartment house, but the memory of 'those filthy tenants', whom she blamed for 'sapping the joy out of everything', was still achingly vivid.[42] The years of being bothered by broken leases, unpaid bills, unmarried couples and drunks, the tormenting difficulty of balancing her landlady responsibilities and her artistic calling, were still fresh in her mind. Her apartment-house stories, containing some venomous portraits of her tenants, were written in a spirit of revenge. They eventually appeared in *The House of All Sorts*.

After 1937 Emily grouped her stories thematically. Like everything she undertook—whether potting, painting, or rug-making—her writing was produced in great quantity. By the early summer of 1937, only months after her attack, she completed her Indian stories, which had been written over a period of eleven years.[43] At the end of the year her apartment-house reminiscences had gone through a first draft. During the early months of 1938 the stories of life in an English sanatorium, originally titled *Chins Up* and later published as *Pause: A Sketch Book*, were drafted, and by the end of that year a group of childhood stories— the first written in 1933—and 'Woo's Life' were finished. In 1939 she completed an autobiographical manuscript of 114 pages that Harris had urged her to write in 1933 (it remains unpublished), wrote more childhood sketches, and revised some earlier ones.[44] The following year she revised 'Woo's Life' and produced still more childhood sketches. In 1941 'Bobtails', 'Birds', and 'Wild Flowers' were written. The last three years of Emily's life were devoted to revising early manuscripts, many written before 1937; to writing an entirely new autobiography, to which she gave the title 'Growing Pains', and to completing fifty short sketches, most of them about her childhood, that she called 'Hundreds and Thousands' (this too remains unpublished).[45] She neglected to write as frequently in the journals she had begun in 1927, having found in her creative writing another companion for her loneliness and an outlet for an active mind that was no longer matched by an active body.

Most of Emily's stories were written between the ages of sixty-three and seventy-one. They have in common many characteristics—crotchetiness, alienation, exaggeration, and sentimentality—that had always been part of her personality but had become more pronounced in her old age. Though Emily attempted to be as true to places and people as she could, and did not choose to write about anything that was not drawn from her own experience, her stories are not accurate accounts of her past. They are a mere reflection, altered and coloured by literary instinct. Chronology is abandoned—especially in her autobiography; incidents are sometimes oversentimentalized into inaccuracy; her age is capriciously recorded; names are misremembered or altered from Drake to Crane or Mayo to Martyn.[46] Where she found gaps in her memory, fictitious characters and incidents were invented to bridge the holes. Most of her stories are told according to a formula in which conflict and contrast, and the struggle between good and evil, are prominent. Emily is usually at the centre of each story as a benefactor—to the Indians, animals, and peasants—or as the victim of apartment tenants, sophisticated English girls, or an overbearing father or sister. If she does not figure in the story, the contrast between Indians and whites, or animals and people, is a frequent theme. Harmony reveals itself only in nature, Indians, and animals—and in herself, as she was in tune with these things.

Emily's nature writing appears in her sketches not as self-conscious set-pieces but as brief, vivid passages that emerge naturally from the narrative. At their best they are objective, deeply felt, and compellingly visualized; but a sentimental anthropomorphism sometimes creeps in, as when she writes of the trees' chatter; white clouds dancing over the blue dome of the sky; ferns, leaves, and twigs doing 'a mad joy-dance'; trees clothed in petticoats or described as old matrons or young children. The splinters left on a stump after a tree had been felled were 'screamers', symbolizing for Emily 'the cry of the tree's heart, wrenching and tearing apart just before she gives that sway and the dreadful groan of falling'; the loggers who cut the trees down were the forest's 'executioners'.[46] Given this tendency, one would expect the animals in her stories to be over-endowed with human characteristics; but their behaviour, while always entertaining, is usually described with restraint.

The humans in Emily's stories are usually stereotypes—even when they are Indians, whom she sought to bring to life as distinct personalities. (Sophie Frank is an exception.) Realizing this, Emily admitted that she 'ought to stick to nature' in writing because she did not 'know humans as deeply', always setting 'their faults above their virtues'.[47] Her regard for white people in general was very low—a reflection of the misanthrope in Emily. Those she considered socially beneath her often revolted her. Her maids, and most foreigners, met with her scorn. Humanity was sinful and she forced it to bear a measure of the guilt she always carried with her. Nature was stable; Indians were innocent victims; and so both were idealized.

Emily's stories are lifted above sentimental nostalgia by literary flair: a sure instinct for telling anecdotes and details; a narrative style that is spare and to the point, and at the same time fresh and homespun; visually accurate and vivid descriptions of places and things; and memorable turns of phrase ('from stir to start'), metaphors ('Millie's stare was the biggest thing in the house'), and similes (nuns 'as dignified as pine trees').[48] One feels her intense love for the West Coast in her evocative descriptions of the scent of the salt air, the sting of campfire smoke in the eyes, the push of growth in the tangled forest, or the forest's overwhelming silence. Emily makes the reader share not only the things she loved but her dislikes—the thoughtlessness of tenants, the hypocrisy of the English, the cruelty of her sisters—all of which she was able to treat comically. Finally, she reveals herself in her stories: her morality, her sentimentality, her prejudices, her love of nature, even her meanness and the childlike side of her character, are all present.

Before 1937 Emily had attempted, with the help of her listening ladies, to publish individual stories. After 1937 she made thematic collections of them—usually no more than a hundred pages in length—and submitted them to book (rather than to magazine) publishers. She insisted that she never expected to publish anything, yet whenever a group of stories was sent off, her expectations for publication rose. The first collection, twenty Indian stories—nineteen of which later appeared in *Klee Wyck*—was submitted to Macmillan of Canada in 1937. A few months later the president, Hugh Eayrs, wrote Emily that he enjoyed the Indian stories but felt that the public would not.[49] He suggested that she send them to Lorne Pierce, editor of the Ryerson Press, which Emily did early in February 1938. Also included in the bundle were six childhood stories. 'I do not know how to write well or express myself in words,' she explained apologetically in a letter to Pierce, 'but what I have earnestly tried to do is to show honestly & sincerely Indians of British Columbia coast as I have experienced them.'[50] Margaret Clay sent a long supportive letter, which said that Emily's submission had received the praise of Ruth Humphrey and Professor Garnet Sedgewick, head of the English Department at UBC.[51] While the manuscript was with Macmillan, Humphrey had suggested that Emily show some other material to Sedgewick. Although not a writer himself, Sedgewick had a reputation as an outstanding teacher and respected scholar. He promised to give Emily a good criticism, and even agreed to edit the stories should Macmillan decide to publish. Emily waited anxiously for seven months before hearing from Sedgewick that while he felt the stories deserved a big and appreciative audience, he feared they would not find one. Though they delighted him, he was very pressed for time and found it

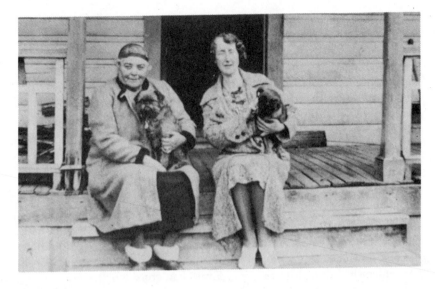

Emily and Flora
Hamilton Burns
at Metchosin,
1939. (Photo:
Humphrey
Toms) PABC.

difficult to provide a critique. Emily was heartened that 'he thinks they are not twaddle', but disappointed that he made only minor changes of punctuation in the manuscript.[52]

The Ryerson Press mislaid the manuscript while moving its offices. Pierce and his executive secretary were terribly apologetic but could find no trace of the twenty Indian and six childhood stories Emily had sent them. Eleven months after their receipt, they were found—at Queen's University, where they had mistakenly been sent and deposited with the Pierce Papers. Three weeks later Emily received a rejection letter. The unidentified house reader said he doubted 'if we could make it into a book with a very wide appeal.' The sketches were uneven in length and quality and many had nothing to do with Indians. He thought the author was 'very observent but one feels she describes objects better than she does persons.' She wrote well, in a rather light style, and some of the descriptions were 'fairly vivid', but the manuscript as a whole left one 'rather depressed—possibly a tribute to the author's skill but rather, I think, to the vision called up of a dying race living in squalor.'[53]

Emily was fed up with publishers, editors, and helpers. 'I hate 'em all,' she wrote, and swore that 'this is the last time I shall hand my manuscript over to others.'[54] But Ruth Humphrey did not give up. When she was in Vancouver in the spring of 1939 she showed some stories to Ira Dilworth, one-time principal of Victoria High School, formerly a member of the English Department at UBC, and now regional director of the CBC in Vancouver. He was struck by their literary quality and appeal. Ruth told Emily to send him some more, and she sent him seven Indian and six childhood stories. They so impressed him that he arranged for Sedgewick to read a selection over the CBC in February 1940, and he himself read some in July. Both events encouraged Emily greatly.

The month before the stories were aired, Emily learned that her landlady wished to sell the Beckley Street cottage. She was dumb-founded. Though many of her friends had criticized her for living in a working-class district, she had been happy there. Over the past four years she had become involved in the lives of those around her. Neighbours had occasionally been treated to a reading of her stories, or invited to assist in producing diapers and nighties for twins born to destitute parents across the street. Though given first opportunity to purchase the house at a very low price, Emily's $500 offer was not enough. But she thought of a more attractive solution to her housing problem: she would live with Alice.

Now her only surviving sister, Alice was seventy and had long ceased teaching. In the summer of 1939 she had moved her belongings to one side of the St Andrew's Street schoolhouse in order to rent the other half, but no renters came forward. The inefficient wood stove, the building's old and dowdy appearance, both inside and out, did not make up for its convenient location close to town. Emily had considered a move to the schoolhouse three years earlier; now it seemed inevitable. 'It will be nice for old age to be so close to each other,' she wrote in her journal, and anyway 'Alice . . . half wants me.'[55] But Alice had not been consulted. Emily simply announced that she was moving in. Alice was speechless, but she weakened and allowed Emily to alter the vacant side of the building to suit her needs. A new bathroom and bedroom were built onto the existing one-floor no-basement structure, the kitchen was renovated, gas installed, storage racks built for her paintings, an aviary constructed on the porch for her canaries, a large portion of the garden fenced off for her dogs, and the house painted both inside and out—all on Emily's half. Alice, now almost blind, was astonished by the swiftness and extent of the alterations and complained that the place was no longer hers. Emily rebuked her, dismissing her remark as mere sentimentality. The alterations continued, with Emily insisting that she could not live without order. She offered to paint Alice's half of the house, but Alice refused, and renovations were confined to one side. Emily, needing space for painting, enlarged her territory. Alice lost the use of her former schoolroom; it was converted, despite its south light, into a studio. Alice's spare room was also usurped for the maid's room. Alice—with her dog Chum, her chipmunk and canaries—moved into the remaining third of her house.

Alterations amounting to between $500 and $600 were completed in late February 1940, and the move was made with the help of Willie Newcombe. 'A new page of life is about to turn,' Emily wrote, 'and my finger is licked to flip the corner.'[56] Moving into Alice's house on the site of the old cow yard, Emily returned to end her life a few yards from where she had begun it.

It will be 'cosy and nice for both of us to be in easy reach of each other,' Emily wrote to Nan Cheney, but there were problems from the start.[57] Not having lived together since they had shared a flat in Paris,

Emily and Alice had forgotten many of their differences. Alice was a vegetarian and 'a monotonous feeder'; Emily ate 'like a squirrel', wanting a 'constant change and all kinds of little odds & ends of variety'.[58] Alice could not tolerate the maximum volume at which Emily, deaf in one ear, played her radio. Emily resented Alice's visits to the studio-classroom. 'She comes in and expects me to *drop everything* and just chatter and *chatter to amuse her*.'[59] On the other hand, Alice felt that Emily had little consideration for her near-blindness. Emily often became voiceless from attempting to outyell the usually quiet Alice, who had been shouting at deaf Emily. Friends observed the situation from both sides. 'Alice was tyrannical,' recalled Carol Pearson. 'She would lock the adjoining door and use a lot of salt on the food to upset Mom.'[60] Alice's friends, the Hennells, saw things differently. 'Emily was definitely the "boss lady of the litter",' either 'as sweet as could be or an abhorrent bitch.'[61]

Yet the two sisters loved and cared for each other in their dotage. In the evening Emily read to Alice, who had not yet mastered Braille. She refused invitations to visit friends in Vancouver because there was Alice to consider. And when Carol Pearson wrote to Emily during the last years of her life inviting her to live with her permanently, she refused to leave Alice. 'Though now and again she gets peeved with me,' Emily replied, 'really she does love me and I believe she'd give her life for me.'[62] As the youngest, Emily had hoped to take care of her older sister. The reverse situation caused her much concern. Considering her near-blindness, Alice managed remarkably, tending to Emily during the night, preparing her meals on the maid's day off, typing letters to Emily's friends when she was unable to herself and—though she did not care for camping—visiting Emily on her last sketching trips.

Emily remained in poor health despite Alice's care and the ease of smaller quarters. During the upheaval of the move she had to take many heart pills, and she had a minor heart-attack just after it. She recovered sufficiently to make a short sketching trip to the Metchosin gravel pits in May 1940. A few days after returning, however, she suffered a major stroke. She was rushed by ambulance to St Joseph's Hospital.

Emily was 'the worst she had ever been', Alice reported to a friend.[63] The right side of her face and her left leg were paralysed, her vision was blurred, and she had lost the use of her voice. She remained in hospital a month, then returned home to the care of Alice and a maid. When she was visited in July by Humphrey Toms—a young schoolteacher who had befriended Emily in 1933 after seeing her work in an Island Arts and Crafts exhibition—he found her still in a critical state. She lay in the darkened bedroom motionless, with her knees drawn up and her eyes closed. There was silence except for the heavy summer rain falling on the big maple beyond the draped window. Toms moved close to where Emily lay and asked her how she was. Speaking with difficulty and stammering over some words, she replied that she was 'a little better', but 'think I should have been allowed to go when I was in hospital.' 'I *want* to go,' she told him, 'I don't feel I'm good for much.' She paid no attention to the scuffling of the griffons in their boxes at the foot of the bed, nor to the squawks of her parrot Josephine. Eyes closed, and her chin sunk in a roll of her neck fold, she lamented that she was incapable of working, of taking care of herself. Moreover, she 'didn't think it was worth patching old people up.' Toms left Emily's bedside depressed. Recalling the meeting later to Nan Cheney, he wrote, 'I fear that we may hear that she has gone one night in her sleep.'[64]

Ten days after his first visit, he found Emily a 'changed woman'.[65] A week later, on the first day of August, Emily was 'out on her back verandah, her hair in pig tails, shouting at Ruby [the maid] who was clearing the yard for a load of wood.'[66] Her left leg was still partly paralysed, but with the help of Ruby she constructed a 'scoot box' by attaching four coasters to a butter box; sitting on this, she was able to push herself with her good leg and get around inside her house. Willie built a ramp over the steps for the box should an outing by car be offered. Emily converted another box into a typewriter desk so that she could type in bed, another into shelves, and yet another into a walker, so that she could move around her bedroom. Mobile, and with most of the feeling back in the right side of her face, she was once again 'full of beans'.[67]

Jock Macdonald, who also visited Emily that summer, reported that she was 'taking her illness philosophically'. He was certain that she had 'at least some years of activity because of the power of her will and her amazing vitality.'[68] Her recovery was not easy. There were long bouts of crying, which she allowed herself to enjoy 'to the full'.[69] She realized that she could go at any time, or creak on for several years. A row with her maid, or an exhaustive outing, could bring on a last fatal attack. There was no longer any ambiguity between sickness and old age; she knew that the first could possibly be cured and that the second could not. But she had no intention of giving up her work.

On his first visit Toms had noticed a manuscript lying on Emily's bed and concluded that 'she must be doing a little work from time to time, recording and correcting her stories.'[70] During the first two months following the stroke Emily had difficulty focusing her eyes and thinking clearly, but she was able to resume work on her stories by August. Dilworth had promised to take a selection of Indian and childhood stories to a publisher in Toronto, and before his departure Flora Burns worked late into the night typing clean copy from handwritten or crudely typed pages and editing the stories for spelling, punctuation, and paragraphing. The deadline was met, and Dilworth left the stories with the Oxford University Press in June. The next month Emily heard from an editor, King Gordon, who wrote that, while he liked them, he considered them more suitable for a magazine.[71] Dilworth persisted, bringing the stories to the attention of the manager, W.H. Clarke, who felt initially that they would never sell. Dilworth pressed him to consider publishing 'a mixed bag' of Indian and childhood stories, and Clarke finally consented.[72] Emily was elated when she heard of this, though she

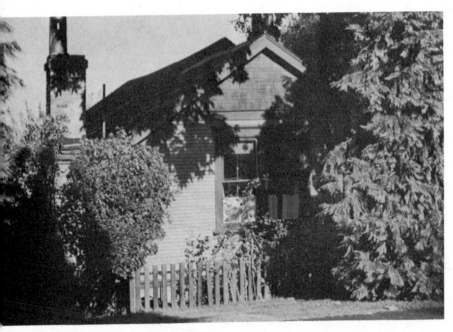

(ABOVE) Alice's schoolhouse on St Andrew's Street, 1945. Courtesy Grant Crabtree.

(BELOW) Inside Emily's studio in Alice's schoolhouse. Photograph by Ken McAllister, taken a few weeks after Emily's death. The painting on the easel is *Gitwangak*.

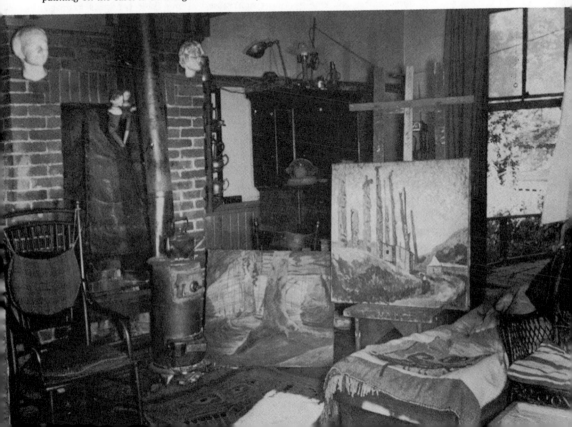

would have preferred to have the stories published thematically.

With the improvement of both her health and her publishing prospects, she asked Ruth Humphrey and Flora Burns to listen to, and correct, the childhood stories she was working on. Dilworth had been sent some new stories, but he was slow to comment on them. Emily waited for him to return her work throughout the autumn and into the winter of 1940. By January 1941 her patience was exhausted. She wrote that, following his 'protestation of interest last summer', it was incomprehensible that he could have let her down 'so completely'.[73] He had not only failed to comment on the group of stories she had given him or on the progress of negotiations with Oxford, but he had not visited her 1940 exhibition at the Vancouver Art Gallery, as promised, or called on her when he had been in Victoria. Dilworth soon discovered Emily's expectations as a correspondent and her vocal response to disappointment. To make amends, he travelled to Victoria early in 1941, agreed with Emily that the Indian stories should appear in a separate volume, and began the first of several working sessions on them with her.

Emily usually read the stories to Dilworth aloud; then he made corrections in spelling, punctuation, and paragraphing. She agreed with most of his editorial changes, expressed faith and confidence in his criticism, and was inspired by his discussion. As she told him at the end of one session:

> I do enjoy going over material with you. So few people are understanding and one gets so embarrassed seeing their thoughts exposed and dissected but with you I don't. I forget even to blush at my spelling and punctuation.[74]

Things moved quickly after this. In late March Dilworth brought Mr and Mrs Clarke over to Victoria to meet Emily. In May a contract to publish a group of Indian stories was signed. By June the stories were at the Press. In September the title, illustrations, and jacket subject had been selected. In October, Dilworth submitted a preface. *Klee Wyck* (the final title, chosen over *Stories in Cedar*) was in print at the end of October—'a real *object* at least even though only in her underwear'.[75] (Emily's advance copy lacked a dust jacket.)

Greatly helped by enthusiastic reviews, the first printing of *Klee Wyck* (2,500 copies) almost sold out by Christmas. Canadians were now sharing Emily's experiences on her first trip to Ucluelet, where she was given her Indian name Klee Wyck, and travelling to the Cariboo, then north with her up the Skeena River and the mosquito-infested Nass, and through the lush growth of the Queen Charlotte Islands. They met the pipe-smoking Mrs Green at Skidegate; the mangy dogs who followed Emily around the swampy burned-over village of Greenville; Clara and William Russ, who told her ghost stories on the beach at Tanoo; and Sophie Frank. Critics were unanimous in their praise of Emily's Indian portraits and admired the way she had succeeded 'in giving one an entirely new feeling for the British Columbia coast, for forests, the mountain backgrounds, the rough waters, and the luxuriant undergrowth spreading over the deserted villages.'[76] But above all they praised her literary style, which to Robertson Davies showed

> . . . a clear, powerful, original and rigorous mind. Her writing is completely free of fripperies and self-conscious fine writing; every unnecessary word has been purged from her descriptions; every thought is as clear as the note of a bell. But she is not a stark writer; on the contrary she employs, perhaps unconsciously, nuances which have never appeared in Canadian prose before. Her pity is great, but severe; her irony is like the slash of a razor. She writes like a woman who has led a lonely life, free from the pretences and flatulent enthusiasms which bedevil literary folk. There is nothing to be said in dispraise of her work; it is the product of a fine mind, complete and strong in itself.[77]

Klee Wyck's publication was celebrated by the Women's Canadian Club of Victoria on Emily's seventieth birthday, the thirteenth of December. Emily expected a gathering of a few Club members when she arrived at the Oak Bay home of Mrs H.E. Young. Instead she was greeted not only by most of the members, but also by representatives of over twenty Victoria organizations, including the Authors' Association, the Victoria Literary Society, the Society for the Prevention of Cruelty to Animals, the Island Arts and Crafts Society, and the Provincial Museum. The Reverend T.A. Laundy opened the celebration with a short prayer. The principal of Victoria High School, Harry Smith, was master of ceremonies and he read many official letters of congratulation, beginning with two from the Lieutenant-Governor and the Premier. Emily, sitting rather bewildered on a pink sofa, listened to letters praising her 'great and distinctive contribution . . . to the art and literature of the province'.[78] She heard the Indian Commissioner of British Columbia and the Indian Agent thank her on behalf of the native people. She received a sheaf of pink carnations, a box of gold and white chrysanthemums, a bouquet of roses, and a corsage of rosebuds. Ira Dilworth read 'Canoe' and 'Juice' from *Klee Wyck*, then tea was served. With Alice on her right, Emily cut the first slice in the enormous cake and everyone sang 'Happy Birthday'.

Feeling that she must respond to the occasion, Emily rose, with the help of Ira Dilworth, and spoke:

> Thank you everybody for giving me such a splendid, happy birthday party and for being so kind to *Klee Wyck*. I would rather have the goodwill and kind wishes of my home town, the people I have lived among all my life, than the praise of the whole world; but I did not write *Klee Wyck*, as the reviewers said, long ago when I went to the West Coast Villages painting. I was too busy then painting from dawn till dark. I wrote *Klee Wyck* one year ago in hospital. They said I would not be able to go about painting here and there any more, lugging and tramping. I was sore about it, so, as I lay there, I relived the villages of *Klee Wyck*. It was easy for my mind to go back to the lovely places. After fifty years they were as fresh in

my mind as they were then because while I painted I had lived them deep. I could sail out of hospital and forget about everything. It was *Klee Wyck* gave my sick heart courage enough to get better and go home to the easy life the doctor had told me I had to expect now.[79]

She sat down to hearty applause, then everyone sang 'Auld Lang Syne', 'For She's a Jolly Good Fellow', and 'The King'.

Emily 'survived and *enjoyed*' the occasion.[80] Her proudest moment was when Ira Dilworth walked across the room to where she sat and gave her a 'kiss for Canada'.[81]

Ira Dilworth was born in 1894 at High Bluff, Manitoba, but grew up in Victoria and knew the Dallas Road cliffs and Beacon Hill Park as well as Emily did. After being educated in the east, he returned to Victoria to teach at the high school, where he is remembered by Max Maynard and Roy Daniells for having awakened their love of the Romantic poets; he was principal from 1926 to 1934, when he moved to Vancouver. In the 1920s he lived on Simcoe Street and often caught sight of Emily, whom he saw as 'an eccentric woman who kept an Apartment House . . . [and] raised English Sheepdogs in kennels in her large garden'.[82] Described as 'intense and creative', and as having a 'somewhat prissy manner', he was a sensitive man with conservative tastes but varied cultural interests.[83]

Dilworth had recognized the quality of Emily's stories as soon as he read them; indeed, he was 'fascinated', even 'enchanted', by them.[84] They took him out of his 'stupid humdrum existence' and let him see 'something exquisite and beautiful.'[85] He denied giving Emily any direct help as an editor, and even felt moved in 1958 to defend his involvement in her work. 'During Emily's lifetime no word in anything she had written was changed without her full consideration.' The corrections he had made in her manuscripts were 'changes simply any editor would make'; he had 'nothing to do with this magnificence of expression that she possessed apparently from the time she was a child.'[86] The genius of the writing was Emily's; the modification of a phrase and the inspiration to continue were frequently Dilworth's. Emily agreed that Ira 'never added or omitted anything without consulting me', and if he made suggestions, 'he made me re-word the thought myself.'[87] Though very busy as regional director for the CBC in Vancouver, and as conductor of the Vancouver Bach Choir, he found time to correct Emily's Indian stories, pay frequent visits to Victoria, negotiate with her publisher, and maintain his half of a demanding correspondence. The friendship that developed between them, partly through letters, flowered under their creative collaboration as writer and editor and transcended Dilworth's initial willingness to assist an undiscovered writer. Basically a lonely man, he guarded his feelings and thoughts from all except a few people: his mother; his adopted daughter Phylis (who was also his niece); and, from 1941 to 1945, Emily.

For Emily, Dilworth fulfilled the role of that long-sought-for 'friend person'. They were '*friends* in the *deepest* sense giving, taking and

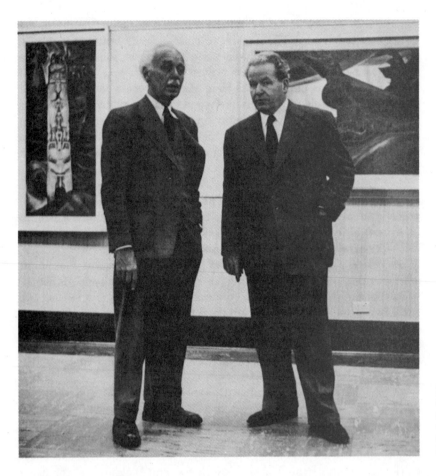

Lawren Harris and Ira Dilworth at the Vancouver Art Gallery, about 1950. CBC.

trusting'.[88] She could express herself freely to him about living with Alice, coping with her maid, and the problems associated with her illness; she could write to him of nature and poetry as she had done earlier only in her journals. Her letters were not merely the outpourings of a lonely old woman. The need for such a friendship was apparent in the early thirties, when she became attracted to Lawren Harris, but he was not nearly so suitable a candidate. Dilworth was single. He had a childhood background not unlike her own and did not live far away. Like Emily, he was solitary and guarded his deepest thoughts from others. He was conventionally religious and believed that religion was closely linked to literature and painting. He harboured hostilities towards Victoria's smugness and eastern Canada's dominance. And he was intensely proud of being a western Canadian.

Theirs was an honest, open friendship that touched every aspect of their lives. It is strange to think of querulous Emily, who claimed that she never fell 'onto men's bosoms with confidences', unfolding so completely with this younger man, whom she remembered as 'a lanky youth' years earlier, mowing the lawn across the street from Hill House.[89] Dilworth was the only person about whom she seldom complained, either in her journals or her letters. There were, of course, small irritations: when a dictated letter from him simply ended 'with regards'; when he failed to answer all her two-to-four letters a week; when he was unable to visit Victoria as often as Emily would have liked. But these were only minor problems. Being able to write to him when she wanted, having his letters and visits to look forward to, enjoying his interest in her manuscripts, delighting in his gifts of flowers, in his poetry program, 'Sanctuary', on the CBC, provided emotional satisfactions and a measure of security in a life threatened by uncertainty.

Had Dilworth lived in Victoria, the relationship might not have blossomed or been sustained; Emily's demands might have been impossible to meet at close range. But in a mainly epistolary friendship, Emily was able to allow a certain flexibility. There were N.N.T.A. letters (not necessary to answer), R.A.L.s (read at leisure), 'Red Hot Specials', 'Week enders', and 'Special Deliveries'. There were letters of complaint; letters written to discuss a painting, an exhibition, or a poem; and letters written out of the sheer need to communicate. 'I just *have* to write,' she told him, 'if the letters bother burn them they've eased me, don't let them annoy you.'[90] She addressed him variously as 'Ira', 'Eye', and when writing to him as her child-self, Small—the name given by Dilworth to the innocent, mischievous, happy *alter ego* of the elderly invalid—as 'My Beloved Guardian'.

In his letters to Emily, Dilworth expressed his deep religious convictions, his fears about the war, his problems as a regional director dominated by eastern-Canadian headquarters, his worries about his ailing mother, and his loneliness and bachelorhood. At a distance it was easy for him to be loving and protective, warning Emily not to overwork, consoling her after a bout of illness, and scolding her for using such words as 'beastly'. He could also share the excitement of her exhibitions and paintings, her book sales, the experience of giving a speech or a public reading of her stories.

Dilworth wrote his letters from his Vancouver home or office, on a plane to or from Toronto, or on a boat travelling up the coast of Vancouver Island. Emily usually wrote hers in pencil, lying on her back. She kept all his letters in a bag near her bed, to read when 'lonely down or crushed or flat'.[91]

The relationship was not without a romantic element. They exchanged rings and frequently expressed their love. 'You will never know', Dilworth wrote Emily in 1942, 'how much your confidence and love have meant to me.' It has been a 'joy to get to know you and to help you say things to other people.'[92] He would give her a written 'bear hug' or sign his letters with 'bundles of love' or 'love in oooooodles'. She had 'crept a little way' under his skin 'as no one else had'.[93] As for Emily, she did not 'give love to many', and when she did love it was 'hard and good & plenty'.[94] Nor was she embarrassed to express it. 'My love for you has been *very strong*, very deep'; she was surprised it was '*so full*'.[95] She attempted to categorize their love as something above the physical and romantic. It was not 'as man loves woman', not *flesh* love, something beyond'.[96] 'It is so rarely that we can share that lovely thing lying just beyond the circumference, nameless, but life itself, formless colorless, substanceless'—which, she added, 'our tongues are too clummsy to express.'[97] Their love was based on a mutual understanding of nature and things, on 'a tuning into things together'.[98] Dilworth was in every sense the companion with whom she could give and take love without fear of being ridiculed. He restored her faith in men. She even said she now preferred men for her closest friends. Women 'get so split up following the careers of their children & chasing around following their husbands', while men had time to absorb books and thoughts and talk about deep things.[99]

Emily's love for Dilworth was a jealous one. She was envious of his close relationship with Phylis, and referred to her coldly. Conversely, she was required to justify her love for Dilworth to those, like Carol Pearson, who felt rather possessive of her; she explained to Carol that she was 'a *sort* of Mother to him'.[100] She did express maternal concern for Dilworth, worrying because he was working too hard and being misused by eastern Canada, and because he seemed to withdraw from his friends after the death of his mother in 1943. She fretted over his bachelorhood—though she referred dismissively to a hypothetical wife as an 'et cetera'.

They probably revealed their deepest feelings for one another in sharing their greatest sorrows. Dilworth told Emily about his beloved sister Pearl, who had died, and Emily told Dilworth about the 'brutal telling', which she had kept to herself for over fifty years. (She also wrote to him about it, as Small.) This confession of her most traumatic experience was the supreme manifestation of her love and trust. Dilworth resisted criticizing Richard Carr. His cool, sympathetic response to the confidence seemed 'to soothe away the old scar'.[101]

Emily would scold Dilworth for not writing; then, ashamed of her impatience, apologize through Small. Dilworth in turn reproached Emily by writing affectionately to Small of her wrongdoings. Thus a balance was kept; feelings both good and bad were aired through the mythical child. In a letter to him of the ninth of August 1943, which Dilworth found in a trunk after her death, Emily wrote:

> Do not be too sad when you and Small unpack the box, let her giggle a bit . . . she has been a joy to us, hasn't she? . . . and if there should be an et cetera who questions 'Who is Small?' say 'Oh, she's just a phantom child, made up of memories and love'. Small's adult outgrew her (as every adult *must* or remain an imbecile) but the child Small learnt the trick of coming back to cheer what used to be her. . . .[102]

She could have added that through addressing herself to her childhood in this way, she had come to a reconciliation with her father. The stories she wrote about Small were based on incidents that occurred before the brutal telling, and she wrote of Richard Carr as she had thought of him then: tall, straight, right, and above all honourable.[103]

Klee Wyck received the Governor General's Award for non-fiction in 1942. W.H. Clarke, writing to McCurry of the National Gallery to suggest a solo exhibition for Emily, stated that Klee Wyck was 'the greatest find in Canadian literature since Maria Chapdelaine'.[104] When it was reissued in a school edition by Clarke Irwin, Emily enjoyed the irony. She told Carol Pearson: 'You know Aunt Betty [Lizzie] always thought me such a poor example for the children at Alice's.'[105] Clarke hoped to publish an Emily Carr book every year and Dilworth was already writing to Emily about a visit to Vancouver to complete work they had begun on the Small stories.

Emily had set the end of her working age at seventy and she was now a septuagenarian. But she did not want to quit. A small advance from Oxford for The Book of Small and the interest expressed in more books were welcomed and her writing continued, entertaining her and easing her discomfort. In June 1942, after having spent much of the winter and early spring in the Mayfair Nursing Home resting, she was strong enough to have a three-week working holiday with Dilworth in Vancouver, where they finished the Small stories. Yet writing fulfilled only part of her creative drive. She had been praised at her birthday party for her painting as well as her writing. She would continue to do both, in spite of the doctor's orders.

13
'Tired very tired'
1942-1945

It was almost two years since Emily had sketched in the forest. Her need to work in the woods again was awakened in May 1942 when Dilworth drove her to Mount Douglas Park, near Victoria. Two months later Carol Pearson, visiting Emily for a few weeks, also took her there. Though Dr Baillie had advised Emily against another sketching trip, on this second visit she booked a tarpaper cottage behind the tea-house in the park for two weeks in mid-summer. Mrs Edwards, the proprietor of the tea-house, agreed to provide meals. Emily would thus be able to manage without a companion.

Mount Douglas Park, which James Douglas had set aside as a Crown reserve almost a century before, lies four miles north of Victoria. The mountain is some 1,200 feet high and its base spreads over most of the park. A flat area on its northeast side runs to the edge of a steep blue-clay cliff that drops to the sea. This was the most frequented section of the park. Here one could have refreshments in the tea-house, picnic at the edge of the cliffs, scramble down the soft clay bank to bathe in the icy waters of Cordova Bay, or just walk on the soft red-needled earth under the massive cedars, which seemed to dominate the area even more than the mountain. It was a marvellous combination of sea, beach, deep forest, and mountain—an ideal location close to town.

Emily was driven to the park by an acquaintance. She arrived armed with her cedar sketching board; her typewriter; the writings of Whitman, Keats, and Emerson; drafts of her stories; and, for company, Dilworth's spaniel Jane. After settling in, she wrote to Dilworth: 'This place is full of cedars; their colors are terribly sensitive to change of time and light [;] sometimes they are bluish *cold* green then they turn yellow *warm* green [;] sometimes their bows flop heavy & sometimes float, then they are fairy as ferns & then down they droop heavy as heart aches.'[1] She could not walk far, but she did not have to because the cedars were everywhere; they could even be seen through the knot-holes of the cottage. It was 'BLISS'.[2] Though Jane had to be watched closely because she ran onto the road, the mosquitoes were bad, and the weather was cool for August, none of these things bothered Emily. Mrs Edwards did all she could to make her comfortable. Breakfast was brought to her in bed; a lunch was packed so that she did not have to leave the woods at noon. (The evening meal was served in the tea-house.) No one disturbed her while she sat at the edge of the cliffs staring across blue Haro Strait to the half-bare San Juan Islands; or while she sat among the cedars, raised her eyes slightly above the trees, and—singing a work-song—let herself be carried into a world where she had no age or sex, where she was just a mindless part of everything around her.

After a day of trying to paint, Small wrote Dilworth: 'Emily has *not* got the cedar rhythm yet nor their particular idiom.'[3] Recording what she saw and felt on paper did not come easily. But with the lush growth all around her and the fragrance of the sea and earth in her lungs, she soon became attuned to the mood and rhythm of the forest. Within a few days her inability to transfer the weight and buoyancy of the cedars onto paper was overcome and she was 'painting like the band'.[4] Sensing that this was probably her last trip, she used every waking minute—painting all day, contemplating the woods and sea in the evening. When there was neither energy to paint nor light to view the landscape, she worked on her stories. (It was here that she wrote 'Mother', perhaps her most powerful autobiographical sketch.)[5]

The painting Emily did on this trip was not a feeble last tribute to the forest. She told Dilworth that she had come back to it 'with added power' and this was true: miraculously she summoned a burst of creativity.[6] Her theme was again the forest interior, but it was not painted in the dark and sombre colours, the slow lugubrious rhythms, of her 1931 Goldstream paintings, nor with short brush strokes reminiscent of the forest-clearing and shore paintings of the mid-thirties. She had not returned to the forest to fall back on an early formula but to combine the strongest characteristics of her earlier work: the mysterious light of her 1909-10 forest interiors done in watercolour in Stanley Park; the rhythm and energy of her mid-1920s experimental work; the monumentality of her 1928-31 painting; as well as the delicacy, joy, and movement of her 1933-6 work. While making use of all she knew, she also found the strength to rise above everything she had done previously and do some sketches that were 'purely experimental'.[7]

The effort quickly drained Emily's small reserve of energy, and after eight days she had to give up. In any case the solitude of the woods had been broken by some 300 soldiers who had set up camp near her cottage and made the woods a battleground for their manoeuvres. Though Emily was exhausted when she returned home, she feverishly began to translate her sketches onto canvas.

Dilworth was the first person to view the fifteen large and many small oil-on-paper sketches—just three days after her return. Afraid that his first impression might sound 'emotional and Flora-Burnish', he reserved his comments for a letter written two days after the visit:

> . . . You have brought back from those woods in your sketches something that is true, exact, highly imaginative and impressionable and yet almost literal too. By which I mean that the work is a fruitful, honest, portrayal of what you knew and felt out there and, if I may be so vain as to say so, what I have seen and felt but what I could never translate to painted canvas or paper and give it currency among my fellow citizens.[8]

These words heartened Emily, and in spite of her exhaustion and insistence that she rest, she continued to work. She painted †*Cedar*, a canvas that is monumental without being heavy, crowded with layers of foliage yet possessing a feeling of space, and rich in interior forest greens yet neither dark nor gloomy. This undertaking, on top of the short trip, nearly ended her life.

Towards the end of August a clot formed on her heart and she was in much pain. She was rushed to the hospital, where for ten days she lay 'weak, morose, blubbering', unable to 'pour out a great bucket-full of cry' to ease her death fears.[9] Dr Archie Herstein, who was looking after her in Dr Baillie's absence, forbade her to paint, write, or even to speak. 'He says I do *everything too violently*,' Emily told Dilworth, 'put my whole self in writing, painting, talking.'[10] Though disappointed at having her painting curtailed, she was thankful that she had 'the manners *not to die* out there' in the park, and happy that the trip had been possible.[11] 'Even if I did come a cropper afterwards,' she told Carol, 'my memories of it are so happy.'[12] Dilworth assured her that 'no one will be able to take away from you and Small the peaceful benediction of those days.'[13]

After two weeks in hospital, Emily was moved to the Mayfair Nursing Home, where she would remain for the next five months. Though prohibited from painting for several months, she was allowed to do some writing. When Bill Clarke visited her in October, he was astounded that, 'although she had been completely unable even to sit propped in bed, she has managed to hold a pad on one knee and to write upon it, even though she cannot see what she writes. . . . After she has completed a sketch in this laborious fashion,' he continued, 'she types it out on a machine which is suspended over her bed.' Emily showed Clarke a draft of 'The Pie', a collection of bird stories. He was surprised that she had written 'almost as much material in the last two months as we used for *Klee Wyck*, and some of it is as good as anything we have seen.'[14]

The Book of Small was published in the late autumn of 1942. A fairly large first printing for wartime—3,000 copies—sold quickly, and it was reprinted in December/January. Clarke reported to Dilworth that bookstores on the West Coast had been 'frightened that a second book may be a flop'. Yet *Saturday Night*, the *Canadian Forum*, the *Winnipeg Tribune*, the *Calgary Herald*, and the *Edmonton Radio Book Review* all acclaimed it as 'the Canadian Book of the Year'.[15] Clarke was naturally eager to see a third book in print. What should be published next? Emily favoured 'Creatures', a collection of dog and monkey stories, but Oxford's editor felt that 'Woo's Life' was not up to standard and that the dog stories were too short to comprise one volume. Emily's second autobiography, given to Dilworth in draft in May 1942, was more tantalizing to Clarke. But Emily wanted that published after her death. Fearful that 'Creatures', her favourite manuscript, would not be published before she died, she asked Dilworth whether another publisher might be approached. Oxford had had the stories for over four months, the time contractually allowed to consider a manuscript without making a firm commitment, and Emily was now free to submit her work elsewhere. Dilworth discouraged her from doing so and Emily waited throughout 1943 and half of 1944 for Clarke to decide what her next book would be. The decision was made to combine the apartment-house and dog stories in one volume to be called *The House of All Sorts*.

Though no book by Emily appeared in 1943, she was given several solo exhibitions that year. By February she was able to spend a few hours each day out of bed and return to her Mount Douglas Park canvases. Together with the fifteen sketches done in the Park, they were exhibited at the Vancouver Art Gallery in June. During the preparations, while Willie Newcombe crated the paintings and Harris and Dilworth hung them, Emily worried that they might look dark and gloomy: they were mostly forest interiors. Dilworth, who did not always trust his own judgement in matters of art, also wondered about the quality of the work. Harris told him that he was 'very much impressed with the strength and at the same time, the delicacy of this later work.' Dilworth was thus able to praise it confidently as 'noble and fine'.[16] Harris expressed gleeful enthusiasm to Emily: 'Golly, gee whiz and jimney cricket, they look and are better than ever each time seen.'[17] The critics agreed; one reviewer even called the exhibition 'one of the most dramatic events ever staged in their gallery'.[18] Emily could not attend the show—or her three other solo exhibitions that year: at the Art Association of Montreal in January, the Art Gallery of Toronto in February, and the Seattle Art Museum in August. She read the favourable reviews as though they were obituaries.

She spent most of 1943 in bed. After returning from the Mayfair Nursing home in February, she longed to be out in the woods and asked Dr Baillie if she could go on another excursion, to be told that she could not. Her only travelling was to and from the Royal Jubilee Hospital. When weather permitted, the staff at the hospital rolled her bed onto the lawn facing Fort Street—a busy thoroughfare that was a world removed from the forest. 'Pray for me and ask for me to die soon & quick,' she wrote Dilworth in June 1943.[19]

Attacks of cardiac asthma often made lying flat in bed impossible. By bending forward over her sketching stool, which was placed in front of her on the bed, Emily could sleep for longer periods, but this posture could hardly have been comfortable. Also, her chest pains were frequent and she had to administer morphine 'hypo stabs' to her thigh and upper arm to ease this condition.[20] Pain pills—which she called 'weepers'—

brought on deep depression. 'It is a toss up,' she wrote Dilworth, 'whether to stay at home and cry from munching "weepers" or be bustled off to hospital for pain.'[21] During 1943 and the early months of 1944 she did both. Her time was spent either at the Jubilee Hospital, the Mayfair Nursing Home, or Alice's. In these circumstances it was almost impossible to continue painting regularly, and certainly difficult to add more stories to the trunk that held her unpublished manuscripts. As for pets, Emily had only Joseph, a budgie, and Chippy, a chipmunk—a sad reduction of the menagerie she had kept before her illness. 'Old age is lonely and bitter,' she wrote to Dilworth, 'when taken sip by sip, to the dregs.'[22]

Like many old people who suffer in the last years of life, Emily flew into a rage over a mere trifle. She attempted to justify her crankiness by claiming that 'if we did not have each other to grunt at, our grunters would grow rusty.'[23] But her outbursts of temper went beyond the bounds of her former grumbling and intolerance. A photograph of the English critic Roger Fry with his mouth open caused her to break into a torrent of written abuse: she hated 'gapping mugs' and his 'head so flat on top'.[24] She vented a good deal of fury on war matters. Her correspondents and visitors were frequently treated to her belligerent views of the 'war-beast'.[25] Girls in uniform made her sick, 'babbling about loyalty', when all they wanted was 'pay and a good time'.[26] Other girls were 'uniform crazy'.[27] The country's 'we're safe attitude' annoyed her too. 'Where were all the fliers they were going to train', which were 'so urgently needed,' she grumbled in May 1940.[28] In 1941 she chafed at not being able to sew 'Bommbed drawers' and pyjamas for the Red Cross.[29] 'If *only* I was within reach,' she wrote, 'how I'd love to give Mr. Hitler a box in the ear or a black eye with my *own* fist.'[30]

Even Alice got on her nerves. Charges that her sister woke her in the night and prepared dreadfully boring meals often appeared in Emily's letters to Dilworth and Pearson. But Alice had complaints too. After *The Book of Small* was published, she 'flared up', claiming that Emily had 'exploited the weaknesses' of the family in order to build up her writing reputation.[31] The nieces echoed this charge. Emily tried to dismiss it by saying they wanted 'syrup not truth', but she took Alice's complaint to heart.[32] Had she been 'disloyal', she asked Dilworth, in making 'fun out of Edith & Lizzie's smug hypocrisy?' By way of justification—though it was untrue—she insisted that 'I *had* to write of those parts to show what drove me to woods & animals.'[33]

When Humphrey Toms visited Emily in 1940 before going into the service, he sensed that 'she simply had to blow off steam about her *grumbles*' to someone, and let her chatter away freely.[34] 'I have no friends they have gone or died,' she wrote to Nan Cheney in May 1941, 'even my enemies have died on me.'[35] In 1940 Edythe Hembroff-Brand was 'neither visitor nor correspondent'.[36] Nan Cheney, with whom Emily had corresponded since their 1927 meeting in Ottawa, had made several excursions from Vancouver to Beckley Street to paint Emily's portrait in

1937,[37] but after it was finished they saw each other seldom, though letters continued. Flora Burns still visited Emily regularly and listened to her stories, but Emily found her 'so dismal so depressing'.[38] Myfanwy Spencer, a young portrait painter, was a welcome visitor; though she moved to New York, she always saw Emily when she returned to Victoria. Lawren Harris came over from Vancouver and these visits gave Emily a 'fresh spurt', but he was often accompanied by Bess, who was an obstacle to their intimacy (as Emily had foreseen years before).[39] Kate Mather promised in 1942 to come to Victoria and help look after her, but at the last minute she was unable to leave Winnipeg, where she was then living. Carol Pearson—who visited her in 1942 and 1944—disappointed Emily when her plans to buy a farm in British Columbia fell through. Eric Brown had died in 1939, Fred Housser three years before. Marius Barbeau was never heard from. Emily's correspondence diminished greatly. Ira Dilworth and Irene Clarke, the wife of her publisher, were the most frequent recipients of letters. (A few acquaintances and admirers of her books and pictures received pencil-written notes.) Emily had an explanation for her neglect: 'Now that people have accepted the books & pictures of me as me,' she wrote in 1944, 'they forget the old derelict shelved away.'[40]

Dilworth—Emily's closest, most loyal friend—found it increasingly difficult after 1942 to keep up the demanding correspondence, and the editing, typing, and publishing chores, that he had so enthusiastically undertaken in the early spring of 1941. His work at the CBC, his own literary endeavours—he was compiling an anthology of English poetry—as well as the failing health of his mother combined to make him less attentive to Emily. Though his visits were less frequent, he did continue to edit her writing. Changes in grammar, punctuation, and vocabulary were made directly onto the typescript; general comments were appended to each story, then mailed to St Andrew's Street. Emily would promptly revise and return a story to him, but he would not deal with it immediately. In 1943 it took him eight months to correct the stories that eventually appeared in *The House of All Sorts*. Emily continued to rely on him, however, and assured him that his 'supervision, comments and suggestions' were essential for her writing. In the spring of 1943 she and Small waited with their 'faces up for a kiss' and their shoulders out 'for a hug' in anticipation of a visit.[41] She had not seen him 'for ages' and she 'needed him badly too'.[42] 'Perhaps Ira is wearied of my writing,' she wrote to him through Small, because it is 'all so much the same (all sort of Biographical).'[43] She observed Dilworth's preoccupation with other matters sadly, though not silently. 'I have felt for a while,' she wrote in 1944, 'how you were rather bored with Emily's ailments & Emily's M.S.'[44] She needed more than occasional written criticisms; she required his presence, his inspiration, his conversation. There was 'no *greater happiness* than going over M.S. with you.'[45]

Emily had become over-reliant on Dilworth's judgement. In 1942 she told him to '*cut out* what & where you think fit, *don't* feel you have to ask me first when there is need for quick action', and she apologized for changes she made to *his* corrections.[46] 'Emily is scard to write,' she wrote to him as Small, because she has so fearfully mussed up your M.S. Bobtails. . . . *Please forgive* her, but she saw *so much* she wanted to alter.'[47] She passed on to him suggestions made by others before considering them herself. When Harris suggested some additions to a draft of her autobiography she had sent him, Emily would not consider them 'without Ira's consent' because, as she told a friend, 'the M.S. belongs to him.'[48] When adding a chapter that was to include excerpts from Harris's letters, Emily asked Dilworth to mark those passages in the letters that he felt should be put into the text. She even consulted him about where she should end the autobiography: 'Do I have to take it to the point where I sit leg-dangling over my grave?'[49] With the last manuscript, 'Hundreds and Thousands', it was little different. Dilworth was given leave 'to cut out any sections' he thought 'foolish or unworthy', and, if he felt they were 'bad', to burn them. 'One's gotta fail sometimes just to make the others seem righter,' she wrote at the end of 1944.[50]

While Emily came to defer to Dilworth more and more about her writing, she retained her independence with her paintings. When he took the liberty of retitling some of them, she did not hesitate to tell him that 'other's names attributed to my canvases always rub this old crank *wrong*.'[51] Emily kept her titles.

In many fatal illnesses there is a period of remission before the end when the condition appears to improve. Emily's reprieve came during the late spring and early summer of 1944. Her easel was once again set up in the classroom-studio, and with the help of a newly acquired maid, Mrs Shanks, Emily was able to devote a few hours each afternoon to painting. In a wheel-chair she saw the flowers bloom in Beacon Hill park. Alice or 'Shanks' usually pushed. These outings must have been a pathetic sight: Emily directing semi-blind Alice along the sloping paths of the park and describing the flowers along the way; or screaming at Shanks, who was terrified of letting the chair run away from her and plunge into one of the muddy ponds. In the summer of 1944 Emily was wheeled to the park by Carol Pearson and posed with her for what was to be a last photograph. Gloved, and well blanketed against the cool sea breeze, she looks happy to be out on the cliffs where twenty years before she had given Carol her first painting lessons.

The last full year of Emily's life was marked by two happy public events, both of which took place in the autumn of 1944. The first was the publication of *The House of All Sorts*. A $300 advance from Oxford, the joy of seeing 'Bobtails' published, and favourable reviews made this her third literary success. At about the same time there occurred the first sale of her paintings in a commercial gallery, arranged by Max Stern of the Dominion Gallery in Montreal. Stern had been in Canada only four years when he discovered' the work of Emily Carr. After fleeing his native Germany in 1937 and attempting to set up the remnants of his

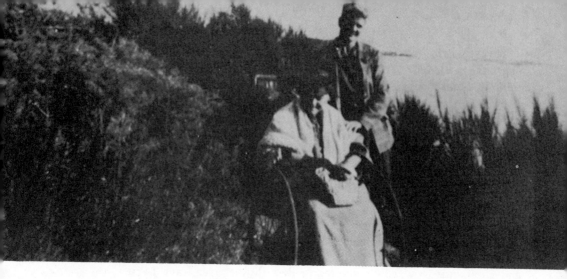

Emily and Carol Pearson on the Dallas Road cliffs, 1944. Private collection.

Düsseldorf gallery in London, he arrived in Montreal with no money but with European sophistication and a certain amount of drive that impressed culturally unsophisticated Canadians. He was hired by Rose Millman of the Dominion Gallery on the understanding that he could buy a partnership in the then-modest business, and on his first western scouting trip in the summer of 1944 he heard of Emily. Having been commissioned by a Montreal doctor to bring back something typically western—and after meeting both Lawren Harris and Ira Dilworth—he arranged an appointment with the Victoria artist through Dilworth.

Stern found Emily sitting on her St Andrew's Street porch, shaded from the August sun by the lattice wall that Willie Newcombe had built in 1940. Almost immediately they went into the classroom studio and Emily began the ever-agonizing task of presenting her work to a stranger. Stern was 'speechless' when he was shown the first canvas, and he found the rest stronger and more emotionally powerful than anything he had seen in North America.[52] His European eye saw affinities with the Norwegian symbolist, Edvard Munch, and the Swiss expressionist, Ferdinand Hodler. Forgetting about his doctor-client, Stern told Emily that he would like to have an exhibition of her work alone. Excitedly he wired Mrs Millman and Arthur Lismer, whom he represented. Mrs Millman answered that she was enthusiastic, but Lismer warned him that 'he would not sell a thing.'[53] Ignoring this remark, Stern rummaged through the studio during the next two days and chose sixty works— largely early Indian and French watercolours. Emily signed each painting and, after consulting Dilworth, agreed to put them out on consignment for one year. Stern's commission would be one-third of the income from sales; Emily would have the remaining two-thirds, less one-third of the transportation and advertising expenses. She was to assume the cost of insuring the paintings in transit. Confident that 'the man seems very interested and very anxious to do right by me', and happy that he also represented Jackson and Lismer, she arranged for Willie to crate and ship her work to Montreal.[54] Within a couple of days Willie had crated sixty

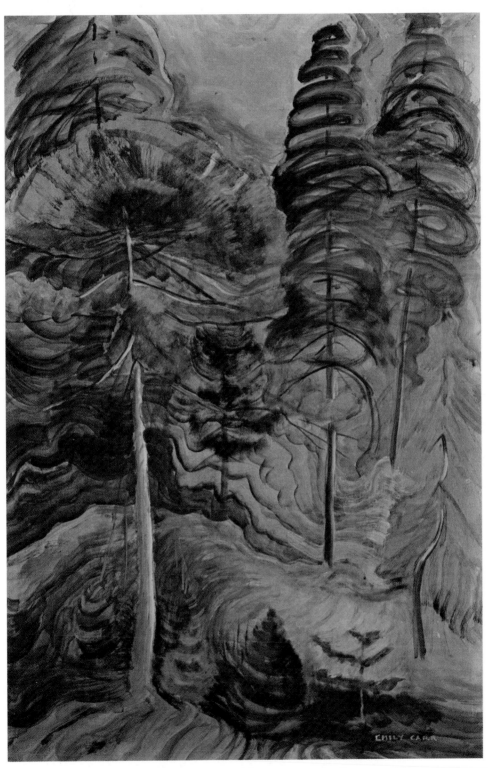

IX—*Forest Landscape (II)*, about 1939. Oil on paper, 36 x 24. Courtesy VAG. NGC.

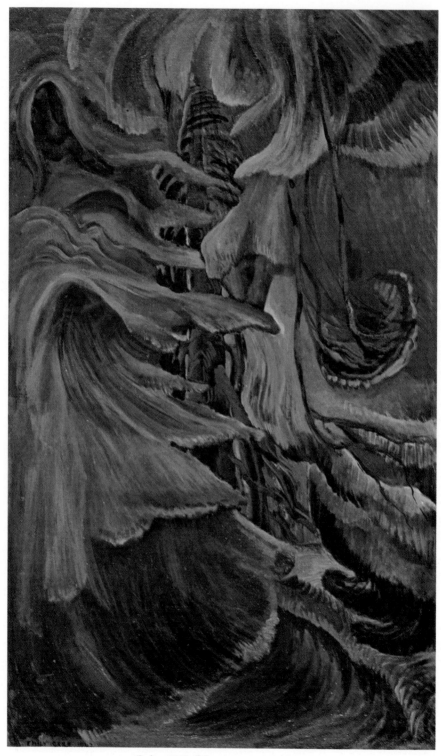

x—*Cedar*, 1942. Oil on canvas, 44 x 27. VAG.

paintings and Stern was returning east by train, reading *Klee Wyck* and *The Book of Small* on the way.

Soon after the opening, on the nineteenth of October, of 'Paintings and Watercolours by Emily Carr' at the Dominion Gallery, Stern reported that thirty pictures had been sold; and before three weeks were up he announced that all but five of the sixty had been spoken for. Though the response had certainly been good, Stern exaggerated the number of sales. Only thirty of the sixty paintings were sold within the first three weeks; and of these, many were bought by Stern himself.[55] The gallery owners were nevertheless satisfied. Watercolours Emily painted at Concarneau had been displayed in the gallery's window, and more French watercolours were hung inside. In the middle rooms visitors could find Emily's paintings of Indians, their houses and totem poles; in the back rooms her forest canvases were displayed. In the catalogue one read that, throughout Emily's studies in San Francisco, London, and Paris, 'her style remained completely independent of any tradition or school.'[56] The legend was established that Emily was an artist who had developed in isolation, unaffected by contemporary art movements.

Within two months Stern had sold thirty-eight paintings and Emily received cheques totalling almost $1,000. She had not expected 'so many sales so soon' and was particularly elated by the purchase of *Indian Village, Alert Bay* by the Art Association of Montreal.[57]

Though Stern had not been the first private art dealer to envision the financial success of Emily's work, he was the first to hold such a large exhibition.[58] And he hoped to repeat it. Attempting to woo the lady who, according to Lismer, hated Montreal, he informed Emily that he would not subtract her share of the shipping and advertising costs from her profits. His gesture was accompanied by a request. As 'we have a growing demand, especially for your watercolours,' he wrote, we 'would be grateful if you could send us a greater number.'[59] Upon hearing that Dilworth and Harris were preparing a publication on Emily Carr's painting, Stern offered financial assistance, 'as this would be excellent advertising for the Gallery.'[60] He had already begun to photograph all her work, including the paintings sold, for use in a book. But Dilworth and Harris did not want to rush their project and in January 1945 Dilworth told Stern that it would 'take a very long time to complete' and that there were 'conditions which made it difficult for the [Oxford] press to publish such a volume.'[61] Though disappointed, Stern was happy to obtain Emily's consent for another exhibition in the spring and Willie Newcombe crated and shipped more pictures to Montreal.[62]

Only a few days after meeting Stern in the summer of 1944, Emily was back in bed. 'It takes little to knock me out these days,' she wrote him.[63] His three-day visit, during which she had shown her work for three to four hours on end, had been exhausting. She tried to get back to painting but jammed her fingers in a door, and soon after this accident she had another stroke. This time it affected not only her body but what she dreaded most—her mind. She lay in the Jubilee Hospital chatting in-

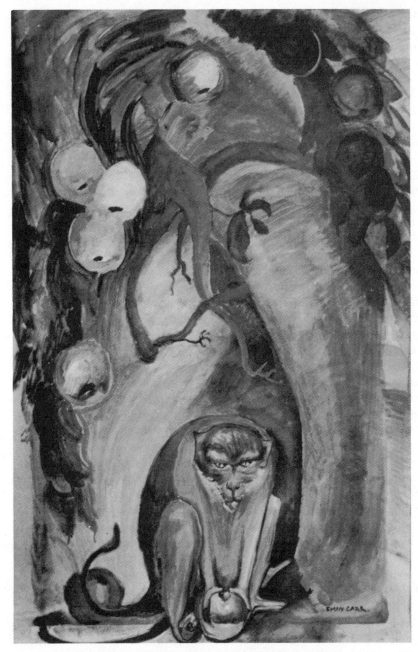

Woo, 1945. Oil on paper, 36 x 24. Emily's last painting. The horizontal line at the bottom suggests that Emily painted a second tail because the lower portion of the painting was originally hidden by a frame. The painting framed can be seen in the photograph of Emily's studio on page 278. (Photo: Saltmarche visual communication—Toronto) Private collection.

coherently to herself about Woo.[64] Alice was afraid she would never hear her sister speak intelligibly again. Dilworth received letters that revealed blurred and muddled thought, yet were lucid enough to express 'shame' for her condition.[65] It was feared that the numbness in Emily's neck, throat, and left arm, as well as her incoherence, might be permanent. But when she showed some improvement, Dr Baillie gave her permission to have a canvas propped against her sketching stool and she attempted to paint—'to *try* and get ahead of myself.'[66] This activity, however slight, along with some comforting letters from Dilworth, gave Emily the encouragement she needed. Her left hand remained weak and her speech was far from normal, but by November she was out of bed painting again, and on her birthday in December she had recovered sufficiently to complain, in a letter to Dilworth, that all her maids had been 'nincompoop vipers'.[67]

On this, her seventy-third birthday, the *Colonist* reported that Emily Carr continued to write and paint, and that she felt she would be all right if she could get outside in the open again.[68] But that December was very wet and cold. In February Emily put the finishing touches on a rather sinister oil-on-paper *portrait of Woo, and touched up several early forest landscapes, but her left arm was now so weak that it would not 'hold . . . steady to let the right hand work.'[69] Nevertheless, Dr Baillie advised her to continue painting, and she did, keeping in mind that Harris and Dilworth had promised to tell her if her work got 'weak & maudling'.[70]

Apart from wanting to help Willie mount and frame some thirty paper sketches for a solo exhibition at the Vancouver Art Gallery in the spring of 1945 (which was never held), Emily had only one wish: that 'I won't out live my reason.'[71] She was not exactly fearful of death, which she had thought about considerably since her first heart attack in 1937, but she quaked at the unknown. She felt that 'tired tired old bodies ought not to be *too* hard to leave . . . it would be frightful to think we had to lug all our ills around forever.'[72] Death would almost be a comfort—a relief from pain and uncertainty, from the fear of becoming senile, and from the knowledge that her painting and all its associations had come to an end.

Emily had begun to prepare for the inevitable end in 1942 when she gave 'quite a number of pictures to various friends . . . thinking that would be easier than willing.'[73] Carol Pearson visited her that year and took care of a number of items that were too personal for Dilworth's eyes but that Emily did not want to be destroyed. Into several boxes Carol packed a pair of men's gold cuff links, small books of poetry, bits of jewellery, small dog collars, faded pictures, a mesh purse, some letters, and numerous other things.[74] Then, following Emily's instructions, she buried the boxes in Beacon Hill Park. (They were never recovered.)

Emily had disposed of her stories, both published and unpublished, and many of her pictures in a less permanent fashion in 1941. Harris suggested that she set aside a 'reserve selection' of pictures for western

Canada.[75] On the fifteenth of July 1941 she added an indenture to her will appointing Ira Dilworth and Lawren Harris trustees of the Emily Carr Trust. Eighty pictures, as yet unchosen, were designated as the Emily Carr Picture Collection. Of these, forty-five were to be put in the Trust and thirty-five were to be sold 'for the upkeep of the housing of the rest'.[76] It was not until the following spring that Harris and Dilworth, with Emily's assistance, chose the forty-five paintings. Two-thirds of those selected were Indian subjects, the rest were predominantly forest; the majority were post 1927. The public was informed that Miss Emily Carr had given the paintings to the nation, or more specifically to the Vancouver Art Gallery on permanent loan. Some thought the location unsuitable because the Vancouver gallery was small, but for Emily it was the logical place to house her pictures. She had had numerous solo exhibitions there and Lawren Harris had been chairman of its exhibition committee since 1941. Of Victoria's response to the disposition of the pictures, not much is known. The Little Centre, progenitor of the Art Gallery of Greater Victoria, was certainly not equipped to handle so large a collection. Emily heard grumblings from a few Victorians to the effect that she had slighted her fellow citizens, but generally they said nothing, which made her 'feel further than ever away from people' when she saw 'how *little* these things matter.'[77] Harris, fearing a Japanese attack, arranged at his own expense to move the pictures east, and they were stored in the basement of the Art Gallery of Toronto.

The Trust pictures were only a fraction of the work that still hung on the walls and filled the racks of Emily's classroom studio: there were also mounted and unmounted oil-on-paper sketches; watercolours from her first visit to Ucluelet, Alaska, and Alert Bay; oils and watercolours of her 1912 trip north; as well as many forest canvases and sketches. These had all been willed to Alice, to be dispersed by her after Emily's death. In an effort to ease Alice's task, Emily drew up a new will in November 1942. In it she designated that 'all my pictures and paintings belonging to me at the date of my death' should go to her trustees. Some were to be sold to cover storage, insurance, and packing costs and to provide for a scholarship fund 'to enable art students residing in British Columbia to study art at some art school or art schools to be selected by the Trustees.'[78] The trustees were empowered to give paintings of their choice to any public gallery in British Columbia. Dilworth was replaced by Willie Newcombe as a trustee of the paintings—an admirable choice, considering his ability to handle and crate pictures, which would certainly have to be moved when Emily died. This new arrangement provided for the disposal by the trustees of all paintings in Emily's studio on her death; it also left none to Alice.

While Dilworth lost the trusteeship of Emily's pictures, he gained custody of her manuscripts. Stories, papers, and letters (not to mention hundreds of paintings) had been committed to fire by Emily when she moved from the apartment house in 1936, from the Beckley Street cottage in 1940, and in 1943 at Alice's. If the manuscripts had not been put into Dilworth's trusteeship, Emily might have had a few more burning sessions. His literary trusteeship meant that provision had been made for the further editing and publication of her stories after her death. While confident that Dilworth could be entrusted with this task, Emily feared that after he died, the editing duties might fall into the hands of Phylis. 'It's not any money that might come from them I want to protect' from her, Emily wrote, 'it's the disposing & arranging & editing the manuscripts themselves that has worried me.' She urged Dilworth to tell her whether Phylis would, in fact, inherit what she called 'my children'.[79] Though there is no record of Dilworth's reply, his will of 1950 left the manuscripts and editing responsibilities to his friend Dean Walter Gage of the University of British Columbia. (A later will, however, gave the editing to Phylis Inglis.)

In the winter of 1944-5 Emily experienced a measure of contentment, not only from knowing that her affairs were settled, but from some reconciliations. Through her friendship with Dilworth she had come to terms with her father and the brutal telling and she was finally convinced that Alice really did love her. Though she regretted that, because of illness, she had been unable to arrange for a marker for Sophie Frank's grave, she was satisfied that the dedication of *Klee Wyck* was her 'monument'.[80] Alice too had been honoured. 'Bobtails' in *The House of All Sorts* was dedicated to her. When Alice was told of this, she kissed Emily and said, 'I am proud of you and your book.'[81] Emily had provided for her by leaving her the Oscar Street house, a painting valued at $500, and all her personal possessions. She had also managed to slip $100 into Alice's bank account that autumn.

Over Christmas 1944, Emily's health began to deteriorate rapidly. On New Year's day she caught a cold and was kept awake during the night by a cough. Her 'hypo stabs' were increased to three a day and now had to be administered by a nurse. However, her weakening condition did not deter her from preparing for the spring exhibition at the Vancouver Art Gallery. Some of the sketches—mostly from the mid-thirties—needed more work. She would prop two pictures on the bed 'to study as I lie'. ('I do a lot of my work that way,' she told a friend.) By February she had still not recovered from her cold but was able to get out of bed and work in a closed-off corner of the classroom-studio from 3:30 to 6:00 in the afternoon. Though she returned to bed 'dead beat', she had enough strength left to write.[82] Carol Pearson, Dilworth, and a few admirers continued to receive short rambling letters, some of which contained reflections on her life:

> I have written & painted to be shure that was because I could not help it. Those things were my life and because it has been a long life (though not so long as old women's lives go now-a-days) and because not love struck my mind was not much distracted with things that did not belong to my work. I am tired *very* tired and 8 years of invalidism have in some ways I am afraid soured me a little.[83]

In these last letters she did not forget who had helped her, though she told the story of her 'discovery' in the exaggerated form that by 1945 had become widely accepted:

> Eric Brown dug me out of the slough of despair in House of A.S. and awakened in me after 15 years of lying fallow, art forgot in despair. Eric took me & my works East & then I met the group men they were all grand to me opened their studios & accepted this raw woman from the west who had turned into a dull old landlady. Lawren had me to his studio twice & his pictures . . . impressed me more than any in my life London, Paris anywhere because they were what was in my heart. I knew I was striving alone in the West for what the group men were striving for in the East and they knew it too & were so helpful . . . [84]

In early February Harris visited Emily for the last time; later that month Dilworth had his final visit with her. On the twenty-fourth of February, when the thirty paintings were ready to be crated for the Vancouver show, Emily took her typewriter, rough drafts of the pieces she wrote for 'Hundreds and Thousands', and left her quarters in Alice's house. The heating in the old house had never been adequate and the chill was unbearable that winter. Also, problems with Shanks had reached an ugly state of constant quarrelling. The decision to move to St Mary's Priory for a rest was a relief to everyone.

The Priory—formerly the fashionable James Bay Hotel—lay close enough to St Andrew's Street to enable Alice to visit twice a day, but it was hardly better heated. Emily was put in a room 'way off down a corridor', where 'nobody ever comes or nothing ever happens'. There was no bell and she complained that 'if anything goes wrong, you go wrong by yourself.'[85] She was not able to work, as she had planned; she was 'too tired to read, too tired to think.'[86] However, this arrangement was better than quarrelling with Shanks. Also, the Priory was not depressing: patients seemed 'to slip off in a merrier mood & make room for the next', the nun-nurses were kind, and there was even an English bobtail, though not well bred and very old.[87] Emily's last letters to Dilworth should have been riddled with complaints—the mounting fluid in her lungs made breathing difficult and the pains in her chest were more frequent—but Emily had just received the news that the University of British Columbia planned to confer the degree of Doctor of Letters on her at their May Congregation. Though she wished it had not been so late, this gave her a great sense of pride. 'If Lizzie was not dead already sh'd die right off,' Emily wrote to Dilworth, 'and Father & Mother? . . . I think the ugly duckling would have given them a *tremendous* surprise.' She imagined that the next generation would 'scoff' at her honours and consider her 'trash', yet that did not matter.[88] So elated was she with the news that she wanted to shout at everyone in the Priory who treated her like a 'half-wit': 'I'm *nearly* a *Doctor*, the University are making me one so there!'[89]

Three days after writing this, another clot formed in her heart, and late in the afternoon of March the second Emily died.

Epilogue

'Suddenly there will be a little clatter of crying, a few flowers and I'll be put away', Emily wrote to Dilworth in 1944.[1] Her funeral was held on the morning of the fifth of March at the McCall Brothers Floral Chapel. The mourners included Alice and her nephew Richard Nicholles, Ira Dilworth, Lawren Harris, Willie Newcombe, several lady friends, as well as representatives of Victoria organizations. The Reverend T.A. Laundy of the Reformed Episcopal Church read the service. The mourners then followed the hearse some three miles to Ross Bay Cemetery, where over fifty years earlier ground had been broken for Emily's mother. The morning was cheerless and grey. The pallbearers—Harris, Newcombe, Dr Baillie, Richard Nicholles, Laundry, and Edward Cridge—carried the coffin to its resting place beside Lizzie, Edith, Clara, Dick, and Emily's father and mother. Thus Emily was buried only a short distance from her beloved Dallas Road cliffs.

Lawren Harris and Ira Dilworth remained in Victoria long enough to hear the solicitor, H.J. Davis, read Emily's will. As designated in 1942, Dilworth became sole trustee of the manuscripts and published books, and Newcombe and Harris were given in trust all Emily's paintings and sketches. The real and residual property, including the Oscar Street house, her personal possessions, and the contents of her safety-deposit box and bank account—which totalled over $2,500—went to Alice.[2] Many not mentioned in the will received mementos of Emily. Her books were divided among Carol Pearson, Flora Burns, Ira Dilworth, and Mark Kearley, the director of The Little Centre in Victoria. Willie Newcombe received most of the baskets, carved grease bowls, and other valuable Indian artefacts collected by Emily. To the Nootka artist George Clutesi, whom Emily had met shortly before her death, went her paints, brushes, and unused canvases. Una Boultbee, Emily's niece, wrote to Alice saying that she wanted Emily's collection of pewter. Anyone who paid a memorial visit to the St Andrew's Street studio was shown around by Alice and usually left with a souvenir.

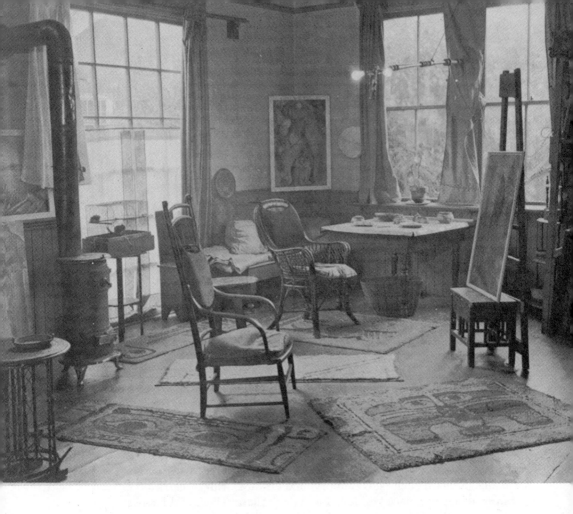

Two weeks after Emily's death, Lawren and Bess Harris travelled from
Vancouver to Victoria to dispose of the paintings that remained. Harris
hoped that Newcombe, also an artistic executor and trustee, would leave
most of the decisions to him, and Willie complied. The several hundred
paintings that were in Emily's studio when she died were therefore at the
sole discretion of Harris. He assigned them to three categories: those that
were to join the Emily Carr Trust Collection; those that were to be sold
through Stern to raise money for the expense of maintaining the Trust
pictures and for a trust scholarship; and those that were to be simply
'discarded'.

Most of the paintings added to the Trust Collection were post-1927
works. Emily's French oils and watercolours went to Stern, who felt that
his Montreal clients preferred her French style. The discards were mainly
paintings done before 1912, though some later forest and seashore oil-on-
paper sketches were included in this category. One observer could not
understand why the 'experts' had condemned some of the paintings for
destruction.[3] Newcombe salvaged many, especially those with Indian
themes, keeping some and selling others to Victoria people. (He

deposited the money from their sale into the Trust.) Alice rescued an early sketch of Richard Carr, and many other watercolours 'full of the past'.[4]

In April W.H. Clarke announced plans for a book of over 100 illustrations of Emily's work. Max Stern hurried to finish building additional storage space at his Dominion Gallery in anticipation of receiving paintings from the Trust. Premier John Hart announced that the government of British Columbia was 'now prepared to buy paintings of the late Emily Carr to form a permanent collection to perpetuate her memory.'[5] Martin Baldwin, of the Art Gallery of Toronto, began plans for a memorial exhibition. And Harry McCurry, of the National Gallery, who was warming to Harris's enthusiasm for Emily's work, suggested that a room be set aside for her pictures in the proposed new National Gallery building; negotiations were begun with Harris to obtain paintings for it through the Trust.[6]

The book Clarke proposed did not appear, nor was an Emily Carr memorial room opened at the National Gallery. Stern, however, did receive many pictures from the Trust and, according to Mortimer Lamb, 'made a killing' from their sale.[7] The province of British Columbia purchased seven paintings for the Archives collection.

Of all the tributes that followed Emily's death, the memorial exhibition at the Art Gallery of Toronto was the most impressive. Though Baldwin had initially hoped to stage a comprehensive exhibition, it was mainly confined to Emily's post-1927 work. It included most of the original Trust pictures and those Harris had added to this category, as well as some works from private collections: 177 oil paintings, watercolours, oil-on-paper sketches, charcoal drawings, and brush drawings, as well as examples of Emily's pottery and rugs. The exhibition opened in October 1945 and was accompanied by an illustrated catalogue, published by Oxford, which contained brief essays by Dilworth and Harris.[8] From Toronto it moved to Ottawa—where McCurry observed proudly that the much-reduced exhibition looked less cluttered in the more spacious rooms of the National Gallery—then to Montreal. (Members of Montreal's Art Association committee had wondered if the exhibition was 'really as important as Harris seemed to think; there had been so much 'propaganda about Emily Carr in the last year or two.' Nevertheless, they accepted it.)[9] Finally it went to Vancouver. There was some talk of sending it to the Tate Gallery in London, and letters were exchanged with New York's Museum of Modern Art, but nothing came of either possibility.

While Harris undoubtedly devoted much of his time and energy to operating the Trust, and one must be thankful that the Trust did not fall into less capable hands, it was unfortunate that he did not save Emily's early work.[10] The exclusion from the permanent collection of paintings done during Emily's early student years in San Francisco and later in France, as well as some that remained from the important experimental years between 1919 and 1927, ensured that the 170 works in the Trust

Collection—the only public body of Emily's work—consisted mostly of paintings completed during the last fourteen years of her life. When Willie Newcombe died in 1960, and the British Columbia government purchased the contents of his home two years later, over 100 paintings— most of them pre-1913—as well as Emily's Indian artefacts, came into public ownership.[11] Thus by 1962 two comprehensive collections of Emily's early and late works became available to the public in the Vancouver Art Gallery and the Provincial Archives in Victoria. By this time many important pictures had disappeared into private Montreal collections through the agency of Stern, or had been sold by the Trustees, or destroyed or dispersed.

When the will was probated in August, five months after Emily's death, Dilworth took possession of the manuscripts, which had been packed in a trunk: 'a great many letters, a number of sketch books, several single sketches in oil and water colour, account books, Emily's journals, a number of manuscripts, and a great many miscellaneous personal items.'[12] He needed to spend little time negotiating with Oxford for the publication of Emily's autobiography. Clarke, who had been interested in the manuscript since 1942, accepted it eagerly.

Growing Pains, dedicated to Lawren Harris, appeared in November 1946. In the words of one critic, it seemed to provide the 'authentic background to the career of Emily Carr', but it owed more to literary art than to the faithfulness of her recollections.[13] The author of *Klee Wyck*, *The Book of Small*, and *The House of All Sorts* did not adopt a conventional approach to the writing of her memoirs—she had no inclination or ability to examine probingly, or to come to terms with, her past—but stayed with the mode of writing that suited her best, and for which she knew she had a receptive audience. Embroidering incidents to give them dramatic emphasis, enlivening them with an ample use of invented dialogue, Emily converted her experiences and impressions, her animosities and resentments, into a series of short sketches, concentrating on her life up to her return from England. (Only the last third of the book is devoted to 1904 and afterwards.) The self-portrait that emerges is of a feisty woman who is independent, unappreciated, and long-suffering. Sympathy is drawn to her because she was usually out of step with the people around her—most of them in some way disagreeable, sometimes comically so—and above all because she remained dedicated to her art through every adversity. Emily had wondered if the autobiography would 'shock or distress' her relatives, and this was probably one reason why she prohibited publication during her lifetime.[14] The account of her childhood did indeed hurt Alice. 'Some parts are really wonderful,' she wrote to a friend after reading *Growing Pains*, 'but her recollections of our childhood days and my own are very different.'[15] To Carol Pearson she wrote: 'I know it is a wonderful piece of literature, but to me the things she says in it are very hurtful, some parts I love and read over and over, other parts I skip.'[16] Perhaps it was in defence of her family, especially her father, that Alice attempted several times to interest Clarke in publishing Richard Carr's diary.[17]

Another Emily Carr book did not appear for seven years—much to the displeasure of Alice, who considered that Dilworth had delayed further publications deliberately. The long hiatus between books was mainly due to Dilworth's uncertainty about his claim to the royalties. Emily's will was unclear on this point. She bequeathed to Dilworth 'all my manuscripts and all the books written by me belonging to me at my death in respect of such of my manuscripts or books written by me and published in my lifetime.'[18] This seemed to indicate that Alice had claim to the royalties of all posthumous publications. Dilworth had been receiving all the royalties since Emily's death but wanted to ensure his legal right to them in the event of Alice's death and before any further books were brought out.

In the late autumn of 1952 Dilworth called on Alice and asked her to insert a codicil in her will that would settle the matter in his favour. (He told her that 'the royalties were so small that they were not worth the time [he] had spent on it.')[19] He pressed her to see her lawyer, which she did, though she was angered by his request. She knew 'nothing about the "law" ', and did 'not feel well enough to wrestle' with the insistent Dilworth.[20] Alice's lawyer told her that the wording in the will 'may be taken either way', but advised her to let the matter be decided in Dilworth's favour.[21] In December he drew up a codicil, which Alice signed, 'to settle the said doubts in favour of the said Ira Dilworth.'[22] Alice was left exhausted, and with a lawyer's bill to pay. But she was relieved that 'perhaps as Ira is to get *all* the proceeds, he *may* hasten the publication of the other books.'[23]

He did. In 1953 two new Carr books appeared: *Pause: A Sketch Book*, published by Clarke, Irwin (of which W.H. Clarke was president), and *The Heart of a Peacock* by Oxford. *Pause* contained thirty sketches and accompanying verse, which Emily had written while she was in the Suffolk sanatorium, with an account of her fifteen months there written much later. The manuscript required little editorial effort from Dilworth, as he had discussed the memoir with Emily. The editing of *The Heart of a Peacock* was less straightforward. Dilworth selected what remained of the bird and Indian sketches; 'Lillies', an attempt at straight fiction; and a long series of pieces about Woo. In some cases several versions of the same story existed and Dilworth used the best portions of each. Other liberties were probably taken, which may partly account for the lack of spontaneity and brilliance in this writing. (The decision not to reprint the book speaks for itself.) Apart from arranging with Oxford for the publication of *An Address* (1955), a transcript of the talk Emily delivered at the Crystal Gardens in 1930, Dilworth did not attempt to publish the remaining contents of the trunk in his possession. It still included a delightful collection of essays entitled 'Wild Flowers', probably too short for publication; 'Hundreds and Thousands', over fifty autobiographical sketches in rough draft; numerous illustrated books of verse; and Emily's journals from 1927 to 1941.[24] When Dilworth died in 1962 he had published only a fraction of what had been left to him. The decision to publish the journals—perhaps the most interesting material remaining—then fell to Phylis Inglis, who had replaced Dean Walter Gage as Dilworth's literary executrix.[25] Mrs Inglis edited the journals, and in 1966 Clarke, Irwin brought out a selection of them called *Hundreds and Thousands*, which was the title Emily gave to her autobiographical sketches. (Emily's preface to these sketches opens *Hundreds and Thousands*. The source of both preface and title, however, is not acknowledged.) Giving Emily's immediate response to people and things, and her working-out of ideas for her writing and painting, these selections from the journals—which Emily most probably never intended for publication—reveal a far less guarded, less 'public', Emily than had appeared in her previous books.

Emily's death had come as 'a dreadful shock' to Alice, even though she had known the grave nature of her sister's illness.[26] She lived among Emily's paintings of the family garden and portraits of Billie and her father. She was soon to pay tribute to her sister by having a bridge erected in her memory in Beacon Hill Park. Three years after Emily's death, she 'still missed Millie very much', though she loved to think of her 'carrying on with her work without the pain and trouble she had here.'[27] She devoted much time to showing guests around the schoolroom where her sister had once painted, and to corresponding with Emily's former friends. She also occupied herself knitting sleeveless jerseys for child war victims; tending to her pets—a squirrel, a dog, and some birds; and partaking in the activities of the White Cane Club. (Despite an apparently successful operation in 1946, her eyesight was almost gone by 1950.) She had a daytime companion, and Willie Newcombe was a frequent visitor—until a disagreement arose between them shortly before her death. Her beloved Hennell boys, Paul and Val, also saw her frequently, and she made an occasional excursion to one of her nieces in Vancouver. In September 1951 she flew there to see the life-size portrait of Emily that formed part of a sixty-five-foot mural on the wall of a downtown bank. Stooped with arthritis, she was unable to raise her head high enough to take it in with her nearly sightless eyes. 'I saw her stockings and shoes', Alice wrote to a friend, 'but not much else.'[28]

Emily's grave had been a worry to Alice because grass did not grow on it for six years in spite of several reseedings. (This was blamed by the gardener on the birds who dusted themselves on it and scattered the seed.) Every birthday and Christmas Alice had a wreath placed on it, and on the graves of her other sisters, her brother, and her parents.

When Alice died in the autumn of 1953, ground was again broken in the family plot and the last of the Victoria Carrs was laid to rest.

Notes

1

CHILDHOOD

1871-1891

1. Provincial Archives of British Columbia [PABC], Richard Carr, Diary of Richard Carr, July 1836 - November 10, 1881, p. 94.
2. Mrs Emily Carr's illegitimacy was established from church records in Long Hanborough, Oxon: 'Baptism, 28 August 1836, Emily, daughter of Ann Saunders (single woman), Freeland.' I would like to thank the Rector of Long Hanborough, the Reverend H.D.L. Thomas, for his assistance.
3. Diary of Richard Carr, p. 84.
4. Richard V. Nicholles (son of Emily's sister Clara) to author, 21 June 1974.
5. PABC, Aural History, Imbert Orchard interview with Miss Flora Hamilton Burns, 18 May 1962.
6. PABC, Aural History, Imbert Orchard interview with Mrs Roberta Robertson, n.d.
7. Diary of Richard Carr, p. 99.
8. PABC, Aural History, Imbert Orchard interview with Mrs Robertson.
9. Emily Carr, *The Book of Small* (paperback ed; Toronto, 1966), p. 130.
10. An advertisement appeared in the *Daily British Colonist*, 2 Oct. 1883, announcing that Miss Withrow was offering lessons to 'young ladies' in oil and watercolour painting, crayon and pencil drawing.
11. Public Archives of Canada, MG 30,

D 215, Emily Carr Papers, Emily Carr to Ira Dilworth, 'Tuesday', n.d. [1942-3].
12. *Ibid.*, Unpublished journals, 'Easter Monday', 1935.
13. *Ibid.*, Unpublished journals, 1935.
14. *Ibid.*, Carr to Dilworth, 'Tuesday', n.d. [1942-3].
15. *Ibid.*, Unpublished journals, 1935.
16. *Ibid.*, Carr to Dilworth, 'Friday' [1942-3].
17. *Ibid.*, Carr to Dilworth, 12 Sept. 1943.
18. *Ibid.*, Attachment to Carr to Dilworth, 25 July 1942; Carr to Dilworth, Dec. [illeg.; 1942].

2

SAN FRANCISCO

AND UCLUELET

1891-1899

1. Emily Carr, *Growing Pains: The Autobiography of Emily Carr* (Centennial ed.; Toronto, 1971), p. 76.
2. The student registers of the California School of Design were destroyed in San Francisco's Great Fire of 1906. Emily's name appears only in the University of California's register for the fall term of 1893. I have established her arrival in San Francisco as occurring in the fall of 1891 for several reasons. Emily says in her unpublished journals that after spending five consecutive summers with the Greens following their mother's death in 1886, Dick

went east to Ridley College and she
went to San Francisco. Second,
Nellie McCormick, who began her
studies in 1891, was at the School
when Emily enrolled. Third, Emily
states that she had been in San Francisco a year when her sisters arrived;
the city directories list the Carr sisters as residents in 1892-3. The
Hayes, whom Emily calls the Pid-
dingtons in *Growing Pains*, accompanied Richard and Emily Carr from
England in 1863 and were later their
guests in Victoria.

3. California Historical Society
   Library, unidentified newspaper
   clipping, c.1878, in 'Mrs. Amelia
   Ransome Neville's Scrapbooks', vol.
   VII, p. 53.
4. Annette Rosenstein, 'Life's Not a
   Paragraph' (unpublished typescript
   in the Bancroft Library, Berkeley,
   Calif.), p. 43.
5. Public Archives of Canada, MG 30,
   D 215, Emily Carr Papers, Carr to
   Dilworth, 'Sunday', n.d.
6. Carr, *Growing Pains*, pp. 22, 33.
7. *Ibid.*, p. 49.
8. Richard (Dick) Carr was at Ridley
   College, St Catharines, Ont., from
   January to December 1892. Ridley
   College to author, 20 Mar. 1975;
   Carr Papers, Carr to Dilworth, 22
   Nov. [1942].
9. Carr, *Growing Pains*, p. 68.
10. Carr Papers, Carr to Dilworth,
    'Epistle No. II, Sunday', n.d.
11. *Ibid.*, '6 p.m. Thursday', n.d.
12. *Ibid.*, Carr to Dilworth, 'Sunday',
    n.d.
13. *Ibid.*, Unpublished journals, 'Love'.
14. *Ibid.*
15. *Ibid.*, Unpublished manuscript
    'Hundreds and Thousands', 'Smash'.
16. *Ibid.*
17. Carr, *Growing Pains*, p. 75.
18. Carr Papers, Carr to Dilworth,
    'Monday', n.d. [1942].
19. *Daily British Colonist* (Victoria), 4
    Oct. 1894, pp. 2, 3. These sketches
    were probably not unlike Emily's
    1895 pen-and-ink sketch of *Rock
    Bay Bridge* (Provincial Archives of
    British Columbia). This—along
    with pages from the sketchbook that
    are now dispersed in various private

collections—is among the few
dateable works between 1893 and
her trip to Ucluelet in 1898. Emily
contributed to the Victoria Fall Fair
in 1895 and won first prize not only
for her pen-and-ink drawings but
for pencil sketches and hand-painted
china. The *Daily Colonist* (Victoria), 18 Sept. 1895, p. 2.
20. Emily Carr, *The Book of Small*
    (Paperback ed.; Toronto, 1966), p.
    70.
21. Emily recalls in *Growing Pains* (p.
    69) that Nellie McCormick shot
    herself shortly after she returned
    from San Francisco in 1893. Nellie
    was still registered in the Mark
    Hopkins Institute of Art in 1895.
22. Sketchbook entitled by Emily 'A
    Bicycle Trip to Lake Cowichan',
    inscribed 'M. Emily Carr, July 23,
    1895'. Private collection.
23. Carr Papers, Unpublished journals,
    'Young Town & Little Girl'.
24. Emily Carr, 'Modern and Indian Art
    of the West Coast', *McGill News*,
    Supplement, June 1929, p. 20.
25. Frederick Ellsworth Walden, 'The
    Social History of Victoria, B.C.,
    1858-1871' (unpublished B.A. thesis,
    University of British Columbia,
    1951).
26. See Alexander Pope, *Essay on Man*,
    Epistle I. Emily copied from line 99
    to the end of the poem in the book
    she gave to Alice, which is now in a
    private collection.
27. Provincial Archives of British
    Columbia, A manuscript by the
    Reverend Melvyn Swartout, entitled
    'Reminiscences'.
28. The Reverend Melvyn Swartout to
    Brother John A. Logan, 25 Feb.
    1899, private collection. Note that
    the house was actually the residence
    of Swartout; but he was at Dogers
    Cove, and his wife in Alberni,
    during the late spring and summer
    when Emily was in Ucluelet. In
    February 1898 Miss Armstrong had
    lost the help of Septice, a native who
    had converted to Christianity,
    which probably brought Lizzie Carr
    to Ucluelet.
29. 31st General Assembly of the
    Presbyterian Church in Canada,

Actions and Proceedings, 1905, 'Indians in British Columbia', p. 173.

30. Emily Carr, *Klee Wyck* (Centennial ed.; Toronto, 1971), p. 4. Emily initially wrote the name as 'Chlie Wyck' (see inscribed photograph, 1901, at the Emily Carr Art Centre, Victoria). Its modern orthography would be *T'le Wek*. I am indebted to Dr Ida Halpern for this information.

31. *Ibid.*, p. 11.

32. Carr, *Growing Pains*, p. 78; Carr Papers, Carr to Dilworth, n.d.

33. Interview with Mrs Gussie Paddon, the second wife of Mayo. Feb. 1975.

34. Carr Papers, Carr to Dilworth, n.d.

3
ENGLAND
1899-1904

1. Carr to Ruth Humphrey, 3 Aug. 1937, in Humphrey, 'Letters from Emily Carr', *University of Toronto Quarterly*, vol. XLI, no. 2 (Winter 1972), p. 109.

2. Emily Carr, *Growing Pains: The Autobiography of Emily Carr* (Centennial ed.; Toronto, 1971), p. 84.

3. Richard Shone, scholar of Duncan Grant, to author, 30 July 1975.

4. John Rothenstein, *Modern English Painters* (London, 1957), p. 290.

5. Provincial Archives of British Columbia [PABC], William Newcombe Papers, Royal Architectural Museum, London, Westminster School of Art Receipt of Registration, 19 Sept. 1899.

6. Public Archives of Canada [PAC], MG 30, D 215, Emily Carr Papers, Unpublished manuscript, 'Hundreds and Thousands', 'Smoking with a Cow'.

7. Mrs Marion Redden is the Mrs Radcliffe in *Growing Pains*.

8. Mrs John A. Farmer to author, Apr. 1977.

9. Mrs Mortimer is the Mrs Denny in *Growing Pains*. Edward Blake established Frederick Redden and Sammy Blake as barristers in an office on Victoria Street, Westminster. The bulk of the practice consisted of looking after Canadian lawyers in London on Privy Council appeals. Mrs A. Armstrong (niece of Sammy Blake) to author, Apr. 1979.

10. Joseph Schull, *Edward Blake: Leader in Exile, 1881-1912* (Toronto, 1976), p. 197.

11. Emily Carr Art Centre, Victoria, Carr to Mrs Frederick Radcliffe, 13 Mar. [1940].

12. Referred to in *Growing Pains* as 'Mildred Compton'. Mrs Lettice Arnote kindly provided details of the Crompton-Roberts family in a letter to the author, 15 July 1975.

13. Carr to Humphrey, 10 Aug. [1937], 'Letters from Emily Carr', p. 110; Carr, *Growing Pains*, p. 91.

14. Richard V. Nicholles to author, 21 June 1974.

15. Carr, *Growing Pains*, p. 214.

16. Emily writes that she was in Scotland one Christmas and during one of her summer breaks. The family she visited may have been that of Polly Anderson (see Carr Papers, Unpublished journals), with whom she later corresponded, or that of a Miss Grant (Mrs Emily English to author, 20 July 1975), about whom the author could find no further information.

17. Carr, *Growing Pains*, p. 137.

18. Note from Emily, 2 Jan. 1900, pasted in William 'Mayo' Paddon's Bible. Private possession.

19. Inscribed in *ibid.*

20. Carr, *Growing Pains*, pp. 140-3.

21. *Ibid.*, p. 142.

22. Inscribed in Paddon Bible.

23. Mayo Paddon, 'Private Journal, 1901', 17 Jan. 1901, p. 6. Private possession.

24. *Ibid.*, 31 Mar. 1901, p. 26.

25. *Ibid.*, 31 Jan. 1901, p. 10.

26. *Ibid.*, 18 Mar. 1901, p. 15.

27. *Ibid.*, 7 Apr. 1901, p. 28.

28. *Ibid.*, 29 May 1901, p. 43.

29. *Ibid.*, 7 Apr. 1901, p. 28.

30. Emily Carr, *Hundreds and Thousands: The Journals of Emily Carr* (Toronto, 1966), p. 163 (1 Jan. 1935).

31. *Ibid.*

32. *Ibid.*, p. 164.

33. *Ibid.*, p. 163.

34. *Ibid.*, p. 85 (28 Nov. 1933).

35. Emily told Carol Pearson that the man to whom she had been promised never returned from the Boer War—likely a reference to Sammy Blake, who went to South Africa around 1900-1 (not as a soldier but to accompany his father) and whom Emily probably never saw again. (Interview with Carol Pearson, Sept. 1974.) See also Pearson, *Emily Carr As I Knew Her* (Toronto, 1954), pp. 54-5.

36. Carr Papers, illustrated poem in handbound book, 'Student Life in London'.

37. *Week* (Victoria), 17 Feb. 1905, p. 1.

38. Carr, *Growing Pains*, p. 157.

39. *Ibid.*

40. *St. Ives Weekly Summary*, 10 Aug. 1901.

41. Florence K. and Bertha Upton used the grotesque black doll, the golliwogg, for a series of illustrated children's books, *The Adventures of Two Dutch Dolls and a Golliwogg*, which first appeared in 1885, published by Longmans, Green, London. The style of printing, as well as the pen-and-ink-outline and coloured drawings in the Uptons' books, may have served as a model for Emily's sketch and verse.

42. See the untitled poems in the St Ives sketchbook among the Carr Papers at the PAC.

43. Carr, *Growing Pains*, p. 168.

44. *Ibid.*, p. 173.

45. A.G. Falliott Stokes, 'The Landscape Paintings of Mr. Algernon M. Talmage', *International Studio*, 33 (Jan. 1908), p. 188.

46. Carr, *Growing Pains*, p. 173.

47. *Ibid.*, p. 176.

48. Herbert von Herkommer, 'Preface', in Lucy E. Kemp-Welch, *In the Open Country* (London, 1905), p. 11.

49. Carr Papers, 'Bushey Sketch book'.

50. Carr, *Growing Pains*, p. 176.

51. Carr Papers, Carr to Dilworth, n.d.

52. Carr, *Growing Pains*, pp. 182-3.

53. *Ibid.*, p. 183.

54. *Ibid.*, p. 184.

55. Schull, *Edward Blake*, p. 219.

56. Jane Walker Hospital, formerly the East Anglia Sanatorium, Essex, 'Register of Patients', p. 24.

57. *Ibid.*

58. Pierre Janet, *The Major Symptoms of Hysteria* (New York, 1920), p. 10; Carroll Smith-Rosenberg, 'The Hysterical Woman: Sex Roles and Role Conflict in 19th-Century America', *Social Research*, vol. 2 (1972), pp. 652, 660, 662-3.

59. Carr, *Growing Pains*, p. 190.

60. Angus MacPhail, 'A Survey of Shock-Therapy', Institution of Electronics, *Proceedings*, vol. 14 (1949), p. 31.

61. Carr, *Growing Pains*, p. 191.

62. Jane H. Walker, *A Book for Every Woman* (London, 1897), p. 47.

63. The medical officer in charge during Emily's confinement was Miss Ethel Maud Stacy and the Matron, Miss Ethel Lewis. Dr D.F. van Zwanenberg to author, 28 May 1974: Emily wrote variously of Dr McNair and Dr McGregor, but her descriptions of them do not match their life models. See Emily's account of sanatorium life in Emily Carr, *Pause: A Sketch Book* (Centennial ed.; Toronto, 1972); Carr to Humphrey, 14 Jan. 1938, in 'Letters from Emily Carr', p. 118.

64. Emily Carr, *Pause: A Sketch Book* (Centennial ed.; Toronto, 1972), p. 3.

65. *Familiar Wild Birds* (London, 1901), inscribed on fly leaf as 'The gift of "Crummie" (Mildred Crompton Roberts)'. Private possession.

66. Carr, *Pause*, p. 61.

67. *Ibid.*, p. 43. There are two versions of the fate of her birds. In *Growing Pains* (p. 190) and *Pause* (p. 148), Emily says that she chloroformed them when her 'severe' treatments began. In *The Heart of a Peacock* (Toronto, 1953; p. 74) she suggests that some survived: 'only one pair of my bullfinches got out to Canada with me.'

68. Carr, *Growing Pains*, p. 192. These verses appear in *Pause*.

69. Carr, *Growing Pains*, p. 193.

4
VANCOUVER
1904-1910

1. Ms Jocelyn Carew-Gibson to author, 16 Feb. 1977.
2. Emily Carr, *Growing Pains: The Autobiography of Emily Carr* (Centennial ed.; Toronto, 1971), p. 200.
3. *Ibid.*, p. 197.
4. Public Archives of Canada, MG 30, D 215, Carr Papers, Unpublished manuscript 'Hundreds and Thousands', 'Smoking with the Cow'.
5. *Ibid.*, Unpublished journals.
6. *Ibid.*
7. *Week* (Victoria), 17 Feb. 1905, p. 1.
8. *Ibid.*
9. *Ibid.*
10. *Daily Colonist* (Victoria), 2 Sept. 1905, p. 6.
11. 'The Vancouver Ladies' Art Club' is Emily's phrase; there are no records to indicate its membership or purpose.
12. *Greater Vancouver Illustrated* (Vancouver, n.d. [1908]), n.p.
13. *Daily News-Advertiser* (Vancouver), 16 Oct. 1904, p. 5.
14. Carr, *Growing Pains*, p. 206.
15. *Daily News-Advertiser* (Vancouver), 30 Jan. 1906, p. 6.
16. Interviews with Mrs M. Daniells, spring 1975, and Mrs Irene Rogers, fall 1974; correspondence with Mrs Pauline Taylor, Apr. 1975, and Mrs Mary Cherniavsky, Oct. 1975. All were pupils of Emily in Vancouver.
17. Mrs Mary Cherniavsky to author, 19 Oct. 1975.
18. Interview with Mrs M. Daniells, spring 1975.
19. Mrs Pauline Taylor to author, 14 Apr. 1975.
20. Interview with Mrs M. Daniells, spring 1975.
21. *Province* (Vancouver), 30 Mar. 1907, p. 28.
22. *Ibid.*, 1 Apr. 1908, p. 9.
23. *Ibid.*, 31 Mar. 1909, p. 9.
24. *Ibid.*, 1 Apr. 1908, p. 9.
25. Emily Carr, *Hundreds and Thousands: The Journals of Emily Carr* (Toronto, 1966,) p. 284 (14 Mar. 1937).
26. Carr Papers, Carr to Dilworth, n.d.
27. Register of Vancouver Tax Records, vol. I, p. 116. The assessed value of the five lots was $750 and the yearly taxes were $45.
28. Carr Papers, Unpublished journals.
29. *Ibid.*
30. *Province* (Vancouver), 24 Apr. 1909, p. 3 and 13 Oct. 1909, p. 12.
31. Carr Papers, Carr to Dilworth, 'Saturday Night', n.d.
32. Michael S. Kennedy, 'Alaska's Artists: Theodore J. Richardson', *Alaska Journal*, 3 (Winter 1973), p. 40.
33. Carr Papers, Unpublished journals.
34. *Victoria Times*, 28 Sept. 1910, p. 7.
35. Wilson Duff, *The Indian History of British Columbia*, Vol. I: *The Impact of the White Man* (Memoir Number 5; Victoria, Provincial Museum of British Columbia, 1964), p. 84.
36. Carr Papers, Unpublished journals.
37. Interview with Miss Grace Judge, Aug. 1974.
38. *Ibid.*
39. *Province* (Vancouver), 26 June 1909, p. 3; Bernard McEvoy, 'Art in British Columbia', *Opportunities*, 24 (Dec. 1910), p. 24.
40. Judge interview; Mrs Mary Cherniavsky to author, 19 Oct. 1974.
41. Mrs Pauline Taylor to author, 13 Apr. 1975; Judge interview.
42. Carr Papers, Unpublished journals.
43. *Ibid.*; Vancouver City Archives, Parks Board, Stanley Park files, Superintendent Report II, 12 Aug. 1908, p. 2, reports the donation of a vulture, probably 'Uncle Tom', by Emily.
44. Carr Papers, 'Billie's Calendar, 1909' ('written' by Billy).
45. Emily Carr, 'Bill', an illustrated poem. Private collection.
46. Interview with Mrs Tina Cole, a young friend of Sophie's, May 1974.
47. Carr Papers, Unpublished journals.
48. Interview with Mrs Faith Halse, a niece of Ann Batchelor, spring 1974.
49. Mrs Pauline Taylor to author, 13 Apr. 1975; interview with Mrs M. Daniells, spring 1975; *Province* (Vancouver), 10 June 1910, p. 5.

5
FRANCE
1910-1911

1. Public Archives of Canada, MG 30,
   D 215, Carr Papers, 'Sister and I
   from Victoria to London'. Sketchbook [1910].
2. Emily Carr, *Growing Pains: The
   Autobiography of Emily Carr*
   (Centennial ed.; Toronto, 1971), p.
   215.
3. *Ibid.*, p. 216.
4. *Ibid.*
5. William Gaunt, *The March of the
   Moderns* (London, 1949), p. 97.
6. Lucy Carrington Wertheim, *Adventure in Art* (London, 1947), pp.
   32, 33.
7. Gertrude Stein, *The Autobiography
   of Alice B. Toklas* (New York,
   1960), p. 117.
8. Sir Alfred Rose, 'Gertrude Stein and
   Painting', unidentified clipping in
   Lucy Wertheim Papers. Private
   possession.
9. Wertheim, *Adventure in Art*, p. 31.
10. C. Holland, 'Lady Art Students in
    Paris', *International Studio*, 21
    (1904), p. 228.
11. André Salmon, *Modigliani: A
    Memoir* (London, 1961), p. 105.
12. The Fine Art Society, *J.D. Fer-
    gusson, 1874-1961* (London, 1974),
    n.p.
13. Haldane Macfall, 'The Paintings of
    John D. Fergusson, R.B.A.', *In-
    ternational Studio*, 31 (May 1907),
    p. 207.
14. The Fine Art Society, *J.D. Fer-
    gusson, 1874-1961*, n.p.
15. Art Gallery of Ontario, John Kyle to
    Charles Scott, 15 July 1945.
16. Interview with Flora Hamilton
    Burns, Apr. 1974.
17. Stein, *The Autobiography of Alice
    B. Toklas*, p. 140.
18. Emily Carr, speech at Crystal
    Gardens, Victoria, 4 Mar. 1930, in
    Emily Carr, *Fresh Seeing: Two
    Addresses* (Toronto, 1972), p. 1.
19. Carr, *Growing Pains*, p. 221.
20. E.H. McCormick, *The Expatriate:
    A Study of Frances Hodgkins &
    New Zealand* (Wellington, 1954), p.
    126.
21. Alexander Turnbull Library,
    Wellington, New Zealand. Frances
    Hodgkins to Mrs Rachel Hodgkins,
    27 Nov. 1911.
22. C. Hay Thomson, 'An Artist of the
    Moderns', *Everylady's Journal* (Mel-
    bourne), 6 Jan. 1913, p. 12.
23. Alexander Turnbull Library,
    Wellington, New Zealand, Frances
    Hodgkins to Mrs Rachel Hodgkins,
    27 Nov. 1911.
24. McCormick, *The Expatriate*, pp.
    132-3.
25. Anthony S.G. Green, 'Reflections
    on the Hodgkins Exhibition', *Ac-
    cent*, 5 (Dec. 1969), pp. 29, 43.
26. McCormick, *The Expatriate*, p. 141.
27. E.H. McCormick interview with
    Miss Hannah Ritchie, a student of
    Frances Hodgkins in Concarneau in
    the summer of 1911, Apr. 1955. I am
    indebted to Dr McCormick, who is
    soon to publish a biography of
    Frances Hodgkins, for his generous
    sharing of his notes.
28. Raymond Nancenta, *School of Paris*
    (London, 1960), p. 49.
29. Société du Salon d'Automne,
    *L'Exposition de 1911: Catalogue des
    Ouvrages de Peinture, Sculpture,
    Dessin, Gravure, Architecture et
    Art Décoratif* (Paris, 1911), p. 77.

6
VANCOUVER AND
THE NORTH
1911-1913

1. Interview with Mrs Molly Underhill,
   spring 1974.
2. *Province* (Vancouver), 25 Mar.
   1912, p. 8.
3. *Saturday Sunset* (Vancouver), 30
   Mar. 1912, p. 12.
4. *Province* (Vancouver), 27 Mar.
   1912, p. 13.
5. *Ibid.*
6. *Ibid.*, 8 Apr. 1912, p. 5.
7. Interview with Miss Grace Judge,
   Feb. 1977.
8. *Province* (Vancouver), 'Against
   French Art', 3 Apr. 1912, p. 12.
9. *Province* (Vancouver), 8 Apr. 1912,
   p. 5.

10. H.N.W. Toms to author, 2 Apr. 1974.

11. Interview with Miss Grace Judge, Aug. 1974.

12. Emily Carr, *Hundreds and Thousands: The Journals of Emily Carr* (Toronto, 1966), p. 160.

13. In January 1912 Emily sold the five Hastings townsite lots she had purchased in 1909. She made a nice profit of $575, part of which was no doubt used for this trip. Deed of Land No. 92759 dated 15 Jan. 1912, Vancouver Land Registry Office. A note about Emily's excursion in the *Queen Charlotte Islander* (Prince Rupert), 22 July 1912, refers to her being 'on the staff' of the Grand Trunk Pacific while she was on her sketching trip.

14. In her unpublished autobiography (Public Archives of Canada, Emily Carr Papers), Emily refers to Grier's visit as being in 1913; it was more likely in 1912. Emily could have met Grier in London through Sammy Blake, a boyhood friend.

15. *Queen Charlotte Islander* (Prince Rupert), 22 July 1912, p. 2.

16. Harold Sands, 'The White Man's Angry Heart', *Canadian Magazine*, 34 (Jan. 1910), p. 276.

17. Public Archives of Canada, MG 30, D 215, Emily Carr Papers, Notes from Apr. 1913 talk at Drummond Hall.

18. Muriel Brewster, 'Some Ladies Prefer Indians', *Toronto Star Weekly*, 21 Jan. 1928, p. 52.

19. Carr Papers, Notes from Apr. 1913 talk at Drummond Hall.

20. Emily Carr, 'Modern and Indian Art of the West Coast', *McGill News*, Supplement to June 1929, p. 4.

21. Carr does refer to Clara Russ as 'Clara' in 'Two Women and an Infant Gull', *The Heart of a Peacock* (Toronto, 1953), p. 62.

22. Emily Carr, *Klee Wyck* (Centennial ed.; Toronto, 1971), p. 63.

23. Carr Papers, Unpublished journals.

24. Compare the watercolour *Tsatsisnukwomi Tribe, Klawatsis* (illustrated), with the intervening photograph 'Kwakiutl Village of Tsatsisnukwomi' (illustrated) and the finished oil painting *Kwakiutl House* (Vancouver Art Gallery, 42.3.33) to see the use of a photograph to define in oil the base figures of the left and right outside columns that are missing from the watercolour sketch.

25. *Daily News-Advertiser* (Vancouver), 15 Sept. 1912, p. 19. The article also quoted Emily as saying she was 'hoping to have some of her sketches of the B.C. totem poles hung . . . in the Salon . . . next year', but she apparently never again referred to this as an eventuality.

26. *Province* (Vancouver), 14 Sept. 1912, p. 8.

27. *Vancouver Sun*, 10 Oct. 1912, p. 3.

28. *Province* (Vancouver), 12 Oct. 1912, p. 42.

29. Provincial Museum of British Columbia, Curatorial Files, Carr to H.E. Young, n.d.

30. *Ibid.*, Young to Carr, 7 Nov. 1912.

31. *Ibid.*, Carr to Newcombe, n.d. [Sunday, autumn 1912].

32. *Ibid.*, C.F. Newcombe to Kermode, 17 Jan. 1913.

33. Provincial Archives of British Columbia, C.F. Newcombe Papers, Carr to Newcombe, 'Sunday', n.d.; Lt G.T. Emmons to Newcombe, 25 Mar. 1914; Philip Drucker to W.A. Newcombe, 14 Dec. [1935].

34. *The Home of the Salish and Dené* (Toronto, 1907).

35. Carr Papers, 'Lecture on Totems', Apr. 1913.

36. *Province* (Vancouver), 16 Apr. 1913, p. 13.

37. Provincial Museum, Curatorial Files, Carr to Young, n.d.

38. Carr Papers, 'Lecture on Totems', Apr. 1913.

7

CHRYSALIS
1913-1927

1. *Daily Colonist* (Victoria), 25 Oct. 1913, p. 17.

2. Public Archives of Canada, MG 30, D 215, Emily Carr Papers, 'Friday Night', n.d.

3. Provincial Archives of British Columbia [PABC], Flora Hamilton Burns, 'Emily Carr An Immortal of Canada' (typescript, 1966), p. 12.

4. *Victoria Times*, 'Arts and Crafts Exhibition', 18 Oct. 1913, p. 11.

5. *Daily Colonist* (Victoria), 19 Oct. 1913, p. 16.

6. Emily Carr, *The House of All Sorts* (Centennial ed.; Toronto, 1971), p. 92.

7. Edythe Hembroff-Schleicher, *Emily Carr: The Untold Story* (Saanichton, B.C., 1978), p. 66.

8. See PABC, Newcombe Papers, where Emily transcribed portions of James Deans, *Tales From the Totems of the Hidery* (Chicago, International Folk-Lore Association, 1899). Crest and tatoo symbols were copied from texts such as James G. Swan, *The Haida Indians of the Queen Charlotte Islands* (Washington, Smithsonian Institution, 1874).

9. Emily Carr, *Klee Wyck* (Centennial ed.; Toronto, 1971), p. 6.

10. *Daily Colonist* (Victoria), 25 Oct. 1916, p. 8.

11. PABC, Aural History, Imbert Orchard interview with Mrs Kate Mather, 20 June 1962.

12. Interview with the late Mrs A.G. Cowie, Oct. 1973.

13. PABC, Aural History, Orchard interview with Mrs Mather.

14. Interview with Mrs Elizabeth Ross about her late husband, William Ross, Aug. 1975.

15. Carr, *House of All Sorts*, p. 9.

16. PABC, Aural History, Orchard interview with Mrs Mather.

17. Emily Carr, *Growing Pains: The Autobiography of Emily Carr* (Centennial ed; Toronto, 1971), p. 230.

18. Carr Papers, Carr to Dilworth, n.d.

19. Flora Hamilton Burns on 'CBC Wednesday Night', 9 Apr. 1958. Typescript in private possession.

20. Carr Papers, Carr to Dilworth, 22 Dec. [no year]. In recounting the incident, Emily refers to Mayo as 'Martyn'—the same name she uses for him in *Growing Pains*.

21. *Ibid.*, Carr to Dilworth, Dec. 1942.

Emily wrote to Mayo Paddon in 1936 and learned from him that he had remarried after twenty-six years of 'bachelorhood' and had an eighteen-month-old son. He also told her that he still loved her. (Emily Carr, *Hundreds and Thousands: The Journal of Emily Carr*, Toronto, 1966, p. 223.) Mrs Gussie Paddon has told the author that she remembers her husband receiving this letter.

22. Carr, *The House of All Sorts*, p. 144.

23. *Ibid.*, p. 129.

24. *Ibid.*, p. 148.

25. *Ibid.*, p. 122.

26. 'Closing Kennels', an advertisement in the *Daily Colonist* (Victoria), 3 Aug. 1921, p. 12.

27. Emily contributed cartoons to the *Western Woman's Weekly* from 20 Dec. 1917 to 4 Oct. 1919.

28. *Western Woman's Weekly* (4 Apr. 1918), p. 1.

29. *Ibid.* (9 Nov. 1918), p. 3.

30. Mrs Elizabeth Ross to author, 10 Mar. 1975.

31. Interview with Mrs J.A. Burchett, spring 1977.

32. Emily Carr Art Centre, Victoria, Emily Carr to Mrs Frederick Redden, 9 Dec. 1923; interview with Flora Hamilton Burns, 1973.

33. Emily Carr Art Centre, Emily Carr to Frederick Redden, Sept. 1924.

34. National Gallery of Canada [NGC], H. Mortimer Lamb to Eric Brown, 24 Oct. 1921.

35. Art Gallery of Ontario, H. Mortimer Lamb to Barbara Swann, 14 July 1945 and 2 Aug. 1945.

36. NGC, Lamb to Brown, 24 Oct. 1921.

37. *Ibid.*, Brown to Lamb, 23 Nov. 1921.

38. A.Y. Jackson, *A Painter's Country: The Autobiography of A.Y. Jackson* (Toronto, 1964), p. 113.

39. *Daily Colonist* (Victoria), 26 June 1921, p. 3.

40. Letter from Eric Brown to the British Columbia Art League, cited in Vancouver City Archives, British Columbia Art League, Minutes, 13 Mar. 1925.

41. *Province* (Vancouver), 8 Feb. 1925, p. 19.
42. Interview with Mrs Viola Patterson, Oct. 1975; Mrs Patterson to author, 5 Oct. 1973.
43. Mrs Viola Patterson to author, 5 Oct. 1973.
44. *Modern French Painters* (London, 1923). Emily's copy is inscribed 'M. Emily Carr, Victoria, B.C., January-March 1924'. Private possession.
45. *Ibid.*, p. 31.
46. *Ibid.*, p. 33.
47. *Ibid.*, pp. 80-1.
48. *Some Work of the Group of Twelve* (Seattle, 1937), n.p.
49. Emily Carr Art Centre, Victoria, Emily Carr to Frederick Redden, Sept. 1924.
50. *Seattle Post-Intelligencer*, 4 Apr. 1924, p. 13.
51. *Daily Colonist* (Victoria), 24 Oct. 1924, p. 12; see also PABC, *Fifteenth Annual Exhibition of the Island Arts and Crafts Society*, 20-5 Oct. 1924.
52. *Catalogue of the 48th Annual Exhibition of the San Francisco Art Association at the California Palace of the Legion of Honor*, no. 82, Apr.-June 1925.
53. *Seattle Post-Intelligencer*, 6 Mar. 1925, p. 12.
54. *Daily Colonist* (Victoria), 17 Aug. 1926, p. 5.
55. Vancouver City Archives, British Columbia Art League, Minute Book, Gallery Committee, 26 Oct. and 25 Nov. 1926.
56. *Ibid.*, 9 Dec. 1926.
57. *Province* (Vancouver), 22 Oct. 1926, p. 15.
58. Extract from a letter from Emily Carr to Marius Barbeau, 23 Oct. [1926]; Marius Barbeau Collection, Canadian Centre for Folk Culture Studies, National Museum of Man, National Museums of Canada, Ottawa.
59. *Ibid.*, Carr to Barbeau, 3 Nov. [1927]. Emily refers here to Barbeau's having written to her the previous year.
60. PABC, Island Arts and Crafts Society, *Sixteenth Annual Exhibition*, 1925.
61. Mrs Kate Mather to Mrs C.S. Band, 21 Nov. 1956. In possession of Mrs C.S. Band.
62. Carr, *Growing Pains*, p. 231.
63. *Ibid.*
64. PABC, Aural History, Orchard interview with Mrs Mather.
65. N. de Bertrand Lugrin, 'Women Potters and Indian Themes', *Maclean's Magazine*, 15 Mar. 1927, pp. 7, 9.
66. Carr Papers, Carr to Dilworth, 'Saturday Night', n.d.
67. Carol Pearson, née Williams, recalls that it was 1917 when she, her parents, and brother Brock, moved to Victoria (letter to author, 8 Jan. 1976). Captain Williams does not appear in the Victoria directories until 1920 and I have no evidence of Carol Williams' having resided in B.C. before 1921. Ms. Margaret Glide of Queen Margaret's School, Duncan, informed me (16 Feb. 1976) that Carol Williams' name appears in the register for September 1921. Alice reopened her St Andrew's Street school in September 1922—when the Hennell family, with whom she was employed, moved to New Jersey—and it is probable that Carol and Brock Williams boarded there during the summer of 1922.
68. Carr Papers, Carr to Dilworth, n.d.
69. *Ibid.*, Carr to Dilworth, 'Friday Morning', n.d.
70. *Ibid.*, Carr to Dilworth, 'Saturday Night', n.d. [1942].
71. Flora Hamilton Burns, 'Emily Carr', in Mary Quayle Innis, ed., *The Clear Spirit: Twenty Canadian Women and Their Times* (Toronto, The Canadian Federation of University Women, 1967), p. 231.
72. *Emily Carr As I Knew Her* (Toronto, 1954). I am grateful to Carol Pearson for her recollections, and for the use of her collection of Emily Carr letters. Interviews with author: spring 1974, autumn 1975.
73. Thomas J.W. Nute to author, 11 Feb. 1975.

8
DISCOVERY
AND ITS EFFECTS
1927-1929

1. *Daily Colonist* (Victoria), 14 Sept. 1927, p. 1.
2. National Gallery of Canada [NGC], *Exhibition of Canadian West Coast Art* (Ottawa, 1927), p. 2. The exhibition moved from the National Gallery to the Art Gallery of Toronto, then to the Art Association of Montreal.
3. Public Archives of Canada, [PAC] Lawren Harris Papers, 'Fine Canadian Art for Public Institutions', *Toronto Daily Star*, clipping in Harris scrapbook, VI (1922-60), Feb. 1927.
4. Marius Barbeau, 'The Canadian Northwest', *Magazine of Art*, 24 (Mar. 1932), p. 331.
5. NGC, *Exhibition of Canadian West Coast Art*, p. 2.
6. Art Gallery of Ontario, Barbeau to G.R. Grieg, 23 Feb. 1927.
7. F. Maud Brown, *Breaking Barriers: Eric Brown and the National Gallery* ([Toronto,] Society for Art Publications, 1964), p. 103.
8. *Ibid.*; Brown to author, 11 Jan. 1976; interview with Mrs Brown, Sept. 1974.
9. *Daily Colonist* (Victoria), 14 Sept. 1927, p. 1.
10. NGC, Brown to McCurry, 17 Sept. 1927.
11. NGC, Barbeau to Brown, 3 Oct. 1927. Walter Walker accompanied Marius Barbeau to the Inlander Hotel in Hazelton in the autumn of 1927. In an interview (June 1974), he recalled that this was the first time either he or Barbeau had seen the work of Emily Carr.
12. Glenbow-Alberta Institute, Marjorie Dallas interview with Walter J. Phillips, 1962.
13. National Museums of Canada, National Museum of Man, Canadian Centre for Folk Culture Studies, Marius Barbeau Collection [hereafter Barbeau Papers], Barbeau to Jackson, 4 Nov. 1927.

14. NGC, Carr to Brown, 1 Nov. 1927.
15. F.B. Housser, *A Canadian Art Movement* (Toronto, 1926), p. 146.
16. *Ibid.*, p. 24.
17. *Ibid.*, p. 40.
18. *Province* (Vancouver), 8 Apr. 1912, p. 5.
19. Emily Carr, *Hundreds and Thousands: The Journals of Emily Carr* (Toronto, 1966), p. 3 (10 Nov. 1927).
20. Carl F. Schaefer to author, 21 Dec. 1975.
21. Carr, *Hundreds and Thousands*, p. 5 (14 Nov. 1927).
22. *Ibid.*, p. 6 (16 Nov. 1927).
23. *Ibid.*, p. 6 (17 Nov. 1927) and p. 7 (18 Nov. 1927).
24. *Province* (Vancouver), 8 Apr. 1912, p. 5; Carr, *Hundreds and Thousands*, p. 7 (17 Nov. 1927).
25. Carr, *Hundreds and Thousands*, p. 7 (17 Nov. 1927).
26. *Ibid.*, p. 8 (18 Nov. 1927).
27. *Ibid.*, p. 10 (22 Nov. 1927).
28. *Ibid.*
29. *Ibid.*, p. 11 (27 Nov. 1927).
30. *Ibid.*, p. 12 (5 Dec. 1927).
31. Interview with Nan Cheney, 16 Oct. 1973.
32. *Ibid.*, p. 11 (5 Dec. 1927).
33. *Ibid.*, p. 12 (5 Dec. 1927).
34. Provincial Archives of British Columbia [PABC], Edythe Hembroff-Schleicher Papers, Carr to Hembroff-Brand, n.d. [Sept. 1938].
35. Carr, *Hundreds and Thousands*, p. 13 ('Montreal').
36. See: Madam Blavatsky, *The Secret Doctrine* (London, 1928).
37. Lawren Harris, 'Art and Life', CBC 'Science and Art' typescript, 31 Mar. 1921. Author's copy.
38. Carr, *Hundreds and Thousands*, pp. 17-18 (12 Dec. 1927).
39. *Ibid.*, p. 16 (12 Dec. 1927).
40. *Ibid.*, p. 17 (13 Dec. 1927).
41. Housser, *A Canadian Art Movement*, p. 15.
42. Lawren Harris, 'Art in Canada: An Informal History', CBC Wednesday Night (typescript), 21 June 1950.
43. Carr, *Hundreds and Thousands*, p. 5 (14 Nov. 1927).
44. NGC, Brown to Carr, 14 Jan. 1928 (copy).

45. Barbeau Papers, Barbeau to Carr, 11 Jan. 1928 (copy).
46. *Ibid.*, Carr to Barbeau, 22 Jan. 1928.
47. Emily Carr, *Growing Pains: The Autobiography of Emily Carr* (Centennial ed.; Toronto, 1971), p. 237.
48. PAC, MG 30, D 215, Emily Carr Papers, Harris to Carr, n.d. [probably Mar. 1930].
49. The National Gallery purchased three pre-1912 watercolours: *House Post, Tsatsisnukwomi; Gitwangak;* and *Alert Bay.* Barbeau and the Museum each bought one painting. Emily received a total of $425.
50. Muriel Brewster, 'Some Ladies Prefer Indians', *Toronto Star Weekly*, 21 Jan. 1928, p. 52.
51. NGC, Carr to Brown, 29 Apr. 1928.
52. Barbeau Papers, Carr to Barbeau, 12 Feb. [1928].
53. NGC, Carr to Brown, 11 Aug. 1928.
54. Barbeau Papers, Carr to Barbeau, 12 Feb. 1928.
55. Walter Walker interview, June 1974.
56. In 1905-6 the Indians of Kitwancool played an active part, with other Gitksan villagers, in resisting the attempts of the Federal Fisheries Department to restrict their fishing. In both 1909 and 1911 they expelled a group of provincial land surveyors from their valley; this was why Emily was warned not to go there in 1912. Reuben Ware, 'A Sketching Trip to the North Coast, 1928: A Letter by Emily Carr (1871-1945)'. Research paper for History 899, History Department, Simon Fraser University.
57. NGC, Carr to Brown, 11 Aug. 1928.
58. Carr, *Growing Pains*, p. 237.
59. Canada, *Sessional Papers*, 1929, no. 26, 'Report of the Deputy Superintendent General of Indian Affairs', p. 9.
60. Emily Carr, *Klee Wyck* (Toronto, 1941), p. 102.
61. NGC, Carr to Brown, 11 Aug. 1928.
62. Ina D.D. Uhthoff, typescript memoirs, n.d. Private possession.
63. NGC, Carr to Brown, 1 Oct. [1928].
64. NGC, Tobey to Buchanan, n.d. [received 15 Apr. 1957].
65. This painting is no longer extant.
66. See Paul S. Wingert's fine discussion on the art of the pole in his 'Tshimshian Sculpture', in Viola E. Garfield and Wingert, *The Tshimshian Indians and Their Arts* (Seattle, Wash., 1966).
67. See Maria Tippett, 'Emily Carr's "Blunden Harbour" ', in NGC, *The Bulletin*, No. 25 (1975), pp. 33-7. Another example of Emily's use of a photograph for a painting of a village she never visited is *Heina* (about 1928, NGC), which an x-ray has revealed to be an overpainting of a literal copy of an 1884 photograph by Richard Maynard, now in the possession of the Provincial Museum of British Columbia.
68. Interview with Mrs Viola Patterson, Oct. 1975; interview with Philip Amsden, Aug. 1975.
69. Carr Papers, Unpublished journals, 24 Nov. 1930.
70. NGC, Tobey to Buchanan, n.d. [received 15 Apr. 1957].
71. Carr Papers, Harris to Carr, n.d. [Mar. 1929].

9
SPIRIT AND THE LAND
1929-1933

1. Public Archives of Canada, MG 30, D 215, Emily Carr Papers, Harris to Carr, n.d. [1929].
2. Emily Carr, *Growing Pains: The Autobiography of Emily Carr* (Centennial ed.; Toronto 1971), p. 254.
3. *Ibid.*
4. Carr Papers, Unpublished journals, Port Hardy, summer 1930.
5. *Ibid.*
6. Carr Papers, 'Renfrew, August 14, 1929'.
7. Emily Carr to C.S. Band, 17 Apr. 1937. In possession of Mrs C.S. Band.
8. Emily Carr, *Hundreds and Thousands: The Journals of Emily Carr* (Toronto, 1966), p. 287 (17 Apr. 1937).
9. It seems that Emily did not go to Washington, D.C.

10. Interview with Yvonne McKague Housser, Oct. 1974.
11. Artist clipping file, National Gallery of Canada Library, undated [May 1930].
12. Interview with Mrs Doris Spiers, Sept. 1974.
13. Edythe Hembroff-Schleicher, *Emily Carr: The Untold Story* (Saanichton, B.C., 1978), p. 88.
14. Carr, *Growing Pains*, p. 242.
15. Yvonne McKague Housser interview.
16. Carr, *Hundreds and Thousands*, p. 22 (26 Nov. 1930). Georgia O'Keeffe's *Lawrence Pine Tree, with Stars* likely influenced Emily's untitled painting of the same subject (VAG, 42.3.166).
17. *Koskimo*, a charcoal sketch (VAG, 42.3.119); a watercolour, *Zunoqua* (VAG, 42.3.101), and an oil, *Zunoqua of the Cat Village* (VAG, 42.3.21) of 1932-3.
18. Carr Papers, Carr to Dilworth, 'Epistle No. I, 14th February'.
19. *Ibid.*, Harris to Carr, 'Day after Christmas' [probably 1930].
20. University of British Columbia Library [UBCL], Nan Lawson Cheney Papers, Carr to Cheney, 22 Dec. 1940.
21. Carr Papers, Harris to Carr, 4 Nov. 1932.
22. Carr, *Hundreds and Thousands*, p. 86 (8 Dec. 1933); Carr Papers, Unpublished journals, 22 May 1931.
23. Cheney Papers, Carr to Cheney, 20 Mar. 1932.
24. *Ibid.*, Carr to Cheney, 15 Mar. 1938; Carr, *Hundreds and Thousands*, p. 71 (31 Oct. 1933); Carr to Humphrey, 25 Apr. 1938, in Ruth Humphrey, 'Letters from Emily Carr', *University of Toronto Quarterly*, XLI, no. 2 (Winter 1972) p. 128.
25. Cheney Papers, Carr to Cheney, 20 Mar. 1932.
26. Interview with Dr Emma M. Smiley, fall 1974. Dr Smiley was closely associated with the Unity Centre at this time.
27. Carr Papers, Unpublished journals, 22 May 1931.
28. Christina M. Killen, 'The New Cycle Philosophy', typescript (n.p., n.d.), Lesson I, p. 2. Notes handed out to students attending the New Cycle Philosophy Course. Private possession, Victoria.
29. *Ibid.*, Lesson VIII, p. 1.
30. *Ibid.*, Lesson V, p. 2.
31. *Daily Colonist* (Victoria), 2 June 1934, p. 10.
32. Carr, *Hundreds and Thousands*, pp. 93-4 (29 Jan. 1934).
33. Carr Papers, Unpublished journals, Port Hardy, summer 1930.
34. Provincial Archives of British Columbia [PABC], Newcombe Papers, Dr Erna Gunther to William Newcombe, 5 Sept. 1930.
35. Carr Papers, Unpublished journals, Port Hardy, summer 1930.
36. *Ibid.*
37. Carr, *Hundreds and Thousands*, p. 21 (23 Nov. 1930).
38. D.H. Lawrence, *St. Mawr and the Man Who Died* (New York, 1953), p. 146. Emily's typed transcription of the passage is in the Carr Papers, 'Typed Notes'.
39. Carr Papers, 'Typed Notes'.
40. Mary Cecil Allen, *Painters of the Modern Mind* (New York, 1929), pp. 76-7.
41. *Ibid.*, pp. 47, 55. Emily's typescript notes from which these quotations are taken are in the Carr Papers, 'Typed Notes'.
42. Allen, *Painters of the Modern Mind*, p. 61.
43. *Animals in Art* (London, 1929), p. 64.
44. Carr Papers, Harris to Carr, 'T'Other Emily', n.d.
45. *The New Art* (London, 1922), pp. 68, 82.
46. Carr, *Hundreds and Thousands*, p. 25 (18 Jan. 1931).
47. Carr, *Growing Pains*, p. 238.
48. Carr, *Hundreds and Thousands*, pp. 28-9 (17 June 1931).
49. Carr Papers, Unpublished journals, 28 Sept. 1931.
50. *Ibid.*, Harris to Carr, 20 Dec. 1931.
51. Carr, *Hundreds and Thousands*, p. 22 (26 Nov. 1930).
52. Carr, *Growing Pains*, pp. 264, 265.
53. *Ibid.*, p. 265.
54. George A. Ross, of J.J. Ross & Sons,

to author, 19 June 1975.

55. Carr, *Hundreds and Thousands*, p. 107 (5 Apr. 1934).

56. PABC, Hembroff-Schleicher Papers, Carr to Hembroff, [Nov. 1936]; Carr Papers, Harris to Carr, 19 May 1933.

57. National Gallery of Canada, Carr to Brown, 4 Mar. 1937.

58. Carr, *Hundreds and Thousands*, p. 31 (12 Nov. 1932).

59. *Ibid.*, p. 30.

60. Spiers interview.

61. Carr Papers, Harris to Carr, 19 May 1933.

62. *Ibid.*, Bess Housser to Emily, n.d. [June 1933].

63. *Ibid.*, Harris to Carr, 19 May 1933.

64. Carr, *Hundreds and Thousands*, p. 34 (27 Jan. 1933).

10
NEW FRIENDS AT HOME
1930-1934

1. National Gallery of Canada [NGC], Brown to Carr, 19 Mar. 1928. The poor review appeared in the *Vancouver Sun* (Vancouver), 21 Feb. 1928, p. 14.

2. *Province* (Vancouver), 21 Nov. 1929, p. 6.

3. Provincial Archives of British Columbia [PABC], Hembroff-Schleicher Papers, Carr to Hembroff-Brand, n.d. [Sept. 1935]; University of British Columbia Library [UBCL], Cheney Papers, Carr to Cheney, 22 Oct. 1932.

4. *Seattle Sunday Times*, 30 Nov. 1930, p. 6.

5. *Art News* (New York), 27 Dec. 1930, p. 26.

6. *Town Crier* (Seattle), 3 Dec. 1930, p. 26.

7. *Art News* (New York), 27 Dec. 1930, p. 26; *Arts Digest* (New York), 1 Jan. 1931, p. 26.

8. Public Archives of Canada [PAC], MG 30, D 215, Emily Carr Papers, Harris to Carr, 'Day After Christmas', n.d. [1930].

9. Emily Carr, *Hundreds and Thousands: The Journals of Emily Carr* (Toronto, 1966), p. 33 (25 Jan. 1933).

10. Muriel Brewster, 'Some Ladies Prefer Indians', *Toronto Star Weekly*, 21 Jan. 1928, p. 52.

11. 'West Coast Art', *Daily Colonist* (Victoria), 27 Mar. 1928, p. 9.

12. *Daily Colonist* (Victoria), 24 Oct. 1928, p. 5.

13. Lodewyk Bosch, 'Victoria Artist Who Does Inspired Work' in *ibid.*, 2 Mar. 1930, p. 13.

14. Emily Carr, *The Heart of a Peacock* (Toronto, 1953), p. 205. Courtesy Clarke, Irwin & Company Limited.

15. Carr Papers, Unpublished manuscript 'Hundreds and Thousands', 'So Big, So Little, So Shy, So Brave'.

16. *Daily Colonist* (Victoria), 5 Mar. 1930, p. 7.

17. *An Address* (Toronto, 1955). This was later republished—with the 1935 Victoria speech, 'The Something Plus in a Work of Art'—in *Fresh Seeing* (Toronto, 1972). Courtesy Clarke, Irwin & Company Limited.

18. *Daily Colonist* (Victoria), 6 Mar. 1930, p. 7.

19. Carr, *The Heart of a Peacock*, p. 206. Emily gave another talk on modern painting six days later for the Business and Professional Women's Association, the Kumtuks Club. *Daily Colonist*, 11 Mar. 1930, p. 15.

20. Interview with Max Maynard, Sept. 1974.

21. Frederick Brand to author, fall 1974; Bob Allen, 'New Picture of Shadbolt Takes Form', *Province* (Vancouver), 21 Nov. 1973, p. 15.

22. Edythe Hembroff-Schleicher, *M.E.: A Portrayal of Emily Carr* (Toronto, 1969), p. 48.

23. Interview with John Macdonald, summer 1976.

24. Hembroff-Schleicher Papers, Carr to Hembroff-Brand, 8 Dec. 1936.

25. *Ibid.*, n.d. [Dec. 1937].

26. Quoted in Allen, 'New Picture of Shadbolt Takes Form', p. 15.

27. Hembroff-Schleicher Papers, Carr to Hembroff-Brand, n.d. [Thanksgiving 1936].

28. Jack Shadbolt, *In Search of Form* (Toronto, 1968), p. 64.

29. UBCL, Exhibition catalogue, University of British Columbia, Mar. 1933.

30. PABC, Carr File, Art: Shadbolt and Maynard'. Unidentified clipping labelled 1932, probably written by Mabel Mackenzie.

31. Hembroff-Schleicher Papers, Carr to Hembroff-Brand, 11 Oct. 1935.

32. Dilworth Papers, Carr to Dilworth, n.d. [received 2 Oct. 1941].

33. Hembroff-Schleicher Papers, Carr to Hembroff-Brand, n.d. [1933].

34. Carr Papers, 'Saturday' [Oct. 1937].

35. Interview with Max Maynard, Sept. 1974.

36. Ronald Bladen to author, n.d. [Jan. 1974].

37. Edythe Hembroff-Schleicher, 'My Friend Emily Carr'. Typescript in PABC, p. 3. For two different versions by Hembroff-Schleicher of her meeting with Emily Carr see: M.E.: A Portrayal of Emily Carr, pp. 1ff. and Emily Carr: The Untold Story (Saanichton, B.C., 1978), pp. 12ff.

38. Frederick Brand to author, fall 1974.

39. Cheney Papers, Carr to Cheney, Jan. 1938.

40. Hembroff-Schleicher Papers, Carr to Hembroff-Brand, 'Thanksgiving', n.d. [1936].

41. Cheney Papers, Carr to Cheney, 15 May 1932. Hembroff-Schleicher states in both M.E.: A Portrayal of Emily Carr (p. 27 and p. 31) and Emily Carr: The Untold Story (p. 125) that she sketched with Emily in May 1931 at Cordova Bay and in September 1931 at Goldstream. Evidence shows that during May 1931 Emily was attending Harry Gaze's Applied Psychology lectures (see Carr Papers, Unpublished journals, 22 May 1931) and during September of the same year she stayed with Mrs McVickers at Metchosin (see ibid., 28 Sept. 1931). I can find evidence for only one sketching trip shared by Emily and Hembroff-Schleicher: in May 1932.

42. Hembroff-Schleicher, M.E.: A Portrayal of Emily Carr, p. 30.

43. Frederick Brand to author, fall 1974.

44. Hembroff-Schleicher, 'My Friend Emily Carr', p. 10.

45. Cheney Papers, Carr to Cheney, 22 Oct. 1932.

46. Maynard to author, 12 July 1973.

47. Daily Colonist (Victoria), 9 Oct. 1932, p. 18.

48. Victoria Times, 12 Oct. 1932.

49. Maynard to author, 6 Sept. 1973.

50. Cheney Papers, Carr to Cheney, 22 Oct. 1932.

51. Ibid.

52. PABC, W.A. Newcombe Papers, Typescript of Carr's speech of 14 Dec. 1932.

53. Ibid., Typescript of circular letter, Dec. 1932.

54. Cheney Papers, Carr to Cheney, 22 Oct. 1932.

55. Daily Colonist (Victoria), 15 Dec. 1932, p. 6.

56. Newcombe Papers, Typescript of Carr's speech of 14 Dec. 1932.

57. Daily Colonist (Victoria), 15 Dec. 1932, p. 6.

58. NGC, Carr to Brown, 15 Dec. 1932.

59. Ibid., Brown to Carr, 21 Dec. 1932 (copy).

60. Cheney Papers, Carr to Cheney, 7 Jan. 1933.

61. NGC, Carr to Brown, 20 Jan. [1933].

62. Ibid., Carr to Brown, 3 Jan. [1933].

63. See Hembroff-Schleicher, M.E.: A Portrayal of Emily Carr, p. 60.

64. Daily Colonist (Victoria), 18 Jan. 1933, p. 8.

65. Ibid., 29 Jan. 1933, p. 9.

66. NGC, Carr to Brown, 20 Jan. [1933]: 'Ideal' is enclosed.

67. Carr, Hundreds and Thousands, p. 92 (16 Jan. 1934).

68. Hembroff-Schleicher, 'My Friend Emily Carr', p. 11.

69. Ubyssey (Vancouver) 14 Mar. 1933; 22 Feb. 1935.

70. Art Gallery of Ontario, Clay to Grace Pincoe, 4 Aug. 1945.

71. H. Mortimer Lamb, 'British Columbia Painter', Saturday Night, 14 Jan. 1933, p. 3.

72. Cheney Papers, Carr to Cheney, 16 Feb. 1938.

73. NGC, Carr to Brown, 9 Mar. [1928].

74. NGC, McCurry to Carr, 23 May 1928 (copy).

75. National Museums of Canada,

National Museum of Man, Canadian Centre for Folk Culture Studies, Marius Barbeau Collection (hereafter Barbeau Papers), Barbeau to Carr, 14 Apr. 1928 (copy).

76. Barbeau Papers, Carr to Barbeau, 5 Mar. [1928].

77. Cheney Papers, Carr to Cheney, 14 Dec. 1931.

78. *Ibid.*, n.d. [spring 1932].

79. *Ibid.*, 14 Dec. 1931.

80. NGC, Carr to Brown, 19 Oct. [1934].

81. Cheney Papers, Carr to Cheney, 25 Oct. [1935].

82. NGC, Brown to Carr, 14 Jan. 1928 (copy).

83. PAC, Harris Papers, V, 'Miscellaneous 21', pp. 1, 2.

84. Emily Carr, *Growing Pains: The Autobiography of Emily Carr* (Centennial ed.; Toronto, 1971), p. ·239.

85. Carr Papers, Carr to Dilworth, n.d.

86. Cheney Papers, Carr to Cheney, 9 Dec. 1938.

87. *Ibid.*, 7 Feb. [1932].

88. A.Y. Jackson, *A Painter's Country: The Autobiography of A.Y. Jackson* (Toronto, 1964), p. 112.

89. Carr Papers, Additional notes in unpublished journals.

90. Hembroff-Schleicher Papers, Carr to Hembroff-Brand, n.d. [1937].

91. NGC, Lismer to McCurry, 20 June 1935.

92. Cheney Papers, Carr to Cheney, Sept. 1937.

93. So reported to the author by a close friend of Varley's.

94. Cheney Papers, Carr to Cheney, n.d. [Oct. 1935].

95. Carr, *Hundreds and Thousands*, p. 98 (18 Feb. 1934).

96. Hembroff-Schleicher Papers, Carr to Hembroff-Brand, 17 Nov. 1933.

97. *Ibid.*

98. Carr, *Hundreds and Thousands*, p. 77 (10 Nov. 1933); p. 79 (17 Nov. 1933).

99. Cheney Papers, Carr to Cheney, 22 Dec. 1940.

100. Carr, *Hundreds and Thousands*, p. 78 (17 Nov. 1933).

101. Car Papers, Carr to Dilworth, 19 Apr. [1942].

102. Carr, *Hundreds and Thousands*, p. 79 (17 Nov. 1933).

103. Carr Papers, Carr to Dilworth, 19 Apr. [1942].

104. Carr, *Hundreds and Thousands*, p. 79 (17 Nov. 1933).

105. *Ibid.*; Carr Papers, Unpublished journals, 7 Feb. 1934.

106. Carr, *Hundreds and Thousands*, p. 87 (12 Dec. 1933).

107. Cheney Papers, Carr to Cheney, 22 Dec. 1940; Carr Papers, Unpublished journals, 7 Feb. 1934.

108. Carr Papers, Carr to Dilworth, n.d.

109. Carr, *Hundreds and Thousands* (29 Jan. 1934), p. 94.

110. Carr Papers, Harris to Carr, 10 Feb. 1934.

111. *Ibid.*, Bess Housser to Carr, 20 Feb. 1934.

112. *Ibid.*, Unpublished journals, 11 July 1934.

113. Carr Papers, Unpublished journals, 1934; Carr to Mrs Katherine Daly, 11 Feb. 1945. Private possession.

114. Carr Papers, Unpublished journals, 11 July 1934.

115. *Ibid.*

116. *Ibid.*, Carr to Dilworth, n.d. [Sunday, Epistle No. II].

117. Cheney Papers, Carr to Cheney, 22 Dec. 1940.

118. Carr Papers, Carr to Dilworth, n.d. [July 1942].

119. *Ibid.*, 25 May 1944.

120. Carr, *Hundreds and Thousands*, p. 138 (5 July 1934).

11
FRUITION
1934-1937

1. Emily Carr, *Hundreds and Thousands: The Journals of Emily Carr* (Toronto, 1966), p. 269 (19 Dec. 1936).

2. *Ibid.*, p. 19 (25 Dec. 1927).

3. *Ibid.*, p. 212 (24 Dec. 1935).

4. Public Archives of Canada, MG 30, D 215, Emily Carr Papers, Unpublished journals, 8 Dec. 1934.

5. *Ibid.*, Sept. 1931.

6. *Ibid.*, 8 Dec. 1934.

7. Interview with Eleanor Sinclair,

Aug. 1974. See also Carr, *Hundreds and Thousands*, p. 320 (25 Feb. 1940).

8. Carr, *Hundreds and Thousands*, p. 191 (6 Aug. [really 26 Aug.] 1935).

9. M.E. Coleman, 'My Friend Emily Carr', *Vancouver Sun*, 12 Apr. 1952, p. 14.

10. Carr, *Hundreds and Thousands*, p. 63 (Oct. 1933).

11. *Ibid.*, p. 68 (18 Oct. 1933).

12. Coleman, 'My Friend Emily Carr', p. 14.

13. Carr to Molly Frame, 1 Dec. 1935. Private possession.

14. Carr, *Hundreds and Thousands*, p. 108 (16 Sept. 1933).

15. H.N.W. Toms to author, 2 Apr. 1974.

16. Carr to Molly Frame, 27 Dec. 1935. Private possession.

17. Carr Papers, Unpublished journals, 31 Jan. 1931.

18. Emily Carr, *Fresh Seeing*, (Toronto, 1972).

19. Interview with Mrs Doreen Radcliff, Mar. 1974; Mrs Radcliff to author, Apr. 1974.

20. Carr Papers, Unpublished journals, 22 Oct. 1935 [misdated as 19 Oct. in Carr, *Hundreds and Thousands*, pp. 202-3].

21. Philip Amsden, 'Memories of Emily Carr', *Canadian Forum*, 27 (Dec. 1947), pp. 206-7; interview with Philip Amsden, Sept. 1975.

22. Carr Papers, Carr to Dilworth, postmarked 2 Oct. 1941.

23. *Ibid.*, Unpublished journals, 19 Aug. 1930.

24. Carr, *Hundreds and Thousands*, p. 88 (19 Dec. 1933).

25. Carr Papers, Unpublished journals, 12 Aug. 1934.

26. Flora Hamilton Burns, 'Emily Carr and the Newcombe Collection', in Hudson Bay Company, *The World of Emily Carr*, Exhibition Catalogue, 1962, p. 11.

27. Carr Papers, Unpublished journals, 3 Sept. 1933; Amsden interview.

28. Provincial Museum of British Columbia, G. Clifford Carl to Bert Hudson, 25 Nov. 1963.

29. Bert Hudson, 'Victoria's Gentle Servant of the Arts', *Daily Colonist* (Victoria), 6 Sept. 1964, p. 4.

30. Provincial Museum, Carl to Hudson, 25 Nov. 1963.

31. Interview with Erna Gunther, Oct. 1975.

32. Emily Carr to Ruth Humphrey, 22 Aug. [1937], in Humphrey, 'Letters from Emily Carr', *University of Toronto Quarterly*, XLI, no. 2 (Winter 1972), p. 113.

33. University of British Columbia Library [UBCL], Cheney Papers, Carr to Cheney, 12 Sept. 1938.

34. M.E. Coleman, a friend of the Carr sisters, states that Emily 'first showed me her writing' in the early twenties and they discussed the possibility 'of her doing a book about her experiences'. *Vancouver Sun*, 12 Apr. 1952, p. 14. Emily also sent her manuscripts to Lawren Harris, Fred Housser, and Katherine Pinkerton and read them to others, like Frederick Brand and Philip Amsden. See Emily Carr, *Growing Pains: The Autobiography of Emily Carr* (Centennial ed.; Toronto, 1971), p. 268.

35. Provincial Archives of British Columbia [PABC], Aural History, Imbert Orchard interview with Flora Hamilton Burns, 18 May 1962.

36. Flora Hamilton Burns, 'Emily Carr—An Immortal of Canada' (typescript in Provincial Archives of British Columbia), p. 18.

37. Interview with Ruth Humphrey, July 1973.

38. PABC, Aural History, Burns interview.

39. Emily Carr to Ruth Humphrey, 22 June 1937, in Humphrey, 'Letters from Emily Carr', p. 193.

40. Carr, *Hundreds and Thousands*, p. 265 (1 Nov. 1936).

41. Carr Papers, Carr to Dilworth, 'Friday', n.d.; PABC, Hembroff-Schleicher Papers, Carr to Hembroff-Brand, n.d. [Nov. 1939].

42. Carr Papers, Unpublished journals, 3 Oct. 1939.

43. Carr, *Hundreds and Thousands*, p. 331 (21 Feb. 1941).

44. PABC, Hembroff-Schleicher Papers, Carr to Hembroff-Brand, n.d. [Nov. 1929].

45. Carr Papers, Carr to Dilworth, 20 June [1941].
46. Carr, *Hundreds and Thousands*, p. 310 (3 Oct. 1939).
47. Amsden, 'Memories of Emily Carr', p. 206.
48. Hembroff-Schleicher Papers, Carr to Hembroff-Brand, 7 Aug. 1937.
49. Carr Papers, Harris to Carr, n.d.
50. Carr to Mrs C.S. Band, 17 Apr. 1937. In possession of Mrs C.S. Band.
51. Carr, *Hundreds and Thousands*, p. 36 (7 June 1933).
52. *Ibid.* Courtesy Clarke, Irwin & Company Limited.
53. *Ibid.*, p. 35 (7 June 1933).
54. Cheney Papers, Carr to Cheney, 25 Oct. 1935; Carr, *Hundreds and Thousands*, p. 118 (14 May 1934).
55. Carr to Humphrey, n.d. [23 May 1938], in Humphrey, 'Letters from Emily Carr', p. 131.
56. Carr Papers, Unpublished journals, 20 Aug. 1933.
57. Carr, *Hundreds and Thousands*, p. 50 (19 Aug. 1933).
58. *Ibid.*, p. 54 (8 Sept. 1933).
59. Carr Papers, Unpublished journals, 12 Sept. 1933.
60. Carr, *Hundreds and Thousands*, p. 219 (28 Jan. 1936); Cheney Papers, Carr to Cheney, n.d. [May 1932].
61. Carr Papers, 'Art Notes' (typescript).
62. *Metchosin*. Collection of Mr Alan Gibbons, Ottawa.
63. Carr Papers, Harris to Carr, 3 May 1936.
64. Cheney Papers, 'Talk on Art', by M. Emily Carr, 22 Oct. 1935, p. 6.
65. Carr, *Hundreds and Thousands*, p. 154 (1 Nov. 1934).
66. 'World of Art', *Saturday Night*, Vol. 51, no. 5 (7 Dec. 1935), p. 27.
67. Carr, *Hundreds and Thousands*, p. 256 (16 Aug. 1936).
68. *Ibid.*, p. 144 (30 Aug. 1934).
69. *Ibid.*
70. *Ibid.*, p. 224 (16 Feb. 1936).
71. Hembroff-Schleicher Papers, Carr to Hembroff-Brand, n.d. [May 1935].
72. Carr, *Hundreds and Thousands*, p. 218 (28 Jan. 1936).
73. After Lizzie's death, only months following the move, Emily received income from the rental of the Carr home. She also agreed, at this time, to accept $15 a month from her Vancouver nieces, an offer she had previously refused.
74. Carr, *Hundreds and Thousands*, p. 235 (26 Apr. 1936).
75. Hembroff-Schleicher Papers, Carr to Hembroff-Brand, 8 Mar. [1936]; Carr, *Hundreds and Thousands*, p. 219 (28 Jan. 1936).
76. Hembroff-Schleicher Papers, Carr to Hembroff-Brand, 8 Mar. [1936].
77. Emily Carr to Molly Frame, fragment [1936]. Private possession.
78. Carr, *Hundreds and Thousands*, 'Later', p. 252 (5 Aug. 1936).
79. Interview with Eleanor Sinclair, Aug. 1974.
80. Carr, *Hundreds and Thousands*, p. 273 (9 Jan. 1937).
81. PABC, W.A. Newcombe Papers, Carr to Newcombe, 'Tuesday', n.d. [1937].
82. Carr Papers, Unpublished journals, 21 Jan. [1937].
83. National Gallery of Canada, Patricia Keir to Eric Brown, 26 Jan. 1937.
84. *Ibid.*, Brown to Grigsby, 27 Jan. 1937 [day/letter telegram]
85. Ruth Humphrey to author, 29 July 1974.
86. Carr, *Hundreds and Thousands*, p. 278 (29 Jan. 1937).
87. Hembroff-Schleicher Papers, Carr to Hembroff-Brand, n.d. [Feb. 1937].
88. Carr, *Hundreds and Thousands*, p. 278 (29 Jan. 1937).
89. Eric Brown was largely responsible for the private sales, which were of paintings that were among those he had requested Newcombe to ship to the National Art Gallery in January 1937.
90. Cheney Papers, Carr to Cheney, Feb. 1937.
91. Carr, *Hundreds and Thousands*, p. 282 (14 Feb. 1937).
92. Carr to C.S. Band, 17 Apr. 1937. In possession of Mrs C.S. Band.

12
WRITING AND IRA
1937-1942

1. Provincial Archives of British Columbia [PABC], Hembroff-Schleicher Papers, Carr to Hembroff-Brand, 'Wednesday Evening', n.d. [Feb. 1937].
2. Emily Carr, *Hundreds and Thousands, The Journals of Emily Carr* (Toronto, 1966), p. 280 (9 Feb. 1937).
3. University of British Columbia Library [UBCL], Cheney Papers, Carr to Cheney, 13 Apr. 1937.
4. Carr, *Hundreds and Thousands*, p. 303 (4 Sept. 1939).
5. *Ibid.*, p. 331 (21 Feb. 1941).
6. Cheney Papers, Carr to Cheney, n.d. [June 1939].
7. *Ibid.*, Toms to Cheney, 8 June 1939; Carr to Cheney, 'Monday', n.d. [July 1939].
8. G. Campbell McInnis, 'World of Art', *Saturday Night*, 3 Apr. 1937, p. 8.
9. Emily knew and admired Van Gogh's work, but insisted that though they were after the same thing—unity in movement—she had 'not come by the idea through him'. Carr, *Hundreds and Thousands*, p. 106 (4 Apr. 1934).
10. McInnis, 'World of Art', p. 8.
11. NGC, Carr to Brown, 4 Sept. 1938.
12. Carr to C.S. Band, 12 June 1938. In possession of Mrs C.S. Band.
13. NGC, Carr to Brown, 4 Sept. 1938.
14. *Ibid.*
15. *The Times* (London), 15 Oct. 1938, p. 10.
16. *Manchester Guardian*, 15 Oct. 1938. Signed N (probably Eric Newton).
17. Eric Newton, 'Canadian Art Through English Eyes', *Canadian Forum* (Feb. 1939), p. 345.
18. National Gallery of Canada [NGC], Brown to Carr, 30 Nov. 1938 (copy). It should be noted that only one of Emily's recent oil-on-paper sketches, *Sky*, was exhibited in this exhibition; the other three works were from her 1929-31 period.
19. Carr, *Hundreds and Thousands*, p. 301 (31 Nov. 1938).
20. Cheney Papers, Carr to Cheney, n.d. [summer 1939].
21. *Province* (Vancouver), 13 Oct. 1938, p. 28.
22. *Ibid.*, 2 Nov. 1938, p. 18.
23. NGC, Macdonald to McCurry, 18 Nov. 1938.
24. NGC, Cheney to McCurry, 10 Nov. 1938.
25. Reg Jessop, 'Faculty, Student Review Emily Carr Exhibition', *Ubyssey* (Vancouver), 4 Nov. 1938, p. 1.
26. NGC, Cheney to Brown, n.d. [Nov. 1938].
27. Cheney Papers, Carr to Cheney, 19 Oct. 1938.
28. NGC, Carr to Brown, 24 Nov. 1938.
29. Hembroff-Schleicher Papers, Carr to Hembroff-Brand, 'Wednesday' [Nov. 1939].
30. *Ibid.*, Carr to Hembroff-Brand, 'Saturday' [July 1939].
31. Cheney Papers, Carr to Cheney, 'Saturday' [postmarked 25 July 1938].
32. Arthur Lismer to C.S. Band, 25 May 1940. In possession of Mrs C.S. Band.
33. Notes taken during the Shadbolt lecture at the Vancouver Art Gallery, 24 Oct. 1941. Private possession. Shadbolt had, however, made similar remarks five years earlier. See his 'The Artist and His Means of Expression', *Canadian Author and Bookman*, 14, 14 Dec. 1936, p. 11.
34. *Vancouver Sun*, 25 Oct. 1941, p. 6.
35. *Province* (Vancouver), 23 Oct. 1941, p. 24.
36. Public Archives of Canada [PAC], MG 30, D 215, Emily Carr Papers, Carr to Dilworth, 'Saturday Night' [1942].
37. Carr, *Hundreds and Thousands*, p. 322 (5 Mar. 1940).
38. Cheney Papers, Carr to Cheney, 'Sunday' [Mar. 1938].
39. Hembroff-Schleicher Papers, Carr to Hembroff-Brand, 'Wednesday' [Nov. 1936].
40. Cheney Papers, Carr to Cheney, Monday' [15 Mar. 1938].
41. Carr to Katherine Daly, 17 Jan. 1945. Private possession.

42. Hembroff-Schleicher Papers, Carr to Hembroff-Brand, 'Monday' [Dec. 1937].

43. Emily told several friends, including Ira Dilworth, and spoke publicly (see note 78), of writing the Indian stories only after her first heart attack in 1937. For a more complete discussion of *Klee Wyck*, see Maria Tippett, 'Emily Carr's *Klee Wyck'*, *Canadian Literature*, no. 72 (Spring 1977), pp. 49-58.

44. Carr Papers, Harris to Carr, 24 June 1933.

45. 'Chins Up' became *Pause: A Sketch Book*; the childhood stories, *The Book of Small*; the second autobiography, *Growing Pains*. Some of 'Woo's Life' and 'Birds' appeared in *The Heart of a Peacock*. 'Wild Flowers', 'Hundreds & Thousands', and the first autobiography remain in manuscript in PAC, Carr Papers.

46. 'Mrs. Crane' in *The Book of Small* (paperback ed.; Toronto, 1966), pp. 41-52; 'Martyn', in *Growing Pains: The Autobiography of Emily Carr* (Centennial ed.; Toronto, 1971), pp. 140-5.

47. Carr, *Hundreds and Thousands*, pp. 326-7 (20 Dec. 1940).

48. Emily Carr, *Klee Wyck* (Centennial ed.; Toronto, 1971), p. 45; *Ibid.*, p. 43; Carr, *Hundreds and Thousands*, p. 274 (15 Jan. 1937).

49. Hembroff-Schleicher Papers, Carr to Hembroff-Brand, n.d. [Oct. 1937].

50. Queen's University Library, Lorne Pierce Papers, Carr to Pierce, n.d. [Feb. 1938].

51. Sedgewick did not see Emily's stories for the first time in 1937; Frederick Brand had shown him samples of her work in the early 1930s. Carr to Humphrey, 10 Aug. [1937], in Humphrey, 'Letters from Emily Carr', *University of Toronto Quarterly*, XLI, no. 2 (Winter 1972), p. 111.

52. Hembroff-Schleicher Papers, Carr to Hembroff-Brand, n.d. [Oct. 1937].

53. Pierce Papers, 'Memo: Twenty-five Indian Sketches'.

54. Cheney Papers, Carr to Cheney, n.d. [5 May 1938]; Carr, *Hundreds and Thousands*, p. 311 (3 Oct. 1939).

55. Carr, *Hundreds and Thousands*, p. 312 (17 Jan. 1940).

56. *Ibid.*, p. 317 (23 Feb. 1940).

57. Cheney Papers, Carr to Cheney, 26 Feb. 1940.

58. *Ibid.*, Carr to Cheney, 9 Jan. 1941.

59. Carr to Carol Pearson, 7 May 1943. Private possession. Alice was not indifferent to Emily's work. She now actually preferred the more modern paintings because 'the big splashes of colour were easier to see'. Interview with Paul Hennell, May 1974.

60. Interview with Carol Pearson, Sept. 1974.

61. Hennell interview.

62. Carr to Pearson, n.d. Private possession.

63. Cheney Papers, Toms to Cheney, 9 June 1940.

64. *Ibid.*, Toms to Cheney, 12 July 1940.

65. *Ibid.*, Toms to Cheney, 22 July 1940.

66. *Ibid.*, Toms to Cheney, 1 Aug. 1940.

67. *Ibid.*

68. NGC, J.W.G. Macdonald to McCurry, 30 July 1940.

69. Cheney Papers, Carr to Cheney, n.d. [1 Aug. 1940].

70. *Ibid.*, Toms to Cheney, 12 July 1940.

71. Carr to Humphrey, 2 July [1940], in Humphrey, 'Letters from Emily Carr', p. 134.

72. Ira Dilworth, CBC Wednesday Night', p. 14; Cheney Papers, Toms to Cheney, 28 Sept. 1940.

73. Carr Papers, Carr to Dilworth, 2 Jan. 1941. Dilworth had written to her on 1 Oct. 1940 but had not returned her stories.

74. *Ibid.*, Carr to Dilworth, 30 Apr. 1941.

75. Cheney Papers, Carr to Cheney, 27 Oct. [1941].

76. C.H. Sanderson, *Selections From Twelve Important Reviews of Klee Wyck by Emily Carr* (Toronto, n.d.), n.p.

77. Robertson Davies, 'The Revelation of Emily Carr', *Saturday Night*, 8

Nov. 1941, p. 18.

78. *Daily Colonist* (Victoria), 14 Dec. 1941, p. 6.

79. Emily Carr, *Growing Pains: The Autobiography of Emily Carr* (Centennial ed.; Toronto, 1971), p. 274. Courtesy Clarke, Irwin & Company Limited.

80. Carr to Pearson, 2 Jan. 1942. Private possession.

81. Carr, *Growing Pains*, p. 275.

82. Ira Dilworth, 'Emily Carr: Artist— Author', *Saturday Night*, 8 Nov. 1941, p. 26.

83. James K. Nesbitt, 'Kindness, Drive, Energy, Characterized Ira Dilworth', *Vancouver Sun*, 27 Nov. 1962, p. 13; Peter L. Smith, *Come Give a Cheer, 1876-1976* (Victoria, 1976), p. 82.

84. Dilworth, 'CBC Wednesday Night', p. 14.

85. Carr Papers, Dilworth to Carr, 3 Nov. 1942.

86. Dilworth, 'CBC Wednesday Night', p. 14.

87. Carr, *Growing Pains*, p. 269.

88. Carr to Pearson, 17 Oct. 1942. Private possession.

89. Cheney Papers, Carr to Cheney, 13 May 1941; Carr Papers, Carr to Dilworth, n.d.

90. Carr Papers, Carr to Dilworth, 'Jubilee Hospital', n.d. [1943].

91. *Ibid.*, Carr to Dilworth, 'Sunday', n.d. [1942].

92. *Ibid.*, Dilworth to Carr, 14 Nov. 1942.

93. *Ibid.*, Dilworth to Carr, n.d.

94. *Ibid.*, Carr to Dilworth, n.d. [1942].

95. *Ibid.*, Carr to Dilworth, 29 Aug. 1943.

96. *Ibid.*, Carr to Dilworth, n.d.

97. *Ibid.*, Carr to Dilworth, 19 Jan. 1942.

98. *Ibid.*, Carr to Dilworth, n.d.

99. *Ibid.*, Carr to Dilworth, 29 Aug., n.d.

100. Carr to Pearson, 17 Oct. 1942. Private possession.

101. Carr Papers, Carr to Dilworth, 'Tuesday', [1942].

102. Emily Carr, *The Heart of a Peacock* (Toronto, 1953), p. xv. Courtesy Clarke, Irwin & Company Limited.

103. In a letter to Dilworth, Emily wrote: 'If I have made people respect and honour father through the *Book of Small*,' perhaps that 'in some way atoned for all of my years of bitterness.' Telling Dilworth of her childhood trauma, then writing of those years before it, 'sort of squared me with father.' Carr Papers, Carr to Dilworth, 'Tuesday', n.d.

104. NGC, W.H. Clarke to Eric Brown, 16 June 1941, mistakenly addressed to Eric Brown, who had died in 1939. McCurry replied that 'we have a definite rule against "one-man" shows of the work of living artists'. McCurry to Clarke, 17 June 1941.

105. Carr to Pearson, n.d. Private possession.

13
'TIRED VERY TIRED'
1942-1945

1. Public Archives of Canada, MG 30, D 215, Emily Carr Papers, 'Small' to Dilworth, 'Tuesday, Mount Douglas', n.d. [1942].

2. *Ibid.*, Carr to Dilworth, 2 Aug. 1942.

3. *Ibid.*, 'Small' to Dilworth, 'Tuesday, Mount Douglas', n.d. [1942].

4. Emily Carr to Carol Pearson, 'Thursday Evening, Mount Douglas Tea Room', n.d. [1942]. Private possession.

5. Though originally written as another 'Hundreds and Thousands' sketch, 'Mother' was eventually incorporated into *Growing Pains*.

6. Carr Papers, Carr to Dilworth, n.d. [1942].

7. *Ibid.*, Carr to Dilworth, fragment [1942]; see the painting *In the Woods. British Columbia*, Montreal Museum of Fine Arts.

8. Carr Papers, Dilworth to Carr, 13 Aug. 1942.

9. *Ibid.*, Carr to Dilworth, 'Saturday Afternoon', n.d. [1942].

10. *Ibid.*, Carr to Dilworth, n.d. [1942].

11. *Ibid.*, Carr to Dilworth, 'Saturday Afternoon', n.d. [1942].

12. Carr to Pearson, 11 Jan. 1943. Private possession.

13. Carr Papers, Dilworth to Carr, 24 Aug. 1942.
14. W.H. Clarke to B.K. Sandwell, 28 Oct. 1942. Files of the Oxford University Press, Toronto.
15. Carr Papers, Clarke to Dilworth, 7 Nov. 1942; Clarke to Carr, telegram, 6 Dec. [1942].
16. Carr Papers, Dilworth to Carr, 1 June 1943.
17. *Ibid.*, Harris to Carr, n.d. [1943].
18. J. Delisle Parker, 'Emily Carr—Victoria Painter Artist', *Victoria Times*, Magazine, 1 May 1943, p. 7.
19. Carr Papers, Carr to Dilworth, 4 June 1943.
20. *Ibid.*, Carr to Dilworth, 'Sunday', n.d.
21. *Ibid.*, 'Small' to Dilworth, 13 Apr. [1943].
22. *Ibid.*, Carr to Dilworth, 'Sunday', n.d. [1944].
23. *Ibid.*, Carr to Hembroff-Brand, 'Saturday December', n.d.
24. University of British Columbia Library, Nan Cheney Papers, Carr to Cheney, n.d. [postmarked 26 Feb. 1941].
25. Carr to Pearson, Aug. 1944. Private possession.
26. Carr to Pearson, 13 Dec. 1942. Private possession.
27. Carr to Pearson, Aug. 1943. Private possession.
28. Cheney Papers, Carr to Cheney, 25 May 1940.
29. *Ibid.*, Carr to Cheney, n.d. [postmarked 30 May 1941].
30. Carr Papers, Carr to Walter Gage, 6 Dec., n.d.
31. *Ibid.*, Carr to Dilworth, 12 Dec. [1944].
32. Carr to Humphrey, 2 July [1940], in Humphrey, 'Letters from Emily Carr', *University of Toronto Quarterly*, XLI, no. 2 (Winter 1972), p. 134.
33. Carr Papers, Carr to Dilworth, 12 Dec. [1944].
34. Cheney Papers, H.N.W. Toms to Cheney, 28 Sept. 1940.
35. *Ibid.*, Carr to Cheney, 30 May 1941.
36. *Ibid.*, Carr to Cheney, 7 Nov. 1940.
37. Nan Cheney's portrait of Emily was left to the National Gallery of Canada in 1948 by J.F.B. Livesay. 'I loathe the picture', Emily said in a letter to Eric Brown (National Gallery of Canada, Carr to Brown, 26 Mar. 1939).
38. Carr Papers, Carr to Dilworth, 23 Feb. 1942.
39. Cheney Papers, n.d. [postmarked 30 May 1941].
40. Carr Papers, Carr to Dilworth, 'Sunday', n.d. [1944].
41. *Ibid.*, Carr to Dilworth, fragment, n.d. [1943].
42. Carr to Pearson, 9 May 1943. Private possession.
43. Carr Papers, Carr to Dilworth, 4 Aug. 1943.
44. *Ibid.*, Carr to Dilworth, 'Sunday', n.d. [1944].
45. *Ibid.*, Carr to Dilworth, 'Sunday Morning', n.d.
46. *Ibid.*, Carr to Dilworth, 6 May 1942.
47. *Ibid.*, 'Small' to Dilworth, n.d.
48. Carr to Humphrey, 29 Oct. 1943, in Humphrey, 'Letters from Emily Carr', p. 146. Emily had named Dilworth her literary executor in the autumn of 1942.
49. Carr Papers, Carr to Dilworth, n.d.
50. *Ibid.*, Carr to Dilworth, 15 Dec. [1944].
51. *Ibid.*, Carr to Dilworth, fragment, n.d.
52. Max Stern, 'Portrait in Memory of Emily Carr', CBC Wednesday Night (typescript), 9 Apr. 1958.
53. Interview with Max Stern, Oct. 1974.
54. Carr Papers, Carr to Dilworth, 'Friday Night', n.d. [1944].
55. Provincial Archives of British Columbia, W.A. Newcombe Papers, Stern to Dilworth, 28 Oct. 1944; see *ibid.*, Stern to Carr, statement, 6 Dec. 1944, for the number of paintings sold.
56. Dominion Gallery, Montreal, *Paintings and Watercolours by Emily Carr, October 19 - November 4* [1944].
57. Dominion Gallery, Montreal, Carr to Stern, 1 Nov. 1944.
58. Harry Hood of Vancouver's Art Emporium had tried to get an exhibition throughout the 1930s.
59. Newcombe Papers, Stern to Carr, 1

Dec. 1944.

60. *Ibid.*, Stern to Dilworth, 27 Jan. 1945.
61. *Ibid.*, Dilworth to Stern, 29 Jan. 1945.
62. This exhibition was not held until after Emily's death, in November 1945. It was called the 'Emily Carr Memorial Exhibition'.
63. Newcombe Papers, Carr to Stern, 11 Aug. 1944.
64. Interview with Ruth Schroder, a former nurse at the Royal Jubilee Hospital, Aug. 1974.
65. Carr Papers, Carr to Dilworth, n.d. [1944].
66. *Ibid.*, Carr to Dilworth, n.d. [1944].
67. *Ibid.*, Carr to Dilworth, 13 Dec. [1944].
68. *Daily Colonist*, 8 Dec. 1944, p. 7.
69. Carr Papers, Carr to Dilworth, '3:30 AM', n.d. [1945].
70. Cheney Papers, Carr to Cheney, 10 May 1942.
71. Carr Papers, Carr to Dilworth, n.d.[1944].
72. *Ibid.*, Carr to Dilworth, 12 Nov. 1942.
73. Carr to Pearson, Aug. 1943. Private possession.
74. Humphrey Davey, 'Artist's Treasures Hidden in Woods Here Were Buried by Emily Carr's Lifelong Friend', *Victoria Times*, 11 Jan. 1955, p. 11.
75. Carr to Pearson, 6 July [1941]. Private possession.
76. Newcombe Papers, 'Indenture', 1941, between Carr, Ira Dilworth, and Lawren Harris; Carr to Pearson, Apr. 1942. Private possession.
77. Carr Papers, Carr to Dilworth, 30 June 1942.
78. Newcombe Papers, copy of will, 30 Nov. 1942.
79. Carr Papers, Carr to Dilworth, '3 AM', n.d.
80. *Ibid.*, Carr to Dilworth, 18 Jan. 1945.
81. *Ibid.*, Carr to Dilworth, 'Friday Noon', n.d. [1944].
82. Carr to Katherine Daly, 4 Feb. 1945. Private possession.
83. *Ibid.*, 17 Jan. 1945.
84. *Ibid.*, 11 Feb. 1945.
85. Carr Papers, Carr to Dilworth, 'Tuesday' [27 Feb. 1945].
86. *Ibid.*, Carr to Dilworth, n.d. [1945].
87. *Ibid.*, Carr to Dilworth, 'Tuesday' [27 Feb. 1945].
88. *Ibid.*, Carr to Dilworth, n.d. [1945].
89. *Ibid.*, Carr to Dilworth, 'Tuesday' [27 Feb. 1945].

EPILOGUE

1. Public Archives of Canada, MG 30, D 215, Emily Carr Papers, Carr to Dilworth, 'Sunday', n.d. [1944].
2. Emily's bank books are in the possession of H.J. Davis, Victoria.
3. Provincial Archives of British Columbia, W.A. Newcombe Papers, Flora Hamilton Burns to W.A. Newcombe, 8 June 1945. Reference to discards is also found in a letter from T. Daly to his parents, 10 Sept. 1947. Private possession.
4. Alice Carr to Katherine Daly, 13 Dec. 1947. Private possession.
5. *News Herald* (Vancouver), 14 Mar. 1945, p. 1.
6. National Gallery of Canada [NGC], McCurry to Harris, 10 Dec. 1945; McCurry to Harris, 26 Dec. 1945.
7. H. Mortimer Lamb to A.Y. Jackson, 14 May 1959. In possession of Dr Naomi Jackson Groves.
8. *Emily Carr: Her Paintings and Sketches* (Toronto, 1945).
9. NGC, President of the Committee of the Art Association of Montreal to McCurry, 29 Nov. 1945.
10. In 1961 Harris resigned from the administration of the Trust; Newcombe had died the year before. Alistair Bell and J.A. Parnall were appointed in their place. The trustees chose the scholarship winners and issued the funds. The Trust fund, amounting to over $12,000 in 1946, was able to provide an annual scholarship to young British Columbia artists. The first recipient was Joe Plaskett in 1946 and the last was Anna Wong in 1966. Because of Alistair Bell's concern to have the Trust pictures become the permanent possession of the Vancouver Art Gallery, and

through his efforts, legal title was transferred from the Trust to the Gallery in March 1966.

11. The pictures in the Newcombe Collection came not only from the 1945 discard pile but also from the original purchases of Willie's father, C.F. Newcombe.

12. Ira Dilworth, 'Preface' to *The Heart of a Peacock* (Toronto, 1953), p. xi.

13. Donald Buchanan, 'Growing Pains', *Canadian Art* (4 Mar. 1947), p. 83.

14. Carr Papers, Carr to Dilworth, 'Sunday', n.d. [1942].

15. Alice Carr to Daly, 13 Dec. 1946. Private possession.

16. Alice Carr to Carol Pearson, 4 Jan. 1947. Private possession.

17. Alice Carr to Daly, 14 July 1952. Private possession.

18. Newcombe Papers, 'Will of Emily Carr', 30 Nov. 1942.

19. Alice Carr to Daly, 11 Dec. [1942]. Private possession.

20. *Ibid.*, 19 Nov. 1952; Jan Zach to author, 5 Jan. 1976.

21. Alice Carr to Daly, 11 Dec. 1952. Private possession.

22. Newcombe Papers, codicil to will of Alice Carr, 15 Dec. 1952.

23. Alice Carr to Daly, 11 Dec. 1952. Private possession. Had the will been contested and judged in Alice's favour, the royalties from Emily's posthumous publications might now be the property of Alice's heir, the Queen Alexandra Solarium for Crippled Children in Saanichton, B.C., rather than of the two adopted daughters of Ira Dilworth, Edna Parnall and Phylis Inglis.

24. The unpublished material mentioned is now in the British Columbia Archives. The trunk, and perhaps some very valuable contents, still reside with J.A. Parnell, who refuses scholars access to it.

25. Codicil to Ira Dilworth's will, 26 Nov. 1958, appointing Phylis Inglis to replace Dean Walter Gage. Dilworth had edited about 90 pages of the journals before his death in 1962, according to Edythe Hembroff-Schleicher, *Emily Carr: The Untold Story* (Saanichton, B.C.), p. 296.

26. Alice Carr to Daly, 4 Feb. 1945. Private possession.

27. *Ibid.*, 13 Dec. 1947.

28. *Ibid.*, 14 Sept. 1951.

Index

Entries given italicized page numbers are illustrated.
Colour reproductions are indicated by Roman numerals.

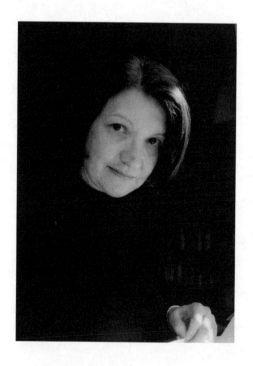

About the Author

Dr. Maria Tippett is one of Canada's most prominent cultural historians and the author of many books on art, culture, and history. She has lectured extensively on Canadian art and culture in North and South America, Japan, and Europe and has curated exhibitions in Canada and abroad. Her books have won numerous awards, including the Governor General's Literary Award for Non-Fiction and the Sir John A. Macdonald Prize for Canadian History. A Fellow of the Royal Society of Canada, she was for many years a Senior Research Fellow at Churchill College, Cambridge, and a member of the Faculty of History at Cambridge University. Her next book, a biography of Yousuf Karsh, will be published by House of Anansi Press in 2007. Maria Tippett lives with her husband, historian Peter Clarke, in British Columbia.

Karsh of Ottawa
A Biography
by Maria Tippett

Karsh of Ottawa tells, for the first time, the full story of how a young
Armenian immigrant living in Ottawa in the 1930s became the most
prominent portrait photographer of the twentieth century. In this ground-
breaking biography, acclaimed writer and historian Maria Tippett reveals
the consummate skill with which Yousuf Karsh (1908–2002) built and
maintained his reputation over six decades. With each photograph he
took, he relied not only on his brilliant mastery of the camera but equally
on his gracious manners and shrewd psychological insight into human
nature. Tippett explores his fascination with power, authority, and fame
along with the entrepreneurial skills of his two business managers, spous-
es Solange then Estrellita, and the carefully cultivated patronage of the
Canadian government. *Karsh of Ottawa* will be illustrated throughout with
black and white images from the artist's life and work.

Available from Anansi in 2007

ISBN-10: 0-88784-198-8
ISBN-13: 978-0-88784-198-9